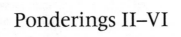

Ponderings II–VI

Studies in Continental Thought

Martin Heidegger

Ponderings II–VI

Black Notebooks 1931–1938

Translated by
Richard Rojcewicz

Indiana University Press
Bloomington and Indianapolis

This book is a publication of

Indiana University Press
Office of Scholarly Publishing
Herman B Wells Library 350
1320 East 10th Street
Bloomington, Indiana 47405 USA

iupress.indiana.edu

Published in German as Martin Heidegger *Gesamtausgabe 94: Überlegungen II–VI (Schwarze Hefte 1931–1938)*, edited by Peter Trawny
© 2014 by Vittorio Klostermann GmbH, Frankfurt am Main
English translation © 2016 by Indiana University Press
All rights reserved

The paper used in this publication meets the minimum requirements of the American National Standard for Information Sciences—Permanence of Paper for Printed Library Materials, ANSI Z39.48–1992.

Manufactured in the United States of America

Library of Congress Cataloging-in-Publication Data

Names: Heidegger, Martin, 1889–1976, author.
Title: Ponderings : Black notebooks / Martin Heidegger ;
translated by Richard Rojcewicz.
Description: Bloomington : Indiana University Press, 2016– | Series:
Studies in Continental thought | Includes bibliographical references.
Identifiers: LCCN 2015035416| ISBN 9780253020673 (vol 1
cloth : alk. paper) | ISBN 9780253020741 (vol 1 ebook)
Subjects: LCSH: Heidegger, Martin, 1889–1976—Notebooks, sketchbooks, etc.
Classification: LCC B3279.H48 S36213 2016 | DDC 193—dc23
LC record available at https://lccn.loc.gov/2015035416

1 2 3 4 5   21 20 19 18 17 16

CONTENTS

Translator's Introduction

This is a translation of volume 94 of Martin Heidegger's *Gesamtausgabe* ("Complete Works"). The German original appeared posthumously in 2014.

The volume inaugurated the publication of Heidegger's "Black Notebooks." These are small (ca. 5 × 7 in.) notebooks with black covers to which the philosopher confided sundry ideas and observations over the course of more than forty years, from the early 1930s to the early 1970s. The notebooks are being published in chronological order, and the five herein correspond to the years 1931–1938. In all, thirty-three of the thirty-four Black Notebooks are extant and will fill up nine volumes of the *Gesamtausgabe*.

Heidegger gave a title to each of the notebooks (these first five to be published are "Ponderings") and referred to them collectively as the "black notebooks." The published series begins with "Ponderings II"; "Ponderings I" is the lost notebook.

As can be imagined regarding any notes to self, these journal entries often lack polished diction and at times are even cryptic. Nevertheless, the style and vocabulary are mostly formal, not to say stilted, and are seldom colloquial. This translation is meant to convey to an English-speaking audience the same effect the original would have on a German one, with the degree of formality varying pari passu with Heidegger's own. A prominent stylistic peculiarity I was unable to render in full, however, is the extensive use of dashes. Heidegger often employs dashes not merely for parenthetical remarks but for any change in the direction of thought. Sometimes dashes separate subjects and predicates, and some dashes even occur at the end of paragraphs. Due to differences in English and German syntax, I could not include all the dashes without making for needless confusion and could not place them all at the exact points that would correspond to the original text. This admission is of course not meant to imply I did capture the varied styles of the notebooks in all other respects.

The pagination of the notebooks themselves is reproduced here in the outer margins. All of Heidegger's cross-references are to these marginal numbers. The running heads indicate the pagination of the *Gesamtausgabe* edition. I have inserted myself into the text only to alert the reader to the original German where I thought it might be helpful (for example, as indicating a play on words I could not carry over into English) and to translate any Latin or Greek expressions Heidegger leaves untranslated. I have used brackets ([ ]) for these interpolations and have reserved braces ({ }) for insertions by the editor. All the footnotes in the book stem either from me, and these few are marked as such, or from the editor and are then placed within braces.

I am indebted to Charles Bambach for an insightful review of an earlier version of this entire translation; the changes he recommended have substantially improved the final text.

Richard Rojcewicz

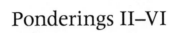

Ponderings II–VI

The entries in the black notebooks

are at their core
attempts at simple designation—
not statements or even sketches
for a planned system.

INTIMATIONS X PONDERINGS (II)
AND DIRECTIVES

October 1931

M. H.

πάντα γὰρ πολμητέον[1]
Cf. pp. 19 and 132.[2]

---

1. ["For all things are to be ventured."—Trans.] {Plato, *Theaetetus*, 196d2. *Platonis Opera*, ed. John Burnet (Oxford: Clarendon, 1900).}

2. [All cross-references cite the pagination of the notebooks themselves, indicated here in the outer margins.—Trans.]

What should we do?   1
  Who *are* we?
  Why should we *be*?
  What are beings?
  Why does being happen?

Philosophizing proceeds out of these questions upward into unity.

*   *   *

1

What we extol as blessing depends on what afflicts us as plight.
    And on whether *plight* truly urges us on, i.e., *urges us away* from
staring at the situation and talking it over.

Greatest plight—that we must finally turn our backs on ourselves and
on our "situation" and *actually* seek ourselves.

Away from detours, which merely lead back to the same beaten paths;
sheer *evasions*—remote and desultory—before the ineluctable.

The human being should come to himself!   2
    Why? Because a human being "is" a self—yet is *in such a way* as to
lose or indeed never win himself and to sit somewhere otherwise captivated and transported—we still scarcely see all this great being and
potential for being as we gaze at wretched imitations and dried up and
incomprehensible exemplars—proffered "types."

But: how does a human being come to his self?
    Through what are his self and its selfness determined?
    Is *that* not already subordinated to a first choice!
    Insofar as the human being does not choose and instead creates a
substitute for choosing, he sees his self
    1. through reflection in the usual sense;
    2. through dialogue with the thou;
    3. through meditation on the situation;
    4. through some idolatry.

Supposing, however, that the human being had chosen and that the   3
choice actually struck back into his self and *burst it open*—

i.e., supposing that the human being had chosen the disclosability of the being of beings and by this choice was placed back into Dasein,[3] must he then not proceed far into the stillness of the happening of being, a happening which possesses its own time and its own silence?

Must he not have long been silent in order to find again the power and might of language and to be borne by them?

Must not all frameworks and specialties be shattered here and all worn-down paths be devastated?

Must not a courage, one which reaches very far back, attune the disposition here?

4   Someone who sticks fast to the foot of the mountain—how will he ever even see the mountain?

Only more and more rock faces.

But how to come upon the mountain?

Only through a leap from another mountain; but how to come upon that one?

Already *to have been* there; *to be* someone placed on the mountain and ordered to be there.

Who was already so? And *is* it still because no others can drive him away?

Beginning and re-beginning of philosophy!

2

5   We stand before nothingness*—to be sure, but in such a way that we do not put nothingness and this standing into effect, do not know how to put them into effect—cowardice and blindness before the opening of the *being* that bears us into beings.

* Indeed not before nothingness—instead, before each and every thing, but *as nonbeings* (cf. p. 50).

---

3. [Heidegger's term, in the most literal sense "thereness," for the beings we ourselves are, thematized specifically as places (*da*) where occurs an understanding of what it means to be (*sein*) in general. When hyphenated, Da-sein, this thematization is emphasized.—Trans.]

3

Must the great lone path be ventured, silently—into Da-sein, where beings become more fully beings? Untroubled by all situations?

Has it not long been folly and confusion and groundlessness to run after the "situation"?

"Situation"—at the beach and in the sand, small mussels are splashed about, into them we wriggle and see only wrigglers but never the waves and the upsurge of beings!

4   6

Nothingness—which is higher and deeper than *nonbeings*—too great and worthy for any individual or all together to stand before it.

Nonbeings—which are less than nothingness—because expelled from the being that negates all beings.

Less—because undecided, neither amid beings, since these latter are more fully, nor amid nothingness.

5

A disregarding of the situation is to be set in motion, but out of the positive aspect of the ineluctable—the disregarding of the situation and the justification for doing so.

We first are our situation when we no longer ask after it.

Back into the "unconscious"—i.e., not into "complexes" but into the truly happening and necessary "spirit."

This devilish—or rather deified—farming of the situation! The *semblance* of seriousness.

6   7

Mankind no longer knows what to do with itself—and consequently conjectures "everything" in the end.

7

Mankind believes it must do something with itself—and does not understand that Da-sein has already done something with it (beginning of philosophy)—from which mankind fled long ago.

This—the fact that *in Dasein* beings have being—i.e., become more fully beings and more fully nullified—is the mission [*Auftrag*] of humanity in this happening.

8

Being and Time I[4] a very imperfect attempt to enter into the temporality of Dasein in order to ask the question of being for the first time since Parmenides, cf. p. 24.

9

Objection to the book: I have even today still not enough enemies—it has not brought me a Great[5] enemy.

10

8

Thoughtlessness toward the "tradition" and disdain of the contemporary belong to the keen-hearing diffidence before the past.

11

Jaspers writes three slapdash and uninformed volumes about that which philosophy—in creative individual works, and only so—bears in silence (silence-bearing), namely, the fact that philosophy goes to the issues. And thus every common barker and writer is handed the formula to talk on and on even about the philosophically ultimate. And thus the impotence of "contemporary" persons for philosophizing—indeed even only for a return to antiquity—is not only proven but also justified. Even "being" is now brought into the longest-winded idle talk, and each one may with equal justification maunder on about what strikes him.

12

Yet "say" it to yourself daily in your taciturnity: be silent about bearing silence. Cf. p. 17.

---

4. {Martin Heidegger, *Sein und Zeit*, *Gesamtausgabe* (GA)2 (Frankfurt: Klostermann, 1977).}

5. [Regarding capitalized adjectives, see the editor's afterword.—Trans.]

13

The essence of truth must first be transformed and must be transposed into a new sharpness and hardness so that beings may find admittance.

To admit beings—let them through "through" Da-sein. Ambiguity of the "through" ["*Durch*"].

14

Therefore, it was a mistaken view that *Being and Time* could overcome "ontology" *directly*. The appalling "result" is indeed only that the prattle about "being" has increased and has become *still* more groundless.

14a

Everything is to be set still deeper; thus first made ripe for transformation.

Everything—i.e., first and only the beginning of philosophy.

15

We are not strong and originary enough to "talk" truly *through* silence and diffidence. Therefore, one must *talk* about everything, i.e., prattle. (Cf. p. 93.)

16

10

Being is to be set more deeply into Dasein through the actual question of the essence of *language*.

Thus with Dasein a transformation of truth and being is to be compelled.

That is a happening of history proper; for this history the "individual" is inconsequential and counts only inasmuch as he secures for himself in *effective* work a possibility of repeatable impulses.

17

Being not without language—but precisely therefore *not* "logical." Language not without being.

18

The law-awakening must happen out of the depth of Dasein through the fully assumed conditionality of an individual human being.

What is human resides in trusting to the depth of Dasein! The adverse criticism of human partiality is to be endured.

What is effective is *not* that which is deemed worthy of agreement.

11

19

The one who must philosophize "today"—and by that I mean someone under the irrevocable power of the *beginning* of Western philosophy in antiquity—has the assignment of maintaining constantly effective a dual attitude in all hardness and decisiveness: *on the one hand*, the *interpretation* of the ancients, as if what mattered was nothing else than to let *them* alone come into words (beginning and history of the question of being), *and then* the attitude of the most broadly and deeply interpretive questioning out of the ground of Dasein—as if at issue was nothing other than to help "being" to a bursting forth in actual work and in a first solitude (overcoming of the question of being).

This duality, however, is *one* (cf. p. 14)—this one nevertheless is the grace of the calling to an incomparable fate.

20

We are merely plowing the field, so that this fate might find a place where it could bring the seed to itself in safekeeping.

21

Or rather: we are merely gathering stones and weeds in a devastated field and are clearing it so that the plow will find an unobstructed path.

22

The time is not ripe for understanding the *question of being*, neither in terms of a living inner mastery of its proper and full history nor in terms of its essential power of attack on the possibilities of Dasein (art—faith—nature).

12

Still less, however, is the time strong for that which the question of being actually only prepares: *its overcoming* in the sense of an actual re-beginning with the beginning.

The presentiment itself lies far from the fact that the essence of truth must first be transformed again and become actual in Dasein by way of a work.

23

Only if we are actually errant—actually *go* into errancy, can we strike up against "truth."

The deep, uncanny, and thus at the same time great attunement of   13
the errant ones as a whole: *the philosopher.*

24

Only with increasing depth does genuine breadth expand.

But also only that depth closed up again in the configured work will in the future encompass the breadth.

25

Yet whither the philosopher presses forward and what to him beings as a whole newly become—that is his ultimate, and he must be able to make it precisely the originary and first. Precisely this is denied again in a necessary way.

And therefore he is precisely from his deepest depth originarily able to be overcome.

To know this gives for the first time fruitful and clear position *in* the work to the work and thereby to the effecting and disdaining of what is ineffective.

26

14

The essence of *time* is to be questioned disclosively in order to find ourselves in our moment.

27

Need to consider history truly, i.e., that which remained *un*done and henceforth shut itself off, so much so that the semblance could arise that it is not at all there and never was.

28

The freedom which indulges that undone history is to be awakened once again.

Not as if the earlier could be retrieved—but so that it can come to us now and quickly out of ourselves according to our necessities.

29

Inquisitiveness and craftiness never allow a thing to show its essence.

30

The philosophy to come must be an *exhortation*—exhortation to the being of the "there." Cf. p. 11.

31

The great difficulty of the new beginning: to let the voice exhort and to awaken attunement; but at the same time for the creating ones—to think all this in advance with clarity and to bring it into a creating concept.

15   The exhortation exhorts humanity to its higher affiliation and deeper rootedness.

32

This exhortation—of philosophy—is the *poetry of being*. The poetry of being earlier than beings (for us) and yet only in order to propound beings as older. The bursting forth of being in the packings of its poetry.

"Poets"—They poetize "only" beings in each case! and yet in that way also *being*!

33

Or must not philosophy a fortiori poetize beings? Yes, and even beings *as such*—as a whole.

34

Which poetizing? If yet no creating—poetizing for Da-sein—only there does *being* in general occur. Being becomes poem; therefore finite! Not the converse—to poetize beings and *thus* first empower them; i.e., to make Dasein at the same time mature for power and in the service of power!

35

The poetizing exhortation leads before something cor-responding—what cor-responds to the poetized—this "responding" manifests itself thus for the first time.

36

Can an individual still compel something essential?

Does that not lack the community of the few who endure it?

Where is the simplicity of preparation for taking something essential and thereby persevering?

Yet are these not questions stemming from a merely *semblant* thoughtfulness?

Must not a responsibility simply be accepted?

What is a responsibility?

To pledge oneself for something and sacrifice oneself!

Pledge oneself for what? For Da-sein to become powerful in humans and their measure and might!

But how to bring about this pledging?

Depth and breadth of the engagement of Da-sein in the question of being!

Whither with the asking of this question? Into the ᚺ.[6]

The whither is not the concerning-what! Instead, the concerning-what belongs to the questioning itself, which as a whole—as this whole of the question concerning being—has its whither.

But the ᚺ must be borne in silence through the questioning and in the attuned *silence* must be gained by struggling toward grace. Cf. p. 8.

37

This whither is the striven for in disclosive striving.

38

First thoroughly fathom the silence, in order to learn *what* may be said and *must* be said.

39

Science: do we still need science—i.e., what passes for it today? Who are the "we"?

Who needs essential science (like passion)?

The leaders and guardians—who are these—where should they stand as which persons?

Science still only an acrobatics of methods, a trust in the carrying on of learned pursuits, and the cocky presumption of transmitting and offering.

---

6. {Unfamiliar symbol.}

40

"Science" like passion and leadership. ["Wissenschaft" *wie Leidenschaft und Führerschaft*].

41

How is the *pledging* supposed to become effective? It has its own—hidden—mode of radiating out. And in the end this is a subordinate question.

More than enough if the responsibility is accepted.

42

Pledging as beginning of the origin—originary beginning!

17

43

Science must once again take its course—anew out of the originary pledging—and thereby it alters in its being and estimation.

44

Philosophy—is it for the sake of *cultivation* or for mere *factual knowledge*? Neither the one nor the other; as much the one as the other.

That means: it can never be grasped originarily from them—because its descendants as well as its origins are of a deeper stem.

45

Only *charged* concepts—ones that anticipate and *engage*—are "formative." *"Space and time"*—a long-since-familiar wordplay which still signifies only a neutral schema of forms, thanks to Kant and science.

But: "People without space"[7] and their most singular individuals without time.

What is "space" here?

What is "time" here? Origin of *H*. Is that also *space* as time for a "people"?

Space and time not the juxtaposed, which is simply "given," but instead the opening and upsurge of being, which must be striven for.

---

7. {Hans Grimm, *Volk ohne Raum* (Munich: Langen und Müller, 1926).}

46

How today everyone must immediately dispose of every half-thought he has in fact swindled out of someone or other and must store this up in "great works"—instead of keeping for himself genuine insight—such that the insight would produce something essential and would itself thereby disappear. Only if much does *not* come to light, is held back, do we have *some* evidence that the occasion has been created for something great to take form.

47

The ridiculousness of a "philosophy of existence," not a jot better than "philosophy of life."

48

To philosophize: to be under no superior.
     The new, not inceptual, end-like *beginning*.
     Philosophy! Finally its essence is up for discussion: it is to bring:
     Dasein into silence (positively)

being into words (language—truth)

     and the pretense about humanity into silence—thus it is to hazard humanity (positively). Cf. p. 21.
     But: to bring being into words means something altogether differ-   20
ent from erecting and disseminating an "ontology." (Cf. p. 22.)

49

Today (March, 1932) I am in all clarity at a place from which my entire previous literary output (*Being and Time*, "What is Metaphysics?,"[8] Kantbook,[9] and "On the Essence of Ground" I and II[10]) has become alien to me. Alien like a path brought to an impasse, a path overgrown with grass and vegetation—a path which yet retains the fact that it leads into Da-sein as temporality. A path on whose edges stands much that is contemporary and mendacious—often in such a way that

---

8. {Heidegger, "Was ist Metaphysik?" in *Wegmarken*, GA9, 2nd ed. (Frankfurt: Klostermann, 1996) 103–122.}

9. {Heidegger, *Kant und das Problem der Metaphysik*, GA3 (Frankfurt: Klostermann, 1991).}

10. {"Vom Wesen des Grundes," in *Wegmarken*, 123–175.}

these "path markings" are taken as more important than the path itself. (Cf. p. 102, 104.)

To be sure, up until now no one has comprehended the path—no
one has traversed it back and forth—i.e., no one has sought to reject
it. For that, it would be necessary to understand the "goal" or, more
prudently, the space (the "there") into which it wanted to lead and to
transpose. But this condition has not been met, despite everything of
"ontology" crying out as all too familiar.

21   And it is good that, above the confused enthusiasm, the ignorant
discussion and praise come slowly to an equally widespread "rejection," one certainly just as blind and removed from every confrontation, i.e., precisely from a more originary formulation of the question.

Yet why still record this, since to me myself the question is becoming ever more problematic. Cf. p. 22, 44.

50

Out from the foolishness of the idle talk about the situation, need to
"reflect" on the most remote preservation of the power of the origin.
(Cf. p. 81.)

Empowerment as preservation. (Cf. p. 24.)

51

We must philosophize ourselves out of "philosophy." (Cf. p. 19 bottom, 35
top, *89.*)

52

To be the leader—not: to go in front, but: to be able to go alone, which
means, however, to bring the aloneness of Dasein to silence and to do
so positively versus the pretensions of individual "existence."

22   ### 53

If the question of being had been grasped, even if only in a crude way,
i.e., grasped at all as *the* question (from Plato up to Hegel there is no
other, and what comes to be added makes no matter whatsoever), then
Being and Time could not have been misinterpreted and misused as an
anthropology or a "philosophy of existence."

It has scarcely been seen that the emphasis on the individual and
on the individuality of existence is merely a counterthrust to the
misinterpretation of Da-sein as "consciousness," "subject," "soul," or

"life" and that the individuality of the existing individual is not the problem but is only a contingent passageway to the alone-ness of Dasein, wherein the all-oneness of being happens.

(Cf. s.s. [summer semester] 1932, p. 25ff.[11])

54 23

I would give entire many-volumed "philosophies" for the single hard statement of Anaximander—even if only because this one statement compels us, i.e., compels us to examine whether and to what extent we summon up the power to *understand* or, in other words, to be at home *in* the questioning of being and therein to consent *to* being.

Since we can so easily become engulfed in later and contemporary things of every sort all around us, therefore even the most powerless person can still capture a crowd and accordingly step to the fore and do so with a cleverness which can feign an essentiality, especially if an "existentiell seriousness, " indeed meant in a quite valid and genuine sense, is standing behind this and over and above it.

That thereby, however, the least thing is happening for philosophy, I severely doubt.

But "politically" it is always incumbent from the first to side with the genuinely "existentiell" ones versus the "scientific" philistines.

55 24

Concerning *Being and Time* (cf. p. 7).—If I spoke as the learned "they," then I would have to say: to publish the book in a new edition would mean to rewrite it, but for that I have "no time," I have other tasks.

Would that that were an error! *Other* tasks in philosophy besides the question posed there—even if at first only partially worked out? The question of being. There is no other option except to write this book and only this book *again and again*. At the risk of remaining a *homo unius libri* ["person of one book"]. Beyond this *unum* ["one"], there is no *aliud* ["other"].

Therefore have to work out the question with more penetration and only just that; not at all the answer. The arrival of its answer at the end something quite peculiar! In the working out as semblant *analysis* the unique valid and lasting *empowerment*!

---

11. {Heidegger, *Der Anfang der abendländischen Philosophie: Auslegung des Anaximander und Parmenides*, GA35, (Frankfurt: Klostermann, 2012), 74ff.}

56

Philosophy merely the retuned reverberation of the great poetry. Re-tuning into the concept—i.e., retuning of being.

57

Retuning into an all-embracing disclosive questioning—but for what? For what? Why the entire hardness and coldness of the concept? In order to impart to beings their | full empowerment and to lead humanity to a more originary *poetry*—i.e., to one by which humanity can become great and can experience the bliss of high spirits.

Individuals!—and the many? They may go as they came.

58

The many now prattle everywhere of a "new concept of science" and do not realize that such can never be devised, especially if all power for concepts is so fully lacking, and this again because that which is to be grasped in the concept (being) is not understood.

59

Originariness, hardness, and determinateness of the *totalizing concept* [Inbegriff] signify something quite other than the semblant rigor of operating with mathematical symbols and promulgating the ideal of mathematical cognition.

60

What I imagine by an actual "*logic*"! (Cf. p. 35.) λόγος not "assertion"—| but the self-positing interrogative addressing of beings as such, which means that the *pronouncement of beings in being* is a basic happening in the "essence" of truth (ἀ-λήθεια). (Cf. s.s. 34.[12])

61

Not a doctrine regarding *content*, a doctrine to which an agreement must be established and which could bask in some sort of validity—but just as little the idle submitting of possibilities for selection—the

---

12. {Heidegger, *Logik als die Frage nach dem Wesen der Sprache*, GA38 (Frankfurt: Klostermann, 1998).}

frivolous and noncommittal relinquishing of one thing for another according to circumstances. *Instead*, achievement and empowerment to *one* decisive attitude that does not remain empty and formal but rather has its decisiveness in making fast and "grounding" the truth of beings in quite determinate horizons of vision and spheres of action.

This requires the highest conceptuality of the *"logic"* of the totalizing concept.

62

Slowly—and precisely for that reason without undergoing the genuine jolt—one will bring oneself to unite the understanding of being with what for *us* is the essentially possible essence of the—existent—human being and thence begin *to be* the much-discussed "whole" person.

63

Where existence, there question-worthiness of *being*, and vice versa. (Transformation of language.) The arresting of both is originary and arises *in the movement into the free domain*—since freedom forms itself—whereby for the first time struggle and preservation and the disappearance of mastery and rank.

64

If being is questioned disclosively, what forms first is concealment. Philosophy creates the concealment.

Language changes essentially—not primarily in vocabulary—but the mode of saying and hearing.

65

How first *in being* to beings! and formerly?

The fact that philosophy by essence places itself under its own *"critique"*—namely—in the basic question of how broadly through being beings may be liberated, i.e., newly *poetized*.

66

Philosophy:
    highest certainty of the way: through being to beings—
    innermost bond to the issues—
    most originary attunement—

hardest conceptuality—(totalizing conceptuality)—
inexorable simplicity—
deepest essentiality—
and yet—all this may already be present and still there is no success. Cf. p. 29.*

67

Earlier only weapons were burnished, and indeed very harmless and
short-range ones—now only "instruments" are tuned, perhaps quite
cheap and crude ones—and everything slurps tunings.

29   This burnishing and tuning make the concert, and the public even
believes that it is entertained and that it hears something.
When will we finally play and play on to the struggle?
Enough of tuning and burnishing! Or indeed not enough?
And in all this only a *writer* of words.

*All this is to be brought to conveyance through the pure pertinence
of the theory; if need be—piecemeal.

68

This uncanny knowledge of the possibilities of the past great one and
the tasks of liberating and configuring the possibilities—and yet the
equally powerful *necessity* of newly retracing the way oneself.

30   ### 69

All my labor always turning in two directions—*on the one hand*, only
as continuation on the way and preparation of the way—and it is inconsequential what thereby—in breaking through—falls to the side—
and is shoveled away.
On the other—this that is "brought out" for itself as "result" left behind—which to be sure never allows one to finish with the way and
the digging and to make for oneself an image of them—nor indeed
of the inner thrust (and the inner, ever self-transforming outlook) of
the entire advancement.

70

The world is in reconstruction (cf. p. 36)—but the poetizing power is
still in darkness—and yet it is there!

Who will liberate it? Not: who will quickly discover the cure through urgent trial and error in order to extol this power to just any arbitrary individuals; but only: who knows the law of the origin and I acquiesces to that law.

And *thereby* inserts himself into the dispensation of the soil of an inherited essence.

31

71

Only someone who is German can in an originarily new way poetize being and say being—he alone will conquer anew the essence of θεωρία ["theory," "beholding"] and finally create *logic*.

72

In labor always a clear planning and taking hold, even a finishing off, and what is properly attained thereby, what happens, is still never to be seen *all at a glance* or even seen cursorily—indeed for the most part it is not to be seen at all; always to dig and break loose in the foreground—but without this the concealed never attains its appropriate (i.e., precisely mysterious) liberation.

* * *

A great faith is passing through the young land. Cf. p. *41*.

73

32

Being, "our" being, is to be poetized more originarily.

"*Our being*," i.e., the being (happening through us and in us) of beings as a whole.

"More originarily"—to ask (indeed in advance and in an altogether more comprehending way) the unasked question.

74

In philosophizing, *never* to think about the "others" or about the "thou," but just as little about the "I"—only about and for the origin of being. This holds equally of the matter at issue and the way. ↗

75

The error of those of today: they do not know of the long, restrained growth of things and believe they can compel this growth overnight to produce any useful object they like.

76

Essentiality without groundedness remains frail—groundedness without essentiality becomes otiose.

77

Write out of a great reticence.

33

78

If I say philosophy is not science, then the scientific character—the essence of this character—is not taken from philosophy—but rather is preserved from the start in the only possible way.

Philosophy is scientific *in a way* that a science can never be.

And this is true of it *as* philosophy—therefore such a designation is a misunderstanding—of the same stripe as speaking of the "philosophy of life" or the "philosophy of existence" (cf. p. 34).

For the rest, the treatment of such "questions" is useless—if the work does not from the start testify to contemplation, claim, measure, and *ability*.

79

Clearer: not "origin," but instead *happening of being and happening of truth*—not "transcendence" only, but *the world's becoming world*, its beginning and existence.

80

How rapidly and thoroughly the growth of being in antiquity stalled and became petrified.

34   The disclosive questioning of being requires the essential leap ahead, i.e., demands a glimpse which makes a path for itself in the leap and in this path opens being. Essential components here: "modalities" and "copula"—already the terminology indicates a misunderstanding of the issue.

81

Philosophizing: *formative release of the happening of being.* The setting up of truth ahead of individual truths, the transforming of traditional "truth." (Cf. p. 36.)

Such release of the happening of being requires predominating clarity of the concept in its riches—this clarity in turn compels the opening through struggle of what cannot be comprehended.

Thus philosophizing effectuates the inner enhancement of both the happening of being and of Dasein in Dasein's breadth and depth.

The release can be for us only one that repeats—in every postulation it already accepts "beings" and proceeds into their history—accordingly philosophy *is* in itself history—not only incidentally—but in its very conduct.

82   35

Philosophical activity—discernible in what?

Whether such activity describes things and classifies opinions,

whether it improves the things handed down and displaces them,

whether it articulates and organizes everything knowable,

whether it grasps what is current (the situation!) and yet lags behind.

How all such undertakings must be justified from the outside—through the taking over of accomplishments in education, in "universal refinement," in "world view," and in "basic science."

All such only superficial and subsequent outer "aspects." (Cf. p. 21.)

83

"Logic" (cf. p. 25).—A person whose Dasein is *not* attuned to the essence of beings as a whole and to their chasms and "grounding" does not need—and does not deserve—any "logic." Such a one manages very well at all times with his "healthy" thinking. But one who exists in the essence must demand "logic" for himself. For it is—rightly understood and not as formal technique—the power and intrinsic exercise of the liberation of truth.

Therefore, perhaps a *correct* lecture course on logic—not the usual   36
old "dead" logic which never did live—for the most serious and "gifted"—not for the ungifted and those without resource in thinking. They are past help.

84

The world in reconstruction. (Cf. p. 30–31, 45.)

What seeks to become—in which *tasks* it thrusts itself forward—which perspectives compel these tasks; which happening (being—truth) is here at work—need to catch sight of and liberate this "work" in its fore-working.

85

Philosophy is never "of" or "about" something—always only *for*—for *being*.

All questioning is disclosive questioning; all investigating and analyzing, a fortiori and in the first place all projection and forming of a *work*, constitute an *effectuating*. (Cf. p. 40.)

But this not primarily a "working" "on" something; practical!—instead, the work is effectuated in that being brings it about. That holds in a derivative sense also of science. Therefore, already a mistake to start with "object" and "theme" and remain there.

37   First out of such an originary calling of the work and only out of it the first consecration and inevitability of the clear hardness of the concept.

86

We first find God again when we lose the *world* no longer and truly exist in the power of *world-formation*.

87

Why do eager reviewers and writers so uniformly and definitely *shirk* when it comes to the decisive treatise, "On the Essence of Ground"?

Enough already here with the reckoning up of "influences" and of the dependencies on Husserl, Dilthey, Kierkegaard, and whoever. Here the task was—if anything—to put into effect a confrontation with antiquity and with the retrieved problem of being. Instead of which, manifest prattle keeps piling up from week to week.

And now even idle talk about "philosophy of existence."—The masters may let themselves be "influenced" indeed by Kierkegaard, Kant, Hegel—; it is easy to see where this gets them. It is the peculiarity of

38   an "influence." | When people repeat Hartmann or Cassirer or anyone else, or even when, as is mostly the case, they repeat some rootless and homeless "general opinion,"—they mean that that is no influence. But such idle talk is never to be eradicated.

88

The being of beings and the history of "truth" have the same *"time."*
The extinguishing of being as "nihilation" of *"beings."*

89

Forward thrusts (projectively formative ones) *into* the happening of being and *outbreaks from* it.

90

Philosophy is *the* science, and precisely for that reason it makes no sense to speak of *"scientific philosophy."*

The "sciences" are "philosophies" (Aristotle). Therefore, if I say philosophy is not a "science," it does not merely mean not an "individual science" but also not one of the *pluralistic philosophies.*[13]

"Science" not the higher concept for philosophy; instead, the latter the concept of the former.

The concept of science cannot be drawn out of the factual organization of the extant "sciences," but only out of the idea.

91   39

Necessary in order to rebuff the entire perverted labeling of my endeavors as "philosophy of existence" or "existential philosophy":

1. clarification and grounding of the concept of existence;

2. clarification and grounding of the concept of philosophy. Cf. above, p. 33.

92

The usual (*today only fallen into the mere opposite*) idolization of *science* and of its accomplishments. Upon closer inspection, as regards the superficial, the technical, and the task and compilation of immediate "results," there is agreement everywhere and there is "progress"—but as regards everything *essential*, where the issue is *knowledge* in the proper sense, everything splits apart and is primarily a matter of a lamentable dilettantism.

Thus philosophy has no occasion at all to accept this science—not even mathematics—as a model; cf. the uncertainty and brittleness of the "foundations" of mathematics.

---

13. [The sense would seem to call for "pluralistic sciences."—Trans.]

Nor does it help to take what is lamentable and accidental of the operation and through "contemplation" and mere (artificial) "rootedness," replace it in the "people"—on the contrary, what is decisive here is only the might of the possibility of "existence"; (*not* in the ethical sense).

40   93

In Jaspers, a false, ungrounded respect shown to the (quite unpersistent and intrinsically brittle) "compellingly knowable."[14]

94

Staunchly into the ineluctable!

95

Autumn—not deterioration and dying, not the over and done—quite to the contrary, the fiery, glowing entrance into the certain silence of a new time of waking to the unfolding—the acquisition of the restraint of the established jubilation of the inexhaustible greatness of being [*Sein*] at its bursting forth.

96

Since philosophy has no "object" (cf. p. 46 bottom) and being is also never a "theme," therefore the philosopher, in all questioning and laboring, can never undertake "mere" investigations (cf. p. 36); on the contrary, he labors only if he thinks within the work to be effectu-
41   ated; admittedly the work-formation can I and must constantly change, until it is transformed into a sweeping blow. And the latter is then always at the same time renunciation of other possibilities. The greatness of the renunciation must lend to it a proper verve and an unrelenting hardness. The renunciation acquires greatness when the task is traversed in its manifold possibility.

The work-formation is neither "the system" nor the "book to be written."

_____

14. {Cf. Karl Jaspers, *Philosophie I: Philosophische Weltorientierung* (Berlin: Springer, 1932), 147.}

97

You are to ground the ground! From the grounding of the ground. *Cf. p. 80!*

98

Knowledge and belief—I can not and can never know that I know—if I know—but can only believe that I know. Yet this *belief* is then that originarily attuned familiarity with the ground—the Grounding vibrancy in the basic attunement. Therefore nonsense: to set absolute certainty qua self-knowing knowledge (evidence) as the measure for being and for the question of being.

Out of this belief (grounding of the ground) the poetizing thinking in the disclosive questioning of being. Cf. p. 31 bottom.   42

99

We discuss eagerly and loudly what we are to do, but we do not pay attention to what we are *to let go*. In the end, for us the main burden is that which we should "let go"; especially where the issue is the formative work. Yet such "letting go" is indeed *never* merely "negative"; on the contrary, it is basically only the reverse side of the way we stand toward authentic power and genuine "knowledge."

100

Every question a pleasure [*Lust*]—
    every answer a loss [*Verlust*].

101

What counts is the *empowerment of being*! and of this alone. And such empowerment is not to be carried out through a presentation of "ontology" or the like, but only through the formative stamping of the essence of being itself. Cf. p. 48.

Can humans do this? They *must*. Otherwise, they go to *ruin* on their indifference to Dasein—which means, however, *it continues on in that way*.

102   43

Philosophy least of all is capable of eliminating the already all too severe plight (the external one) or even of pointing out ways to that end.

On the contrary, philosophy must remain hard against the plight and keep itself hard to the wind of *its own* storm. For momentary and eager fussing over the situation demonstrates only that such fussing is always without importance.

For all too long already in "philosophy" there has prevailed an eager flight from its task; for all too great a distance there has spread an unlearning of the capacity to wait for the growth of the essential things. And this because fraternizing with the inessential is still all that guides the word and could make us believe that this fraternization will in the end still bring us to the essence.

Only one who remains *hard* to the wind of the first ineluctability "experiences" for himself the right to hardness and to the semblance of unconcern over the present condition of the nation.

44   Philosophy can—at best—be transferred to the margin of the possibility of staunchness in the ineluctable.

For the most part, however, things remain in the well-tended swamp of the actuality of the changing inconsequentialities.

103

The task is to place *Being and Time*—as a book—into the shadows by way of an effectuating of what is intended in it but in the actual "work" is in many ways unsuccessful. That would be the proper refutation.

104

The power of the simplicity of the pledging in the staunchness toward the ineluctable.

105

The highest steadfastness in the guise of mere "relevance"; indeed the former to be achieved only through the latter.

106

The "liberal" sees "connectedness" in his own way. He sees only "dependencies"—"influences," but he never understands that there can be an influencing which is of service to the genuine basic stream of all flowing and provides a path and a direction.

45   He does not understand that to such effectuating the craving for originality is a frivolous pastime that has long been irrelevant.

107

Once more: the world is in reconstruction toward itself. We are again approaching the truth and its essentiality—we are becoming mindful of everything the truth requires to take it up and to take a stand within it—to become ones who are indigenous, who stand on native soil.

The one who can be indigenous is the one who derives from native soil, is nourished by it, stands on it—this is the original—that is what often vibrates in me through body and disposition—as if I went over the fields guiding a plow, or over lonely field-paths amid ripening grain, through winds and fog, sunshine and snow, paths which kept mother's blood, and that of her ancestors, circulating and pulsing. . .

The other indigenous ones—to them this root has withered, but they persist on the way back to the soil and to esteeming the soil.

108

46

The running around has an end—the progress has become satiety—we want to come to a stop.

Halt! And here is the originary limit of history—not the empty super-temporal eternity—instead, the steadfastness of rootedness.

Time becomes space.

But the originary time becomes the fore-space of the duration.

109

Where there is growth, there is silence and not the noise of bustle and of loud demands, of ardent student bodies, of the participating throng.

The one who bases growth on things like that or even (which is equivalent) grieves over their lack—he comprehends nothing and has in himself no task.

110

Empowerment of being—not to seize subsequently in concepts and stretch open that which we already possess anyway, but to effectuate for the first time that which does not yet occur. By essence, therefore, philosophy has no object [*Gegenstand*]. (Cf. p. 40, 101.)

47   ·   *111*

"Configuration of a new actuality"? Employing old, obsolete means and aims—without knowing or even questioning what is signified by actuality here as a mode of being. Yet have earlier generations done this? Certainly not—but their configuration was also appropriate and was never so much on the verge of nothingness as we are today. Here there is no—still so eager snatching after Christian and Protestant doctrines and ways.

                                        112

The essential is to be championed to the last!

But have we even only surmised it, let alone taken hold of it—and are we inclined to involve ourselves all the way to the last?

To name only one—Nietzsche! He is pillaged arbitrarily and accidentally—but no effort to set his most inward intention on a ground, in a work, on a way.

48   *113*

The *empowerment of being*—through treatises? Certainly not—but only through that happening which comes to maturity and is granted place in the thrown understanding required by the treatises.

The task is to indicate *the* empowerment of being *in this way* at the same time and to set it in motion thereby. Cf. p. 42.

The empowerment—nothing an individual is capable of—also nothing appropriated by a community—not even the rootedness of a community in its indigenousness.

For all this must already "essentially occur" in that one individual—otherwise he would not be an individual but only the inflated case of an empty universality. And so to march out community and "communication" here is merely a misunderstanding.

For there is a hidden communication through the *essence*—a communication which is therefore not to be named so. The alone-ness of the individual out of the essential ground of things cannot be pressed into the "individuality" of a community, even if this latter is ever so
49   zealously based on | the "thou-relation" and ever so apparently avid for "authority."

These are indeed only pretexts for the ultimate emptiness of a first essentiality.

If this primally arising essentiality of a person in his ineluctable individuality is *also* called "liberalism," then not only is this catchword being used too freely but it also demonstrates how little one is summoned to traffic in the essential—despite all of the zeal.

The one who publicly accedes to the "configuration of an actuality" must not speak of "new orders of value" as his end-all and be-all; he runs the risk that there will come to light a great incapacity which will no longer let itself be concealed by ever so much objective knowledge, cleverness, and zeal.

114   50

In the end, we have not undergone any trial at all, indeed have not even prepared for one—we even lack the knowledge of the way to such a preparation for a trial. Instead, there has been an escape into Christianity, or some other frenzy has instituted itself; one gads about in the superficial and babbles on. All this in a casual ignorance of being; under these circumstances, how are beings as a whole supposed to concern us at all?

There is talk of nothingness and of us being set into nothingness—as if that were a word, or meant something, whereby the most groundless indifference no longer appeared.

We have indeed no longer anything to champion—even this possession of our Dasein—the antiquity of the Greeks—must first be conquered by us—how should we truly await here | the coming might of   51
being.

115

The human being—a steep path in an ever stronger wind!

116

That the *Greeks*—so entirely without *"science"* and *"prior to"* it—created *philosophy*! They were not yet exposed to the reproach of "mere speculation," a reproach deriving from sciences in decline, whereby philosophy is discouraged and constantly distrusted. Thus there spreads a leveling down to the "respectable work" of science, which at the same time allows its techniques and its entire apparatus to come into play—and thus scarcely any possibility of not falling victim to this ever-lurking falsification of philosophy. Philosophy has quite lost its own inner form, *because it no longer has its own questions and, thus impoverished, merely chases after the sciences.* (Whence also the will to "system" and the yearly more comprehensive books, which are "new" only by sporting the latest hairstyle.)

52   The *essence of being*: it occurs as the partitioning into possibility, actuality, and necessity—on the basis of the empowerment of the ineluctable. Cf. below*!
        Empowerment as poetry.
        Poetizing and thinking. (Cf. p. 88.)
        The first task is once more—no matter whether it amounts again to
"science"—to create grounded horizons and make them familiar, so
that out of them can arise an experiencing and a first speaking. Today, on the contrary, these are mere expedients, and one must practically apologize for using them; one would like best to manage "very
well" without them.

Insufficient and consequently misleading are: (cf. p. 62)
        a) the attitude toward being which merely describes it and ana-
lyzes its meaning as presumably an unprejudiced and therefore "originary" attitude;
        b) the regress to the conditions of possibility perhaps on the basis
of a "constitutive" consideration, whereby still beyond this the very
dimension of regress is unclarified and ungrounded—instead, some-
53   thing like a mere | "logically" driven return to further conditions—;
        c) the classifying systematization of thereby acquired or otherwise
gleaned and improved determinations of being (categories) in a "doctrine of categories";
        d) not even the questioning back to the dimension of constitution
and systematization, a questioning explicitly undertaken on the basis
of such initial steps (a, b, c). Cf. Kantbook: dimension of origin;
        e) also not at all something like the envitalizing of these consid-
erations through a linkage to "existence" or "life" in a further moral-
practical sense. (Enmoralizing of scientific comportment.);
        f) just as little the superficial ascent to the absolute, taken over from
Christian tradition. (Cf. p. 66);
        > *in this way*, everything that is pushed back and forth into direc-
tions of questioning and materials, ones taken over or simply snatched
up, remains some sort of exchanging of that which has never
"newly"—i.e., originally—been the "old." This in any case gives the
54   facile impression of progress and of "nearness to life"—| but ultimately
gapes at one in an irresponsible inconsequentiality.
        Instead, what matters is:

117

to configure the *empowerment of being* toward the preeminently
dominating and impelling experience and procedure; therein and

thereby everything that was genuine in those previous initial steps is first worked out and is incorporated into its free accomplishment.

Yet this is an entirely untrodden path, although in the beginning and as the beginning of philosophy the first and most proximate space for it and for its broaching was created.

To take the path means: to reckon ever again with relapses and with the increasing difficulty of the steps, especially since every step is effectuated only in a piece of work and of utterance—above all because the articulation of the path must be ready and manageable in advance and constantly. (Cf. p. 76.) "Church fair" 1932.

The effective tuning puts everything here on another course.   54

Yet the course must remain under wraps—it comes to light only in the soberness of the work.

118

The human being *is to be hunted throughout* the entire foreignness and alienating character of the essence of being in all the essentiality of that essence.

Need to effectuate both in one: the *alienating character* of the essence and the *ineluctability* of the essence.

And this hunting up and never resting is simply "only" through a growing and pertinent disclosive questioning—the basic attunements in the view and the attitude, but never in words!

To hunt up into the (first) ineluctability.

To hunt through the full foreignness.

To hunt down the entire alone-ness of the human being—

and then commences the hunting of the empowerment.

The ineluctability of being! Being itself as ineluctability. (Cf. p.   56
69, 105.)

119

The long-extant irresponsibility in talking on and on about being and its "meanings" does, despite all, proceed apace and is now for the first time actually raised to a principle through so-called ontology and a fortiori where ontology is denied (Jaspers) and precisely there is also not understood.

120

"*Science*" is at an end and precisely for that reason it can least of all be taken positively as "compelling knowledge" and the latter as leap to

God Almighty. In that way sciences receive Christian sanction at any time in their entire wretchedness—and this is the opposite of a philosophical overcoming and transformation.

Who could say what will move into the place of science?

This alone is certain: it depends on whether and how we once again involve ourselves in being.

121

It is an unspiritual representation of *Dasein = the effectiveness of philosophy*, if that means philosophy is effective only in case it is mediated and passes over into "actuality." What they here call "actuality"—precisely that thrust which, lost in itself, grasps nothing.

The effectivity of philosophy is not in those doubtful uses of a lexicon, that adornment of common ponderings with propositions read up in philosophy books.

The "effectivity" *effects* nothing—but consists instead in testifying to the start of a transformation of beings out of empowered being.

And this testimony testifies only in the effectuated work, which necessarily stands in itself, gives away nothing of itself, transmits nothing of itself; on the contrary, it sooner only draws to itself—in order to repel. But this movement is the unsettling of the hitherto, an unsettling that will not be admitted and is therefore falsified. There is no accommodation between philosophy and "actuality."

122

How far advanced are the Greeks over us; there is accordingly no returning to them—only a catching up. But that requires the power of throwing oneself forward in a primally arisen disclosive questioning. And that means simply to liberate the Da-sein in today's humanity.

123

The *distant injunction* [*ferne Verfügung*] in which philosophizing takes its course! (Cf. p. 85.)

124

A sketch of the whole: (cf. p. *61*)
    The liberation toward Dasein—   (*)
    The empowerment of being—
    The truth of the essence.

10-18-1932

124a

*The gathering up toward Dasein,
  in order to empower being by way of sustaining it
  and thus to let truth happen.
The greatness in all this: all backstairs and purposes and "senses"   58
become otiose.

125

The human being is neither ordained toward "grasping"-"hearing" nor "born to see," "bound to behold"—but instead is thrown into attunement, called to being—i.e., so that he might empower being.

Long and bitterly enough have beings been affected by the "haptic" *and* "optic."

The confrontation with antiquity, i.e., with the beginning, is worth *both*!

126

The failure—the other writings and *Being and Time* have not in the least succeeded even only to nudge in the direction of questioning, let alone produce an understanding of the question, an understanding which would lead to a retrieved questioning. Instead, only inane idle talk.

Yet how one with such a huge failure nevertheless for a while can   60
be on everyone's lips and on the nib of everyone's pen and can thereby make a "name" for himself.

How dreadful that is—not for the one concerned, who has and retains *the* task—indeed grasps still more firmly his new task—but rather for those who totter about in such idle talk and next year must already be on the lookout for something new to chatter about. Yet—there must be persons (*"scriptores"* ["writers"]) who make a vocation out of this and a business as well.

127

Handed down propositions about being . . . (Cf. p. 75 top.)

128

Dismantling of the adopted "laws of thought"*
  Regress to the origin, which is thereby "shown."
  Construction of that which those "laws of thought" "genuinely" say
  out of the origin into the empowerment.

*cf. treatise on the "Principle of Contradiction."[15]

61   *129*

Highest clarity
innermost attunement
broadest essentiality   } in the disclosive questioning of being—
purest simplicity   as the silence of the essence.
hardest inexorability

This disclosive questioning may swing out—better: swing in—to the question-worthiness of being, a question-worthiness effectuated by this very questioning. Deeming worthy *in this way*, the questioning empowers being.

Thereby the absence of all the false rigor of the cheap and broad systematization of what is said very often and just as superficially; free from the intention to spread cheap edification; untouched by all excited "existentiell" pretense.

Only: awakened alertness for disclosive questioning in Dasein; thus solely to unconceal the latter itself and, in it, the concealedness of beings.

Questioning in the deepest—immediate—connection to the beginning of philosophy through the Greeks.

62   *130*

Write down the concealed dialogues of language.

131

(Cf. p. 152.)—Not return into the ego; instead, transition to the world. In the transition, at the same time an entrance into Dasein.

Not lostness in formally abstract being; instead, gatheredness in the whole of attuning being.

Not sticking tight to an actuality; instead, binding to the bindingness of the partitioning.

Therefore, neither *construction* of the "logical" (categorical) nor *intuition* of something "real"; instead, a disclosively questioning projection of the projected-attuned-attuning project.

---

15. {Heidegger, "Der Satz vom Widerspruch," to appear in GA91.}

132

To take being out of the ἔστιν, *the "is" (cf. p. 119)*—was of inmost necessity to the Greeks.

For they were to be the first to take being into understanding (which for them, e.g., for Parmenides, was νοῦς, apprehension). In such a horizon was grounded their existence in the midst of beings as such.

Why, however, precisely presence—from the *present tense* of the verb? Because presence the most proximate and the enduring.

Opposed to nothingness—opposed to the "not" and the "no."   63

The beginning necessarily an immediate assertional "yes" to continuance, constancy, and circle.

The constancy maintains itself in all variations and extension in Plato (μὴ ὄν ["nonbeing"] as ὄν ["being"]) and Aristotle (δύναμις—ἐνέργεια, κινήσις ["potentiality—actuality, motion"]).

This understanding of being was incorporated by Christianity (Augustine—Thomas) into the horizon of an eternal creator-God. The understanding of being was thereby implanted into a realm of faith and became entrenched—*lumen naturale* ["natural light"].

Yet thereby for the first time the innermost act of beginning and questioning on the part of the Greeks was bent over toward results and—still more—toward the first truth.

The mathematical idea of knowledge at the start of modernity—itself basically ancient—now brought a grounding and new confirmation to the philosophical system. This renewed obstruction of the beginning found its conclusion in Hegel. His historical construction, which expressly took antiquity as *thesis*, became in this way a fortiori the suppression of the beginning.

Christianity and idealism, especially in their intermediate and decaying forms, supported the nineteenth century and its "science." Historical science and natural science found justification in the understanding of being (ἔστιν, presence) that had long been self-evident. The past merely the present-at-hand lying further back. Nature the present-at-hand currently graspable.   64

Thereby indifferent—positivism or idealism: for both, beings are what has presence.

Nietzsche was the first to see the doom, specifically in terms of *morality*. He saw: the *meekness* before the ἀεί ["eternal"], the prostration before the object—the perversion of the once-erect, battling, dominating way of questioning into the serfdom of self-absorbed science. Nietzsche alone saw "today's situation," and he could do so because he foresaw something else.

He thereby created a completely different attitude for humans—one of looking forward and demanding.

This superhuman labor had to break a man. (Cf. s.s. 32.[16])

65   Nietzsche did not go so far as to transform being and I create a new horizon; ultimately because he himself did not understand the ancient problem of being. He could not *in this regard* break the hegemony of the tradition. Hence his fatal opposition between being and becoming, an opposition dating back to his early years (1873).

But he also remained misunderstood here; the "unscientific" philosopher. Everything remained as of old. The phenomenologists (Husserl and Scheler) did manage this one achievement: they awakened the immediate perception turned toward the things themselves (intuition—essence). In other words, they awakened something of the attitude characteristic of antiquity. But rootlessly and in subjection to the nineteenth century, i.e., within its schemata and "problems."

Alongside this, in desultory and accidental consequence of Nietzsche, a multifarious unrest, confined to individuals and groups; the war——

And subsequently: 1.) historiology of and for the present

2.) worldview, and that as "presupposition" for science

3.) demand that science be close to life

4.) "philosophy of existence" (Jaspers).

66   But all this out of antiquity—indeed back into it—cf. Jaspers, whose "system" offers the most genuine philosophical presentation of this half-measure.

"Science" (entirely nineteenth century; Max Weber)

"existence" (Kant—Kierkegaard—philosophy of life)

"transcendence"—Christianity.

Everything remains as of old—indeed "science" and "transcendence" were even devalued in favor of existence—i.e., relativized toward it. Being is constantly under discussion—and yet the question of being is not surmised in the least, let alone comprehended. Consequently the way has not even been paved for this question. On the contrary, the work has been looking backward.

("Dialectical theology,"[17] on account of its inconsequentiality and swindle, does not deserve attention. It is the worst deployment of Protestant Jesuitism.)

---

16. {*Der Anfang*, 45f.}

17. {Strain of Protestant theology deriving from Karl Barth's commentary of 1919 on the epistle to the Romans.}

What should happen? Taking action—*creatively* acting and only "speaking" of it to oneself.

The task is now:

To win back the beginning—to question again within its most in-   67
trinsic questions—; admittedly, that is possible only if we ourselves have appropriated the *questioning*. What does not help here is merely to modify or append.

For instance: instead of being, becoming (Nietzsche).

> instead of the present-at-hand, the past, and in-
> stead of the elevated "eternal," the so-called present.
> instead of spirit, the soul and the *body*.

rather:

> the task is to disclosively question the full essence of
being—wherein presence (the "is") is positively fused, and at the same time its predominance is struck within its limits.

Being must unfold its horizon further and now indeed fully (time). That means: the attunement.

The partitioning must determine the attunement—it must form the horizon for being—(space—time).

Not the "it is," but the "let it be" (thrown projection) and specifically the "let it be" of the original taciturnity.

133   68

The essence of being is truth (ἀλήθεια); therefore truth is to be questioned disclosively in its ground and origin. Yet precisely for that reason it is *erroneous* to grasp being on the basis of the "true" proposition (judgment); for such is not *the* truth.

134

Crisis of science and of the concept of science!

Indeed we still do not at all possess the space and the perspectives in which a genuine and fruitful crisis becomes possible.

If we do not succeed in actually doing something again with the beginning of Western philosophy, then the end is inevitable. Why? Cannot something later likewise serve to stimulate and lead? Must there always be this going back?

Indeed a going back cannot actually be carried through, since we exist in a tradition insofar as we exist at all. It is not a matter of choice.

Yet why back to the beginning? Because to us more than ever, and to Western philosophy already for a long time, simplicity, essentiality, and a sense for the originary are lacking.

69   The like can be understood and genuinely appropriated only under the power of an actual *exemplar.*

Quite apart from the issue of *that about which* we must philosophize, the *how* of the questioning, the how of treating the questions, must first be accorded rank and measure.

Yet no less the *what*, that which we have to question, for here the *how* requires and leads to the proper and unique *what*: the question of *being.*

135

The essence of being: a *taciturnity that conceals.* The essence of being is truth I partitioning—and the latter? Taciturnity that conceals, ineluctability. *Silence-bearing*—(cf. p. 62 top, 79, 90 bottom ff.).

136

A *vast amount of the correct* in philosophy and a *scarcity of the true.* For that sort of correctness is always untrue—insofar as it unconceals nothing essential but, instead, conceals everything essential—; the correct is arbitrarily repeated and altered, mostly in extrinsic parroting of what is noised abroad, without the soil and approach, horizon and concept, in the least prepared or grounded.

70
137

If, beyond the beginning, beyond the grounding of the understanding—in general—of being, the understanding—as such—of being becomes a problem, then the question of *being as such* (not only of beings as such) is broadened and deepened.

Yet if the *understanding of being* becomes problematic in that way, it means that *existence* as such is coming into question, and thereby so is the *human being.* But not in the usual "existentiell" sense.

This questioning transformation, however, in and through the question of being.

Only *in that way* does the reversion into *existence* happen historically.

138

We must place ourselves back into the great beginning. (P. *109,* 126.)

139

The basic philosophical question of being (p. 131) is not the question of the human being—"philosophy of existence"—on the contrary, the question of being first provides the possibility, and thereby especially the limits, of the question of the human being—already because this being must necessarily be grounded anew in his essence by way of the question of being. Therefore, that essence never simply lies at hand for philosophizing to snap up.

140   61

Philosophizing: projection of being out of the plight of the distant injunction, a projection that builds *forth*.

Not a *"mere"* projection as the plan of "research tasks," but building: driving piles, setting beams and crosspieces.

Building on being, whereby already as building the basic attitude is different. Cf. p. *114*.

Not watching and considering "creatures"—but also not merely becoming conscious of what is—and thereby meaning that because knowledge is a "more" and an "in addition" it therefore would already be a transformation—on the contrary—thereby only the binding to the decayed and crippled is secured while at the same time the illusion remains lucid that one is in fact beyond these—. The erroneous opinion of Idealism, above all of German Idealism: consciousness would be a higher and transforming level of being—but also the countererror: it is enough to leave the "world of consciousness" as it was in order merely to build it back into the "soul."

Yet *how* accomplish this projection that builds forth? Perhaps   72
through the writing of the thickest possible books? No! But must there indeed be communication?

Yes! But not mass communication.

Instead, simple, slow, surveyable and yet precisely inexhaustible and perpetually afflicting communication.

Good signs for philosophy, which to be sure promise it nothing positive.

The great uproar of the last decade, which no one with insight could take seriously, is giving way to a weary murmuring. And already resistance is bestirring against this "excess of philosophy"—and rightly so. For on the one hand this was and is no philosophy, and on the other hand it thrives only if it has gained acceptance. A "philosophically interested" epoch is the death of philosophy.

It bodes well for the future that German youths deeply reject "philosophy" and "science," for only *in that way* will I these youths be able
to experience all this again essentially and indeed want to experience
it—they would then no longer be German. Such rejection the first actual deed.

To begin, to "know" less and know less often, in order to experience the wretchedness of this mere cognition.

141

Two weights have long been burdening our existence and today press
down on it even more because they are no longer felt as such.

1. the entrenchment and trivialization of the ancient understanding
of being (an understanding which is itself already alienated) in the
Christian "worldview" and in the secularization of that outlook;

2. the mathematization of knowledge, the concern over certainty
and over so-called provability and relevance.

Both these weights belong together intrinsically, and only through
philosophy can they be radically sprung open and productively sup-
planted. Cf. p. 104.

Yet that indeed means: to "believe" in a completely new beginning
of philosophy! Implying in turn: to become equal to the first beginning and—confrontationally— I to start with it?

In building forth, to demolish; in demolishing, to build forth. These
are *one*, and only as this unity does each have right and power and
possibility.

142

The unconditioned basic attunements as forces of the bursting forth
of being.

The essence (a) [*sic*; a = *activ*, "active"?] of being as the silence-bearing empowerment of the ineluctable (i.e., time).

143

How arduous is the path into what is due: no longer to concern oneself with the "philosophy" at hand and so to overcome all misinterpretation.

This indeed signifies nothing other than *corresponding* to the essence
of being! That is the meaning of authentic existence, which *Being and
Time* still presents much too "existentielly" and extrinsically. It does
so because even the question of being still wallows in erudition and
the concomitant dross. (Cf. p. 104 top.)

144

The philosopher as one who travels alone; but not alone with his small "self"—on the contrary, with the world, and the latter *prior* to all "with one another."

145

75

Need to transform the traditional propositions about being into questions and put back the questions as maelstrom into the grounding of the empowerment.

146

The silence-bearing empowerment of the great intimations in the opened road.

147

At the earliest—because already in the beginning—what becomes senseless in philosophy is the so-called constant researching on and on, as well as the correction of "mistakes," and the contribution to an overall goal. Where something like that is sought, the empowerment of beings has already been renounced—indeed thereby we see that such never was operative.

148

Care—not the trifling worry of humans over their daily troubles, but the aggrandizement of Da-sein in the fearfulness of the essence of being (partitioning).

149

Therefore, need to understand care and *language*. (P. 97.) The *pronouncement* out of this fearfulness of the breadth and abyss of the (modal) partitioning. Bursting forth and acceptance—projection—attunement.

150

76

Mankind and Being (cf. p. 94.)—that would merely be the title of a thoroughly erroneous task, no matter whether being was referred back to humans (sheer subjectivizing of the understanding of being) or whether humans as beings among others were placed under being. In either case, the *possible* existential essence of mankind—*empowering swing into the happening of being*—does not get liberated.

Here—with such a swinging in—humans forsake their usual humanness—and a greatness is effectuated in which humans disappear and *beings are.*

What is first in this regard is to experience in general the existence and transcendence of mankind—and insofar as these are supposed to be "shown," the task and the accomplishment of *Being and Time* are justified. Otherwise, however, the book is erroneous in many ways and not equal to the genuine question. Thus the title is *still* warranted. (Cf. above, p. 52f., and 91f., 94 bottom.)

151

The enduring-projecting swing-in is to be brought to indigenousness; all the rest—thus especially every sort of "effectivity" and "noteworthiness"—is inessential, i.e., inconsequential and at the same time a danger to the essence, because thereby the essential is rubbed away and dispersed.

77   Need to find the breadth and depth and direction of Dasein and make its task indigenous and binding on Dasein. It is of little help to say: step up to the things and leave the "schools"—the listening and reading—; for the things could be all too graspable—without thinghood and projection—so that more than enough of what is actual—and yet no being.

152

Absence of the essential affliction:

Signs of it: the lack of a Common will and knowledge; the lack of a ground and soil and path and air for these—the lack especially of a commonly experienced, and above all commonly desired, actuality. This because everywhere and for a long time the *impotence for an indicational excitation of being has been reigning.*

153

There is said to be a new actuality now: the political will of the young people. What is "the political"? (Cf. p. 81.) In every case, something essential resides here—insofar as it is not a mere "reaction" to the extrinsic and typifying self-comparison against other possibilities, circumstances, and eras.

This desire to come again onto a soil I augurs an awakening but   78
likewise stands in a double danger: either "the political" is altogether
absolutized, or it is all too facilely incorporated into an apparently renewed Christianity and into the cultural assets of Christianity.

But: labor camps, battle teams, colonists—

Thereby this awakening is without indicational power toward a
distant injunction—not equal to the burdens—not needing the clear
coldness of the concept and the sharpness of the affliction of the essential fearfulness of being. Thereby everything falls back at once into
the old concepts and valuings—pessimism/optimism and the like.

People without work—above all, without a calling.

More fateful: without a will to these things; without the constraint
of the growth to such volition.

Once again have to become *subservient* to the *mystery* of fallow
ground and seed, germination and growth, wind resistance and fruitfulness.

Preserver of the excitation of being in the depth and breadth of being. Tradition of such preparation and preparedness. Therein resides
the mysterious ordination of the individual to his I people, such that   79
as mature he would become the guardian of the blessing of Da-sein;
this blessing merely endures the fearfulness of being; and that fearfulness presses toward blessing.

The—mysterious—*harmony* of these preservers and guardians: to
rouse oneself and individuals to it and to secure oneself therein. First
of all need to open space for this, prepare the ways, and send in advance the directions—such is the arousing of the happening of being.

Only if and only as long as this originary *aloneness* of Dasein is experienced can true community grow indigenously; only thus is to be
overcome all publicness of those who have come together and are
driven together.

154

"Existence" as pledging [*Ein-stand*] and acknowledgment [*Eingestän-
dnis*] in being; "in" being, toward beings; this is to be conducted up
to mankind.

Question of being—the disclosive questioning of beings.

155

Who knows in what we have become mired?

80

156

The *essential fortuitiveness of being* (partitioning) is the fearfulness of its essence and likewise the concealment of the blessing.

On the "ground" of this—namely, *the* fortuitiveness as such in being—the entire superficiality of the *sciences*—causal research—first becomes visible, and therein is manifest how much they foster the semblance of truth and do so merely in a previously dimmed realm.

157

How the "principle of sufficient reason," ever since the αἰτία ["cause"] in ἐπιστήμη ["knowledge"], is concerned with the *presentification* of the semblance of the partitioning—and properly bears in itself a withdrawing from the essence of being and henceforth always promotes this withdrawing. Precisely because the whole mob of those with understanding and reason will protest against this, the fortuitiveness in the essence of being must belong to its truth.

Fortuitiveness and groundlessness and width and breadth of the future of being. (Cf. p. 41.)

81

158

This appeal to the situation is perpetuation of the superficial and the run-of-the-mill. In any case it is completely unable to determine the standpoint of the admission (acknowledgment)—for precisely the *mania for the situation* dispenses indeed with the exertion of the projection of the track on which the human being stops, a projection that stems from far back and that disposes far ahead. This mania indeed plays only with the givens, and it intends and contends that this is "actuality."

159

The political stirring of the young people (not of youth).

Youth is essentially participating.

This happening of today:

1.) is suspected under the label of "party politics," and so the old keep their distance from it with the slogan: menace to the objectivity and pertinence of "science";

2.) or—which is still more fatal, because more deceptive—it is falsified into something harmless—"political instruction"—"the individual and the state." | Moreover, the demand of "timeliness" is supposedly satisfied thereby.

82

3.) Or one falls prey to a reduced imitation of party activity. Not only a misleading of political stirrings, but a self-disintegration.

Yet all this merely the aberration and roiling of a nascent coincidence and of an incipient jointure. For which the indication is this:

The stirring not a fleeting tickle—instead, the emergence of an agility in the appropriation of beings—the enduring of an early hardness, the approaching of a free cultivation—awakening bond with that which afflicts. Work—people—cultivation—state—| opening up of the world.

All this perhaps still confusedly in dispersing and disapproving of what has been handed down and has become rigid, and yet *the one*— the other; remaining absent and left behind are mere self-dissection and self-comparison—self-exclusion as a typical possibility versus many others—overcome is the miring in consuming and crippling "analysis" and in false theorizing.

On the other hand, there remains the error of an extrinsic separa-   83
tion between "actuality" and "ideology"; neither the one nor the other—i.e., the originary nexus of the happening of being is not recognized and grasped, and precisely therefore all knowledge as such is misinterpreted and devalued and, in correspondence, easily-mouthed "doctrines" are gullibly accepted.

All this because no attunement growing into the ground, an attunement in which the absence of the essential affliction could be experienced. Therefore, no exposedness to beings as a whole—no conducting into beings—no acknowledgment.

And yet again a forward-bearing superiority in that acceptance of beings—all the more pressing if it is supposed to be preserved and at the same time expansively acquired, the reacceptance of the stirrings in the affiliated track of the happening of being. Cf. p. 77.

Acceptance of beings in and through the cultivation of the empowerment of being. This as the disclosive questioning of the (partitioning). This youngest unexpected stirring of young people in unity with the most exceptional oldest people—the latter, however, more originarily | transformed. But already, as long since, of no use is the refer-   84
ence to some sort of higher or highest actuality—Christianity—; invented myths of whatever sort—; and this not because they have become powerless, empty, and uprooted—without the conclusiveness and force of something grown in fruitfulness and blessing—but because mankind and we in particular (as delegates) cannot measure up to beings as such.

What counts is to bring to acknowledgment (existence) something higher than all this—being itself in its expanding breadth and depth.

As with the inexorableness of that stirring, so with the *strangeness* of this first task of all; to make *it* binding and indigenous in us. The basic question—(cf. p. 78, mystery . . .).

N.B. Obviating two misunderstandings:

1. as if at issue here were a philosophical substructure for some sort of political action in the narrower sense;

2. as if in general this were still an occasion to form some sort of "philosophy."

85   Even if only a few experience it: we are already catapulted too far from the outworn groove of the satiated comfort which allows itself to be content with improvements and with the reconfiguration of what has been handed down; we are too tenaciously seized in our essence for us still to be moved by such things. We come to terms with the radically dominant hostility against philosophy and take this widespread pretense (bearing the title of philosophy) as a swindle. We can do so only if and only as long as we have subscribed ourselves to the inexorableness of essential questioning.

The world is in reconstruction; mankind is awakening.

160

The *struggle over antiquity* (the Greeks, the early Greeks) will be waged not as a dispute about accepting or rejecting something or other there, about the degree and kind of the distribution of something that has been—but instead as a *struggle over the beginning,* over the grasp of the beginning and over the acknowledgment of the unavoidableness of the act of beginning and thereby over the theme of a distant injunction—the catching up to the latter. (Cf. p. 58, 89, 132f.)

86   ### 161

The full questionableness of being as the blazing of the flame at the hearth of beings. (Cf. p. 97 bottom.)

162

"Ideologies" have now been discovered, and they are immediately made out to be "illusions," in contrast to the "actual," which is restricted to the everyday and to external need. Thereby a comparable error arises; in both respects, beings and being are not grasped. Instead, the actual is now given a religious and indeed Protestant title, people are chased into church, and this is called meditation on "existence." The literati now enthuse not over "spirit," which they reject, but over "countryside" and "people," and the wretchedness of these doings is even greater than before.

163

Science: The sciences are quick to appeal to the rigor and invulnerability of their *method* when they sense, and want to conceal, the meagerness and shabbiness of the matter under consideration; whereas on the contrary the essentiality | of the matter creates for itself its method,   87
yet at the same time does not allow that method independence but, instead, absorbs it into itself, so to speak, *in such fashion* that even the way, as belonging to the matter at issue, becomes essential.

164

Need to think forward in advance into the mission of the acceptance of greatness and so, in one, to plant the action back into the powers of what is incalculably ineluctable.

(Happening of being.)

165

The law of the essence (a) of the simple deep breadth of Dasein—*being* essentially occurs.

In the empowerment of the essence, have to leap over everything, whereupon we indeterminately strive to take everything in, whereby we think, confusedly enough, to liberate and bring to conveyance all that afflicts and compels us.

Harmony is to be made operative in such empowerment.

166

Philosophy is to be grounded in itself of its own essence, not Da-sein on it; but indeed precisely in service to a grounding of humans out of beings and into them!

167   88

Thinking and poetizing. (P. 121.)
    Thinking is . . .
    Such delimitation itself poetizes; for, what thinking is is nowhere to be found and picked up—instead, it opens itself only to the pre-

scribing-configuring projection; this means here: the outreach into the concept.

Such outreach, however, is interpretive and thus a matter of thinking.

Therefore: poetizing and thinking entwined in each other, and so what they are would be acquired in a determination that both joins and separates them. Indeed such a procedure unavoidable precisely at the outset and yet only a first grasp of something primarily groundless and without prospect—what there still is here of the utterance of the word.

A question: where and how does the original oneness of that intertwined unity have its happening, its necessity, and its mission? In the essence of philosophy—as disclosive questioning of the essence (a) of being.

(Poetry as myth
Poetry as poetry in the narrower sense. "Poesy."
Poetry as philosophy.)

89   *168*

Must we today in the end *break off philosophizing*—because people and race are no longer equal to it and because its power is thereby diminished even more and reduced to impotence.

Or is the breaking off not at all necessary, since already for a long time there has no longer been a happening?

Therefore, flight into faith or into some sort of wild blindness, even if only that of rationalizing and technologizing.

Or must the *breaking off* be *carried out*, just as much as the beginning—so that this stopping must become a happening in the most proper sense and an ultimate exertion—

But what will be broken off and ended? Only that inceptually poor running on of the history of post-Greek "philosophy." | The dismantling a "breaking off."

So that this breaking off would become the opening up of the beginning, the re-beginning of the beginning (cf. p. 85). The greatness of the going down would be reached—not as a disvaluing—but as a seizing of, and persevering in, the innermost and outermost mission of what is German. (Cf. p. 21.)

90   *169*

Need to find the most proper mission and, by transforming it, to join it back into beings as a whole.

Not the curiosity-rousing individuality of the "personal," but the collected greatness of the work.

Markings: how far labor and attitude keep themselves away from the pull of "trends" and designations;

how strongly insensible to the everyday semblant urgency of what is present;

how sure in rejecting the misleading claims of today.

Must not confuse oneself with the "publicly" delineated and urged "self."

Must enter into the fearfulness and tediousness and into the blessing of essentially occurring being.

170

Against the priority of being over beings!

(Understanding of being; the usual question of being.) And thence: altogether against being!

171   91

Connection to the conclusion of Being and Time I (p. 437f.). After that, the "investigation" is "underway" in the kindling of the question of being.

Underway on which way? Over the understanding of being—Dasein—temporality—time, and toward the "meaning of being."

And being? In which schema?

1) Unarticulated and unexplicit: the questions of traditional ontology, the modes of being of the (regional) domains, the modalities, the copula—everything considered and pervaded by the understanding of being oriented to this ontology.

2) The "expansion" of the Greek ὄν ["being"], οὐσία ["substance," "estate," "property"] (qua constant presence and against "becoming") to everything that is not nothing.

3) Being as so grasped related to understanding.

4) Being at the same time taken back into the "existentiell."

This "underway" on a way which simply takes its course somewhere? Or paved according to signs (εἶναι—νοεῖν—λόγος ["to be—to apprehend—discourse"])—without considering (cf. p. 95: semblance of being) that this way might already be a wrong way, indeed that I even "being" and beings wrongly have this priority. The inceptual way offers at once a prospect on beings, and this prospect is now definitively taken as the goal of the way—very well heeded even later in the entire tradition up to Hegel and Nietzsche.

92

In order to secure this way and indeed to compel taking it up again, I have recourse to the greatness of the beginning and thereby to an essential predelineation of the mission.

And yet—there is a nagging doubt as to whether in the end everything is not aberrant—or if not that, whether precisely out of this beginning and its continuance we are not faced with a task completely different than that of "repetition."

At first the breaking off, which must not escape into the dismantling that indeed merely remakes "the way." On the other hand, no possibility of starting everything all over again, out of a void; on the contrary—*still* more originarily bound to the beginning out of the essential mission and therefore *freer* in relation to the beginning.

93   The task is a poetizing compression of the essence, in order thereby to bring "being" to disappearance (cf. p. 101). For that, the previous labor (especially since *Being and Time*) must be preserved as sharpest opponent and made even stronger.

Earlier, the way was for me still much too easy, almost a game which things fell into—then a struggle. The currently acquired opponent also that which alone is communicable—but not as such—instead, precisely only in itself—; already thus there is opposition to the traditional forgottenness in the question of being.

Now the sayable word found, behind which the proper fruitful silence can unfold. (Cf. p. 9, 69, 115.)

172

What is *onerous* (full of inconveniences and obstacles) is still not *heavy* (from weight); what is heavy is still not necessarily *deep* (pointing into the abyss). And what is deep still not ever need be *serious*.

173

94

Mankind and being. (Cf. p. 76 above, 116, 119.)

This "relation," provided it is one at all, is completely obscure. Neither from the one (mankind) nor from the other (being) is a resonant unison to be perceived or even imagined. And so how they might be connected is still unquestioned—despite—indeed precisely because—the "subject" has long been fastened into the theme of philosophical questioning, no matter whether only in detachment from the "logical" or with the aim of leaving human beings behind, on the way to "consciousness in general" or the like.

Unavoidable above all: a sufficient even if one-sided clarification of being, and not merely an *understanding* of being.

"Mankind," on the contrary, seems sufficiently discussed already. But that is mere seeming, for in aiming at the relation, precisely the *understanding of being* is overlooked as a basic happening and is merely co-included subsequently under alien psychological rubrics and faculties (*ratio*, reason).

Therefore *against* anthropologism, *for* mankind; against the "existentiell," *for* existence—standing-out as the standing-forth endurance (persistence) of beings—*against* existence, for Da-sein; "against" Dasein, for being; | against being, for the essence.   95

In the essentially occurring essence toward the *uniqueness* of the *isolation* of being in nothingness.

Need to let humans go *in themselves* along with the understanding of being, but this "inwardness" is the outside—and in the innermost the outermost grows. The unavoidable.

The deepest is the widest.

The outermost, however, remains being, even if at first only in its *semblance*:

a) as the most universal and emptiest—; the palest and the blown apart of that which is valid for many and for all; the quantitative;

b) as the mere "concept" and "the abstractum";

c) even as the ground—qua condition of possibility in the homelessness of the so-called a priori;

d) as what is intensely and constantly present (οὐσία);

e) as the perpetual and incessant sayability of the "is" and of its *obtrusiveness* over and against "beings."

The beginning must fall victim to this *semblance of being* (cf. p. 91) such that in general being gets caught in the question of being and no longer allows denser compression. (Cf. p. 119 bottom.)

Philosophy arises while held in the power of this semblance. It   96 stands and at once falls—in that it becomes "science"; or an independence is thought up by which philosophy is posited "next to" religion and art. Out of this independence philosophy seeks to *give* and to ground but in the end only takes and must admit its subservience to another.

What is this other? Not faith and its treasures—instead, that which philosophy forsook as it had to entrust itself to the semblance of being and become blind to the fortuitiveness of being itself, qua that in which the highest and sharpest necessity of the poetry of the essence lies closed up.

But is this decline to be carried out again in reverse—certainly not—as long as we are no longer equal to the beginning and do not bring the greatness of this semblance into the open so as to enkindle the mission by it.

That semblance of being, however, places itself around and before humans, and they are reflected therein as beings among others. Then 97 the delusion I arises that it is impossible to step outside of the relation of mankind and being, which yet one must do in order to question disclosively the whole of this relation. Except that one would step into nothingness. Yet as long as this is allowed merely as something mis-thought, contrived, it is only the semblance of that semblance.

Yet if the outermost is only the innermost of the human being, then the outside becomes the inside of the innermost and deepest, becomes that place where the human being has forsaken himself the longest and in the highest mission of his essence has found himself.

Have to come back from there as a complete alien and bring along— set down—the most alien.

174

The alien (*the human being*) *and* the great fortuitiveness (*being*).

The throwing into being and the trembling of the thrownness into the essence as *language*.

Language: the hearth of the world (*cf. p. 75, 117*). *Here* the uniqueness of the revealing-concealing isolation in the simplicity of the alone-ness of Dasein. (The unison.)

98

175

Science: despite—indeed *because* of—all the obtrusiveness of science over and against beings, how much we are turned away from beings and relegated to our self-alienation. Yet even so we remain thrown into being.

This running behind the sciences by "philosophers" is as ludicrous, pitiful, and customary as the centuries-old nipping at the heels of the respectively current "philosophy" on the part of theologians.

176

How far removed from *nature* must natural science be, such that it con-siders one of its successes the raging of technology, a raging grounded on that science?

Whither has *history* escaped from us, such that newspapers and fac-tions can boast to be its preservers?

177

Folks whose noses will still smell the day after tomorrow, and who still have on their tongues the day before yesterday, behave like ones who had known and configured the "new actuality."

178   99

τὰ γὰρ δὴ μεγάλα πάντα ἐπισφαλῆ, καὶ τὸ λεγόμενον τὰ καλὰ τῷ ὄντι χαλεπά.[18] "Everything great wavers and wobbles, stands in a storm. The beautiful is difficult."

The latter portion is an old dictum (Solon?); together with the former, it expresses the entire essence of the Greeks. Both are gathered in the δεινόν ["uncanny"] (cf. Sophocles's *Antigone*).

The beautiful is difficult to open, to endure, and to safeguard. This difficulty announces the greatness which wavers. In all this, the measure of beings as such. In Plato, only still a vestige of it, and after him and already through him it decays into the empty and rootless *convertabilitas* ["convertibility," "equivalence"] of *ens, verum, pulchrum, bonum* ["being, true, beautiful, good"]—or else it is even squandered in the infernal catchphrase: "the true, the good, the beautiful."

The attunement of the beginning is to be experienced on the basis of that dictum. *The concealed deep mourning over the veiled decaying of the essence into being as presence.* (Cf. place, time, discourse, outward look, "view.")

179   100

On clandestine ways to God who is "dead." (P. 109.)

Some humans lose themselves in a timeless and spaceless ground-laying occupation. Here the "grounding" alone is still "the actual," and even this eats itself up. Ever thinner and emptier but also ever more arrogant becomes this unrolling into a mere revolving. Here the ultimate ground-laying is to occur, which is then supposed to be followed by an unshakable progression of collaborative research by many. Here scarcely yet something actual which can still be relieved of actuality.

Others throw themselves into the "situation" and make the same "God" (transcendence) and the "world" (compelling knowledge) subservient to moral (stoic) existence and persistence. Here everything remains as of "old," i.e., as before in an average Kantianism. Here no rolling on, but instead an empty, increasingly blind treading in place,

---

18. {Plato, *Res publica*, 497d9.}

and what there still might be beyond this is degraded to a "cipher" for an "x," and this back and forth of ciphers is left to some sort of empty frenzy.

101 Both groups are without future and without past and therefore possess only the semblance of the present. For the former, philosophy something producible in correspondence to the "sciences"; yet even these are not so and today are all the more an aberration—why the ground-laying here? For the latter, an occasion for a moralizing psychology of various occurring human possibilities of philosophizing.

Everywhere an evasion of history; *thus* the clandestine ways to something which is supposed to be allowed to stand *over* all that.

Someone starting out indeed needs to know these occurrences, but he must not for a moment be diverted into *"refutation."*

180

Need to conceal and preserve being while *sheltering* it, so as to help beings to power thereby.

The sheltering concealment in the reticence of the essence; but the reticence requires precisely disclosive discourse about being. The question of being is necessary, but only as the most proper service to the sovereignty of the essence.

102

181

That most vain modesty, which takes itself merely as a pretext in order to guarantee completely the unruly puffing up and the public preening—in order to veil the loathsome self-praise of one's own wretchedness in the sheen of a pretended virtue.

182

Psychiatry deals with the "experiment" that lets beings themselves happen with regard to the relation of being and nothingness.

183

Being and Time (cf. p. 20)—what was there a *means and way* to pose the question of being for the first time is made into a goal and result by all who claim the intention was a "philosophy of existence." It is so easy and satisfying, therefore also reassuring, to ferret out the many borrowings from Kierkegaard; in the consciousness of this "detective" achievement, one goes into retirement or gets on one's "high horse" and relegates the genuine problem—indeed then to whom? To no one—since the problem is not at all seen, on account of the blindness induced by existential philosophy. But why upbraid these I contemporaries—if that is what this is—when the author himself stupidly held back the main point! Or was it an "unconscious" prudence, thanks to which this main point was saved from being minced into a great mash of "situation," "existence," and "decision"?

The hysterical bother over existence, and what is bound to this bother and follows from it, cites Kierkegaard and Nietzsche and proves thereby that it seeks support from those in whom is visible an incapacity to philosophize in the grand style but who continue to philosophize further, along with the others, the remaining, inept individuals. Neither Kierkegaard nor Nietzsche had the courage and, above all, the power—if anything—to break off with philosophy—but such is, as in all human creations, something positive, by no means a mere running out and ebbing, and Hegel, who brought to completion, utterly did not posit the end—because he no longer grasped the beginning.

184

104

Being and Time on its way—*not in its goal and task*—did not become master of three ambient "temptations":
1. the *"ground-laying"* attitude of neo-Kantianism (cf. p. 113);
2. the "existentiell"—Kierkegaard—Dilthey;
3. "scientificity"—phenomenology (cf. p. 73, *133*).
Thence also the "idea of dismantling" *determined.* (Cf. p. *128f.*)

The "criticism of the book" sees only *these* dependencies individuated and believes it can from them also reckon up the goal and the task (it does not see the ineptness to the task).

Have to show how those three conditions themselves arose from an[19] inner deterioration of philosophizing—from a forgetting of the basic question—and that *therefore*—not at all because they merely stand in place of something contemporary—they must lack every suitability to clear precisely the *way* for the basic question. (Cf. p. 107.)

Whether what is disclosively questioned in the basic question can by itself demand and determine the way; for that, it must previously be empowered sufficiently in the essence—thus already thoroughly questioned—why then still seek the way? That is the way of the work.

We say *too much* about the analysis of the inessential, we say *too little*   105
about the empowerment of the essence.

---

19. {*Phä Zhng* [*sic*] {?} written between the lines.}

185

The *absence of the affliction* through being. (Cf. p. 122.)

The distorted essence of being has rubbed away all being. What has remained: the transience of all beings and, in correspondence, this easiest capacity to get hold of the most arbitrary things.—Nothing stays, but also nothing escapes.

186

The forgottenness of being is the untrammeled gaping which spreads emptiness through all things.

The forgottenness of being has uprooted beings and allowed them to degenerate into the indifference of the sundry. *The neglecting of the recovering question is the erroneous presumption.* Nietzsche said: "God is dead"[20]—but this is spoken exactly in the *Christian* manner, precisely because it is *un*-Christian. And that is why the "eternal recurrence" is merely a Christian expedient—to give the inconsequential "life" once again the possibility of importance. And this remains an attempt at salvation in "beings" versus the nihilism of beings. And therefore this traditional understanding of being is furthermore taken over in full exaggeration; "power" and so on.

106   But—we can encounter the distorted essence of being only on the basis of the essence. We must go back to the place where the human being *throws himself adrift* into the essence of being. And re-find the swinging arc of the throwing; clear this track for humans.

But the essence can never be "intuited." (Cf. p. 55.)

187

To the *mania for ground-laying* corresponds the aiming at the *fabrication of a universal*—comprehensible to everyone—"*worldview.*" And *both* can be surmounted or "grounded" through the "*question of being.*"

And if the question of being is to be renounced? Already even because it does not pass by the miserable rummaging in wretched human nature?

But what to put in its place? Must philosophy still be? End! But actual ending? Then a fortiori "anthropology."—or else the actual poetry of being.

---

20. {Friedrich Nietzsche, *Die fröhliche Wissenschaft, Werke,* vol. 5 (Stuttgart: Kröner, 1921), 163.}

188

The *"ground-laying"* as question of the *"conditions of possibility"*—this respect of questioning rests completely on an understanding of being in the semblance of being, an understanding fabricated on presence (ἀεί—a priori). Thereby the "ground" is secured in advance, and, through the mode of questioning, the horizon of possible "understanding" is also already circumscribed. Understanding aligned to "producibility," established on this as its sovereign domain. But what kind of "producing"? An uncreative one—for in advance—better: in reverse—the "conditions" at hand are already postulated.

A question: how must matters "basically" be, so that we understand the starting point as the understanding of being and as the outcome of the understanding of being? Which is *our* understanding—that we here make the measure of elucidation—whereby we are "satisfied"? Origin of this entire way to question? On the basis of the sovereign understanding of being! (Circle!)

| Kant—Leibniz—Aristotle—Plato |

How in each case the stock of conditions and the field of conditions— how far themselves secured or only snatched up and inner-logically{?} —contradictionlessness of thinking—εἶδος—ὕλη—λόγος—ἐπιστήμη— τέχνη ["form—matter—discourse—knowledge—technology"] | discussableness—*contradictionlessness*—possibility—essence. (Cf. p. 111: presence according to Parmenides.)

189

Whither the human being throws himself adrift, there he unfolds the *presentiment* of his directionality, and "there" the "there" arises, the originary open spaciousness and thence also space. Through this space is thrown the swing of time—the world forms itself "in" space-time {?}.—Herein the partitioning essentially occurs.

The contingent is included in such projection—the essence (a) in its happening not at all the origination (presented in the reverse direction) of something producible. Thus would be grasped only what is graspable in *such* an understanding—something concocted—where nothing which comes entirely from itself and thrusts into the essence can play in.

190

The *originary silence* as *further* silence in and out of the pre-sentiment of language. But that silence is not inactive—rather, the initially opening listening into (beings).

191

Partitioning: collapse and excess. Bent into unity out of one another.

192

The human being is jostled out of (himself), which serves as testimony to the throwing of his throwing (himself) adrift, wherein that move was thrown forth. Throwing oneself adrift and *errancy*.

193

Why must we place ourselves back into the beginning? (Cf. p. 121.)

Because we have been thrown off the *track*. The evidence of it is the absence of the affliction (p. 105). The track, however, is that of the self-throwing adrift of humans into the (essence); on this track, the essence of being is opened to him (p. 106). Only on this track and in the momentum of the directionality of its throwing is the question of being to be raised—perhaps as a dismantling question.

But the *absence of the affliction*—why not leave it at that? Already because we experience it and say it—we are not at all "beyond it"— instead, we still stand in the *after-sentiment* of the *directionality of the throwing of thrownness*.

The return—which is necessarily a conquest—into the beginning is thus not striving for any improvement of philosophy—as a reparation for something neglected by antiquity—or the setting forth of an exemplar—or the like. For—| the fate of philosophy remains entirely open—perhaps the result is its end and the mission of its stopping.

That after-sentiment is still a faint recollection of the erstwhile greatness of humans in upsurge—and perhaps this greatness must come again, so that things can go to the "end"—an end—which indeed can become a new great beginning.

194

Need to stand—i.e., question—in the after-sentiment and pre-sentiment of the greatness of humans as ones who throw themselves adrift (p. 121) *and therein build oneself firmly and completely—*

So as to drive back there, among other things, the current humanity—and attune the disposition in the questioning that bears silence. Thereby then—what we so name—the transience and the merely psycho-bodily—are to be taken in the extrinsic sense—of course without dealing *with it*. (Mistake in w.s. [winter semester] 29–30.[21])

195

How the first throwing oneself adrift in that which it opens (being—presence—apprehension—view) is *snatched up* and held fast. (Cf. p. 124ff.) Following up the priority: of the uniqueness and unity of presence (cf. also p. 107 bottom). The absence | remains repudiated; this   111 questioning does not become master of it, under the predominance and superior force of presence. The essence, apparently unique-unified-clear, is so severely confined to presence that conversely only on the basis of this latter is all "essence" once again posited. (ἀεὶ ὄν ["eternal being"]—eternity and the like; cf. even the ἄπειρον ["the limitless," "that which contains no contours"] of Anaximander!)

This constrained essence never allows the absence repudiated by it to be grasped further and more deeply than merely formally and negatively—let alone to be gathered back into the essence. (But Parmenides; Diels, fragment 2: λεῦσσε . . . , cf. s.s. 32![22])

Only as "parts" of time and as μὴ ὄντι ["nonbeings"] do they, with Aristotle, come into their own in a very remarkable way. Yet what *thus* was established back then about being (essence) and time—is only the pronouncement of the snatched-up beginning, at which it had to stay—as a new entrenchment resulted—despite finiteness and "salvation of the soul" and "history"—indeed precisely through these—a fortiori through Christianity. How "modernity" did not find out—but, rather, utterly entangled | in the dialectic, supposed itself   112 "liberated"; how Kierkegaard and Nietzsche—assisted themselves in that they completely abandoned the question, turned their backs on everything, and thereby remained precisely in fetters—how today, with all that, everything completely totters in great confusion and obliviousness.

Yet absence is not merely to be incorporated for itself in a subsequent retrieval; instead, the essence is to be transformed—indeed first to be attained as such.

And absence is richer, more mighty, and of a more originary essential force than overdone presence. Absence as beenness and as future.

---

21. {Heidegger, *Die Grundbegriffe der Metaphysik: Welt-Endlichkeit-Einsamkeit*, GA29–30 (Frankfurt: Klostermann, 1983).}

22. {*Der Anfang*, 174ff.} [There Heidegger renders the fragment as follows: "Behold now how what was previously absent has steadfast presence for apprehension."—Trans.]

Both as the originary bending apart of the essence and as essentially occurring unity. And ultimately presence only a forgetting of these.

196

How in the throwing oneself adrift the *essence* springs forth—what is to be known of that and in what way. In the essence spring up truth and errancy.

113

197

The *intention toward "ground-laying"* (cf., among others, p. 107) merely simulates a "radical" questioning—but in fact remains mired on the surface of *that which* is to be grounded here. The "ground" and the return to it are already "settled"—i.e., determined, secured, and agreed upon.

This deceptive occurrence takes possession of the sciences almost from the beginning (Plato: ὑπόθεσις ["hypothesis," "something laid down underneath"]) and thenceforth (Descartes . . .). And one now accounts for "philosophy" conversely from these—philosophy becomes innocuous—a supposedly ever increasing depot of secure cognitions | which, should any one of these alleged cognitions persist, merely have the drawback that no devil, let alone a human being, bothers about them. Yet this scientific philosophy even has an explanation for that: it is not at all necessary that truths be valid for themselves—therefore let us leave them and, along with them, their tiresome guardians. But at times their treasures appear tiresome to these guardians themselves—they then slink away from them and pursue wild polemics—supposedly to vindicate their philosophy, which no one lays hands on.

114   And these {sciences} already as components at the heart of culture—(Christian truth—*sapientia* ["wisdom"]). The philosopher concerned with ground-laying becomes in this way a "grounder." Now one gives oneself—more or less well—the role of one on whom the further progress of the world must wait in order then to be erected definitively; but in case the world does not do this favor, it is explained as blind, unintelligible. "Philosophers" of this sort, however, are not ridiculous figures, because they have even taken on the background of a ridiculousness.

115

198

The philosopher is never someone who grounds—he leaps ahead and stands there to the side and instigates the clarity of questioning and tends to the hardness of the concept and thereby administers the space-time of free poetizing in the empowerment of the essence toward the grounding of humans in soil—work—struggle and downgoing.

199

Questioning is *more provocative* and harder than all the empty sharpness of "thinking"; it is *more thrilling* and attuning than all sentiments lashed down to make them secure.

200   116

The image of the effectiveness of philosophy in general has been formed on the basis of the historical "effect" of Plato and Aristotle on the Christian West. But what if here the opposite of philosophical effectiveness existed; indeed what if there were no such thing as philosophical "effectiveness"?

Philosophy cannot be effective—as little as can a way or a track—; it can only open up and keep sharp the need and risk of having an effect.

What results from this for an "appointed teacher of philosophy"? He cannot communicate philosophy through instruction; still less may he, by playing with philosophy, "existentielly exhort"; still less may he belabor philosophical cognitions; on the contrary, he must gather himself up and: philosophize—come what may.

In philosophizing, however, he must be in genuine dialogue with philosophers—of his choice. And what then finds expression in words is always only the—to be sure, necessary—superficies. (Cf. p. 93, *123 bottom.*)

201   117

The animal and the human being. Animals do not know, provided the disclosability of beings pertains to knowledge. Because no truth, so also no need to question which "world" of individual animal or of species is "truer" than the others among themselves or in relation to humans.

Yet the animal is indeed sentiently "related to . . ."—not only in the so-called sense-organs—but in and as an entire corporeality—a surrounding field thus in a certain way "open"—scent and color, e.g., for bees—but we do not know what is open here and how it is so—; we speak and question even here on the basis of our own world—except that we do not meditate on how unavoidably this unspoken point of departure requires a clarification and a securing—apart from the categorial preconceptions under which we posit the research "object" that bears the name of animal.

Although a basic experience of animality and life does hold good, we yet find ourselves involved in a great and deep detour to reach the animal—it is always a matter of *taking back from the human being*—but not such that the animal would be "reduced" from humans as a by-product | through a remainder method.

Instead, necessary:

1. Adequate gaze at the human being—soul—body.
2. From this (1), looking ahead to animal—life.
3. The guiding wayposts of going backwards, to and fro.
4. Therein the inversion of the throwing oneself adrift.
5. The positive element in the retrograde modes of determination.

202

Sensibility seen only in a *Christian* way by Kant, i.e., on the basis of *thinking*, and the latter taken as "spontaneity." Thus sensibility merely "receptive." Entirely wrong—the body is "active" without it qua animal and a fortiori in the throwing oneself adrift is concomitantly carried into the throwing—henceforth the body lives while configuring a world and creating in the empowerment of the essence—: language (p. 97).—The body acquires with the throwing a quite new, transformed deployment of power.

203

No polemic! But not due to conciliation or even snobbery—instead, because filled and fulfilled by *struggle* against the distorted essence of being.

204

The animal and the human being. The latter, as standing into being, has already very early prepared his throwing himself adrift—not first after a supposed conclusion of mammalian "development"—instead, this development is already a reversion of the basic form of humanity.

If animals, and living beings in general, could "recognize"—they would never have a capacity to live. They would have been immobilized by beings and themselves determined as beings. Because this happened to humans, however, humans have not reached a goal or end—but instead possess a quite different task of world-*formation* and incorporation of the body in the (now for the first time appropriable) beings. In the throwing oneself adrift commences the projection—

and in the projection as such—with it and not as a later result—commences the thrownness as manifestation of fearfulness. Thrown projection as opening up of the partitioning—empowerment of the essence.

205

120

The human being—where we seek him (cf. p. 3):
   whether we subordinate him to God, the God of the Christians—
   whether we take him as one human being *to another* in their history—and human being only as goal—
   whether we take him as the last sediment of living things—
   or whether we grasp him as leap into being, i.e., accept the empowerment of being—(leap into Da-*sein*).

206

Does the human being have a goal? If so, then it is the goal of having no goal, such that his possibilities are not tied off or even constricted. Since when has the human being been given goals?

207

How the question of being (cf. s.s. 35[23]) is conspicuously decoyed to "being" (cf. p. 62) as verbal noun derived from "is." What is here called a verbal noun—what lies in this "grammatical" "category" as regards the understanding of being and, above all, as regards the impotence of being or {?} the *echo of being*? How from here semblance comes to predominate, as if being were originarily related to | the "under-   121 standing" and consciousness (ego *cogito* ["*I* am thinking"]). Why does λόγος take possession of being; why is λόγος seized into "logic"; why does the theory of logos become the theory of "thinking"?
   Which restriction, emptying, and deception can be traced to the grasp of "being" in terms of the verbal noun? (Cf. p. 95.)

208

The suspected—prostration before so-called facts—the agreed—common—appeal to something that apparently makes otiose the task of an originary legislation. Where this idolatry predominates—not only in so-called positivism, but also precisely in those who keep house

---

23. {Heidegger, *Einführung in die Metaphysik*, GA40 (Frankfurt: Klostermann, 1983), 58ff.}

with "ideas" and "values"—there every projection-truth must be suspected as incidental and as phantasy.—But even with insight into its
essential priority, it is still difficult to carry out the projection as such
with the appertaining certainty. (Cf. p. 51.)

209

122 I could now begin to be less distrustful of my own work—for the opposition is now complete and united—and everything that I joins up
there—but even the disdaining of these "opponents" would still have
to take them seriously even in the smallest matter—although they do
not deserve it.

They would like to rescue their "exact" philosophy, which is too
harmless to be endangered. And so, *despite* the unanimous opposition, the distrust must remain and for essential reasons must become
stronger—such that the struggle remains ongoing.

210

To give oneself up to the distant injunction (p. 109f., *121*)—that is the true
basic relation to the *beginning* and signifies *even* the re-beginning of
the beginning—that beginning is thoughtful poetizing (p. 88) in its
essential necessities, a poetizing that throws itself adrift—art—polis—
philosophy—the gods—nature—world-formation and its first failure
along with its entanglement in presence. The strengthening of the
question of being.

Might we again *dare* to learn about the Greeks and from them? So
that in the re-beginning we come to struggle *against* them.

123   ### 211

The end—the decay of the essence pertaining to being. (Cf. p. 105f.)
Being is forgotten, precisely because still constantly known and
used—in a casual way. Being is squandered in a hodgepodge of rootless concepts, exhausted in a whirl of all (easily) arranged "dialectical"
relations of concepts. Being has become the arena for the play of all
sorts of systems and "scientific philosophies"—ones which even have
the fatal semblant merit of being mostly *correct*, yet on no account in
the least *true*. But this travesty of philosophy only the result of the
decay of being. On account of that decay, *Dasein is thrown off the track*
and set down in the dull rest of a manifold insulation from danger—
wherein everything great is consumed, without measure or direction—cut to pieces and formless and without the inner law of the nation—. And where this decay breaks out, the genuine discipline and

training to be competent for it (in mind and body) remain something supplemental whose facile disposing of the worst bungling is taken as a matter of course.

How find the way out of this? The first thing is to grasp that it is useless to try and improve any aspect whatever of that which lies on the surface, instead of bringing into salience the most extreme and broadest plight: the decay of being. But how experience this plight? Is | it necessary that many, the many, experience it? No—that is even   124
impossible. The "situation"—not what passes for that today, but the place of the track of the essence of being—should and can be known only to a few, and they must be silent if they are to act in the power of this knowledge. The shuddering together before self-refusing beings must not become a public affair. But what is even less needed is a fabrication of the plight and of the affliction through a false memory of the mythical or through rummaging around in the unconscious, or the like. All that is indeed merely the same misunderstanding and the counterpart to the impotence of "spirit."

Because nothing escapes contemporary people, because they have a facile and correct answer for everything, whereby they throttle everything as already having been, the essential must therefore remain in silence now and for the future—but all the harder and clearer may be what is said in the power of that silence. (Cf. p. 115.)

212

In the clarity and relentlessness of the *end*, the beginning is illuminated and the re-beginning becomes the plight. (Cf. p. *93*.) The empowerment of the essence as the distant injunction into which we dovetail.

213   125

Beginning and end. (Cf. s.s. 31, supplement to p. 5c.[24])

Being, once the *lightning* that suddenly bursts and draws all things into its light according to their measure and law and import—now a weary semblance allowing all import and measure to steal away.

Being—a gift, a jubilation and a shudder, a question—the beginning.

Being—an exhausted possession, an object of prattle, a bore, a name—the end.

---

24. {Heidegger, *Aristoteles, Metaphysik* Θ *1–3: Vom Wesen der Wirklichkeit und der Kraft,* GA33 (Frankfurt: Klostermann, 1981), 28ff.}

214

Being as the lightning flash of the essence and afterwards the abiding semblance of the essence.

The beginning and the history of the disempowerment of the essence in being.

"*Ontology*" as the entrenchment and sanctification of the disempowered essence.

215

The *dismantling* [Destruktion] (cf. *Being and Time*) only a subordinate task in the service of a recollective presentation of the history of the disempowerment—because the question of being is indeed not itself the basic question—instead, only a first stoppage of the disempowerment and a preparation for the conversion to the empowerment of the essence. "Ontology" does not at all know the question of being—; where the *transition* of the latter to "ontology"! *Plato—Aristotle—precisely through their greatness the ambiguity of their philosophizing is intensified.*

126

216

The essence must already become inceptually entangled in being— the *entanglement of the essence* introduces the disempowerment of the essence and grounds the priority of being. Being, however, entangles itself in the object; the entanglement as a happening of the essence is formative. The object forms its "over and against" in the "is," and from there "being" shifts into the assertion—λόγος—thinking—subject—consciousness.

Thus the human being slipped out of the essence, and being merely shifted "over" itself (ἰδέα ["idea," "something seen"]), lightened itself, and released itself so as to be the beings themselves.

This flight indeed ushers in the "truth" of "theoretical" knowledge but also the disempowerment of the beginning. The pushing away of beings—having them over and against in intuition—will then carry over even to God—as the creator; the *ens creatum* ["created being"], however, now compels the question—how it might be accessible to the *ego—ego cogito* ["I—I am thinking"]. The advancing secularization brings about a complete detachment from the beginning—now at once arises the semblance that it would again be the beginning, whereby the latter—in revivals of antiquity—is drawn in even by name. Thus everything moves—especially because of Kant—more and more to the end | precisely because a certain greatness resides in these exertions toward pure philosophy. Only on this basis can the

127

breadth and depth of the failure be estimated. The great attunement has long since been withdrawn from philosophy; instead, a scientificity and moral endeavors regarding culture and refinement.

The rebellion of the "is" against being and essence and beings as object and appearance. (Cf. p. 111 bottom.)

How slowly and seldom do we master the pre-effective past, with what difficulty we *remain* equal to it. What is called for is not to throw away and get rid of but to reconfigure the past into the struggle, especially when we take possession of the past as the beginning.

217

The essentialness of the essence can be empowered only in and from the essentiality of the essence—terror and blessing, the great attunements which incorporate humans.

218

The inceptual priority of being, however, must not in any way be misinterpreted as "errancy"—on the contrary, the entire greatness of the inescapability of the entanglement of the essence | must remain unfolded and thus also the semblance of being—only in that way does the beginning receive and retain its greatness and essentiality, and only *in that way* does the "nevertheless, the empowerment versus the disempowerment" acquire its entire force of ineluctability.   128

Anything else may happen, apart from continuing the beginning in its entanglement—especially since it cannot at all be decided whether an empowerment of the essence is to be effectuated over and beyond the beginning.

Quite to the contrary, however, the exclusive entrenchment in the "is," an entrenchment originating in the disempowerment of the essence, must be retracted—whereby this entrenchment still retains its necessity.

The question of being remains the necessary way of the swing back into the beginning—for only in snatching up the beginning can the empowerment of the essence repeat itself.

Philosophy belongs in the history of beings—therein philosophy has its measured portion: to keep open the question-worthiness of the essence, to maintain the hardness of the clarity of the concept, and thus to preserve the deep breadth of the great attunements.

No philosophy for the sake of itself.

Neither the immediacy of the "total" state, nor the awakening of the people and the renewal of the nation, a fortiori not the salvation of "culture" as supplement to people and state, and utterly not the   129 flight into Christian faith and the frightful scheme of a Christian culture could or should be determinative first and last.

Instead, the ineluctability of the work of the empowerment of the essence, an ineluctability amply nourished out of what is concealed, must be experienced and secured in the few individuals. The confiding guardianship over the possibility of the effectuating of such work must be secured unconstrainedly. Precisely because the issue cannot be to accomplish a "ground-laying" but instead to bring beings as a whole *to the space and track* of a great Dasein. (P. 131.)

Without that, everything remains accidental and boundless strain and small comfort without degree or rank—despite all the awakening of the masses to the developed unity of people and nation. If we do not bring ourselves so far that our history becomes a gaining through struggle of the consolation of an essential breadth and depth 130 of Dasein out of the reticent essence of being, then I we have effectuated the end and indeed a small and ridiculous end.

To be sure, this does not mean the perpetuation of the institutions for the care and preservation of the spirit, institutions which have become empty and rootless. Here there can be change only out of that original transformation of Dasein—out of it such that the transformation is set going and set to work. Yet *one* presupposition among others for accepting this inner mission consists in a renunciation of the reckoning with generations and the playing off of one generation against another—that remains a branch of the superficial planning according to typology and psychology; a basic defect in the knowledge of the maturity and the progressive growth of the spirit—; *mere youth* is here just as little summoned as is the occupancy of the "key positions" of the "institutions."

219

Prometheus (Aeschylus) and the beginning of philosophy.
 The beginning and the world-event.
 The world-event and human Dasein.
 The history of Dasein and the decay of being.

131

220

Ontology is unable to master the question of being, indeed not because any question of being endangers and ravages being—but rather because λόγος does not allow an originary relation to ὂν ᾗ ὄν ["being qua being"], since the being-question itself is only the forefront in the empowerment of the essence.

The question of being is an ontological question only in the entanglement.

221

Ambiguity of "ontology":

1.) If this title signifies *any* questioning *whatever* of ὄν ᾗ ὄν, without an indication of the horizon or the like, then the question of being, qua question, is ontological.

2.) But if this title signifies at the same time an orientation of the interpretation of being toward λόγος [*logos*], then indeed the later beginning in Plato and Aristotle (already in Parmenides and Heraclitus) is onto-logical, and so are all doctrines of categories—a fortiori transcendental philosophy.

3.) Only if ontology in the broader and narrower senses is grasped according to origins and limits, can it be shown how the question of being presents merely the forefront of the empowerment of the essence. The empowerment a fortiori not related to existence—on the contrary, related to the human being in Dasein.

222

132

Weary and used up are all great attunements as well as constancy in them. Therefore, the questioning power as world-happening is completely closed off. The fact that facile superiority of faith—a superiority which is only cowardly mendacity full of borrowings in philosophy—or the semblant vivacity (whose spiritual impotence cries to heaven) of the political.—

Therefore, what matters before everything and for everything is only the one task: to open up the world-place and its great attunements of disclosive questioning—the power of being.—

Furthermore, to strive only so that *the work shall stand* and only that. (P. 128.)

The many, however, may be calmly awakened into a people and even rescued—still others may be relinquished to today's strident theologians and theological writers.

223

The *question of being* to be anchored *not* in *"existence,"* but rather in the *beginning* as the throwing oneself adrift into the essence (cf. p. 70). That is the *world-event* as such—into its vibrancy are admitted the humans of our history, to be sure without their surmising what is unprecedented in the event—unprecedented as emergence of nothingness and decay into nullity.

224

The German ἄτολμος ["uncourageous"] (cf. p. 85).

That is to be said precisely of the Germans, because the acceptance of the distant injunction of the beginning awaits them alone.

The protracted impotence for insertion into the availability.

This impotence can be seen:

1.) in the groundless impatience with regard to all finding the way back to an essential growth;

2.) in the measureless dissolution of all actual questioning into one or several "psychologically" explainable and "historiologically" deducible views;

3.) in the unanimous diminution of every approach to the building up of the magnitude of the human world;

4.) in the stealing away from the breadth and depth of every world-affliction;

5.) in the unruliness of the prattling on and on about things from which the prattlers have in advance been closed off.

ἄτολμος: without the force to involve oneself in the ineluctability of the distant injunction of the happening of being, without the great breadth to retain even the foreign and the hostile.

225

The *beginning* as distant injunction for the postulation of the question of being is to be developed quite differently than before. Thereby removed just as much from extrinsic "dismantling" as from "existence."

The human being—i.e., our Dasein must be projected out from the distant injunction of the beginning and for that availability.

Out from and in the τόλμα ["courage"] of the disclosive questioning of the essence (cf. p. 140).

Out of the *beginning* effectuated *in that way* as its own, the essential truth of the beginning is to be brought to light; this was previously called the *"ontological difference."* (Cf. □ and s.s. 32.[25])

---

25. {Heidegger, "Ontologische Differenz und Unterschied," in *Zum Ereignis-Denken*, GA73.2 (Frankfurt: Klostermann, 2013), 901ff.; *Der Anfang*, 31f.}

226

The earlier effort, in *Being and Time*, to move from a preconceptual understanding of being to a *concept* of being was not sufficiently original or necessary—on the contrary, it was superficial and formal, a perverse striving after "science." Even insofar as something true does reside there, the conceptuality was not adequate. Moreover, the existentiell tonality of the "totalizing concept" remained insufficient and not *inceptual* enough—since the beginning and the arrangement were effective only extrinsically. (Cf. p. 104.)

The totalizing concept along with the self-throwing adrift did already happen | in a concealed way, signified an involvement in the essence, and developed first and normatively as an opening up of being in perceiving and saying—*the world-event*. Soon, however, the hiddenly governing totalizing concept for knowledge was dissolved into the order and *koinonia* [κοινωνία, "association"] of "ideas" and "concepts" and was then completely destroyed by the Christian renunciation of the world and division into *creator* ["creator"] and *creatum* ["created"]—precisely this even with the help of these ideas and concepts. The rest is then the ever-increasing flight into dialectics (Hegel) or into Schelling's destitute separation into positive and negative philosophy, in which Christianity and retained antiquity and idealism (rationalism) are supposed to be tied together.

227

Precisely in its great beginning, *philosophy* did not ever have the hegemony we like to attribute to it by thinking of the sovereignty of modern science since Descartes.

The task is to philosophize philosophy out of this empty, unfruitful, merely semblant hegemony—in order to give back to philosophy the greatness of the certainty of its rank. This greatness | resides in leading through the superior ability to step back—back to the hearth of being. This is of course far from the now popular "restriction" and elimination of philosophy on the part of a supposedly renewed Protestantism—a fortiori it has nothing in common with the equally blind struggle against "intellectualism" and "rationalism."

This revocation of philosophy, however, not something "negative" or even its self-emasculation—instead, the safeguarding of its power—even more—it is finding one's way back into its essence and thus into the beginning—*"happening of being."*

228

The momentary urging of the most immediate needs and the slowly prepared dovetailing into the distant injunction of the beginning have *their* respective time and precisely *in that way* stand in the most intrinsic connection.

229

Are we able to experience and question disclosively which priority fate has meted out to our people? The exposure to beings (thrownness) must be accepted inceptually and reconfigured in its hard individuation and interrogative clarity!!

137   Will philosophy first of all find the power to step back into the preparedness and preparation for the configuring appreciation of this dignity of the people and of the extension of their rank, the rank they are supposed to come into?

How few are those who have at all grasped the actual horror in the lack of any spiritual preparation. What do we know of ourselves— who are we? *Who is the human being?*

How utterly we at once place this question in cold storage, in that we turn it into "anthropology"—instead of experiencing the fact that precisely the asking of this question transforms everything anew and deprives us of all domiciles and specialties and customary practices— i.e., lets them crumble away.

230

The people: the guarding and carrying out of the empowerment of being. The empowerment out of the fearfulness of thrownness, whose first essential *individuation* remains precisely the people—and their great *individuals*. The essence of these individuals to be grasped out of and in the individuation as people.

138   ### 231

How everything has become accessible to "meditation" and reflection today! Nothing can any longer resist analysis or withdraw from it. Yet—still more fatally—we believe we would come in this way to the ground and soil, whereas we merely suck the blood out of the last impulses and forces of active and constructive questioning.

Should everything be swallowed up in analysis? Or do we come and finally bring ourselves—each one with his own mission—into the thrilling and unfamiliar moment of populist[26] [*volkhaft*]-spiritual action?

232

The harm of the human sciences, the sciences of the spirit—how they inundate, destroy, and disempower everything spiritual.

233

Only two ways lead out of this whole misery:
1. relentless awakening of the beginning and of, among other things, its exemplariness;
2. the necessary work that stands in the availability of the beginning.

234   139

Taking a line through Hegel, one believes that meditation on and consciousness of the presuppositions of science would be the higher and authentic science—I *cogito*—*me cogitare* ["I am thinking—of myself thinking"]—"consciousness" is a *higher level of being*—if the "finite" were known, then it would already be infinite.

Whereas at work in Hegel is only the final lostness in the end with Christian-spiritual-absolute makeup. An attempted salvation—typical for today—which believes it is preserving "science" (—monstrosity) if it incorporates the very "presuppositions" of science into such science. The deterioration and the deviltry of the groundlessness of the deterioration in "potency."

"In the consciousness of the restriction lies a going beyond it."[27] This Hegelian proposition holds only if precisely consciousness is regarded—in the manner of Descartes—as "higher."

---

26. [Heidegger employs in these notebooks three adjectives derived from the noun *das Volk*, "people": *volkhaft*, *volklich*, and *völkisch*. I have rendered them respectively as "populist," "communal," and "folkish" and have placed the German term in brackets at each occurrence. The term *völkisch* has racial overtones. It is up to the reader to determine Heidegger's attitude toward the overtones of each term.—Trans.]

27. {Georg Wilhelm Friedrich Hegel, *Vorlesungen über die Philosophie der Religion*, part 1, *Collected Works*, vol. 15 (Stuttgart: Frommann, 1928), 184.}

Who can guarantee that such consciousness does not harbor a slavery with respect to the "restriction"? Why is the "beyond" already the higher?

140

235

Boundless knowledge and unsupported conviction—overrun each other perpetually and in that way squander all the reticent force of the empowerment of being toward increasing work and toward the awakening world—toward a ravishing destiny.

236

People are perpetually shocked by my "figurative language" ("throwing," "pre-running," etc.). As if language would be spoken differently each time.

And precisely philosophical language! E.g., λόγος, which people so readily appeal to against all presumed "irrationalism."

λόγος is λέγειν—glean [*lesen*]—gather—and

οὐσία—is estate—property—

ἐπιστήμη is—stand before, stand above—etc.

But why strive to correct the rampant stupidity and impudence—let them lie, let them go to perdition.

141

237

The *act of re-beginning with the beginning*—should *not* falsely turn the beginning into an end or goal—but instead preserve it in its inceptuality—i.e., let it come into action in view of the distant injunction which radiates forward out of the beginning and was concealed for too long in its necessity, such that it was replaced by something accidental and secondary.

Not a revival of antiquity—that is not needed—instead, a revival of our people and of their task. For that, however, we must set ourselves out into the clear hardness of the affliction of the beginning.

238

But one will soon be in a great hurry with a "German philosophy"—indeed a "society" for that has already been founded—and what is

"German" about it will be that the standards and difficulties of the mission will be abandoned and replaced by "Germanism."[28]
 Or will the connection to the Greeks first be reestablished?

---

28. {The "German Philosophical Society" existed from 1917 to 1945. In 1933, it explicitly declared allegiance to Hitler.}

{Index}

PONDERINGS AND INTIMATIONS III

Fall 1932   Martin Heidegger

1

1

A marvelously awakening communal [*volklich*] will is penetrating the great darkness of the world.

2

The actual work should exist—once again in posing the question of being—and should configure that questioning in its entire originality and breadth for the remote fate of the age, in order thereby to join back into the great beginning the most secret communal [*volklich*] mission of the Germans.

3

The incomparability of the world's current hour, a chamber in which German philosophy should strike up and resound.

4

But—we must first ripen to philosophy, and the soil and storm and sun for this ripeness must first be prepared—the communal [*volklich*] happening *could* press on to there—will it?

2   Yet in no way can "philosophy," |which indeed does not exist, now be plugged into the "political"—still less the case with a "new" science which, if at all, could only arise out of philosophy.

The entire degeneracy of the age now flowing away can be seen in the fact that it can elicit as a countermovement nothing more than the dabbling idle talk and din of "political science."

5

The communal-civil [*volklich-staatlich*] happening is to be unfolded in its actuality in order to attack all the harder and sharper and fuller the floundering (rootlessly and without rank) of the new spirit—i.e., in order to guide the awakening actuality of German Dasein to its greatness for the first time, a greatness concealed to this Dasein and waiting for it, a greatness around which the most fearful storm is raging.

The Δεινότης ["Uncanniness"] of the extreme fate of the greatness of the Germans.

6   3

Where is the gathering advance mission of Dasein in the prevailing world of the German, a mission rooted in the basic attunement and one constantly reaching higher and broader?

The throwing oneself adrift in the partitioning (being) of the exposedness of Dasein.

7

What is difficult and fateful in our labor for the university is that we must largely act by way of "talking," and all accomplishment forfeits its simple certitude in passing through the viscosity and sponginess of the ones who are to be formed here.

8

Pressed to assume the rectorship, I am acting for the first time *against* my innermost voice. In this office, at most I might possibly be able to *prevent* one thing or another. For building up—assuming such is still possible—the personnel are lacking.

From the time as rector   4

9

Need to be made surer and suppler by every struggle. What is unsuccessful is a doctrine; with opposition, make the strap more firm!

10

The great experience and fortune that the Führer has awakened a new actuality, giving our thinking the correct course and impetus. Otherwise, despite all the thoroughness, it would have remained lost in itself and would only with difficulty have found its way to effectiveness. Literary existence is at an end.

11

Relentless in the hard goal,
    supple and changing in the ways and weapons.

12

The new university will arrive only if we *sacrifice* ourselves *for it*; this is our lot, even if only to form an advance image of it for ourselves.

13

No programs, no systems, no theory, and a fortiori no empty "organizing."

   Instead, to create the actual, the proximate, the possible—not to evade the actual—this is *the new courage for fate as the basic form of truth*.

14

The meeting of the solitary ones can happen only in solitude.

15

The world-moment of our history; the resoluteness of that moment. We are not able, and do not want, to calculate the future or even know what is to come. Quite to the contrary, we must and indeed want to create anew our futurity and thereby our entire temporality—the new courage.

16

The preparation and directedness toward the "revolution" as such toward "production."

17

Be ready, with a broad will, to be frustrated by the everyday bustle.

18

Finally: incorporated into the creative joint-responsibility of the truth of folkish [*völkisch*] Dasein. Basic attunement.

19

The mission—if precisely this were the mission: the full imposing and first proposing of the new essence of truth?

The essential uncertainty in assuming the mission—averting the fatal opinion that what is coming could be calculated and could simply be compelled by sheer will!

On the contrary, the highest willing and thoughtful clarity will precisely increase the incalculability and the danger of withdrawal and consequently will demonstrate: with regard to the mission no resting in possessions but instead the full breadth of the exposure to the whole.

20

How through leading and following—the highest mission in the state and in the people is disbursed, interwoven, and in each case individuated by being *thrown to each respectively.*

21

The mission—not an impotent "idea" we think of now and then, not a floating image we have intuited hitherto, | but that which has been   7
assigned Dasein in its ground—to *bear*—just as if Dasein stood in a stream flowing against us.

"The least fatigue, and we are torn down"[1] and fall into the common understanding of short-sighted pretense—the mission is no longer there for us.

It is *preserved* only in struggle (cf. Heraclitus).

Mere images do not bind.

22

The *worthiness for power* and for the possession of power.—Does it derive from *"rights"*—because one has "rights"? And why is one in the right? Because of having power?

The worthiness for power out of the greatness of Dasein—and Dasein out of the truth of its mission.

Whether Dasein is equal to its fate! Here not to be raised to the ultimate rules and ultimate prescriptions.

23

"The masses"—not a community of the people.

---

1. {Unidentified citation.}

The masses destroy—are not actual—totter in an empty present—without history—constantly "outside themselves"—susceptible to every "sentimentality."

8   *24*

The mission: the new truth is not the ultimate—instead, the new truth is precisely the concealedness of the new truths and so the concealedness of beings and of being:
The most proximate, wherein the most remote is secured.

                                            25

National Socialism is a genuine nascent power only if it still has something to withhold behind all its activity and talk—and only if it operates as strongly holding back and in that way has effectivity into the future.

But if the present were already that which is to be attained and striven for, then only a dread of the downfall would be left over.

                                            26

National Socialism not a ready-made eternal truth come down from heaven—taken in that way, it is an aberration and foolishness. Such as it has become, it must itself become in becoming and must configure the future—i.e., it must itself, as a formation, recede in favor of the future.

9   *27*

Rule: to create wholly unconditioned out of what is to come, to sustain the foreign land of the future—to take from there, without condition, the measure and rule and on them to carry through to the claims.

                                            28

The thrust of the question:
    not to run after in analyzing and "typifying"—
    not inner possibilities, for something stably present at hand, toward its higher stabilization—
    but rather: in demanding—exposing—compelling.

29

The end of "philosophy."—We must bring it to an end and thereby prepare what is wholly other—metapolitics.

Accordingly also the *transformation of science.*

30

We need a new constitution of the university—the single spiritually political leadership made secure—and why? Not to give what is present at hand a "build-up" and a new gloss, but to destroy the university. This "negativity," however, lwill be effective only if it finds its task   10
in the education of a new species.

Such a constitution would be senseless and detrimental if with its help one desired to hold fast to existing conditions and merely "adapt" to the times.

Such a constitution would be a weapon of struggle if all that mattered were to create for the new generation and for its truth a free path and to bestow on them the genuine tradition.

The current institution of higher learning is still merely a temporary waypoint.

31

Ever-increasing hardness in the attack.

Guarantee of superiority in frequent predicaments of having to lead.

No flight, no weariness, always on the attack.

Not to have full powers, but to *be* the power!

32

Metaphysics as metapolitics.

33   11

According to everything the students offer now at the start of this summer semester, it must be concluded that they are disappointing all along the line—not primarily with regard to the reconstruction, but already with regard to the revolution *within* the university.

Ever so much courage and enthusiasm cannot compensate for the complete spiritual immaturity. Science would not be necessary for now—but indeed a considerable measure more of knowledge and understanding of the tasks and possibilities of a university education, more than that offered by the highest faulty recollection of a seminar once attended as an auditor.

Nevertheless, the will to vague yet certain claims on the part of the students must be kept alive and shown the way.

But to effectuate is of no use for the university.

12

34

The only possibility resides still in the rising generation and in the few young ones among the old. But this rising generation must no longer grow up as before.

Yet even thereby nothing guaranteed—since there is still the possibility that the university hitherto will altogether disappear—that the constant movement in the faculties of medicine, law, and education will create separate professional schools. The danger of the earlier encapsulation in blind specialized activity would thereby no longer be so dire; for the impetus and the setting of goals would be political—; the question is how much it would not become a mere institution for cramming and an ill curtailment of knowledge to the "practical." This "practical" is admittedly the purest and worst "theory," since there is no such thing as this "praxis." It all depends on the directors of these schools.

Next to this, or over it and under it, the leader schools of the various party organizations must be built out and all schooling aligned to a
13   *Reichs-university*; the latter not as a separate academy—yet lindeed under the highest political and spiritual demands and impulses of the people and of the configuration of the state.

35

The impending concordat[2] with the Catholic Church is supposed to be a victory, for it is to drive the priests out of "politics."

That is an illusion; that incomparably well-coordinated organization will remain—and also the power of the priests; their power will merely be made more "sanctified" and will be wielded more slyly.

36

Much organization all around—often good ideas—but arranged as if we were already at the goal; and then at once everyone is named and

---

2. {The so-called concordat with the Reich [*Reichskonkordat*] was the one concluded on July 20, 1933 between the German empire and the Holy See; it regulated the rights of the Catholic Church in state affairs.}

"grasped," and after a few weeks a universal failure; for neither are people brought up nor are the forms made to grow *in genuinely sustained* seeking and touching.

37

Supposing the spiritual power is sufficient, then only *two things* could help a forward movement: 1.) the new construction of one sole university 2.) in unity with that, a teachers school.

38

14

Need to stay in *motion* and keep everything in motion with *resolute patience*.

The establishment of the will—to keep Dasein and beings as a whole projected in such and such a way; correspondingly, to compel and secure the question and the way of seeing—to construct in advance the concepts that serve to open up.

"Motion"—but not directionless, desultory, capricious trial and error and quick reabandonment.

Not organization and an occupation of positions, and then a return to or continuance in humanity as hitherto.

Genuine motion—without pathos, but from passion.

39

The *inadequacy* of the current more or less great remainder of the ill-bred masses will always persist and will drag down—and mislead—all volition.

The danger of the inadequacy will even increase if these remainders—branded as "battlers"—put on airs in the party, and if out of permanent positions they obstruct, internally cripple, and annihilate everything that strives to go beyond their stubbornness.

40

15

Only where a *strong* will—its *law* and *opposition*—only where creative power, only there allowance and agreement and affirmation. This latter, however, will not create the New actuality—but perhaps might confirm and strengthen it.

Can actualities such as school and its configuration be *commanded*? Certainly—if the command is not the dictating of something proposed—but the impressing empowerment of ordaining and ever-increasing powers.

41

Despite all oppositions, inversions, and reversals, must not deviate or wane.

But *why* the *attempts in an out-of-the-way corner*?

42

If the dawning German Dasein is great, then it bears millennia before itself—we are constrained by that to think in advance corresponding—i.e., to anticipate the arising of a completely other being and to prepare its *logic* for it.

16 We must not take our standards from the puffed-up bourgeoisie; we must not consider the creators of the coming time to be the philistines who mutually appoint themselves "Führers."

We have to keep ready a deep and sharp suspicion as long as everything is pressed around the confrontation with Christianity.

We must not—despite all "results" and "numbers"—esteem according to the present.

We have to strive to grasp the whole only on the basis of the few and thereby consider that precisely these few—if indeed in them something great is at work—exist beyond themselves—and yet *are* quite differently from the way they act and speak.

43

We are involved in rebuilding the ways of the transition—but that is our fate—and if we assume this fate it will unfold as that which excites:

What counts here is

not only to be hard and to bear oneself forward into the dawning
17 being—to act entirely in this being | and to grasp and know oneself in concomitantly acting out of it—but thereby still to sustain the opposite of what was hitherto—which again strives to give itself off as delay—and to recognize that we never get entirely loose of it and that often precisely the most effective action in the field of the hitherto as well as the highest passions, according to its forms and means, must be confirmed.

44

A far-reaching spiritual-historical will to the future must become awake and secure and must prepare the next half-century step by step, at least as regards its spiritual constitution.

45

Education—the effective and binding realization of the power of the state, taking that power as the will of a people to itself.

46

Is that the right way: in constant dealings, in maintaining the bustle, in diverting the all-too-great countereffect, in eliminating |personal   18 squabbles, in the back and forth of momentary trial and error and of undertakings—in all this is the right way a *crippling of oneself* in the genuine power and a barring of oneself from the actual spiritual task?

What is the point of lecturing here and there, since the lecture will not be understood?

To be away from dealings—which others can accomplish much better—does not mean to stand apart from the movement. Will our people after a few years starve to death on the constant slogans and catchphrases—or will we create an actual spiritual nobility, one strong enough to configure the tradition of the Germans on the basis of a great future?

Is it a natural consequence that today by necessity the form of the future spirit is misunderstood and that within the National Socialist movement one must misunderstand those beginnings that in it press on to an actual developed transformation of powers, ways, and works?

47   19

Only those long prepared can also build far in advance.

Only those radically decided and constantly placing themselves in the decision can also decide centuries in advance.

48

The preparation for the transformation of knowledge will take decades. It requires an originary strong *tradition* of the essential in a forward direction. It needs a mode of knowledge cultivation [*Wissenserziehung*] that will appear in real teachers and in a teaching community and will create paradigms to which the rising generation can and must be bound. The driving, farsighted, and creative powers must converge in a knowledge academy pointing *forward* and setting standards and rules.

And what do we have instead?! Only an uncreative floundering in daily whims and a verbose din over demands already obsolete thirty years ago and never vitally rooted.

20

49

The complete misunderstanding of the poly-lawfulness of the great powers in a creative people brings this people into a disastrous mediocrity and inner impotence.

Certainly—there is much to be retrieved in institutions and measures, but that is not the only thing, and—if not continually drawn from new sources—it is not at all essential. "Organization"!

50

"Organization"!—No organization without a previous clarification of the will, without a spiritually provident awakening of a mission, without a completed preparation for the genuine, sustained, and not quickly spent powers.

Organization in the genuine sense is never a mere "technical," extrinsic institution—it *can* awaken by itself and can elicit and thrust forth something new—but precisely for that reason it can also thwart, suppress, cover up, and immobilize and can let one slide down into a perplexity breaking out overnight.

21   Once again: we have much to *retrieve* and to go along with in the daily grind—and yet all this must *not surpass* our genuine, most intrinsic, and broadest folkish [*völkisch*] being—otherwise we shackle ourselves all too blindly to the current times.

There is also a blindness that sees.

51

If the *university* is to appertain henceforth to our people, then the university's mission of *knowledge cultivation* must—*still* quite differently—be originarily rooted, clarified, and sharpened—out of the *need for knowledge* as a basic character of the being of our people.

The goal is not scientific progress in itself nor its equally impossible appendage of "specialized" professional training and technical preparation—instead, the goal is teaching as *education*. Leading—guiding—steering of *knowingness* [Wissendsein]. *Mastery* and handing down of the people's knowledge in genuine questioning: these are decisive.

Knowledge cultivation in a selection—education and leap in advance.

22

52

The breeding of high—and of the highest—*sorts of thought* comes first, prior to all mere communication of cognitions.

The *high sort of thought* and the nobility of Dasein—not bound to class or vocation or status! But can be unfolded in status.

How is a high sort of thought bred? Through the constant constraint of a determinate questioning bound to a mission; firm promptings!

53

"Socialism":

as mere pleasure in egalitarianism—

as predominance of those who merely drag down—

as mere carrying on of the common welfare—

as the obligation (one of various parts and levels) of all to their respective mission after their guiding and sorting in the entirety of the people.

54

The *metaphysics of Dasein* must become deeper in accord with the innermost structure of that metaphysics and must expand into the *metapolitics "of" the historical people*.

55

"Classical philology" now has the single task of making Greek and Roman civilizations available for a confrontation (one as hard and l essential as possible) of the Germans with them, i.e., of unfolding antiquity to its highest possible power.   23

56

The Germans would have to fall from their innermost essence if in the future they are not seized by a restless hunger according to the questioning and configured depth of Dasein and breadth of the world.

And on what should they then feed—into what should youth grow? Will the youth in the manner of plants merely put forth a flowering which the frost at night will dispatch—or will there be erected truly, i.e., in struggle, a work on which generations can build? And where is the great opponent in this struggle, the struggle to which the coming generations must be equal and which they must take upon themselves and configure? Where should the great propelling opposition be, if not in us, to the extent that on behalf of the coming generations we sacrifice ourselves as a transition not simply to be pushed aside?

24   *57*

The university is dead; long live the future advanced school of knowledge cultivation of the Germans!

First we will be driven into a great plight with regard to knowledge, a plight little tracts and brief indoctrination camps will not ameliorate but will rather make still more pressing and severe.

58

Under which presuppositions is any leading of the university possible at all? (Cf. p. 28f.) Under the following:

1.) that the present will of the leader is thrown far in advance with regard to the spirit and the people, and that the movement of striving for knowledge is provoked and constrained out of the impending powers of Dasein;

2.) that this happening, which bears, seizes, and determines the leader, arises originarily from a transformation of being pure and simple;

3.) that the will of the leader can be shared by others; that therefore the impelling basic powers grow and so does the simplicity of the task;

25   4.) that a sufficient *philosophical* education becomes common property everywhere, allowing a first upsurge into the essential;

5.) that the will of the leader in slinging bridges can build in the company of the will of the followers and not remain completely without supports;

6.) that an originary, high, effective thinking is desired;

7.) that in general the possibility of a leading in the spiritual-historical domain is inwardly conceded;

8.) that this leading unfolds out of its *own* law and does not become a mere emulation of other relations of leadership;

9.) that the leading does not start with the office and only then must be carried through—because in that way there is already effective from the first a mistrust of the official "superior" and of the alleged power holder;

26   10.) that a tradition of *powers* does not come down to a mere passing on of cognitions and rules.

59

We are stepping into an age which must bind us again to the original powers by way of tradition. Not the *liberating* configuration in the work, but the *binding* and backward-building effectuation—; therefore the comparison with ages of enlightening liberation and of its free accomplishment is misleading from the very start.

60

All possible and impossible tasks are attached to and dependent on the university, yet the tasks of knowledge cultivation, as the only matter proper to this school, are now a matter of concern only incidentally, if at all.

61

The projection of being qua time overcomes everything hitherto as regards being and thinking; not idea, but mission; not loosing, but binding.

The projection does not break loose to pure spirit but instead first opens and binds blood and soil to a preparedness for action and to a capacity for work and for *effectivity*.   27

62

To trust—to liberate the other for his task and his volition, which is thereby *never* entirely understood—in the sense of a reenacting grasp. Despite this, to accompany and to follow are decisive. Not necessary here is an agreement in the same opinion with regard to the issues— nor a sharing of the same standpoint.

There is trust from below and from above—both are borne and arched over by a historical knowledge of the world.

63

The more originary and far-reaching an upheaval, all the more necessary the knowledge that builds in advance—the more resolved toward the state, all the more essential the confrontation with the encroaching powers.

64   28

The less the individual ego matters, all the more pressing is it to require *mastery* in everything. Only mastery creates the tradition of powers and claims, for it binds to the tasks and it makes permanent everything essential and simple. Thus what was peculiar multiplies of itself, and what seldom was proliferates.

65

The end of the university and the beginning of the new knowledge. Both belong together; the latter terminates the former. Very few surmise something of both—but not those and precisely not those who move in apparently revolutionary machinations.

66

How far away are the "students" from their new and necessary essence as *workers*; how fundamentally do they mistake this mission; how content they feel in whatever forms conceal to them the genuine circumstances, hinder every engagement, and yet persuade them that they are involved.

With every spiritual threat, people go off the path and feel bored through the constant repetition of the same | slogans, which now have also become common on the lips of the reactionaries and the most apathetic.

The strongest reaction sits in its own camp, since it has already concluded an unconscious pact with the visible reactionaries:

The agreement and the reciprocal validation in the same spiritual apathy and mediocrity.

67

Knowledge and science.—It is in *philosophy* that all great and full knowledge finds itself and thereby disseminates the essence in the power and duration of that essence. Philosophy is the basic presupposition and tribunal for the coming to be, passing away, and mere drifting along of science—insofar as the latter does in *one* way make knowledge itself an institution and a task.

Accordingly, the new knowledge must first create for itself its philosophy. But this philosophy is not to be sought where, with the most problematic means of the nineteenth century, a confused worldview is made legible for the | new configurations.

This new philosophy requires its own long preparation which makes ready for the great confrontation with what is strongest and greatest, i.e., with what once was philosophy and gathered its entire power for the last time in Hegel. Only if the new philosophy actually starts to become *can*—but by no means must—the science bound to it come to be.

Yet the opinion today: there is now precisely science; it makes a good impression as a cultural possession; it is commonplace and useful. And we must now merely polish up in some way this that is present at hand and quickly clamp it into a cheap dogmatics—i.e., write around it a semblant philosophy compiled from the murkiest sources, and make it utilizable.

What if the much-discussed struggle of the student body to conquer the university had concerned an institution which was already long ago in decay—; indeed what if this struggle, which is now supposed to be "propelled" I further, were only a participation in the conservation of an appearance of decay—therefore the worst (because no longer master of itself) reaction; cf. the position of the student societies—especially if they are supposed to be "reorganized" into *one* student body.

31

68

Which institutions and strivings now (December 1933) determine the university (cf. p. 68):

1. the German student body;
2. the German academic staff (grasped in formation);
3. the S.A.[3] office for higher education.

These organizations, according to their own formation of will and their own attitude, do not operate out of the actual historical life of the individual universities but rather approach them from the outside, from deliberated claims. These "organizations" labor within the individual universities only by way of functionaries whose prime duty is to conform to the leadership. The gaze at the respective proper tasks I of a university—in each case different according to region, history, teaching staff, and kind of student population—becomes unfree; i.e., properly *political* decisions cannot at all be carried out. Lacking are the suitability and power for meditation on the situation; lacking above all is any genuine far-reaching will in advance.

32

A scattering and a tying up in momentary "action" are unavoidable—especially since what indeed is demanded is that something "happen."

4. the National Socialist medical confederation;
5. the National Socialist legal confederation;
6. the National Socialist teaching confederation.

These professional organizations secure for themselves an essential domain of influence on the university. They concomitantly determine the selection of teachers, the establishment and apportionment of the curriculum, and the configuration of the examinations. They concomitantly set the standards for work and judgment in the actuality

---

3. [Paramilitary *Sturmabteilung*, "storm division."—Trans.]

of the university. Even here, the decisions are not made politically out of the respective necessities, circumstances, levels of development, and oppositions, | but instead out of the calculated total needs of all the professional claims.

7. The ministries are taking over the university administratively. They call for, regulate, and level out all the endeavors, proposals, and demands of the aforementioned institutions. The rector's position is inserted in the university as a safeguard; it is supposed to ensure a leadership of the school. But the rector is becoming simply an intercessor for those organizations. He has at most the problematic task of assuming responsibility for everything drawn into the university. It is only of relative—not absolute—importance that the rector be a National Socialist or not. In the latter case, even the aforesaid organizations work more easily, because already from mere prudence, if not indeed anxiety, everything is affirmed and carried through.

8. The university itself no longer summons up a genuine "self-assertion"; it no longer understands this | demand; it gets lost in the mere continuance of the usual bustle along with the now unavoidable synchronizations [Gleichschaltungen] and reforms. It no longer finds its way back to experiencing originarily the necessity of knowledge and configuring its task on that basis. It knows nothing of the fact that a self-assertion would have to mean no less than a fundamental confrontation with the great spiritual-historical tradition insofar as that is still today our *actuality* through the worlds of Christianity, of socialism as communism, and through modern Enlightenment-science.

9. But all the previously named (1–7) institutions and positions also know nothing of all this; therefore they reconcile themselves perfectly with the dominant scientific activity, provided the latter merely guarantees a certain political education as a necessary by-product. Still more: there is not only a toleration of the essential character of the prevailing science, but what dominates and is even cultivated is an aversion to all | spirit which had previously been misinterpreted as intellectualism. The disinclination to every spiritual struggle counts as strength of character and as the sense of a "nearness to life." But this is at bottom only a philistinism laden with retrograde feelings. It would even be unimportant if it did not unwittingly force the entire movement into a spiritual impotence which completely accounts for the lack of any sharp and hard weapons for the impending spiritual struggle by calling that lack an unburdening of intellectual baggage and of empty theories.

10. These circumstances in their entirety may be an immediately disappearing transitional state, seen from the narrow viewpoint of the destiny of *one* university in the scanty time frame of one year. But

they can also be taken as the beginning (that keeps feeding quickly and without being heeded) of a great neglect in the commencement of the most pressing task in the education of the German youth: the commencement of nationally and historically spiritual knowledge | cultivation, for which the meaning of knowledge is no longer the un-committed possession of cognitions but rather a *mode of being*—the be-coming equal to the great and thus difficult future of our people, a be-coming equal that is self-grasping and that is seized in the concept.

36

11. What are we supposed to do in these circumstances?

a) Immediately collaborate in the harsh actuality by pressing for-ward, i.e., not become entangled in the forms of so-called leadership positions and thereby deprive ourselves of the genuine effectivity, one dependent on germinating and ripening. Therefore: assume the leadership for oneself, stepping out from the crowd and reconfigur-ing it in struggle, and in silence prepare for what is coming in its ap-proach, stepping out from small domains.

b) Where possible, press for few, simple institutions and for their creation, which are to be retained in the flux, and which *above all* of-fer a guarantee that in their order new beginnings will be formed and genuine powers united, whereby slowly | yet continuously the high-est spiritual standards are posited, made familiar in disposition and attitude, and led into appearance in word and work.

37

c) In both ways, we can act and carry on to the end only by deny-ing the university as already present at hand while affirming the mis-sion of the entirely other knowledge cultivation.

Only by grasping the fact that reactionism, which clings to what already prevails, as well as the new organizations, which merely re-arrange what already prevails, immediately work toward an irresis-tible dissolution and final destruction of the university. As long as this insight is lacking, all work for the new knowledge cultivation cannot come into the open realm and rest on fertile soil.—

Historical-spiritual worlds and powers are not overcome by turn-ing one's back on them or by putting them in irons by way of arrange-ments.

The basic defect of today's "political education"—a tautology—is not that too little is done and is so only hesitantly and unsurely, but that too much is done and is so too hastily and wants to be made as something new in the twinkling of an eye. As if National Socialism were a coat of paint that is now quickly spread over everything.

38

When will we grasp something of the simplicity of the essence and of the cau-tious persistence of the unfolding of the essence in generations?

We ever struggle only in misguided and conventional aims which are anticipatory merely in semblance.

Need to recognize variegated tasks and grasp them in their necessity and rank, while yet holding fast to the *one* most proper vocation. No infidelity with regard to the non-everyday, originary certainty of the *creative*. The latter not to be confused with the *machinational*.

No "classes"; but rank.

No "strata"; but superiority.

39   *69*

A popular remark: National Socialism was not first developed as *"theory"* but instead began with praxis. Fine. But does it follow that "theory" is otiose? Does it follow even that we merely "otherwise," "for the rest," deck ourselves out with bad theories and "philosophies"? It is not seen that "theory" is here taken in two senses—according to need—and that we are therefore "theoretically" mistaken precisely in the interpretation of our own doings; for if the many "speeches" in the struggle were not "theories"—what would then happen but this: a reeducation of the people and fellow members of the nation to other viewpoints, e.g., with regard to one worker versus another, with regard to economics, society, state—ethnic community [*Volksgemeinschaft*]—honor—history?

"Theory" as mere detached thought that is simply entertained in the mind and "theory" as anticipatory demand of knowledge must not be lumped together; in each case the meaning of praxis is also different; engagement is not mere praxis; nor do mere breaking forth and lashing out constitute engagement. This misconception of "theory" can have the most disastrous consequences on the practical level, for praxis then becomes mere "bustle" = badly understood "organization."

40   Yet now is not the end-condition—nor simply a sector of a mere diffusion of that condition in the entire people, over and above party— on the contrary, what is called for now is precisely engagement in this that is allegedly *theoretical*—because here all basic attunements are rooted and out of them the historical world must be created.

The more originary and stronger are the symbolic power of the movement and its work, so much the more necessary is knowledge. But the latter not in its propositional consistency and its calculability—but instead as the power of the superiority of the world with regard to the basic attunement.

70

We do not desire to underpin National Socialism "theoretically," not even supposedly so as to make it in that way for the first time durable and endurable.

But we do want to provide the movement and its proper power possibilities of world-configuration and of development, whereby we know that these projects as such—i.e., falsified into "ideas"—do not possess any effectuality; but indeed they do if they are *language* and interrogative attitudes, ones thrown in the power of the movement | and arisen in the field of that power and persisting therein.   41

The power of the projection to attune and to create images is what is decisive—and that cannot be calculated. Attunement and image—but these must encounter the closed will to configuration on the part of the people.

71

Is it any wonder that flourishing on all sides are philistinism, conceited half-culture, and bourgeois pseudorefinement and that the inner demands of German socialism are not at all known and thus also not striven for—least of all on the basis of much-invoked character? The most facile platitude as thinking tied to a people! Such states of affairs, however, cannot be avoided. Mediocrity must exist—but one must not aim to improve it; it is censured enough; most severely in that it knows nothing of its wretchedness and in accord with its own law must not know it.

72   42

Spiritual National Socialism is nothing "theoretical"; nor is it an "improved" or even "authentic" one; yet indeed it is just as necessary as the National Socalism of the various organizations and professions. Whereby it must be said that the "mental laborers" are not less removed from spiritual National Socialism than are the "manual laborers."

Therefore, need to *bear up* with the spiritual demands, even if this aspiration is so often and so easily ridiculed from above as something supplementary and, according to good Marxist thought, is dismissed as something merely for "fellow travelers."

73

The danger that the movement might become something bourgeois is in essence nullified precisely in that a spiritual National Socialism destroys the bourgeois spirit as well as the "spirit" (culture) administered by the bourgeoisie.

74

The *proper, but most remote goal*: the historical greatness of the people in the effectuation and configuration of the powers of being.

43   The *more proximate goal*: the *coming to themselves* of the people on the basis of their rootedness and their assuming of their mission through the *state*.

The *most proximate goal*: the provisional creation of the community of the people—as the *self* of the people.

Work and leadership.

The *most proximate goal of all*: the capacity of *all* countrymen for *Dasein* and for work—creation of the joy of work and of the new will for *work*.

These goals, connected in series, require in each case various levels of configuration, and these in turn are determined by the respective breadth of experience, by the motives of the leading generation, and by the will to revolution on the part of the youth.

None of the configurations of the goals can be effectuated immediately—in each case, roundabout ways and setbacks. But the sequence of configuration in the actualizations is to be established all the more strictly the higher the reaching out to the most remote goal—the more originarily the latter (although closed off) is announced in the basic attunement.

44   Where in all this resides our most proper task: the creation of the new claim to knowledge in the postulation of the new way of seeking and questioning?

The *danger of the relapse* of the university into the previous bourgeois bustling about—despite all the synchronization [*Gleichschaltung*] and additional assimilation of the political.

The *danger of the snatching up* of these relapses into the fixed domains of the world of Christian thought and of the previous Western-modern technological science.

In opposition, we must find and traverse ways and modes for knowledge cultivation and for the awakening of the will to knowledge, ways and modes which are already pervaded by the kind of actuality announced in the genuine goal. And, for that, the motives of procedure must arise from the concealed *basic attunement* which is itself awoken and implanted not in talking about it but rather in the attitude toward it. For this, however, other forms of work in *common* and of the attitude toward work are altogether necessary.

45   The will to knowledge and the service to knowledge must be anchored in basic attunements and in passions; these not as additions and embellishments of a false vivacity—but rather according to the essence of *attunement*—that which determines by attuning. Only in

this way is knowledge set to rights—not at all extrinsically—from its previous institutions and their cultural significance—but from the essential depth of being.

The kind and the passionateness of the basic attunement of the motives and intentions are decisive for the happening. And the reeducation must in advance base everything on that.

The passionateness and attunement of knowing and questioning are decisively intended in the "rectoral address."[4] Here the essence of "theory" in the previous sense is shattered.

The essence of the finitude of being and of Dasein implies that what is effectuated at any time always lies *under* the height of the original beginning—whence it follows: we must always begin *as high as possible* and must persevere in this beginning; for otherwise only setbacks.

To be grasped with clarity is the economic and also immediately   46
political unprofitability of everything spiritually creative. Only the platitude of an opinion all too "close to life" can conclude from this that the spiritual is dispensable and otiose, or, what is even worse, can lead astray to the view that—from the fear that in the end one will appear to be quite unrefined—one should precisely tolerate the spiritual with a smile; whereby one has simply fallen back into bourgeois conventionality.

To lead means to educate others toward autonomy and self-responsibility; and *to lead spiritually* means to educate others for leadership and to awaken their creative powers.

Leading and following can by no means be accommodated to the relation of the above and below. *This* order does not at all take form. *Rank* is inconspicuous encompassing power which nurtures the essential precisely in others and lets it unfold there. The radicality of a movement can be *preserved* only where this radicality must always be created anew with the most clarity and depth—viz., in the spiritual; whereas the realization of goals in every case drives on to an end state in which I one settles down and is secure.   47

The unholy danger of the reputable platitude in the spiritual domain (Krieck[5])! It suffocates everything, gives mediocrity a justified self-consciousness, and kindly removes all suffering from those feeling inferior. And this society is then supposed to prepare a historical world of the people!

---

4. {Martin Heidegger, "Die Selbstbehauptung der deutschen Universität," in *Reden und andere Zeugnisse eines Lebensweges, Gesamtausgabe* (GA)16 (Frankfurt: Klostermann, 2000), 107–117.}

5. {Ernst Krieck (1882–1947), rector in 1933 of the Johann Wolfgang Goethe-Universität in Frankfurt, influential pedagogue; see his *Philosophie der Erziehung* (Jena: Diederichs, 1930).}

We do not want to be beneficiaries and trustees of the achievers—
we are unleashing a new struggle, one which does not have the advantage of publicness and of visible sacrifices—where one can easily
shirk unnoticed and where on the other hand the means of struggle
must first be created.

/ To divert machinations, to settle disputes, to reconcile and confirm institutions, to superintend the routine course—all this has
nothing to do with leadership. /

The *first task of the leader* in *knowledge cultivation* is to set the goals as
a whole, to bring onto the way, and to create the weapons.

That leads at all events to a "reform of the university," which makes
an end of the university and creates an origin.

48   75

Motto for the rectorate: you must not evade the constant disillusion-
ments; they clarify the situation and strengthen the genuine volition.

The will to be leader is other than *the drive to dominate*; the latter is necessary for reassurance in daily successes and for the constant striving
toward them. It finds satisfaction in equilibrium—and does not know
the unrest of genuine volition. But the satisfaction does not satisfy the
one hungry for dominance—he would like his success to be noticed
and extolled—he must concoct new machinations, so that they do not
drop out of the public eye. Necessary for him are soundness of administration, dexterity in negotiation, lightheartedness throughout *great*
questions and tasks, pleasure in undertakings, and a certain ability
to run with the wolves.

76

We cannot overthrow the previous "science" as long as the new one
has not been created. And that is not to be created without the awakening of a new passion of the desire for knowledge. If this does not
49   come about, I then the supposedly overthrown previous science
merely becomes more wretched and problematic than before.

77

"Science," as the decisive beginning of modernity, was a certain "will to
power"—in the sense of the mastery of nature—as "world" over and
against the anxiety before the mystery of forces—a determinately directed mode of unveiling, a mode that maintains a determinate level.

Now knowledge and science must so to speak undertake the *in-
verse* mission:

The restraining and thus "liberating" arousal of the world and thereby of historical Dasein. What binds is only effective work as existentiell labor.

Will and engagement toward the empowerment of powers. The attuning insertion of Dasein into the thrusting projection and content of the happening of a people.

What does this restraining empowerment presuppose existentielly? First and last: a change in the understanding of being! Time!

Through which tasks, and modes, of education are these presuppositions (thrown projection and anticipation) created? (Cf. p. 89.)

New claims of grounding—originary knowledge, in order to awaken the ground.   50

Ground and empowerment; knowledge and *work*.

Work as empowerment and grounding.

The attuning—basically attuning will to empowerment, however, as tradition, i.e., as confrontation with what is great toward a carrying over into the projective domain.

78

The disparagement of National Socialism as a *"gimmick"* with the help of which, as a new lantern, one now seeks through the previous science and its matters and, newly illuminated with corresponding promptness, throws them onto the market. That has, besides easy possibilities of success, also the advantage that one counts *as* a National Socialist and is commended to the masses by the newspapers. Through all this, one introduces into the movement a rigidity—under the semblance of spiritual vitality.

The rigidity creates a destitute state of affairs—i.e., thwarts all anticipatory impulses and attunements | and displaces into a placidity   51
that has been brought into line and is worse than the previous one. Last but not least, one creates for oneself cognitive circumstances from which one can calculate in a superior way that indeed National Socialism actually always already was there and has been prepared. And thence one is absolved completely of the basic attunement of assuming a quite new and unprecedented spiritual mission.

79

What is still decisive is whether the spiritual-historical outward reach and basic attunements are so originary and at the same time so clear that they compel a productive recreation of Dasein—; and the presupposition for it is that National Socialism remains a *struggle*—in the condition of having to accomplish itself and not merely "spreading" and "increasing" and asserting.

Where *stands the enemy*, and how is he *formed*? In what direction the attack? With what weapons?

Is everything stuck in the state of asserting what has been achieved, of prematurely putting on the finishing touches? Heed the excessive 52   emphasis on the *previous* struggle as if I struggle were now at an end.

The one who merely still asserts himself, and thereby falls into a hollow superiority, is least of all immune to that lack of judgment which one day will indiscriminately swallow and extol everything that earlier was ostensibly struggled against.

80

We are now entering the time of a quickly adapted "ideology" for National Socialism; today it is especially easy. The danger of this "ideology": what turns immediately into a denial of the spiritual is carried out *on the one hand* inconspicuously and precisely for that reason misleads the many, on the other hand it is done more conspicuously and then is rejected by others. Everything indeed moves in bourgeois-liberal forms of representation.

81

One can already speak today of a *"vulgar National Socialism"*; by that I mean the world and standards and demands and attitudes of the presently appointed and respected newspaper reporters and makers of culture. From there, naturally under a brainless appeal of Hitler's *Mein Kampf,*[6] a quite determinate doctrine of history and of humanity pro-
53   ceeds to the people; this doctrine can best I be designated *ethical materialism*, which does not refer to the precept of sensual pleasure and living life to the full as the highest law of Dasein; by no means. The designation serves as a deliberate contrast to Marxism and its *economic-*materialistic conception of history.

In the designation above, the term materialism signifies that so-called *character*, which indeed is not identical with brutality and narrow-mindedness, but which does count as the alpha and omega, is determined precisely like a thing around which all else turns. "Character" can indeed mean bourgeois philistinism or, on the other hand, capacity for engagement, a capacity that is ready for engagement, inconspicuously restricted to, and firm in, the work of character and its pertinent knowledge. It can also mean cleverness in all machinations which are on the lookout for something and which well cover

---

6. {Adolf Hitler, *Mein Kampf,* vol. 1, *Eine Abrechnung* (Munich: Eher, 1925); vol. 2, *Die nationalsozialistische Bewegung* (Munich: Eher, 1927).}

over the meagerness of ability and—in case they are lacking—the seriousness and maturity of contemplation. In short: character is indeed not present at hand like a stone or automobile—nor is it simply formed in brief indoctrination camps—| instead, it unfolds in a confirmation   54
within history, one which the character itself *co*-configures in this or that way—though to be sure not alone—in any case not as present-at-hand power—but if at all—then as being-in-the-world—i.e., the power of the capacity of a knowledgeable, spiritual, and natural confrontation with beings.

This *ethical* materialism—indeed stands above economic materialism—insofar as one places morals *above* economics—which indeed must first be grounded and which cannot be decided by "character." This ethical materialism is therefore in no way invulnerable to economic materialism—especially due to the fact that it regards itself as substructure and as bearing and determining and from the outset misinterprets everything else as "superstructure."

This extremely bourgeois pretense over character, a pretense which one day could founder on its own incapacity—now joins up with a *dismal biologism* providing indeed the correct "ideology" for ethical materialism.

The insane opinion is now spreading that the spiritual-historical   55
world ("culture") *would grow like a plant* out of the "people," assuming only the clearing away of obstructions—thus, e.g., the bourgeois intelligentsia constantly maligns, and grumbles about, the incapacity of science.

Yet what alone is gained thereby? The "people," rescued in this way from the "intelligentsia," falls by way of its obscure urge into the most desolate philistinism and presses to imitate and appropriate bourgeois privileges and prestige; the availably present-at-hand dominating force is snatched up in order to bring oneself to dominance; "one" shies away from the struggle which presses forward into the uncertain and which knows that only through closing off and suffering can greatness be disclosed by the few and the individual. Whereby we still quite leave aside the question of how much an originality of the "people" can be attained on such a path today—through halting the intelligentsia, through fetching back the obsolete folklore, etc. There then remain | always the masses of the *petty bourgeoisie* and the masses of   56
the *proletariat*—these can be recreated only in a historical process and not through voting. Although these groups can no longer be divided into classes or organized into parties, yet they are still there as historical attitudes and communal [*volklich*] powers and will be overcome only very slowly: on the one hand, by the youth, and then through the spiritual-historical basic attunement and passion of our Dasein, and finally through an essential change in work and possessions.

And all this is supposed to be created without "spirit" and preached only with "character"? And all this is supposed to arise "of itself" out of the people—without having to be decided and taken up into a discipline for knowledge.

Nothing at all—let alone something great—ever arises from the mere removal of restrictions; what is productive is only anticipatory struggle—i.e., suffering and danger, which is to say, *knowledge*!

57   *82*

The point of knowledge cultivation: not to maintain our scientific prestige at international congresses, but to awaken our people's innermost power of Dasein—not to promote our "culture," but to gain through struggle the clarity of the will of Dasein—not to secure the co-consideration of spiritual needs in the community of the people, but to acquire the sovereign breadth of our essence—not to provide the filling of the bored leisure of those who have possessions, but to set into work the labor stemming from an innermost need—not to let arise a "spiritual superstructure," but to find the basic kind of communal [*volklich*] being.

This task, seen from our current outer and inner need, is perhaps not apparent and not immediately useful—but that only means it is to be carried out all the more silently, with simple means and without hubbub.

58   The struggle for the conquest of the university is coming to an end—one sets oneself to obtain, and hopes to attain in most facile way, teaching appointments, lecturer positions, and professorships. One feels thus permitted to speak down from a rostrum. One falls unwittingly into the trammels of the world one is supposedly struggling against. One is content there, except that one brings to the task inferior qualifications, capacities, and abilities. One has no inkling that what was conquered with so much outcry against ossified professors is already in itself decisively at an end, nor does one have an inkling why this is so, and, more than that, one even sets oneself to perpetuate this end, under the aegis of the new university. And what alone is in fact new here—; in any case, the bureaucratization {?} of the student body and instructors; the astonishing skill in giving legs to everything possible and impossible—not only to that which is properly supposed to happen at this university, viz., *knowledge cultivation*. Supposed to happen, assuming the university has not become an arena for mov-
59   ers and shakers and windbags desirous of showing off—ones I who are as far removed from spiritual responsibility as from any genuine possession of knowledge which could give them the right to have a word to say here.

All this may go on undisturbed. Where it happens most superficially and noisily, there one seeks the university, "where the action is." One has no inkling of the danger one is already sinking into: through continual negation, to make oneself a slave of the negated; for the lack of something else, to adhere to this and if need be dispose of it in up-to-date packaging to a new buyer.

Thus pure philistinism comes to power and impedes the emergence of any creative, forward-pressing basic attunement, eliminates every possibility of genuine spiritual struggle (one indeed sees no opponents and moreover wants to be undisturbed), thwarts even the most imperfect volition, prevents every possibility of verification and selection, and presses everything down to the level of a bored bustling about with rallies, demonstrations, and the like.

To be sure, no spiritual world arises overnight and to order. But we must not fail to work toward the advent of such a world by creating the transition to it; therefore now: by criticizing most sharply the current circumstances.   60

Only a few, only mastery, only what has already long since grown up, only what possesses the basic attunement and has style can lead here and can introduce an actual rebellion that does not end in slogans and abusive language.

Where no unsolvable tasks are posed and an attunement to them is not required, where everything ends in what can be calculated and a man with a diploma in engineering becomes Führer, there the creation of great possibilities is done for, there the whole becomes *a single staging area to which the front* (cf. p. 62) *and the foe are lacking.*

83

The socialist pretense of the students—silliest romanticism: huddling together with "workers" and boozing with them; inspecting and milling about in | their activities—when one knows very well that one will never live or work for any length of time there—all that is just as silly as a farmer, in the season of tilling or harvest, drawing into the university town and inviting himself to a students' gaudeamus in order to testify personally to the bonds tying people together; meanwhile the fields and the harvest go to the devil—or a few women work themselves to death—socialism? If only the students bothered one bit about knowledge cultivation; then their new tasks would be, in preparation for a genuine co-science along with the knowledge of the people, to be obliging to this knowledge, acting in and out of their own vocation, to cobuild the historical-spiritual world of the people, and to preserve taste from a definitive decay into philistinism, in order to awaken and tend to the genuine needs—through a simply serving   61 exemplarity which, to be sure, requires a long education and can arise only from a high and superior genuine knowledge.

62   Precisely *as "student,"* today's student is no National Socialist, but an out-and-out bourgeois; for in knowledge cultivation he salvages himself relative to the most facile and most usual appropriation of a "knowledge estate" which he procures from somewhere or other— without the cognitive attitude that could intrinsically be called "socialistic"—i.e., one that would be motivated by responsibility, secured through a true superiority, and ready to act.

This "socialistic" pretension is only a cloak covering a flight in the face of the authentic task and one's own incompetence.

84

Programs and institutions are useless, if there is no one who bears an inner directedness; it is time to call off the semblant revolution of the university. (Semblance: 1.) because *what* is supposed to be overturned is no longer there; 2.) because what is stepping into its place is even emptier and more immature.) What remains?

The formation of a front—establishment of the goal of the struggle, determination of the position of the enemy (not merely the all too
63   easily misused "reaction" | to it; today's enemies themselves); development of powers; basic posture of the historical advance.

Yet this is ultimately only educational "programmatics." What alone is needed: the *work* [*das* Werk]. Away with the machinations by which the "authentic actuality" is feigned, as is the field of decisions! There *nothing at all* is decided—instead, only the usually ill bustling is kept in play (Cf. p. 60.)

85

What counts:

1. the work that binds and discloses forward—
2. the mastery deriving from knowledge cultivation and from youth clubs—
3. the unconditionality of the claim and the demands—
4. the exemplary cultivation of steady labor—
5. through all this, that proper X!

86

If the current university is at an end, then the students no longer have anything irritating them and then they equally are at an end, along with their wisdom.

87

The most important section of today's university is the *public-relations office*—wielding the greatest possible authority. It is reported there that such and such a number of S.A. men are fed in the refectory, that the building of the new gym increased employment, that an excursion to the North Sea newly brought together students and instructors, etc., etc.—and so what?

88

We have undergone a global economic *plight* and still stand within it (unemployment), we are held in a *plight* relative to history and the state (Versailles), we have long experienced the concatenation of these plights—but we still sense nothing of the *spiritual plight of Dasein*—and the fact that for *this latter* we are still not ready as regards experience and suffering, i.e., still not great enough for it: precisely that is the *greatest plight.* For we are now in the act of wiping out quickly and crudely every dawning of *this* plight, either through a mendacious flight into a now empty Christianity or through the heralding of a National Socialist | "worldview" that is *spiritually* questionable and of dubious origination. And therefore even the happening is lessened and not made free for its spiritually and existentielly compelling power. Therefore, everything is degraded to a cheap scolding of "liberal science" and the like. As if in our own history there were only what the philistines see.

65

When will we come to the great plight of Dasein?

How will we consummate the great compulsion into the greatest plight? When will we come to terms with the question-worthiness of Dasein and with the great anxiety rising up in the face of the risk? When will we smash the noisy and "unpropertied" small-mindedness that poses as "character" today? When will we create the true encounter of the German "workers" with their German tradition and with that of their people?

89

What if the abusive grumblings against the spirit and thinking—and against the genuine question—were only anxiety in face of the clarity of the deepest breadth of the plight of Dasein—; the self-encapsulation in the bourgeois repose of a noisy lack of spirit?

66

The true presentness of Dasein consists not in losing oneself in what is current and bustling about in the states of affairs at hand—but in experiencing the innermost plight; for the plight in itself grasps *forward* and thereby displaces us into the full extension of the whole of temporality.

In the plight, the futurity of an engagement is rooted; in the plight, what has been comes down to us through genuine tradition.

The mission of Dasein is present only for a seeking of the will of Dasein in and for the plight of this will.

Therefore, this will—qua *seeking*—is the most compelled and originarily most necessary *will to knowledge* and, as such, is already essential *knowledge*.

The true constancy of Dasein is *perseverance in seeking* at the hearth of the question-worthiness of being.

Yet a true grasp—i.e., experience—of all this requires a higher—
67   i.e., deeper—Ι level of *renewed self-reflection*; must not falsely equate current conditions with truth pure and simple and must not make believe that one needs to learn nothing more—because one basically *wants* no more, since the capacities for it are lacking, and one would with this admission make oneself into a mere transition and would renounce self-excellence.

Should the state of the movement of 1933–1934 merely be interpreted and decanted into bottles as "what has been attained"—an end-state— or is this only the prelude to a great future of the people? Only if it is this—which we believe—does it harbor the guarantee of greatness. But then the question comes to the fore: which powers create and unfold this future? Certainly not those powers which are ever satisfied with the hitherto, but also not those that now follow behind as latecomers and "interpret" and make palatable—i.e., harmless—every-
68   thing liberal-spiritual. Seen from here Ι a mistrust of the "old" over and against the "new" is not only justified but is even necessary. Yet if this mistrust blindly extends to all spiritual endeavor and to every seeking already long ago equal to such endeavor and *equipped for it*, and if everything is thereby thrown indiscriminately into a melting pot of "intellectualism" and "theorizing," then it becomes a thwarting and disfiguring of creative happenings.

92

Insufficiency and mediocrity cannot be eradicated; they even *must* go on; but they ought not to be raised up to the highest binding measure.

93

The *parliamentarianism* of the university court and of the faculties has indeed been eliminated, in place of which, however, a *council system* has been implemented, one that makes a leading of the university today still more impossible than before. The determinant powers, disjointed among themselves, none of them with a creative basic goal, have an effect on the "object" university, in each case according to their respective authority, and grind down the whole—I or at best it   69 is a matter of a reheated soup into which all sorts of ingredients have been stirred.

The *consequence of this state of affairs* is becoming more visible daily: out of a (not recognized as such) inner helplessness and a poverty of goals, one escapes into auxiliary tasks of the university—; it is a blind footrace of individuals, such as that of the spas for publicity—; the most impossible things are extolled here—; to say nothing of the tawdriness and mendacity of all these doings.

94

Now therefore the "empire" of the students is founded, and the "Führer" is appointed. Someone troubled the Führer himself about this the day before yesterday. Do the German students surmise anything of the responsibility they have to assume? I do not believe so. For that implies being capable of a spiritual-creative attitude and being able to enter an actual "struggle." But what is happening here is indeed only an evasion of the spiritual I struggle, under the mask of "political ac-   70 tion." And if the futility of these doings ever comes to light, then one will promptly point out: indeed, the professors have surely left us in the lurch.

95

While one busies oneself with the everyday, one falls into the delusion of being involved in an authentic happening. While the everyday grinds on and on, without altering, what is authentic is happening invisibly and is already predetermined in the concealed mission. It would be false, however, simply to raise oneself up over the everyday and wander astray in dreamland, instead of maintaining oneself in the midst of being and seeking and carrying on the future in the everyday.

96

The student body and the "academic staff" are now carrying on the same correspondence with regard to appointments and the filling of vacancies as the evil full professors used to take care of. The only difference is that now:

71   1. many more persons are at present occupied | with such questions and inquiries,

2. consequently the arbitrariness of the ones who are judging and the unverifiability of their suitability to judge are increasing,

3. the ones who are now judging are much more *inexperienced*,

4. and much less than before are they aligned to the university in its entirety—for they do not have a general view of anything,

5. under the aegis of an often very problematic National Socialism and from an unjustified self-assurance, they play at being a tribunal and thus they wholly conceal in advance their complete lack of a capacity to configure; they are on the best path to "organize" an unrivalled mediocrity.

97

The self-deification of today's "young generation" is in full swing— the mad, undiscerning, and affected pomposity which in its zeal does not notice how much it also already robs what is old in the same breath

72   that it reviles it | and brings everything down to the boring level of a stetted "phraseology"; for each of the limitlessly unknowledgeable ones of the current generation, this is perhaps impressive, but at bottom all of it is decrepit—a "culture-sociology and analysis" of the worst sort, already seen through by us a decade ago and never affirmed.

If, for the purposes of placing out in relief one's own presumed significance, one uses as comparison only scoundrels and money-grubbers from a degenerate epoch, then it is truly no great merit to be better. What one demonstrates in this way is only the spiritual blindness which cannot see that the outgoing nineteenth century was prepared in its destiny long ago. To ascertain this end is a fortiori no accomplishment, especially if one overlooks the fact that decades ago, 1910–1919, a far-reaching upheaval was prepared. But what matters is indeed not to evaluate this old time appropriately but only to know which powers alone must be drawn on if indeed the future is not to become a bad counterimage to the most proximate past.

98   73

The *certainty in negating* still does not guarantee the power of the *affir-mative*, anticipatory configuration. And on the other hand the latter is not to be gauged according to the scope of the former but, instead, has its great law in history—not in what is merely current.

99

All power is to be placed in restrained mildness and stillness, and the innermost rest of resoluteness is to be preserved for the playing out of the highest necessities of Dasein from the most intrinsic plight and most extrinsic affliction. Steadfastness of the simple gaze at what is Es-sentially unique—the increasing ability to detach oneself from every-thing whereby "one" can only be "at the point of doing something."

100

What the basic will of the new Dasein seeks in secret is to be brought, in its exemplarity, to cognitive—conceptual—elaboration. The co-seeking in the wakening and yet still distracted essence of the people.

101   74

The essential experience of the rectoral year now coming to an end:
    This is the irresistible *end* of the university in every respect, on ac-count of the impotence for a genuine "self-assertion." The latter re-mains as the ultimate demand, growing fainter without any reso-nance.
    Out of the forms and institutions of the university—especially after the change in the constitution—the still flickering previous doings are withdrawing more and more. What acts as "new" is not equal to the task; the "old" is weary and does not find the way back to any origin; too timid to be exposed once again to the full question-worthiness of previous scientific work; too strictly bound to one's own specialty, niche, and domain of accomplishment, one's little world, for a free willing of results to awaken. Unfruitful benevolence is without value.
    The mere reacting with National Socialist means of power I and   75
with the affiliated functionaries can perhaps from the outside simu-late the assertion of a strong position; what use is it, when the entire structure is intrinsically impotent and, moreover, is denied the influx of new and young powers or even only the retention of adaptive teach-ers?

The point in time of my engagement was too early, or better: down-right otiose; the opportune "leadership" should aim not at inner change and self-education but rather at the most visible accumulation of new institutions or else at an emphatic alteration of what was hitherto. In doing so, however, the essential can remain entirely as of old.

All this must run itself out; the "spectators" must languish in their own boredom; meanwhile, the power of Dasein amasses toward a new grounding of the German university.

76   When that will arrive and on which paths—we do not know. Certain is only that we, for our part, must prepare what is coming. We must not expend ourselves on the continuation of what has been, and we cannot let ourselves deform the secret sight of what is coming. We will also never stand aside where the right volition—and capability—sets to work. We will remain in the invisible front of the secret spiritual Germany.

102

Whoever stands in the creative and *affirmative* "opposition" does not merely risk being constantly rejected; he is required to tolerate, indeed to desire, that the "ideas" and impulses—even if often distorted—are taken over by the rulers and conveyed as their own work.

77   ### 103

Against the leveling and unrestricted application of the *Führer-principle*!

How can a *scientist* ever be "Führer"? How *not*. (This inability is not a lack—instead, it secures a proper strength and at the same time a task for those who enter the domain of scientific work.)

How do untrue and slanted judgments and condemnations arise out of perverse goals and claims?

104

The question of the university can be settled neither by looking exclusively at the "students" nor at the tasks of scientific research on the part of the "instructors"; therefore a fortiori not by artificially juxtaposing the two groups—but only by considering their *respective task*—which is already there prior to them and beyond them, grasped or not.

The poorly veiled "positivism" in all of today's idle talk about the university.

105   78

On the situation. (End of February, 1934)

1. The powers that are capable of effectiveness, that sustain, and that are becoming rooted are all with the *youth*, but specifically not with the students, because it is only polemically, not constructively, that the students are "equal" to the world of the university, a world now entrusted to them.

2. The structure of communal-civil [*volklich-staatlich*] Dasein is creating the movement according to a mode of organization determined by soldiers and engineers.

3. The basic attitude in terms of activity and worldview is just as certain as the concomitant spiritual world remains confused. This attitude largely finds contentment in a problematic assumption of the forms of the nineteenth century and its positivistic biologism, without seeing and grasping that for the last fifteen years this change of the whole of being has been prepared, a change in which the movement must once be rooted if indeed it lis to be able to bring about an appro-   79
priate creatively spiritual world on the planet.

106

This spiritual-historical actuality, visible at first only to a few in its main traits, must be thrown by us onto the path as a block of the configured work for the future of the rising youth. Hereupon this youth must find resistance for that struggle in which alone a great being of a people is kindled.

Thereby we must distinguish and attribute an equal validity to: on the one hand, the impulsive psychic basic attitude with the dragging in of everything hitherto as well as the creatively disclosing and pressing projection, and, on the other hand, being, with all its apparent aloofness and supposed impotence.

Consequently, the demand on those who *work* here:

1. not to let themselves be thrust aside from this mission of the philosopher (a mission lying far in advance) through I the urgencies of   80
what is current and the publicness of the "undertakings";

2. but thereby to involve themselves just as little with the substitutability of "science" and "culture," something which indeed stands on the side yet is today already largely accepted;

3. not to make the mission which lies in advance the exclusive measure of the current endeavors of youth—instead, to come to terms with the problematic character of those endeavors and thus to steer them in the right direction;

4. not to impair and misinterpret the superiority through bureau-cratized positions of leadership, but to draw it back into the incon-spicuous existence of perhaps "useless" spiritual creativity;

5. *never* to lose from sight the essentially *mediate* character of all *spiritual* leadership.

81

107

For years I have known myself to be on the right path in the work of knowledge cultivation and must refuse to let myself be convinced by the foolish chatter of little shavers about a "new concept of science."

108

Need to overcome the error that work *on behalf of* the people and out of the people would exist only in noisy fussing about with organiza-tions, ones which might be important for uprooted city dwellers and contemporaries but which must not palm their form off onto spiri-tual-creative work.

To drag everything into the public square is to eradicate all actual existence.

All this is merely a Marxism set on its head and as such is all the more dangerous, because now the deception—the spiritual one—is espe-cially hidden.

The disastrous opinion that struggle takes place only where there is noise and bustle and the hatching of intrigues.

82

109

By joining the tumult of machinations, we seem indeed to admit that we must first change ourselves; whereas in doing so we precisely fall away from ourselves and from the true task. To be sure, in this way there remains the public semblance that we belong to the "reaction-ism" which stands on the side; whereas we do stand quite differently right in the midst of the happening of Dasein.

The courage to take distance must not be deformed by the ostentatious machinations of a noisy "engagement."

110

Today's organized—yet empty—power of the student body operates such that the actual "instructors" are degraded to tolerated and occa-sionally summoned handymen, because they still do precisely possess "knowledge"—which is now obviously understood as a mastery of "facts" and "figures." The *presumption* of the students is justified, where they appeal, against those who are old, to the certainty of the direction of their own drive and to their own will to press forward. But the presumption becomes ludicrous if it is falsified to the view that I precisely the *students* would construct the future spiritual world. *That* they will *never* be able to do, not only because they now momentarily lack "knowledge" in the sense of the mastery of some craft, but because they are *essentially not* at the age of creative maturity with regard to the spirit and worldview.

It would be a mistake to maintain that the current corps of students will one day of themselves reach that point; for they are completely falling into the track of their predecessors. In whatever "categories" it is thought and questioned, the inner spiritual helplessness can be matched only by the great arrogance. And yet this obscure impetus, thus permeated with everything hitherto, has its historical necessity and significance.

111

We must once have gone all the way to the extreme banalities of the everyday, must have stood in them, in order to grasp how the everyday, as the necessary semblance of being, despite all apparent estrangement from the ineluctable (i.e., time) does nevertheless remain caught up in the very heart of it.

We must once have *gone entirely away* into the mercantile, the merely commercial, in order to experience the remote solitude of the *work* and to undertake fully—and stand within—the contradictoriness of being.

112

A farewell speech. (April 28, 1934)

The "collegial" farewell speeches, ones belonging to an already departed time, are constrained. I would like to say a *companionable* word on the spur of the moment.

They are on the point of a new beginning.

I am standing at the end of a *foundered year*.

This looks like an *opposition*:

there the exciting power of the future unknown;

here the paralyzing burden of something that has been.

Yet both belong together—are *the same*: our Dasein of today, which we must grasp firmly with a simple hard insight—in order to avert a dazzling I bliss of hope as well as a no less blinding disgruntlement.

A foundered year—a lost one—unless *foundering* is the highest form of human experience, wherein we encounter the effective powers of the world in their remorseless effectiveness and learn to sense their play and their arrangement.

Thus the basic experience of this foundering is gathered up as follows: the closed and rooted power for self-assertion *has been* withdrawn from the German university. Indeed it has disappeared from it *long ago*; now the void has merely come to light very swiftly and from all sides:

educational power is confused—
worldview power is atrophied—
cognitive power is scattered.

Thus it happens that overnight the university had to lose its influence and position in the public life of the people; it leads now—up to
86   its definitive end—an "antiquarian" | existence and possesses the dubious role of an institution which within certain limits may still supply to students, as quickly as possible and without much exertion, professional and practical bits of knowledge.

It has already become a matter of indifference today whether a university is "well" or "badly" provided in faculty—that can still count only as a "quantitative" distinction. The limit of "quality," of essential suitability, lies elsewhere.

Such a fate of the German university is not to be lamented. Much more disastrous is something else: the fact that now a *supposedly* forward-thrusting student body and an academic staff imitating the students in "organization" and "attitude" are happy about the mastery over the delivery of professional knowledge and put on the sad drama that passes off the edifice they have inherited, one thoroughly decayed, as a conquered fortress.

87   The danger is not reactionism; for the supposed | "revolutionaries" are even *more* reactionary, since in decisive matters they are less experienced and less capable than those who are "old."

The danger is also not the unbridled eagerness to foist onto the university from the outside all thinkable and unthinkable separate tasks—the idle talk about the surrounding locality—where the inside is entirely hollow.

The danger remains: an imminent veiling of the situation, in consequence of which all plans and measures are in advance displaced into the untruth and every genuine volition must stay altogether outside the very narrow confines of what can be grasped.

Only one thing remains: versus the veiling, to show the actual, and that means to pursue a resolution—out of the self-configuring volition of what is wholly other.

What is sad is not this end—but rather the veiling of its actuality.

113

The end of my rectorate. April 28, 1934.—My resignation tendered, because a justification no longer possible.
Long live mediocrity and noise!

114   88

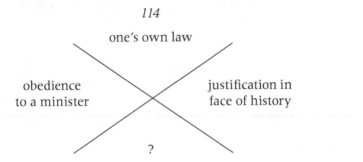

one's own law

obedience
to a minister

justification in
face of history

?

My rectorate was based on a great mistake, namely, my wanting to bring *questions* into the temperament and regard of my "colleagues," questions from which they were at best *excluded,* to *their* advantage—and undoing.

115   89

Need to remain reticent and hard—
    distant and strong—
    entering again into the inmost plight—
    back into the prompting of the distant injunction.
    The great concealed event—
    the remoteness to everything of today.
    The proximity to the inmost vocation of the people.
    (Cf. p. *97f.*)

116

Making Dasein possible through and in care as the effectuation of the essence of being. (Cf. p. 49.)

117

Beyond the inevitability of the "destiny" of Dasein, need to set aside the everyday, so that, by opening up being, all beings may be brought into relief and volition may be enkindled.

90   *118*

The many today: the hasty and noisy,
                 the makers and strivers,
                 the impostors and quibblers.
    Ones who act familiarly with the small and tasteless excitement of
the throng and with its faint pleasure; ones who drift in murkiness
and gape at what is silly.

                            119

The higher compulsion of the earth does not reside primarily in the
everyday and in deeds, but rather already in the creative force of questioning and in the world-configuring power of a people.

                            120

Must the errant leap be taken into the noisy everyday and the maelstrom of its machinations, into the usual inconstancy of the everyday
and its hidden unimportance, so that the unique necessity can be
fully grasped for the first time, whereby one becomes quite alone and
might be equal to the work?

                            121

Where does it lead if "one" takes as actual only what is of *today* and
claims that everything *opposed* to what is of today is "reactionism"?
Yet it could just as well also be a "pro-duction."

91   *122*

There must be those who maintain that a "community of the people"
is equivalent to the crackling unison of a foolish mediocrity, whose
noise they then take as proceeding from adherents.

                            123

A trial: who can bear the incessant degrading of everything inceptual and original—without descending concomitantly; who can look
upon the hollowing out and flattening off of everything substantial
and dense—without becoming a master of platitudes?

124

The *truth of a philosophy* lies in the allegorical power of its work. This power is measured against the force of the fitting subdual of the summoned tumult, against the originality and genuineness of the wakening reattachment to the entire liberated plight of the essence of a historical Dasein. It is out of this work that the enkindling will to questioning must strike forth.

Every rank of accomplishment, every level of claim is inclined toward sinking; this subsidence is accelerated by every widening of the level; then I arises the danger of a complete flatness, whose emptiness offers a resemblance to the simplicity of the essence. But the essence can be encountered in each case only through forceful thrusts in the direction of something unusually ineluctable.   92

125

Those of today totter in the void of mere organization and then—at most—seek behind for a wretched *abundance*, and they believe they could be supplied with this, if only the "organization" were "extant."

126

The *work* of actuality is distinct from all organization and even from the "organic." For it turns out thereby that the creative will is exposed precisely to the overpowerfulness and abundance of the insurmountable, and to preserve *these* it seeks in the structure of the work; the latter does not eliminate what is overpowering but rather liberates it and empowers it. (Cf. above, p. 23.)

127

No quick and easy timeliness!

128

The arising of the *possible*; how it "is there"! But—they mean the reverse—that now the actual is actual—the noisy blind ones, I the ones   93
drunk on the small significance of their machinations.

And how they are completely excluded from the trembling power to endure as destiny the unison of the remoteness of the possible, its remoteness from actuality.

129

Simple, hard, valid, and in measure.

130

In this age, which not only appraises everything according to use-value but also would like to see exclusively along those lines, the demand must be set down to the effect that there is *a knowledge in the knowing ones who are there in a people for the sake of themselves*; this is of course much further removed from "liberalism" than that exploitation of all would-be spirit. Yet we make this demand most fruitfully through such an existence—precisely if it does not succeed in being "heard"—in the end, that would be a requirement which had to run counter to the proper directionality.

94

131

The prevailing madness: the essential—so far as a semblance of it is still graspable at all—is in advance to be made *universal* and something ordinary for a *rough* intelligibility (called "character"), so that it would thereby gain validity.

But it becomes valid only if recognized as something remote and difficult.

132

It is now coming to light that we have already long been living, and will still long live, in the age of the departing gods. The question is whether we will experience in this departure the course of the gods and thus their nearness, one that moves us while escaping from us.

133

The capacity to wait—secured in itself—for the coming famine of the spirit—after the desolate starvation through feeding on chaff.

134

The attaining of the god by way of struggle—the preparation of his abode—in the existence of poetizing and thinking.

In this way, truth first happens, as a lonely forest ridge sweeping through the valleys of humans.

135

The supreme plight of the plightless age: tottering in the forgottenness of beyng,[7] the age holds itself to be secure and to be active in the relieving of needs. Thus the intolerance for poetry and thinking—the obstinacy in face of everything required to endure the mission.

The mania of partiality, the timid jubilation, where only something or other is subdued, shackled, and eliminated—and the blindness toward the greatness of the Lawlessly ungrasped—and the inept aversion to sustaining this other and even to raise it up into beyng and completely carry it over into intimacy.

The outrageous timidity before beyng, in the mistaken regulation of beings in their most proximate usefulness.

136

Ones with knowledge—not scientists—are those who concomitantly bear Dasein as such—and in themselves establish that Dasein is to withstand the tumult of truth—alone, trees rooted in the ground, whose mission is to protrude simply into heaven and, in the structure of the clasping and penetrating roots, to preserve the soil from landslides. (Cf. p. 99.)

137

If a truth lies in the power of "race" (of the native-born one), will and should the Germans then lose their historical essence—abandon it— organize it away—or will they not have to bring it to the supreme tragic denouement? Instead of which, those who are now bred are shortsighted and oblivious!

138

Or is today's convulsion only the precursor of a genuine, complete, and radical turnaround by which the entanglement is resolved into mere *receptacles*?

Still no relations to beyng that persist in an attuning-bearing-exciting way, but only the ingenious penning up of a monstrous sum of receptacles, packed into which all feel secure and well and hardy [*trampelnd*].

---

7. [Archaic form of "being" to render *Seyn*, archaic form of *Sein*.—Trans.]

139

Who and *whose* are we?

140

Must not speak *immediately* and must certainly not write "about"—Heraclitus—Kant—Hölderlin—Nietzsche—but rather must *transform* everything, in concealed thankfulness, to power and density—; only then—may this succeed—are these to be placed back, as something entirely alien, into their most proper greatness; for otherwise we make them share in our half measures.

97

141

First fruits—true ones—are sacrificed, immolated; but they are not passed around and certainly not paid for and transported.

142

Unavoidable: the confused *entanglement* in the massiveness, boundlessness, and hastiness of what is present at hand and in its operative coherence.

Unavoidable: dragging out the mystery into the so-called worldview of the everyday. Therefore, still more necessary is it merely to "know" both the unmastered plight of nature and the historical remoteness—and not to be assaulted by these powers. And this plight conceals the exclusion from beyng, while such exclusion is interment of the conflictual intimacy of the basic happening.

Yet that entanglement is still more confused due to its being unacknowledged *as this*; indeed it gives itself out as *nearness to life*, a nearness that would require "character" and "worldview" to master it. What if this were only the flight from one's own scientific incapacity 98 I and from the spiritual desolation of a vain philistinism?

The entanglement, however, is not supposed to be unraveled—instead, the god requires that the basic happening be opposed to it—while increasing and exaggerating the entanglement—toward a downgoing or a *complete* inversion; but as usual—thus certainly to a sacrifice—; need to place into Dasein the knowledgeable questioning of *reticent* waiting and the world-configuring thinking of the basic happening. (Cf. p. 89.)

143

True *knowledge* includes an awareness of its own essential limits. The mistaking of these limits is an infallible sign of swaggering vanity and also of an incapacity making a lot of noise. The mistaking is *double*: on the one hand, an *excessive* demand that knowledge must immediately lead to so-called praxis and even urge praxis on, and then also an undervaluing of the inner power of knowledge insofar as it can supposedly dispense with the most intrinsic and broadest—constantly open—rigor of grounding and with the free seriousness of questioning.

In the former case, there is a mistaking of what *may* be; in the latter, of what *must* be.   99

Yet to know about limits, and especially *one's own*, requires the highest superiority of Dasein, i.e., the inner suitability for rank and constancy. (Cf. p. 95.)

144

The powers first exert their full force when destiny is seized altogether boldly and properly and the opposition is definitively ventured; then, however, the opposition is beyond all quarrelsomeness and *mere* contrariness.

145

"*Organization*"—is not the substantial unfolding of new buds, but is rather the thorough *boarding up* of all things and of all buds in these things. Yet organization remains a pressing need in view of the untold massiveness and all the handed-down things lying there present.

All the more originary and decisive must become the tension and the counterprojection that affirms the organizing, so a history should still remain possible and an organized sinking preventable.

We can retain as something that has been, while disposing of it,   100
and can let tower up before us as a jutting peak, only that to which we are radically equal and possess in its powerfulness.

In the possession of the great legacy of Greek Dasein, we can venture the swinging over of a sure spirit into the freely binding inauguration of the future.

146

One *is* a philosopher—i.e., a questioner exposed to the tumult of the nearness of the gods—or one is not. But even if one *is*, one can still misinterpret everything, and make everything empty, for example precisely through "philosophical" erudition. But one can also possess the vocation of bearing the actual tradition of philosophy from peak to peak and of preparing the trembling of the future through one's divinely compelled work.

101

147

Nothing halfway or intermediate avails any more—we must make our way completely back into the tumult and thus newly test what is wild *and* what can be grasped and their intimacy. For, even our sobriety has become emptiness and mere expedient constraint, and our passion merely the directionless and spaceless ebullition of shallow waters.

We must make our way completely back into the basic happening—if we are to gain by struggle a true great *downgoing*.

148

Culture? The struggling structure of the historical Dasein of a people and its destiny, a Dasein exposed to the gods.—But struggle πόλεμος ["struggle," "war"].

149

What *saves* us is only the *conversion* into the still not arisen (originary) essence of *truth*, so that in the recurrence out of truth we might surmise what is true and through ourselves prepare an arrival of it—the enduring of an nonunfolded beginning.

102

150

The gaping void in the unsurmised wilderness is to be sustained. (Do not let yourself be talked out of nothingness on account of the wretched certainty of a rootless shrewdness.)

First need to endure an actual questioning and scorn those vain money changers who loudly offer to supply answers, and the most current ones possible, and who in advance justify their half measures, flung into the people, by saying that everything is in development.

151

The many: ones who now speak "about" race [*Rasse*] and indigenousness and who mock themselves in their every word and action and demonstrate that they "possess" nothing of all this, leaving aside the question of whether they actually *are* well-bred [*rassig*] and indigenous.

152   103

Intellectualism is reviled, and talk goes on incessantly—in quite accidental and deficient concepts—"about" the people, the state, science, rights, etc. Yet no one ever considers and questions whether we have such mastery of Dasein that we can for long endure this last and worst chatter. "Positivism"—i.e., the immediacy of the operation of the spirit—goes further, except that one now speaks about "community" and falls head over heels for sheer community. But the masters come in this way into high office, faster than they could have dreamt, with all their incapacity and arrogance. And the much-discussed *people*? That is, the most intrinsic spiritual destiny of the people? Degraded to a dissolution and desolation, such as the Germans have not yet lived through.

153   104

The much-invoked "community" still does not guarantee "truth"; the "community" can very well go astray and abide in errancy even more and even more obstinately than the individual. The people's opinions, convictions, and views have for a long time not been purely and simply the measure of truth and will not become this measure merely because they dominate or are able to breathe and thrust themselves forth. And precisely with the demand for "community," it becomes *even more* difficult not only to bring into power but even just to find the genuine measures and distinctions.

There must be clarity concerning today's mass society and its degeneration—which has been going on for decades, and not merely since November, 1919—in order to sense the full gravity of the responsibility lying in the "emphasis on the principle of community," especially where the cognitive relations are so confused and childish.

Matters which for us have long been unable to become questions   105
are today offered, by those who lack experience and competence, as the newest discoveries and are belabored with unsurpassable bad taste.

154

The most genuine community does not unburden the individual but, instead, demands the highest—i.e., egoless—autonomy of knowledge and of persistence.

155

One noisily decries "intellectualism" and at the same time pushes the awareness and artificiality of "knowledge" so far that one is supposed to create "consciously" out of the "people" and on behalf of the "people."

For does one surmise anything of the fact that in such businesslike destruction of the immediacy of the intrinsically transmissional creativity, one is placing on this latter demands that are excessive, if not absurd? Are *we* then so rich in creativity that we could accomplish 106   this organized awareness | as well as such an arrogance? Or is all this only the abating of a domineering lack of spirit?

156

The task is not to attack what is of today or even to desire its refutation—but, through the founding of an ordained future, to posit the hitherto *as such*, i.e., as having been and thus to place it into a creative downgoing.

157

The superior submission and the great solitude.

158

"*Science*"—the new "catchword"—do not speak about it but work "practically"! One now acts as if "one" had never done so—as if only "professors" had "spoken" "about" science. This new "catchword," however, merely demonstrates that what is at issue here was previously grasped just as little as it is now, where one does not vanish 107   quickly enough into the "practical" or, | likewise practically, concocts the "theory of science" to be "used" in the future. But that "praxis" and this "concoction" are far removed from a *determination* through the happening of knowledge, a happening that bears our historical Dasein and that brings its *own law* to an end, *independently* of what "took place" in 1933, especially as regards the universities.

One acts as if it were only *very remotely* possible that we would *definitively* have to deal in a *creative* sense with a discontinuance of "science"—i.e., with an end—on account of the thrusting of "science," as it used to be, into the domain of the technical-practical and of what are *no longer genuinely* sciences. (Cf. p. 112.) Instead, one does oneself the favor of assuring oneself that "science" will still be pursued in the future, but no longer so "theoretically." One is thereby unaware that knowledge—even if degenerate—can only be "dispatched" *knowingly*—and that entails a new questioning, with new limits and with an *other* truth.

Instead of pursuing further a merely opportune but basically moribund trafficking in slogans, what counts is *self-assertion*, liberation to the essential powers. It is on them I that knowledge *as such*, together   108
with its ground, must newly be established, whereby those powers themselves come to be decided.

159

To what does the most serious, hardest, and most reticent labor of acute questioning lead? To the fact that we are silent more and more, and what is constantly still all too provisional accumulates more and more and needs to be put back—because the wholly simple strangeness has still not been found for that which must be spoken far in advance—which in general opens up the soil and the air and the bridges for questioning and for the capacity to know, out of a changed Dasein and on behalf of it.

160

Perhaps we will succeed in bringing our historical Dasein once again to the nearest borders of the foothills of the domain of philosophical power.

Whoever cannot deal with the fact that philosophy is by essence inopportune, without resonance, and without calculable use, and that it necessarily appears in the semblance of harmless impotence, I may   109
make fun of philosophy or revile it, knowing only that he knows nothing of philosophy. But precisely that is what such a one can never know.

All "nearness to actuality" is vain as long as it is not constrained in *remoteness* from the intimation of beyng.

161

A generation ago, the elementary school teachers fed on Haeckel's "world-riddles"[8] and today feast on Krieck—the difference is only that today the decline into spiritlessness and vanity has progressed even

---

8. {Ernst Haeckel, *Die Welträtstetsel: Gemeinverständliche Studien über monistische Philosophie* (Bonn: Strauß, 1899).}

further and that Haeckel still "accomplished" something in his "sci-ence," which can no longer be said of Krieck.

We no longer have a *spiritual world* (cf. p. 111); we only have its de-bris—of obscure origin—and a utilitarian thinking for crude pur-poses. Within this thinking, the arbitrary is arbitrarily snatched up. Therefore, the most proximate task is to create a spiritual world—in general, a world of Dasein! Precisely this cannot be accomplished to order but must be done only out of plight; and to experience this plight requires a disclosive questioning in which truth as such is newly formed with respect to space and structure.

110   *162*

"Science"—what we so name is indeed no longer science—i.e., an un-folding of knowledge and a binding back into knowledge—but only the running out of a Busy pursuit, one which even brings "profits"—waste waters—which are still taken as self-flowing rivers—and such things as might again be cut to size by today's ignorance and arro-gance.

163

A day is dawning in which all authorities and institutions, all endeav-ors and standards, will be *fused together*—and everything depends on our creating the correct original *fire* and the *thoroughly genuine metal* for the new amalgam and on our making it fluid in the coming Dasein.

This *fire* is the "truth" in the original essence of truth, and the glow-ing, consuming, purifying flame of this fire is *questioning*. But the metal, the genuineness of the ore, is *beyng*.

164

Scientific instruction, i.e., cognitive letting learn—what is it? The knowl-edgeable and constant capacity to learn out of the essential relation to the respective ontological domain and to the world that re-worlds this domain.

111   *165*

The "professorial chairs" have long since become for the most part easy chairs, ones which are now so padded and furnished that they can be occupied in comfort.

166

We are standing entirely outside the new domains of the great spiritual decisions (cf. p. 109):

1. the confrontation with and clear attitude toward *Christianity* and toward the whole of *Western philosophy;*

2. the confrontation with *Nietzsche;*

3. the creative—not merely organizing—relation to *technology;*

4. the new *European* world;

5. the *world of the earth* as such.

All five decisions constitute *the* one decision of beyng, a decision that thereby in itself at the same time is the one concomitant with the entirety of Western history.

The domain of decision must *first be created.*

167   112

I am asked again and again why I do not respond to the reproaches of Herr Krieck!

Answer: such ones, who on account of their shallowness and vanity merely rummage around in everything that was ever formed and thought and who deserve only contempt, can never be *opponents.* In a battle I will face only an opponent, not someone who champions mediocrity.

168

The *sciences* have either been degraded to mere techniques (natural science, medicine, in part jurisprudence), or, in cases that this is not easily possible (i.e., with the human sciences), what dominates is either a desolate increase in literature or a complete perplexity from a lack of questioning—(even here, one is "basically," i.e., superficially, done with everything.) There are indeed now prehistory and similar things, but they are merely transfers of traditional attitudes to daily needs and to previously less elaborated material.

Any sort of essential, original cognitive attitude, which could again   113 determine "science" according to "form," is not there.

A question: then *must* "science" always "go on"? (Cf. p. 107.)

169

Why does one not have the courage to see the university *as it is*: a hodgepodge of groups of professional schools, a hodgepodge shoved together by some ministry?

It is because "one," deep within, thinks "liberally," i.e., becomes enraptured mendaciously with the mere semblance of *"universitas,"* indeed since "one" now has the power and will some day (through whatever channels and as the reward of whatever "organization") receive a place in this sphere called the "university," a sphere constantly reviled in public and hotly striven for in private.

And this is then ideologically confirmed in its lamentable condition through the wretched counterfeits circulated by Baeumler,[9] Krieck, and their cronies.

114 How "reactionary" all this is and how much is the back | and forth thinking—in *its own* sense—the certain working of the Jesuits, who, with the most modern literary means, set down a "literature," over and against which the cry, "Read the National Socialist press," will one day only operate comically—supposing one has not resolved to be a revolutionary also in spirit instead of falsifying the spirit "politically."

170

"Science"—the story goes round that it is *too* "theoretical" and thereby fails in the face of actuality. No! It is not theoretical enough or is *not at all* theoretical; i.e., it has become spiritless and only all too actual—completely political science.

Americanism of conventionality and of bad enthusiasm.—

171

Philosophy: the passion of extreme questioning in the soberness of ordained discourse.

115 ### 172

Male Confederation and Science[10]—a quite cleverly fabricated fig leaf, but one which, despite everything, does not altogether cover the nakedness: male confederation! That signifies a complete lack of manliness of spirit; it is the flocking together and promotion of those who otherwise would fall too short but now enjoy the prospect of making their fortune in a "university career," for which one is always yearn-

9. {Alfred Baeumler (1887–1968), philosopher working on behalf of National Socialism, appointed in 1933 to the newly instituted chair of philosophy and political pedagogy at the Friedrich-Wilhelms-Universität in Berlin.}

10. {Baeumler, *Männerbund und Wissenschaft* (Berlin: Junker und Dünnhaupt, 1934).}

ing (even in vilifying it), in order then to degrade "with power" all distinctions of rank down to a comfortable mediocrity. Then why are there strata! The "eternal feminine" in this male confederation! Just like the metropolitanism in this petty bourgeois "blood and soil."

173

The now usual "socialist" disparagement of everything higher and unique: what is of no service to the community of the people is worthless. But how so? On what path is this service ascertained and understood in general? Does it | not covertly mean: what every ninny cannot swallow immediately and effortlessly and, above all, *would like* to swallow, as appropriate to the ninny's mouth and stomach, does precisely not serve the people.

116

Here is prepared a covert leveling off, and thereby at the same time the "level" is dragged down and made shallow—where, all the same, "science" is already "democratic." To be sure, "philosophy" is also dragged into this "service to the people," a service to which, on the other hand, one allows and does not allow his Christianity.

Similarly: questioning and the raising up of question-worthiness count as mere grumbling—ever inconsequential (i.e., not productive of any immediate concrete truths)—thus as otiose, and sickly to boot! Let us find answers! Stultification as the "primary aim," and true action and power for danger as powerless hesitation and "mere" perpetual deliberation.

174

117

Besides this mania toward ossification in the "normal," i.e., in mediocrity and non-change—the "common"—then the *watchers*:

The *Catholic Church*—it alone "is" Christianity—as always, eager to have its *opponents*—in order to measure itself against them and to remain alert and strong.

It takes the opponents *seriously*, plants itself in them, learns from them up to the semblant disavowal of itself—keeps itself in this way flexible and clever, and constantly makes itself more secure and richer in experience.

This cautious knowing and questioning, this listening to the opponents that apparently is accepting of them, produces at the same time the attractive semblance of spiritual freedom for confrontation, the semblance of being current and modern, and entails the entire sophistry that basically is as rigid as ever in crouching over the already accomplished truth and fitting itself into the presently most beautiful recommendation within the sphere of what one in the precise sense values and desires.

118

175

And in addition still the smooth reformers of what is eternally yesterday's, reformers who perspire in the face of morality and who overflow with conventionality and who find reassurance when throne and altar are again secured against communism, which indeed had above all endangered riches and the cultivation of it in accord with rank. One now again plays the role of the refined and superior person versus the crude laborer, and one is even—so as not to be overly conspicuous—"socially minded." For the rest, one carries spiritual "nonchalance" and barbarity to the extreme under the mask of a custodian of "science." Here resides the greatest obliviousness to what is taking place.

176

The call for a science that would be "close to life" entails a blind turning of the university into an *elementary school* and thereby a destruction of all genuine knowledge, the strangling of every original and persistent desire for knowledge, and the thwarting of any attempt to open up spiritual beyng.

119

177

An age in which a boxer can be acclaimed a great man and be deemed worthy of the usual tokens of honor, in which purely physical virility (brutality) counts as the mark of a hero, and in which the frenzy of the massive is declared to be community and the latter is taken as the ground of everything—where is there still a place for "metaphysics" in such an age?

178

Will we once again venture the gods and along with them the truth of the people?

179

"Heideggerian philosophy"—to the extent that such exists at all—is always only *represented* by other ones, i.e., embedded as a standpoint and assembled into a nullity.

180

The difficulty of the current situation in philosophy does not consist in the fact that philosophy never arrives at the essential questions in a great volition and action; instead, it is the fact that the wretchedness of views is so great that it becomes difficult I to say what actually   120
constitutes this wretchedness.

181

People are waiting for the second volume of *Being and Time*; I am waiting for this waiting to cease and for people to finally confront the first volume.

182

The *confusion in the "spiritual" situation*—this situation does not allow its most proper plight to appear and is so weak (in its semblant strength) that it fears its plight instead of exulting in it.

Meanwhile, positive Christianity is demanded—or conceded—on the basis of the concordat and the universal perplexity and the need for a certain "morality"; besides this—besides those doctrines—there are the all too hasty ones who make a movement out of "belief"; then those who mix an unclear Germanity with a still more diluted Christianity; then those few who form for themselves a standpoint out of sheer Godlessness; and finally the majority, the sheer indifferent ones, who look on and wait for something to which they can "attach" themselves one day.

If all this is not a flight of the gods—if this is not Godlessness—the lack of all art is no wonder!

183   121

The *frivolity* in taking positions.

1. One regrets the absence of *"spirit"* in National Socialism and fears and laments the destruction of spirit. Indeed; but what is understood here by "spirit"? Some sort of unclear vocation to something hitherto—which had validity in its time. This unclear regret and the weak vocation take on a pretense of superiority and eminence—and yet are not able to create anything. One is frivolous with what is happening and with what "should" be "obligatory." And in such frivolity one always easily finds support and nourishment in order to participate continually in such activity.

2. *One simply defends what was hitherto* and assimilates it to what is happening; one pursues a cunning settlement which even looks like a structure and yet is not a venturing, not a putting into effect of an actual *transformation*. One adheres obstinately to something one *has not created oneself* but has only taken over; such a one is not at all in the condition of those who are striving to create that which is coming.

Frivolity goes together with *recklessness*.

122   Instead of a true relation to the extant plight, what dominates is only the morally indignant peevishness of those who are excluded and the narrow and unruffled, yet lively, contentment of the included.

And yet a change is carried out in all this contrariness and smallness of externality {?} and of the unavoidable massiveness. But this change must be taken only as something necessary—not as sufficient; apart from this, there abides a more and more blind calculation of results.

184

German Catholicism is now starting to take possession of the spiritual world of German Idealism—that of Kierkegaard and Nietzsche—and to appropriate the ideas there in its own way and with the clear and fixed means of its tradition. In its own way this Catholicism takes over an essential and vigorous tradition and thereby creates for itself in advance a new spiritual "position," whereas in National Socialism, from the sheer emphasis on what is other and new, one runs the risk of cutting oneself off from the great tradition and going astray in what is makeshift and half-baked.

Yet if, in consequence of the concordat, the battle against the Catholic Church is halted, then no one will perceive the ascendancy
123   of | Catholicism qua "secularizing" power, one that in a certain way is conscious of itself and that easily joins forces with the other powers.

It is senseless to battle against the Church—unless there arises an opposing power of the same type—but it is a basic requirement to resist Catholicism, as a center that is expanding into the *spiritual*-political domain by means of the entire fixed inner cadre of its staunchly ecclesiastical "organization." Indeed this battle requires first of all a corresponding starting position and a clear knowledge of the circumstances.

185

Knowledge and *"specialization"*; question: *how* is the latter to be carried out and borne:

1. as abstracted—derived—individuation which is justified subsequently through results? *Or*

2. as vindication of an essential labor which in itself knows of its essentiality and from there is raised into, thrust into, existence?

The first is escape and flight; the second, attack and steadfastness.

186   124

Knowledge—as genuine oppositionality to action; not the running off into the nearness to life and not the roving about in confirmation of everything mediocre and proximate and of their needs.

187

Infuriated grammar school teachers, unemployed technicians, displaced members of the middle class—as guardians of the "people"—as ones who are supposed to set the standards.

188

Essential for us in the future: the preparation of an originary certitude of choosing and deciding in relation to our past! Not only the fact that we cannot preserve each and every thing in the same way—purely according to the power of comprehension. What is up for decision is the overtaking and pre-taking of the past into what is given as task [*das Aufgegebene*]; the latter stamps what is given as endowment [*das Mitgegebene*] and awakens it thus for the first time in its anticipatory and determinative power.

189

If, in what is called the "university," there were still an originary certainty and faith of spirit, then in | such a time the university would   125
have to blaze up and be consumed in transformation. Instead of which, only the worry that the rigidity could be disturbed.

190

It is said that National Socialism came to be not through thought but through action. Granted; but does it follow that thinking is now to be degraded and suspected? Or does the reverse follow, namely, that therefore thinking must all the more be elevated to an extraordinary greatness and certitude?

191

However backward and "liberalistic" is the supposedly new "philosophy," the problematic "anthropological" "direction," fundamentally overcome in *Being and Time*, is simply taken over and filled with different content, folkish [*völkisch*]-racial content.

192

The ever-greater counterfeiting with regard to what a struggle is, especially a "spiritual" struggle.

126

193

What is *in accord with the people*? That which echoes back to the people (i.e., the many, everyday people) their own opinions and thereby is in service to the people?

There is something truly in accord with the people, and the essence of its accordance lies in the fact that it is *not* brought before the people, indeed can never and must never be brought before them.

The ambiguity in "accordance" ["*Gemäßheit*"] is fateful. The people are not the measure but instead are themselves placed under their measure; everything essential must be in accord with that measure, and thereby a people first *comes to be*.

If accordance with the people, i.e., with the measure to which the people are subject, is assumed to be *popularity*, and if this is meant in the sense of the solidarity of the people, and if that is in turn taken to be the camaraderie of the mediocre ones and of the common pursuit of degrading all that is great and unique, then everything is thrust into untruth and deviltry.

127

194

A current way of talking about written works, which is supposed to be an objection: "*merely produced at a desk.*" Fine; but the question remains: *who* is sitting at the desk, a thinker or a mere writer? If the latter forsakes the desk and enters into the so-called battlefield of "debate," he still does not change from a writer to a thinker—at most, he becomes a screamer. This facile counterfeiting with the desk, as an objection, may one day prove fatal.

195

Race—that which is *a* necessary though indeed indirectly expressed condition (thrownness) of historical Dasein is falsified into the unique and sufficient condition—not only this, it at the same time becomes what is spoken *about*. The "intellectualism" of this attitude; the inability to distinguish between racial education and theorizing about race. *A* condition is elevated to the unconditioned.

196

128

"*The* people"—what is then meant by this? Is the term supposed to represent those who are all too many, the necessarily mediocre ones, those who are easily contented—and at the same time will it pretend to mean the historical determination of the highest possibilities of the whole of a historical Dasein? What holds of the latter does not hold of the former, and vice versa.

"Popularity" of the highest and essential is not at all of service to the "people" and is injurious to the essential and highest.

What therefore is the point of such counterfeiting?

197

Teachers—whoever wants to teach *must be able to learn how*:

1.) to come to an ever deeper knowledge of the essential;

2.) to be silent in face of that which is properly to be taught;

3.) to preserve the gentle superiority of the exemplar and not let oneself slip into a false camaraderie.

198

129

How National Socialism can never be the principle of a philosophy but must always be placed under philosophy as the principle.

How, nevertheless, National Socialism can take up quite definite positions and thus can coeffectuate a new basic posture toward beyng!

But even this only under the presupposition that National Socialism knows itself in its limits—i.e., realizes that it is true only if it is able—only if it is in condition—to prepare and set free an original truth.

199

Three positions toward "science":

1.) "New" science—it is nothing other than the tailoring of the already extant science to fit folkish [*völkisch*] interests; thereby the last remainder of rigor and meditation is lost, and everything sinks into the folkishly coiffed banality of the most desolate American pragmatism.

130   2.) One adheres to the previous "science"—and redeems oneself by referring to its technical indispensability and its necessity for maintaining cultural prestige. Basically, the great *nonchalance* that goes back decades. Philosophy comes under suspicion.

3). Everything is placed in question: through questioning about science back into the essence of knowledge and of truth. It is a matter not of immediate usefulness, nor of the mere maintenance of something hitherto, but rather of the preparation for a transition.

The decision about science in Dasein is at once the question: what can "worldview" be—at all something ultimate?

131   *200*

"*Political science.*"—The cart placed before the horse.

If the sciences had truly been sciences—if they had been "political" in the genuine sense, and if they did not at all have need of this aim. Nowadays—that is done superficially—in a forced folkish-racial way.

And it is thereby supremely unpolitical—for what this pursuit has already *effectuated* extrapolitically—not only with regard to emigrés—cannot be calculated; and intrapolitically what is taking place is a *degeneration*, an *adjusting to irreverence*, and a breeding of mediocre persons.

201

We are now constantly engaged in *expending*.—According to the demand: "Everything for the people!"—what was previously attained and preserved is now brought under the people—very well.

But—nowhere is anything newly gathered up, saved up, *charged* up, worked *up*.

132   No one thinks at all that—precisely here—there must be institutions and possibilities of the new acquisition—and thus of seeking and researching; here only the work of three kinds is minted out—one day, *that* will be at an end and then only the purely *quantitative* will still enter into competition—whoever can most of all build institutes and can apply research endlessly—thus in everything.

What should happen—if everything is furnished downwards—for there *is* a "down below," despite—and in—all community of people.

Everything downward and nothing upward—only more suspicion and more contempt.

What will the standards come to?

202   133

Which paths are to be taken?—Does anyone believe that where the plight of Dasein necessitates, e.g., an actual artist—this artist could create out of other populist [*volkhaft*] conditions, as his own—precisely and only because he is an actual artist? Thus it is of no use at all to speak and behave folkishly [*völkisch*]—and at the same time to degrade "art" to the level of entertainment for the people and of the refinement of even the lower classes.

Instead: what is urgent is *actual knowledge* of great art and of its demands and artistic conditions—only in that way can a cognizant and sustaining art be brought into play and, above all, be experienced as *necessary*. But what if this is trivialized as self-evident and as political indoctrination and indeed as not at all required for formation—in that it is a burden as something unmastered?

203   134

The university is becoming a professional school.—Everything is moving in that direction, for:

1. the university itself lacks the inner metaphysical power of a unitary desire for knowledge, on the basis of which desire the university could *originarily* assert itself as law-giving;

2. the mania for mere applicability and enjoyment is so great that only those concerns count as "service to the people";

3. the result of the former emptiness and the latter sheer emptying must be that this institution will definitively become what it basically already is;

4. yet it would remain to be asked whether there is still the possibility of a normative gathering together of "researchers" as such, ones who do not merely "conduct research" but who *desire knowledge*;

5. but finally—what can still come to be here I if even the *recruits*   135 *and their instigators have at their disposal only the outward look of the officers or that there should no longer be officers at all?*

It might be asked: What is the point of all these considerations? Let it proceed; it will destroy itself. Certainly; but also the other *along with it*—through a mere running out to the end, something else has never come to be—especially not the overcoming of the first.

204

Self-dissection? No. Effective meditation.

To what extent one still stands in a bad self-staring and a discussion of "conditions"—accidental conditions—of Dasein and does not carry out the leap to beyng. But this leap only in virtue of a great impetus in an Open plight.

205

136

Everything is becoming "doctrine" and "standpoint," posits itself on something dry, and is itself drying out—knowledge is not becoming an attitude, and the attitude even less a daring and a pondering. What is this due to? To philistinism and to being ignorant of what is great.

The loud conceitedness and the inner paltriness of the setting of goals.

206

National Socialism is a *barbaric principle*. That is its essential character and its possible greatness. The danger is not National Socialism itself—but, rather, its trivialization into a sermon on the true, the good, and the beautiful (as in an indoctrination session). And the danger is also that those who want to form its philosophy are able to base the latter on nothing other than the traditional "logic" of common thinking and of the exact sciences, instead of realizing that precisely now "logic" is newly coming into urgency and necessity and must spring forth as new.

207

137

If I were now asked again: who is Baeumler? I would answer: a professor—resourcefully and cleverly—"philosophical": an upside-down Ludwig Klages. For the rest: a neo-Kantianism rehashed with National Socialism. In this case, such a characterization by means of catchwords is permitted, because an actual philosophizing is not there—only a playing with snatched-up "positions"—which is also unassailable, as is every "dualism," for by means of this principle everything is easily determined: if it is not the one thing, then it is the other. And that is very gratifying. Moreover, a career can be made out of it.

208

An era of transition; that would seem to be "nothing much." Yet such eras are the only historically decisive ones; in them, that which prevails must be mastered. *To stand right in the midst and yet to be beyond:* what is *only* "new" remains just as fruitless as that which is merely still "old."

209

138

The *people!* Here is what is decisive—to this everything is supposed to be in service.

The people—very well—but *for what* the people?

And *why* the people?

Is the people only a gigantic jellyfish, wallowing around in the world in order then after enough wallowing to be washed up on the shore of nothingness?

Or is it only *here* that the authentic begins?

For what the people?

And *where* is the people?

210

People without space!—to be sure—without an essential world and without essentially occurring truth—in which the people can surmount themselves—in order for the first time—to be themselves. (Cf. s.s. 34.[11])

But not something like "culture"; that is indeed only the fabrication of something earlier!

This established: the values of the people, which are actualized   139
folkishly.

We must outgrow "culture" on deeper grounds—into an essential space.

Culture—is a formation—that has nothing more to do with Dasein.

That would be possible only—where there is "I"—society—where there is "consciousness" and *subjects* and *personages.*

---

11. [Martin Heidegger, *Logik als die Frage nach dem Wesen der Sprache*, GA38. (Frankfurt: Klostermann, 1998), 30ff.]

211

What truly *remains* in history is the unique—*un*repeatable—at once necessary; what can be *"repeated"* in the extrinsic sense—does not *abide*—instead, it vacillates and has no unassailable necessity. It is altogether something else to repeat what is unique—i.e., carry out a proper necessity—and not just calculate.

140

212

Why National Socialism in its current configuration is still hardly a "worldview" and, as long as it insists on this "configuration," can never become one—

because it misunderstands the basic condition of all "viewing"—all intuiting and seeing—and is untroubled by such misunderstanding; indeed it thwarts all striving for such understanding—out of fear for its own bravery.

It misunderstands that everything near and actual is seen, viewed, only on the basis of what is remote.

And that the greatest remoteness of Da-sein is necessary and constitutes Da-sein's own proper grounding.

Can come back to what is near only on the basis of this remoteness.

What is *seen* is first visible on the basis of the remote, only so—in *such* seeing—does the *world* come to be.

141

213

If the frivolous writers and screamers who now "combatively" throw around the catchword "nihilism" could know just *how* nihilistic they themselves are, they would be appalled. Fortunately, however, they are too dense and too timid for such knowledge.

214

Today there are:

1. the mere screamers (consummate ignoramuses—);

2. those who are turned only backward (toward their past—because it is past—ossified ones);

3. the average ones—(who negotiate with both sides and manage very well and evade every decision—properly they are the *worst*, because they take on the semblance of what is "genuine");

4. the rare ones (who act and know originarily, but just for that reason are hated—if recognized—but for the most part are not at all recognized and not confronted);

5. the indifferent ones (these are the majority—who deal with each   142
thing according to circumstances—and sell themselves cheap).

215

In the meantime, nothing has changed in the way of thinking about
the questions to which I am chained. The only thing is that—the misinterpretations and their possibilities have become different, and the
procedures, the dangerous questioning—dangerous for "repose"—are
considered something to be kept at arm's length.

216

Service to the people.—They must always be few, those who know and
can know what, e.g., occurred in Kant's work and *therefore* what will
happen in the future; those who know must remain inconspicuous;
it is enough if they are granted the possibility of handing down their
heritage—I they must have no noise round about them—they bear,   143
as could never be otherwise, something like the bedrock for the existence of the people.

217

The idle talk about "wholeness" proceeds:
    1. in order to conceal the goal—i.e., the goallessness and the im-
potence in setting goals;
    2. in order to disavow the individuals and the unique ones in their
necessity;
    3. in order to deceptively cover over the fact that basically the actu-
alization of everything essential is determined by individuals.

218

The idle talk goes that the "Middle Ages" are precisely now first overcome and brought to an end. I think a Middle Age is beginning; the
one of a perplexed atheism—fruitless and without an Aristotle for it
to take up, indeed even the trace of a power to do so is missing.

219   144

"The Self-Assertion of the German University," or—the little entr'acte
of a great error.

For, already decades ago that which is striving for these goals has been prepared:

The natural sciences are becoming completely technologized.

The human sciences are becoming instruments of politics and ideology.

The *science* of jurisprudence is becoming otiose.

Medicine, as biological, is also becoming technological.

Theology is becoming senseless.

And the university? Not any more a wretched fig leaf for the nakedness of this unstoppable disintegration; a sad occasion for pompous ones who have come too late.

That—which no longer deserves this meditation.

{Index}

Socialism and Catholicism
      [Sozialismus *und Katholizismus*]
      and reactionism [*und Reaktion*],
      115ff.

PONDERINGS IV

Of Da-sein and being

*　*　*

Let the question and the venture

be—beings!

Both are to be possessed at the same time:
Suffering and repulsion
in unity
with the power of the upswing and of the radiance—
which we may first surmise as the grace
of creating—
all other "laboring" is only a
prelude.

1934–1935 (cf. p. *15f.*)

Few things simple great
substantive lengthy strong

* * *

Blaze a trail for beyng
in the concept.

* * *

Preserve the darkness
out of what is clear.

* * *

I ought not compel the answer
but must always only close in on the question—

1

To bring the world as a world to a worlding is to venture the gods once again.

Yet this venturing must conceal itself as a venture and long be silent "about" the gods—the bringing to a worlding, as an act of violence, is simply a deed to do.

In the second beginning, however, this deed must be the demolitional, interrogative, thoughtful swing into an apprehending discourse—the latter as a bursting in and a bursting forth placed into language—the Grounding jointure of the "there"—everything in a simple—hard—strange—reticent consummation.

The capacity to forgo much that could be said; a reticent discourse which silences a surrounding world still in its twilight.

The second beginning near the first like one *mountain peak* to another—

2

The *second* beginning—; merely numbered and extrinsically ordered; but this ordinal number here only as the veiling of the historical relation which must necessarily remain a mystery to us beginners, even if not as something merely present at hand—instead, as the origin of the act of violence.

3

The question is grounded.
The question is unfolded. } the process
The question is carried out.
The concept comes down to an attack.

4

We are still too advanced in being absent, being away;

we are still too young and inexperienced for what is old and for service to the gods.

5

To prepare the second beginning—we are not capable of more—since we only again grasp the first beginning—after it immediately had to go astray.

6

The second beginning possesses the first *concomitantly* in the sphere of its own thrownness, which means also in its historical concealment and distortion—and above all in the strangulation of its character as a beginning.

3

7

The "world" is out of joint; it is no longer a world, or, said more truly— it never was a world. We are standing only in its preparation.

8

Along with losing the gods, we have lost the world; the world must first be [*seyn*] erected in order to create space for the gods *in* this work; yet such an opening of the world cannot proceed from, or be carried out by, the currently extant humanity—instead, it can be accomplished only if what basically grounds and disposes the opening of the world is itself acquired—for *Da-sein* and for the restoration of humanity to Da-sein.

9

The new position—of the "there"—can be acquired only at a remote outpost—where no echo or address can be heard stemming from what was hitherto and is usual. (Cf. p. 38.)

10

The world—as empowerment of the "there"; this the tethered time, without a flight into empty eternity. Yet to acquire this tethering, in order to bring things to a stand, time in its partitioning must first become pressing.

11   4

World overpowers beyng, but only in order to be sacrificed to beyng, never itself coming to presence.

The world worlds, whereby beyng prevails so that beyngs [das Seyende] *might be.* (Event.)

The worlding of the world happens in the world-producing, opening, ordaining authority of administration—care.

The basic way according to which and in which the "there" *is*.

12

The full strangeness of these relations in their simplicity is to be set forth extensively and essentially. In order to

create the beginning of the second beginning; the single rigor, the authority of simplicity; the isolation, of what was earlier, out of the provenance of the beginning; the building and discoursing that conquer.

13

The world is more worlding than beings are being [*seiend*].

14

Space! Where is the "there," such that it is itself the ground of the "where"? (Cf. p. 38.)

15

Who was the caster of this projection?

16   5

World—not a mantle, not an external enclosure; but also not the soul and something interior—quite to the contrary, the vibrant middle of the "there," a grounded middle that *stands* in the clutches and joints of time.

17

Must not run away from the beginning—instead, resolve oneself to it; this compels toward the second beginning. The transformation is due to something abandoned in Concealment.

18

Philosophy: the discursive building in beyng through the building up of the world as concept.

The concept [*Begriff*], however, the anticipatory [*vorgreifend*] attack [*Angriff*] and the adversary of action.

19

How everything on the earth now rolls on so superficially—obliviously, as if veiled in back and reaching forward over all.

20

The *world* as the abyssal ground and the grounding of what is ungrounded. Dasein *inhuman*—as the thrown breaking in, which quarrels with—beings (partitioning).

6

21

The world must first world as the partitioning of the "there"—only in that way is prepared the hour of the suddenness of the unascertainable *overfissure*—the tearing away into the proximity of the gods.

22

The *second* beginning in its struggle with the first. The task: *on the one hand,* an original transformation of φύσις ["nature"], of λόγος, and of perception—i.e., a grounding of ἀλήθεια.

And *on the other hand,* a dismantling of ἰδέα—οὐσία—the a priori and transcendence (seen on the basis of a grounding in thought).

23

The destructive transformation ("dismantling") must precede all other confrontations with Christianity and modernity and with the first "end," and also with the great entr'acte (Kierkegaard-Nietzsche)—because everything is rooted there.

24

The concept of the world—a questioning that pushes itself to its limits, where it experiences itself exposed to what is most question-worthy:

where the "there" opens up abyssally, where the need of preservational disputation necessitates the "there" (constancy), and history, i.e., a people, becomes itself; history is the venturing I of the gods out   7
of a world and for a world; this happening is intrinsically individuation.

25

To *question the concept of world disclosively* = to coground *thoughtfully* the "there" out of the affiliation to such history; not to "research" or explain things, not even "phenomena," not to prove propositions and promulgate a "doctrine," not to offer standpoints—but also not "existentiell" play with all possibilities of comportment and attitudes and world pictures.

26

History—the venturing of the gods is something great only as ruin or victory—; not "duration" essentially—instead, the abyssal character of the gaining through strife—sacrifice and consecration.

27

A question: whether a constancy of the event is still possible; i.e., how it is ventured or forgotten—how the gods in the act of violence of the creating person are compelled to their individuation—and a people is—as history.

The gods indeed only those of a people: no general god for everyone, i.e., for no one.

A question: how to prepare the constancy (gaining the "there" through strife and preserving it); how a grounding of Da-sein?

Whether and how an originary affiliation of the creative ones to   8
the opened core of a people is founded—only in the work—not through planning and extrinsic pressing together in common vicissitudes.

28

World—the opening up of the counterplay between remoteness and nearness, beenness and future: the gods.

The event is the "essence" of beyng: happening of the partitioning.

29

World: space and time appearing in each other. But here space and time as nonapparent—not as that which we think abstractly as a *measure*; rather, as something we take to the measurement and dimensionality of a calculation and computation of "beings" (things present)—not as "empty forms."

30

The *uncanny* thing is closed off to us: the confusion, as original, grants to us today only its shallowest aspect: the *arrogance of the mediocre ones* in the *forgetting* of their own provenance.

But this appearance of the great confusion is not therefore more impotent—instead, only more confusing—so confusing that it even falsifies and weakens the true confusion—the strength of appearances as expulsion of such weakness.

31

The *uncanny* as *doom* [Verhängnis] in a double sense.

32

World is to be grasped only through art as given to the originary event; not first on the basis of knowledge (thinking) or action (deed)—

Yet thereby art is in its essence taken as poetry—the latter itself equiprimordial with thinking—and both originary in *speech*.

Speech and event.

Speech and "nature."

33

Today the uncanny in the measurelessness of the groundless, of the massive, of the rapid, and of the transitory knowledge and attainment of everything.

Here the only help is the *greatest venture* of a poetry that begins anew.

And because we are tottering in this cognition, in this ignorant knowledge, therefore poetry (in the original sense) must be prepared by way of *thinking*.

What is the *process* of this thinking? *A leap into the event.*

Individuals will for long be only an occasion for it.

Therefore, even *art* as an *occasioning of the world.*

34

Philosophy—will not deliver us, will not discover things (through research), will not (after the fact) raise any worldview to concepts—instead, philosophy will again know the πόλεμος—*the event*—and will fathom the ground and the abyss and the deformed ground and thus will become a plight and the necessity—to seize what has been given as task and to conquer what has been given as endowment—to bring history to a happening = to venture the gods once again.

In this way, indeed nothing present at hand or unfamiliar is discovered, but—as more essential and more original—the partitioning is wrested from the closedness of beyng—and truth is changed in essence.

All concepts are recreated inceptually.

35

Words alone no longer suffice—and nevertheless *discourse* remains foundational.

36

All those who are essential are there to be stepped beyond, even if not in straightforward progress. It is well if this "stepping," instead of going beyond them, does not merely pass them by or go around them.

37

With the recognition of Da-sein, the questioning is already far advanced regarding all ending of the subject; for the fact that the subject is grasped in terms of community rather than as an individual is not decisive metaphysically as long as "*subjectivity*" does not altogether drop out. But if the Da-sein of the human being is apprehended, then the questioning arrives without fail at the insight that this—viz., Da-sein—must properly be *mine* to someone or other without thereby becoming in the least "subjective" or egoic in the *subjective* sense.

37a

The age is not without gods *because* we are too "worldly" and so have become godless; on the contrary, it is because we have *no world* and only a confused understanding of beyng. A worldview is merely an expedient and must break to pieces if it does not turn into a world-grounding.

11

37b

Question of being: not to make a transcription of "beings" and do so from the usual problematic perspective—instead, to found beyng in the leap.

12

38

The world is now out of joint; the earth is a field of destruction. What beyng "means" no one knows.

Can we at all know it?

And if yes, *should* we know it?

And if yes to that, how must it *become* knowable?

39

A history of philosophy is to be presented as the history of the great isolation.

40

The decisive basic movement in the affairs of thought: the highest exertion toward the impossibility of leaping over one's own shadow—to build originarily on a newly laid foundation.

41

The fact that we often enough think contrary to our own intention and do not always maintain the correct levels or measure out the necessary carrying distances.

Much exercise is required before you become sure of the courage for your own necessity.

13

42

"*Worldview*"—a late word—originating from the place where one looks back and classifies—calculates in "types." Nothing futural—instead, only a standing still and a tying down—the death of all great and fruitful doubt.

The great doom is nearing, if searching is suffocated and the need for searching is blocked. The concealed errancy in the semblance of the homeland! (Cf. s.s. 36, p. 15f.[1]) (Cf. p. 24.)

---

1. {Martin Heidegger, *Schelling: Vom Wesen der menschlichen Freiheit*, *Gesamtausgabe* (GA)42 (Frankfurt: Klostermann, 1988), 53ff.}

43

The *basically perverse attitude toward "German Idealism,"* as if, from this that is "old" and traditional, something "useful" could be disengaged—positivism—; whereas it is not established whether what is old has already come to us in its essence—as long as we do not retrieve it. Yet this retrieval *demands* that we do not lodge what is "old" in a simple time series but, instead, realize that here every approach is immediately directed to beyng as such. Only on account of an equally strong immediacy and the equal height of solitary peaks can something similar be attained; everything else remains pedantic self-mistakenness at the very heart of the history of the world.

44

14

Where barriers are set to the freedom of abundance, the downfall is at hand.

45

Will we again find our way into the sure simplicity of the essential word? What must happen for us to be capable of that?

46

Philosophical errors do not ever possess any power—to do so, philosophy would indeed first have to be and would have to hear something of the genuine clash of arms.

47

The most intrinsic doom of the *work*: it must stop with that which it itself posits precisely as the possibility of the new beginning.

48

There are things in the world which do not gain anything by being prepared and done "for the people"; instead, these things thereby merely fall prey to inner dissolution and so rob the people of a genuine and secret possession. These things that rob—how long are they still supposed to be up to their old tricks?

15   *Philosophy (cf. p. 39.)*

49

Why and in which limits is philosophy necessary? Where does it have the ground and mode of its genuineness?

50

"Philosophy" is sinking in complete exhaustion. Nonphilosophy is raising an unrestrained outcry, makes noise, and beats about with the borrowed "instruments" of the very philosophy it reviles.

(Mere throwing away!)

51

What does all this say?—The essence of truth and the essence of beyng are distorted and thus are caught up in semblance and in the indiscernability of semblance. Lost is every simple certainty of attitude and of the ordinance of standards.

What is needful?

1. the striking up of the essential basic attunement;

2. the obtaining of essential basic experiences;

3. the grounding of those who ground beyng in the beyng of the ground (event);

4. the determinate opening up of the essence of truth;

5. all this as the grounding of Da-sein in the concept. (Cf. p. 19.)

16   <center>52</center>

The perversions of knowledge (cf. p. 23, 52):

"Knowledge" is perverted to a mere tool, one that is manipulated and so must be on hand.

Consequently, one then demands the corresponding suitability of this tool and wants to have the tool "close to life."

"Life" is understood as the Intelligible bustle of immediate everydayness and of its tangible use and its daily needs.

Such perversion of knowledge proceeds from another one lying still further back—according to that one, knowledge is a self-reliant comportment to the value of truth in itself. The perversion as a tool is merely the consequence of this one and presupposes it.

Both misunderstand—the fact that knowledge is the *happening* of the spirit itself—belongs to Da-*sein*—neither merely a comportment relying on itself—nor a tool. The determination of knowledge must be grounded in Da-sein, i.e., in the ground of the essence of beyng and truth. Yet that requires a transformation of the basic position amid beings in general or, because such is not there, its reacquisition.

Insofar as, by extolling the "new science," a person now bustles   17
about on account of the perversion of knowledge as a tool, he is moving blindly in a peculiar endeavor to philosophize without philosophy. And the public, who know nothing of philosophy and also need to know nothing of it, therefore receive the impression that at present the "true philosophy" would concern that which is loudly endorsed by the newspapers and the elementary school teachers (ones who have become wary of themselves, i.e., have never been self-possessed.)

If this groundless bustling, with some skill and shouting, is kneaded into the truly political happening, it then seems as if this childish din in the field of knowledge does in fact belong together with that happening. And in this pretension, which must be without measure, why should not every student, provided only that he shouts loudly enough, appear to be a hero, especially since students write about heroism every week?

53   18

What is politically right and great, namely, to bring the people back to themselves, becomes, in terms of worldview, something arbitrary and small, an idolizing of the people, who are now extolled as present at hand and in whom everything is formed as present at hand and "organic" and out of whom everything comes forth just as easily and of itself, if one merely has "instinct." This "folkish" [völkisch] animalization and mechanization of the people cannot see that a people "is" only on the ground of Da-sein, in whose truth for the first time nature and history—in general, a world—come into the open and liberate the earth to its closedness.

And only this Da-sein is the possible abode of the plight—in which the flight of the gods can be experienced and the waiting for the ones who will come can be carried out.

54

The great swamp of "organic" thought and speech devours everything, and the dissolvability of everything in this dark pulp is taken as the *unity* of the worldview and is so taken with much approval, since indeed what is easy and current as the correct, and the latter as the "true," always comes down to mediocrity.

19   *55*

The task of the grounding of Da-sein by way of thinking and poetry overcomes the *question of possibility*. That question—How is such and such possible?—is the last implementation of mathematical thinking, which is the result of the dominance of the proposition as such, which in turn is the result of the collapse of ἀλήθεια. (Cf. above, p. 15.)

56

If possibility is taken as the goal of an essential determination and as its answer (essence as the possibility that makes possible, that which *can be thought* without contradiction), then what is here postulated as the *ground* of beyng is the consistency of complete identity; but beyng itself on the basis of *thinking*.

Indeed the questioning of possibility always appears as a return to the origin—and yet it is a deviation into the domain of measures, in which guise pure thinking offers itself in advance. Beyng is not at all the determination and attunement of the need and necessity *of that which* is placed into the question of possibility; beyng is overleaped. Actuality is merely **complementum** *possibilitatis* [*"complement* of possibility"].

The limits and rights of possibility and of the question of possibility are to be established anew on the basis of a grounding of the partitioning in the (event).

The overcoming of the question of possibility radically convulses all ontology.

20   *57*

Now, however, the grounding of Dasein is never rid of the semblance of being an immediate producing of Dasein—and even by way of sheer thought. Here the question concerns:

1. the inevitability of this semblance;

2. the inconspicuous proper procedure of attunement and determination;

3. the originary sharpness of the conceptualization on the basis of the partitioning.

Does this procedure always remain a mere means to allow something else to step into the open and thereby be determined—or is this procedure itself a stage in the happening of the "there"—; *language* and the character of the procedure as work.

58

We are *questioning* in that we are *questioning* the truth as what is true of something true.

We are questioning thus in that *we* are questioning the truth of the people. And the truth of the people brings the people to themselves, in that it liberates them to their plight—brings them into Da-sein.

It is a great thing to give the people back their honor, but honor [*Ehre*] exists only where there is reverence [*Ehrfurcht*], and the latter exists only where there is admiration—

And admiration [*Bewunderung*] exists only where there is the basic   21
attunement toward wonder [*Wunder*]: beyng in the origin.

"Philosophy" in the common view

59

Philosophy is a back-and-forth talking in general concepts about all things. This talking must be carried out on the same plane as discussions about the weather and the latest models of cars.

Since indeed within this everyday idle talk such philosophy *leads to nothing*, one arrives at the practical notion of abolishing it. Excellent.

Except that thereby philosophy is not abolished, for philosophy is not at all at issue here; but a space is created *for* philosophy. It might seem so. Yet at bottom this conclusion "about" philosophy—is already a misunderstanding; for philosophy is there, when it must be there, when it is objectionable and alien even to those who still "live" on its scraps.

60

One now seeks to resist philosophy by dispensing with it. Also a way—into barbarity.

Today the spirit threatens to become what it is taken to be by the   22
common—superstitious—understanding: a "ghost," i.e., a phantom. With the help of this falsification, one then battles against "intellectualism."

Yet admittedly—an appeal to (philosophical) idealism is just as null, since indeed the presuppositions of idealism no longer exist, and it is in itself only an end.

Dasein!

61

Can the Germans abolish philosophy and do so at the very moment they are supposed to become German again? That is to say, can they be there [*da-sein*] without philosophy?

And what about this "abolishing," since philosophy not only is always to be actualized anew—but above all and at the same time is ever again to be conquered anew in its essence?

*   *   *

62

What is "positive" for us is the plight of truth.

23

63

Can we once again—or for the first time—through the productive attunement of beyng (through the event) bring the truth of beings to the origin?

64

The plight of a lack of a sense of plight is basically the concealed ground of the absence of the necessity.

65

How is the plight of beyng to be manifest in and out of the lack of a sense of plight?

How is the forgottenness of beyng to be eliminated—through which recollection?

1. the recollection to Da-sein;
2. the recollection to intimacy.

But all this only as a work and mediately—never as immediate exhortation or the like.

66

The plight that there is *no longer any error*—because errancy circumvented—; one is tired of still *wanting* to know. One provides oneself only with cognitions and schooling.

67   24

"Worldview" (cf. above, p. 13).—Has anyone ever asked to what extent worldview *is* something *first* and last and under what presuppositions it can be so? Quite inconsequential *which* worldview is here "drummed" in.

68

The difficulty: we do not know *where* we are, and we do not have the "there" needed to determine the "where."

Dasein is aberrant; in it we ourselves have gone astray, and as straying ones we in the end obstinately take what is nearest to be the best.

The people as salvation, whereas the people is what requires salvation.

The question and the venture

69

Every question not only desires an answer but above all demands a *venture*. And the ability to weigh and dominate *the* venture is already more than an answer; for the latter is just as impossible as a question for itself.

70   25

The partitioning middle in all things—their gathering together in *concealment* (essence of truth).

The step to Da-sein:

71

The effective *consummation* of the *silence* and of the ever-fainter sound *as* opening up and repositioning of beings with respect to essentially occurring beyng.

But that requires the essential *refusal* to speak of silence and to say anything—unless *reticently*—of the essence of language qua *keeping silent*.

72

The *new* "logic" is *the logic of silence*. But it is completely different in essence and goal from a "logic of semblance."

73

The highest that must be said must become an extreme silence.
    Silence properly as *productive silence*.
26   But is the logic of productive silence then not the betrayal of everything and of nothing?
    Certainly—if it is "read" and followed like the previous logic.

74

Or are we here indeed at a dead end—such that nothing more can re-
volve in a circle?

75

Today philosophy is unimportant!—Completely correct: for the things
of "importance" today.

76

The *interpretation of a work* grasps it in its center and lets the truth of
the work irradiate; this radiating then easily proceeds in many directions into the indeterminate—allowing the latter to resound.
    The art of interpretation now consists in the fact that *as* irradiation
it at the same time creates for itself and maintains a closed circle of
radiance. This circle is then only the radiant core of the work itself.

27

77

At issue is not humanity, but *Da-sein*; and the latter: because of beyng.
    And the latter in the uncanny situation where it does not have to be
wrested from something deep and dark—but, on the contrary, where
through a knowledge of beyng the way to the grounds is to be taken.
Is something like that possible then? It is necessary.
    And this way in the process of silence.

78

To know in a superhuman fashion all great works of thought on the
basis of the new ground, to be acquainted with all fields of beings, to
carry out the most abyssal experience of Da-sein, and yet—all this
only as condition and passageway and something incidental.

79

A terrible aping of Hölderlin's "Hymns" is entering into the semblant poetry of today—without having in itself even the trace of a reason for it or a right.

80   28

The thoughtful steadfastness in the essential word of beyng. (The "system"!)

81

The system of *questions* which are moved by need—what is most question-worthy is beyng; it is most worthy because it possesses the highest rank of all beings and in all beings.

Beyng is the aether in which mankind breathes.

Beyng as (event).

82

God is gone; things are used up; knowledge is in ruins; action has become blind.

In short: *beyng is forgotten*—and a semblance of beings is raging or is fleeing into what was hitherto.

83

The forgottenness of beyng is to be overcome though an internalized recollection, which must *be* an externalization into the broadest and deepest "there": as Da-*sein*.

84

But this overcoming not solely through the *question* of beyng—rather, from the fact that this questioning concerns the essential truth of beyng—concerns that origin which is, and alone *can* be, the *pre-playing* of beyng in our all-knowing | godlessness: art—which means: 29 knowledge of the necessity of art.

85

Fully at the end, philosophy remains only if its end becomes and remains what its beginning is: the question of the truth of beyng.

86

Beyng is the aether in which mankind breathes; without this aether humans would descend to the level of mere beasts and even lower, and all human activity would be reduced to breeding like cattle.

87

We are acquainted with too much and know too little.

88

A "nearness to life" is not what is required; instead, *Da-sein* must again be able to see into its *remote domains*—and so learn to honor its *grounds*.

89

The completely different conditions under which essential knowledge must now operate.

30   *On the situation (cf. p. 33f.)*

90

1. The complete lack of "principles" in philosophy and especially in the sciences.

2. Indeed even the lack of needs in that respect.

3. "Folkish" ["*völkisch*"] "thinking" takes what is a condition and a formative power and makes it into an object and an actual goal.

4. These conditions are reconquered *as such* only if they are placed before great tasks, awakened by these tasks, and tested by them.

5. In that way, the conditions first return to effective incomprehensibility.

6. Where, on the contrary, all this is made an object of the "new" sciences and "worldviews," then it is not only altogether lost but also impedes every genuine formation of principles and every actual questioning.

7. Dasein is in this way cast off into a "reflexive standpoint," one which still surpasses all the "intellectualism" of the nineteenth century.

8. *World*view without world.

*World*view without the basic condition of all "viewing" and without the projection that leaps ahead, in which what is seen first becomes visible.

9. Where a people posits itself as its own goal, egoism has expanded   31
into the gigantic but has gained nothing with regard to domains and
truth—the blindness toward beyng survives in a desolate and crude
"biologism" which promotes a swaggering in words.

10. All this is radically un-German.

*   *   *

Of what use are thinkers in such a boisterous time?

Questioning

91

Certain ones are ill-humored, if not even indignant, over the attitude
and demand of constant questioning. Those who behave in such a way
do not realize that the much-invoked answer is always only the last
step of questioning in a series of many previous interrogative steps.

*   *   *

92

The *concept* is to be propounded for that which is unconceptualized;
and thereby the *essence* of the concept is to be transformed on the
basis of the essence of truth. Originary knowledge in the "concept"
is to be grounded *against* mere *incomprehension* as well as against *in-comprehensibility*.

In every great philosophy, its concealed *way*—and its thrust—to   32
the essential *disclosure* must be followed. But we must never become
fixated on its stated propositions; not as if everything should merely
be dissolved into the way, not as if there would be no Essential truth
in philosophy, but rather because this truth is not a propositional
truth—or, better: because the propositions, the essential ones, have a
different character as propositions than that of a merely correct assertion.

(Cf. Kant's way to the transcendental imagination.)

93

One who would take a *great leap* needs a great *running start*. For that,
he must draw far *back*, indeed all the way back to the first beginning—
if at issue in the leap is the second beginning.

Will we take this leap? It is enough if we clear an essential stretch for the running start and press toward the leap.

The leaper of the leap will come.

Always in transition and forsakenness!

33   94

The *truth* of philosophy—even as possibility—has completely vanished from today's Dasein.

What does that mean? That no *knowledge* about fate any longer holds us truly in a firm grip. That we merely stagger back and forth between an equalization and a crude preaching—; what is unclean and devastated in all modes of thought—which still are only deformed modes, without an articulating law.

                              95

One now "acts" as if there were nothing more to do for "truth."

                              96

(Cf. p. 30, 35.)

1. Everything is groundless and goalless; can a ground and a goal be at all rightly expected and found?

2. We cannot turn back and certainly cannot help ourselves out with snatched-up tatters and patches.

3. Are we moving forward—or are we merely being pushed down a slope, because we do not even have enough weight to fall on our own?

4. Must we at all extricate ourselves from the previous back and forth movement? Whereto?

5. Of what help is the unity of the people—supposing such unity came to be out of the void and in this wasteland?

34   6. Is not all questioning becoming still more pressing and greater and more multifarious for *the people*—is not the wasteland expanding and the void becoming voider?

7. Can a change actually take place without a long preparation?

8. Must not this preparation be carried out radically, from the first and broadest domains of decision?

9. Are not these domains to be opened up in advance *as* the first and broadest ones and incorporated into the structure?

10. For that, must not *thought*—interrogative-poetic knowledge—be affirmed as the highest?

11. Being = time as the presentiment of a preliminary stage of the preparation. (Cf. *Being and Time* II.)

12. Contributions to philosophy.[2] (cf. plan of 7-27-36.)

13. A confrontation with *Being and Time*.[3]

14. The beginning of metaphysics. (Cf. p. 39f.)

Must *not proceed* on the path of doom, but also must *not withdraw* into something earlier—instead, away from the whole path into a second beginning—in the closedness of that path, its simplicity, and its "end."

Da-sein

Earth — World

(Event)

97

Procedure: the simplicity of the thoughtfully designating yet | recol-   35
lected (back to the first beginning) projection.

The projecting as the—ordained—unrest of the thrownness into the plight of a lack of a sense of plight: forgottenness of being and destruction of truth—; the neglect of thinking.

What is at issue

(Cf. running commentary on I, 5
The turn and the overturning.)[4]

98

At issue is a leap into specifically historical Da-*sein*. This leap can be carried out only as *the liberation of what is given as endowment into what is given as task*. And what has to be at issue in all exertions is the learning to be free *toward* and *in* such liberation.

This liberation is the effectuation of the releasement of what is given as endowment and is the holding fast to what is given as task.

But what do we have that is given as endowment? The plightless plight as the plight of a lack of a sense of plight (everything is accessible,

---

2. {Heidegger, *Beiträge zur Philosophie (Vom Ereignis)*, GA65. (Frankfurt: Klostermann), 1989.}

3. {Heidegger, "Auseinandersetzung mit *Sein und Zeit*," to appear in *Zu eigenen Veröffentlichungen*, GA82.}

4. {Heidegger, "Laufende Anmerkungen zu *Sein und Zeit*," to appear in *Zu eigenen Veröffentlichungen*, GA82.}

though used up—everything is spiritless, though arbitrarily displace-
able—no essential thrust and no passion of questioning—everything
is open to lived experience and is likewise devoid of mystery). Where
there is a thrust, only blind seething as something talked into. And
in all this, no plight of the "there" and no knowledge of what is most
difficult. Everything is "fabricated."

36   99

And what do we have that is given as task? That the thrust of what is concealed might thrust originarily and simply and that the projective
jointure might be grasped as a long-prepared work.

That the originary unity of the thrust and of the projection might
become, as equally essential to both, an event. That we do not fall
victim to the allure of seething life and just as little to the allure of a
nongenuine (simulated) rigor of thinking.

That we learn an attuned thinking and its most proper sharpness
and not occupy ourselves with artificial oppositions, spirit as adversary of the soul[5] / or / heroic science (empty glorification of a *previous*
formal thinking).—What is at issue:

The free mastery of the plight of a lack of a sense of plight—not
simply elimination, but rather liberation—out of (the event) and the
changed essence of truth.

* * *

100

This blindness toward the earth and this impotence for the world—
ultimately, this inability to enter into the contention of their strife—
does all that come from exhaustion—or only from a very broad alienation and errancy?

37   How will we know what it is? We will do so I and will experience
what is coming only if we seek a change and indeed in a radical way—
as a second—recollective—beginning; nothing less than that is necessary—even just to know what *is* and what is not—how and whether
being still eventuates to us.

101

Why is it a violation of the essence of philosophy itself to seek to demonstrate mistakes in a philosophy and represent it as partially correct

---

5. {Ludwig Klages, *Der Geist als Widersacher der Seele* (Leipzig: Barth, 1929).}

and partially false? It is because a philosophy can never be *refuted*! Why not? Because it contains nothing refutable; for, what in it is actually philosophy is the opening up of being—world-projection; such can never be refuted, but only replaced and altered—; i.e., every philosophy *remains* and has a corresponding recurrence which can never be immediately established and calculated.

The truth of a philosophy is measured according to the originality of its opening up of the *essence* of truth.

102

The "last human being"[6] is raging through Europe.

103

In the midst of the forgottenness of *beyng* and the destruction of *truth*, it must not be expected that the leap into Da-sein would happen—and be intelligible—immediately. On the contrary: the *supreme alienation*. Therefore, the task is to raise this alienation even more—but in such a way that in it at the same time bridges are slung for a taking hold of steadfastness (cf. above, p. 3.).

104

The *long preliminaries* for the second beginning. It is essential to maintain this *preliminary* character—and not become weak in the sense of a false strength for a supposedly actual and *immediate* second beginning. Yet how in all this at the same time a lack of knowledge is operative.

Questioning—Why is there at all something rather than nothing?—*as the running start* into what is alienating in the alien character of the "there."

Not to give a reassuring-theological "proof" that explains God—not to eliminate the alienation as something extraneous—instead, to make even everything *familiar* seem alien.

Where is God? The prior and more proper question: do we have a "where"? And do we stand within it, such that we can ask about God?

The alien character of the "there" as perseverance of the "where." (Cf. p. 4, 8.)

---

6. {Cf. Friedrich Nietzsche, *Also sprach Zarathustra: Ein Buch für Alle und Keinen, Werke*, vol.6 (Leipzig: Naumann, 1904), 19: "Thus I want to speak to them of what is most contemptible: but that is the *last human being*."}

105

The forgottenness of being and the destruction of truth together effectuate the innocuousness—i.e., the *blocking of what is uncanny*—and
bring about a sequestration from the "there."

39   ### 106

On the other hand, *the statement: Da-sein essentially occurs as the contention of the event.*

107

From the description of existentiell *Da*sein to the grounding leap into
Da-*sein*: "metaphysics" of the (event); historical! But that means: futural.
   "Philosophy" is always only somewhere or other, and at some moment or other, and for someone or other (the few, the unique), like
lightning or earthquake. (Cf. p. 40, 82.)

108

Recollection.
   The recollection *of* the first beginning.
   The recollection into the steadfastness of Da*sein* (*into* the second
beginning).
   The second beginning, as the grounding leap into Da-*sein*, is *"metaphysics"*—in an essentially new—inceptual—sense. Beyond φύσις—
that means: we can no longer begin with φύσις—ἀλήθεια—but are
hurled beyond this beginning—cannot go back and must first seek
and ground the *open place* as such—(φύσις, cf. s.s. 35,[7] not to be misinterpreted as presence at hand—as was the danger in *Being and Time*,
p. 8ff.)
   No longer begin with φύσις *and yet with* ἀλήθεια!*

*But to do this "truly" as Da-sein; yet not as epistemology nor as "fun-
damental ontology."
40   "Metaphysics" can commence only with the second beginning—it
must do so and must as such precisely always recollectively internal-
ize the first beginning (φύσις).
   But the "title" itself says nothing. (Cf. above, p. 34, 46.)

---

7. {Heidegger, *Einführung in die Metaphysik*, GA40 (Frankfurt: Klostermann,
1983), 108ff., 131ff.}

109

Philosophy is the excitation—i.e., the Fathoming grounding in each case of an *impetus*—namely, one impelling away into the essence of beyng and compelling the essence of truth—and in all this an impetus which must be shocking to ordinary thought and activity—and which they experience as insufficient and as ever falling too short, despite all the importunity—and experience not in the brightness of knowledge but in the darkness of a disturbed and reluctant *observation*; presentiment would be said too much and grasped too high.

110

Thoughtful poetizing is the proper precedent questioning—the disclosive questioning of Da-sein—the denominating of beyng. Thoughtful communication built only in and into ordained teaching as *thoughtful linguistic work*. Here, in an essentially other—originary—sense, the "essence" of language is in play; not merely as a means of suitable and comprehensible "expression"—but primarily as the dispositional setting up of Essential knowledge and | ignorance.   41

Such work must "stand" so that times and ages can elapse over it.

That can never be immediately known and "extracted" but is only a mediate origin—to be sure, not of an existentiell attitude—but of an essential knowledge—i.e., of a disclosive questioning and disposing of being and of truth (event).

111

Need to create the (event) of *those* gods with whom we can be friends and to whom we need not be slaves.

112

Philosophy: love of wisdom.

Love: *desire* that beings *be*, being—

Wisdom: mastery over the essentially occurring *unity of creating* (recognizing—teaching—loving) *and of kindness*.

113

Philosophers: those in whom this will is desirous (in the Hindu manner)—, not as *their* will, but as Da-sein.

114

We *become* who we are in that we *are* as the ones we are becoming; by being the ones who are becoming, we acquiesce to the law of becoming, do not force anything, but also do not squander anything.

42

115

The thinking of the thinker is the productive thinking (of a second beginning) which thinks *back* (to the first). Therefore, productive thinking is already not an empty thinking-up out of the blue; instead, a creative denominating.

116

The *transition* from the proceeding of research to the preceding as metaphysics; the *transition* from ground laying (operating back behind) to the beginning.

The transition as changeover: the preparation, the attempts, the preconstruction—all that is indicated in the lecture courses from 1927 to 1936, even though never—intentionally never—communicated directly.

The mask of "historical" interpretations.

Essential here, *inter alia*: the transformation of the concept of existence from the *existentiell* one to the meta-physical. Ex-istence: exposedness out into beings. Further: thrusting forward of the question of truth; again as the openness of the closedness of the "in the midst" as the "in-between."

117

Not measuring up *to* Dasein as "structure," but measuring out *of* Da-*sein* as origin.

This measuring out as such creates the meta-physical moment, as second beginning of an essential history. This measuring out as a tearing away [*Entreißung*] of the forgottenness of being, a tearing away that leaps in and thus is an outline [*Aufriß*] of the essence of truth.

43

118

Philosophizing has become difficult, perhaps more difficult than at the beginning, its first great beginning—because at issue is the second beginning. In such moments, of which many persons have only an immediate feeling, they think of abolishing philosophy; that is called "heroic worldview."[8]

119

What matters is not primarily what serves (i.e., is useful *to*) the people, but what the people must serve, if the people is to *be* a people historically.

120

No *science* ever has even the possibility of demanding the exertion and rigor of *knowledge*, let alone of effectuating what arises in *philosophy*—supposing there is philosophy.

Yet philosophy cannot therefore be called "superscience," for even then it remains measured according to science.

Essential knowledge must be determined and attuned out of the essence of truth. Rigor, however, serves only the exertion toward the leap into the origin—the strife of the "in-between."

121   44

In the age of the "loudspeaker," all that can still essentially be effective is the silence of the inconspicuous in the guise of that which "does not come into question."

Those for whom all sorts of things do not come "into question" never do *question* at all.

122

Da-sein as the most *question-worthy*.

φύσις and the *genesis of the gods*, this genesis [*Entstehung*] not meant as production—rather, to come into position [*Stand*] as to emerge and to rise up [*Aufstehen*]; not causal derivation; nor out of misconstrued "affects" and their impact.

---

8. {Cf. Johannes Mewaldt, "Heroische Weltanschauung der Hellenen," *Wiener Studien* 54 (1936), 1–15.}

123

Must everything that is called "refinement," "spirit," "culture," now be given over to a rescue of the core power of the people? But who is "the people"? Those who used to be called the lower and unrefined classes? Do these, simply because they are unrefined, already guarantee the core power—or is the giving over of all that only a further clarification of the prevailing deterioration as a whole—the coming to light of the impotence, i.e., the weakness {?} and ignorance, for a spiritual struggle (≠ opposition)?

45

124

The secret aim of the other beginning: to establish (as a historical structure) the restraint of the preservation of Da-*sein*—and so to prepare for the (event) as history.

Moreover, a *gathering*: but not only as unification of what was previously scattered and was without opposition; not only sublation of differences; not the middle as mediocrity; instead, gathering: as storage of the actual powers, accumulation of their capacities, and development into structures—creation of the essential *great ability*!

Yet this happens not through the wasting and spending of that which is still salvaged—but through a new action; ability comes only through training; but training only from venturing; venturing only in *questioning*. Questioning only if borne and led by what is most question-worthy (Da-*sein*)—and that happens only if the most originary questioning is at work, and that only where the primal leap [*Ur-sprung*] has been taken, and that only where the necessity of the other beginning has been grasped and conceptualized, and that only where the deepest plight has become a matter of urgency, and that only where the plight is experienced, and that only where the openness of the highest free knowledge and of the actual struggle resides.

Growth into the great opposition—not underhand elimination of what could become uncomfortable to someone in his coziness.

46

125

Actual philosophy always and necessarily stands apart, on the side.

On the side—according to what measure? According to the apparently multisidedness and omnisidedness of the mediocre, the run-of-the-mill, and the immediately needful. In truth, however, actual philosophy stands in the in-between of *Da-sein* and acquires the "there"—for every possible "where," even for the "everywhere" and "nowhere" of the commonplace.

From that perspective, the originary character of philosophy as standing apart must always be misinterpreted—as lack—as presumption, as *isolation*, and as disavowal of "community."

126

"*Meta-physics*"—this name is coined for the knowledge of beings as such—because that is what "physics" is, even and precisely in Aristotle. And that—following upon the beginning—to be sure, as the inability to hold fast any longer.

The disempowerment of φύσις; therefore then ἐπιστήμη φυσική ["knowledge of nature"] and accordingly: μετὰ τὰ φύσικα ["metaphysics," "the things accompanying the natural things"]—i.e., what must be attached to physics, what belongs to it. (Cf. p. 55.)

127

Being itself in plight; *the* plight as the homelessness and hearthlessness of the essential occurrence of being. When will we grasp *this* plight? The fact that the most unique has to compel the most inward! Being and Da-sein! In the intimacy of creativity and I of creative preservation. The homelessness of being—is visible precisely in the *assignment* to "thinking"—representation or some other "faculty"!—and in the lack of every question about being—even in "ontology."   47

128

Philosophy: to put in words the essential occurrence of being.

How in words? As thoughtful designating; as effective discourse of Da-sein. The danger in this discourse!

Philosophy has now been explained "prescriptively" as *Dadaism* and therefore as otiose and nonsensical—this characterization of philosophy is more correct than its advocates could surmise. It does hit the mark—such as philosophy must present itself to the regard of those who are excluded from it. Philosophy then presents its essence only in the most superficial and distorted mirroring. To bring being into words: Dadaism. Where are we, if such has become possible and if this "concept" of philosophy guides the construction of "German culture"?

129

The distress cry for the Essential poet; the grounding of this poet's place (Da-sein).

The plight of the thinker—the one who strives to transform the question of being, without the paths to the instituting of this knowl-
48   edge I in history.

The distress cry for the meta-physical poet; "meta-physical" means: for the poet of the other beginning.

Hölderlin as the "transition."

130

My *basic experience: the essential occurrence of being*—grasped at first as the *understanding* of being; thereby, the danger of an "idealism"; but at any time the countervolition to understanding—as thrown projection; that as Dasein. But this still a wrong way; one which nevertheless first makes it possible now to carry out the inceptually obscure basic experience more originarily and more purely—better: to start to question being, in the supreme leap into the overpowering restraint of standing firm in the essential occurrence of being. But all this in the deepest and most intimate recollection of the first beginning and its tradition.

The basic experience of the essential occurrence of being does not allow the postulation of *one* domain of beings as the standard—or sus-
49   taining—domain, neither that of "spirit" nor of nature ("life"). This basic experience also does not take for decided the openness I and articulation of the ordinary traditional domains of beings—but rather endures in the concealed-disconcealing in-between qua preparedness for the other beginning.

131

The basic experience of the essential occurrence of being is in itself a matter of thinking, inasmuch as at issue are the leap into Dasein and the first grounding of the leap. Thereby the basic experience is not immobilized and abolished—instead, it itself in its essence—uniquely and inceptually—first experiences [*er-fährt*] and acquires the faring [*Fährnis*].

132

That mistaking of the essential occurrence of being qua the understanding of being as well as the condition of possibility of that understanding are connected to the identification of humanity and Dasein ("the Dasein in human beings," *Vom Wesen des Grundes*[9]); indeed, what is intended is a distinction, yet the place of Da-sein is arrested and not reached in a leap as what must first be reached in a leap that grounds the place (space-time); but not an "idealism."

(Cf. leap over and leap into.)

133

The essential occurrence of being as the ineluctability of Da-sein.

134   50

The experiencing and grounding of the future "where" of historical humanity:

the in-between of the Great accident of the (event) in the essential occurrence of being—endured in grounding and preserved steadfastly as Da-sein.

135

Not legislating, but above all determining of the place and grounding of the place; not summarizing, but Precedent instituting of the "truth" of preparedness—finding the path.

136

The question of being as the grounding of Da-sein; the leap into Da-sein as the opening up of the essential occurrence of being.

137

Would that we were able to say *Dasein* productively and truly!

138

Meditation! Meditation? Leave the fact its rights, but come from it directly to an originary meditation on the open concealedness of the essential occurrence of being.

---

9. {Martin Heidegger, "Vom Wesen des Grundes," in *Wegmarken*, GA9, 2nd ed. (Frankfurt: Klostermann, 1996), 164.}

139

Meditation: the steadfastness of the fact.

51

140

Not "plight"—instead, the constancy of the decisiveness of the ineluctability *of Da-sein*.

141

Actual questions—questions as process—are more powerful than answers. With the answer, Da-*sein* comes to a stop.

142

Whenever thinking and the act of meditation fall into the superficiality of the everyday and into the snares of today's measures and standards—the justification of any activity is without prospects. Then recollection must come as a call and must bring that excessive demand by which the thoughtful mode of Dasein is withdrawn into the most extreme solitude. The latter, like an unknown abundance, allows it to happen that only the rare and the few ask about the one.

143

To question?—Very far outside and beyond the limits of the inessential and ordinary, to encounter the most proper essence—as the call to the struggle over the constancy of the great history of Da-sein.

52

144

Science is the explanation of beings.*
    Philosophy is the illumination of being.
    Science must press forward into the Ever clearer as the familiar and commonplace.
    Philosophy goes back into the concealed as the unintelligible and alien.
    Science imparts true things (through correctness).
    Philosophy elicits truth.
    Science takes *Da*-sein as ground.
    Philosophy *is* Da-*sein*.
    The discourse of science is assertional.
    The discourse of philosophy is probative and intimative.

Science confirms—
Philosophy upsets.
Science procures cognitions; builds up.
Philosophy sets into knowledge; grounds the ground.
(On "science," cf. s.s. 37, p. 71;[10] | Working circle, 37–38;[11] cf. *Ponderings* V, p. 92.)

*The counterpart—therefore belonging to science—is the *deduction* out of and according to axioms; "basic" statements [*"Gründ"-sätze*] are different—grasped as *grounding* statements [Gründung*sätze*].

145

Resoluteness—metaphysically conceived—is *originary questioning* in the realm of thought.

146   53

The following must be mastered and be determinative of the attitude: the fact that thoughtful discourse never leads to something comprehensible so as to be documented and proven on that basis—but instead speaks about the incomprehensible, the ineffable, indeed not in order to transform it into the comprehensible, but in order to place humanity back into the strangeness of being. And the following will never be grasped in the ordinary course of things and on the current path, one overcharged with destiny: the fact that the disclosive questioning of what is most question-worthy—the resoluteness toward its *appreciation* and grounding—is to constitute the answer for thoughtful Dasein.

147

Not moral ("existentiell") bother, but metaphysical transformation into Da-sein.

---

10. {Heidegger, *Nietzsches metaphysische Grundstellung in abendländischen Denken: Die ewige Wiederkehr des Gleichen*, GA44 (Frankfurt: Klostermann, 1986), 120ff.}

11. {Heidegger. "Die Bedrohung der Wissenschaft," in *Zur philosophischen Aktualität Heideggers, vol. 1. Philosophie und Politik.* (Frankfurt: Klostermann, 1991), 5–27.}

148

The disclosive questioning of the essence of beyng never becomes "needful"—necessary on account of an essential plight—unless the uniqueness of history is attained—the uniqueness of our situation.

54

149

With the other beginning, are we entering into the "last chapter of the history of the world"[12]?

150

This gloomy autumn, which is not even allowing the leaves to die in their golden colors, can be overcome only by work—provided this work itself becomes an inner illumination of the heart and does not remain mere toil. Indeed we could never compel such illumination, but we can await it. Yet this awaiting must not at all be inaction; on the contrary, it must always become a preparedness for the happening of that which overgrows mere effort. Good hours come only through work itself, through its stretches of failure and its occasional stoppage. Thus work becomes the uniquely genuine way we hold ourselves out to the illuminating ray. To accomplish this holding-out is the mystery of work.

Good and empty hours bring this matter to experience and strengthen the capacity to remain ever close to the things, as on the first day.

55

151

Metaphysics: the history of the essential occurrence of being;
    "metaphysical": relating to the history of being.
    Indeed the name and the concept are thereby overcome. (Cf. p. 46.)

152

Beauty: a metaphysically necessary aberration of the essence of truth, insofar as this essence had to decay inceptually in opening up.
    Philosophy: the eventuating of the essential occurrence of being by way of questioning.

---

12. {Heinrich von Kleist, "Über das Marionettentheater," in *Gesammelte Schriften*, vol. 3. (Berlin: Reimer, 1859), 311.}

153

Philosophy is the grounding and fathoming of linguistic usage, but since philosophy is for the most part not equal to the concealed truth (and truth power) of language, it appears to be mere talk about things which are not there.

This semblance merely confirms—for those who know—the most proper being of philosophy.

154

The *letting-be of beings* is Da-*sein*. This "letting" is not the indifference of indolence or the cowardice of noninvolvement; instead, it is the leap into the "essence," the struggle of steadfastness, the questioning of that which is most question-worthy.

The least attainment of genuine philosophy is the question-worthiness of being and is its unique supreme attainment.

155

The ones projected in advance and therefore necessarily aloof ones and as so projected the *seeking ones*—
    seeking as disclosive questioning—
The aloofness of philosophy not that of a mere keeping away from what is current, but that of a going away as a going ahead in seeking—aloofness not a goal—instead, an essential consequence.

The uniqueness of the necessity of new knowledge for the fathoming of Da-sein.

56

156

The more originary—the more of a leap—is the questioning in thought, all the stronger is the semblance of arbitrariness, and all the harder is the alienation. This semblance must be endured as something necessary.

157

Whether as ontology or as "philosophy of existence," the prattle about being without the *question* of being is growing unendurable.

158

To conceptualize being is not to have knowledge of a "concept," but to conceptualize what is captured in the concept, i.e., to remain essentially exposed to the attack of being.

How can being attack? Attack and (event).

57

159

Nowhere any longer a struggle over measures, no proceeding on new courses.

160

Metaphysical thinking is *inventive* thinking—thoughtful accomplishment—of a change in being. The kind and rank of this change and of the desire for change set the standard by which the greatness of a thinking is to be gauged.

161

The mystery of philosophy is the capacity to wait while questioning, until the simple event comes into clarity unconditionally and creates for itself its place and ground.

162

Has one thinker ever refuted another? Is refutation the form of overcoming appropriate to them? Must there be overcoming here at all? Or does not the one thinker rather situate himself in relation to the other, in such a way that I in this gaining of a foothold they "merely" transform being, without explicitly incorporating the Previous transformation?

58

163

Every great thinker thinks only *one* thought; this one is always the *unique* thought—of being. But to think this *one* thought does not mean to go into retirement with the monotonous sameness of the *one* representation which perhaps was the first to emerge. Nor does it mean simply to "apply" this empty same thought to various domains. On the contrary, the fruitfulness of this thinking of one thought consists in the fact that the uniqueness of this way becomes ever more alienating and question-worthy and thereby unfolds in its originary junctures the fullness of the simplicity—unfolds what is little—into a configuration.

Here is the greatness of thinking, where this simplicity of what is unique may of itself grow into the riches of what is essential and may be transformed. (Cf. p. 59, 66.)

164

Start with something small and yet consider what is great.

165

My lecture courses, which belong to this that is small, | are *all*, and   59
indeed *intentionally*, still only a superficies and mostly even a concealment; this holds as well of those courses which express themselves about themselves and their task.

How should and could it be said pedagogically what the genuine volition desires?

166

Every genuine concept of philosophy is, *as a concept*, gravid with decisions.

167

Every essential thinker always *thinks* about a decisive leap more originarily than he *speaks* of it; and in *that* thinking he must be grasped and *his* unsaid must be said (cf. p. 66). Therefore, interpretation is required.

168

The more clearly and simply, on the basis of a decisive questioning, the history of Western thinking is brought back to its few essential steps, all the more does its binding and anticipating power grow, and this precisely when the issue is to overcome that history. Anyone who claims he could strike off this history by decree is unwittingly struck by it himself and indeed with a stroke from which he could never recover, since it is a blinding stroke— | one that intends to be original,   60
whereas it merely mixes together something traditional, without mastering it, into something supposedly different.

The greater a revolution must be, all the deeper will it attack in its history. (Cf. p. 69.)

169

The overcoming of nihilism—must first grasp nihilism in its hidden depth—as the forgottenness of being and as the collapse of ἀλήθεια— only then is the ground of our history free—
But how then still a grounding?

What would happen if we come to *know* this? The possibility of *reverence*—the self-overgrowing into something great and simple.

170

The one thing necessary: meditation and again: meditation, which means the prior *education toward meditation*. For, meditation is other than "reason" and calculation: it is reverence for the wonder *of being* and is the founding of the nobility of the great Da-sein.

61

171

Through the work of thought, the thrust into beyng is to be given impetus and the thrusting power is to be concentrated therein covertly. In progression and in standstill, the distant position of Da-sein is to be fathomed; that one thing is to be seized, and thereby the event is to be inventively thought.

172

The revolution to Da-sein as effectuation of the truth of being—my one and only volition.

173

Need to assume the highest responsibility, out of the plight of a lack of a sense of plight, for the preparation of a preparedness to be exposed to being.

174

To think ahead and into the future, without ever being able to experience it resounding—that seems to lead to sheer arbitrariness; and yet directive here is a higher law, the origin itself, for even what once was
62 occurring, in case it could be said in advance | and as it were fetched into the present in advance, would never be a proving true of thinking. Beyng is not proven true by beings, but the reverse. Nevertheless, the truth of being is difficult to experience and is rarely experienced;

in this truth the entirety of history—from the beginning to the end—
is always gathered together into one.

We are overly accustomed to acknowledge and to take as true only
what the new day brings, whether we affirm it or take it as a goal—
and its origin does not at all concern us.

175

Plutarch reports the pronouncement of Cato the Elder: ὡς χαλεπόν
ἐστιν ἐν ἄλλοις βεβιωκότα ἀνθρώποις ἐν ἄλλοις ἀπολεγεῖσθαι.[13] "How difficult it is, as a member of a different generation, to defend oneself to
the other."—(Cf. p. 94.)

What is to be done here? Be assimilated, or keep apart? Neither of
these—instead, see that the most proper task unfolds out of the originary ground and attributes to the later generations something inexhaustible.

176   63

Nietzsche once gave—at the end of his journey—in *Ecce Homo*—a
frightful "definition" of the *Germans*—what "German" means: "not to
want to be clear about oneself."[14] Then the acquisition of the German
essence should be sought on the way leading in the opposite direction
from the one that strays into prehistory—on the way of a *future* desire
for *clarity*—a clarity in which everything essential is posed upon the
extreme decision, where the first step, giving the entire movement its
law, would be to carry out a *questioning*. But what sort of witches' caul-
dron is bubbling here—in case it is still only bubbling—Christianity,
"positive" Christianity, German Christians,[15] Confessional "Front"!,
political worldview, concocted paganism, perplexity, idolization of
technology, idolization of race, worship of Wagner, etc, etc.

One *does not want* to be clear about oneself, and how much is there
talk of "wanting."

---

13. {Carolus Sintenis, ed., *Plutarchi vitae parallelae*, (Leipzig: Teubner, 1911),
chap. 15, 4–5.}

14. {Nietzsche, *Ecce Homo. Der Wille zur Macht. Erstes und zeites Buch*, *Werke*, vol.
15 (Leipzig: Kröner, 1911), 113.}

15. {The "German Christians" were a group of Protestants who from 1932 to
1945 subscribed to the National Socialist worldview. The "Confessional Front"
or "Confessional Church" was from 1934 to 1945 the resistance movement of the
Protestant Church against National Socialism.}

177

Only those who are fearless can have anxiety.

178

The genuine "pre-"history: the one that runs before us—or does not.

64

179

Do the new gods come to our encounter?
   Or are we ruined?
   Or is the other beginning the opening for the time of *the last god*?

180

At issue is the development of the power of questioning—i.e., the power to want clarity.

181

The *repetition of the nineteenth century is being carried out*: historicism—merely diverted to prehistory *et al.*

One now also does not want clarity in the essential decisions nor want that which could compel such clarity—questioning.

But one attempts to vilify a hemiplegic Nietzsche with certain notions and ultimately one pursues everything with the unrestrained expenditure of all the means of technology.

182

The complete disappearance of any presentiment of the presuppositions on which the existence of the creative ones stands leads to a misappraisal in the experience of beings in general.

183

That which makes noise does not illuminate. And what is never illuminated cannot clarify.

Only that which clarifies has power.

184

Philosophy?—The fathoming, in thinking, of the ground of the play of being—; what does "thinking" mean here?

185

The inconspicuous but effective way to diminution—one no longer lets anything become great.

186

The style of restraint and the last god. (Cf. p. 70 and 72f.)

187

I am slowly learning to experience the true nearness of the great thinkers in what is most foreign about them.

188

You must learn to grow old very quickly, so you will be able to remain yet at the origin.

189

On the interpretation of Nietzsche's philosophy.—to the extent that finally the insight is dawning that the doctrine of the eternal recurrence of the same not only in fact *is*, but even *must be*, the basic doctrine of Nietzsche's metaphysics, the endeavors in | that direction stem   66
from the sphere of *Being and Time*. There the domain for the understanding of Nietzsche's basic doctrine is first made visible. But the interpretations are *all* insufficient, because they have not grasped—i.e., unfolded—the question of *Being and Time* as a *question*. Ultimately, everything remains at the expedient that Nietzsche returned to the beginning of Western philosophy; but this is precisely his end! And now it must first be reported: *Incipit principium*! ["The beginning is starting!"]

190

If there is something like a catastrophe in the creative work of great thinkers, then it consists not in their "foundering" and standing still, but in their going "further" instead of *remaining* back at the source of their own great beginning. The history of Western philosophy must be appropriated once from this viewpoint. (Cf. p. 59.)

191

Our pride and nobility: questioning into the outermost *and* innermost and still, above all, questioning into the "and"—into the essential occurrence of being itself. This questioning is not without use; indeed for the ordinary bustle it is a disturbance only if that bustle is supposed to be stirred up—a danger. But our questioning is, despite everything, I even as questioning still provisional—it merely prepares. The realm of what is question-worthy must first be made visible again; those who *ground* must be the greater ones.

67

192

The blind and busy! They believe the "they" of "Dasein" is now replaced by the people—or could be at any time; "the people" merely provides a hardening, which means a greater veiling. Besides, the question in *Being and Time* does of course not have the least to do with the prattle about "nationality" ["*Volkstum*"] which is becoming more and more common in science.

193

What is essential in *Being and Time* is up to now still not antiquated and has not previously even once been "new." Instead, it has been mixed into the antiquated and the ordinary and made innocuous.

194

"*Spatial research*"[16]—the new basic form of the sciences? Perhaps it would be good to pursue *temporal* research as well, even if only in the sense of meditation on what at this *time* is actually happening to us. Or does one precisely *not want* any part of *this* clarity?

---

16. {The "federal work group for spatial research" was established in 1935 as a subdivision of the "federal office for spatial order."}

195

Hölderlin—precisely a mistake here slipped in on me. It would be more worthy if for the next hundred years we did not allow that name on our lips or in our newspapers.

196

How little do we know of the riddle and essence of *possibility*?

197

The essential thoughts are to be hunted ever anew through the hardest questions.

198

Pride—is the mature decisiveness of abiding in one's own essential station, the station arising from one's task; it is the certainty of no longer confusing oneself with something else.

199

What we bring forth in the highest clarity of the simplest and hardest configuration can accomplish only this one thing: to allow the concealing to increase and the veiling to become more powerful in its intimacy. And the more exactly we step into clarity, all the more sure does concealment come right behind us and over us. And as this "over us," still unfelt, concomitantly comes into configuration, | the highest is attained—(event).

69

200

In decisive meditations the same experience announces itself again and again: *we are acquainted with too much and know too little.* Are we acquainted with so much because we know so little; or do we know so little from being acquainted with so much? Or are the two relations reciprocal? What is *then* occurring here? In this circle, can our meditation still be free?

Let us forgo acquaintanceship and adhere to knowledge!

201

Through *historiology* we have become weak, uncreative, and useless, or extrinsically imitative—we can be saved only through what is repugnant {?} to us in its falsification—through *history*—and therefore we must allow history to come for the first time to a power effective in advance. This is itself a creation which—in history—not in the mere past—brings new suns to shine. (Cf. p. 60.)

70

202

Who still surmises something of the greatness of the volition which must hold itself in the originary restraint? Who can still experience how originarily this restraint must be assigned to the (event)? (Cf. p. 65.)

203

Perhaps for a long time the new *essence* of truth must become more essential than any individual truths and anything held to be true; for the essence of truth unfolds only as Da-*sein*.

204

In a situation where all spiritual goals have disappeared, every willing of a goal has become weak, and all thinking unsure and unclear, where all powers are confused, all levels intermingled, and any standpoint is apparently impossible—there one cannot set out immediately from any individual question or goal. At such a moment a meditation on standpoint, in the broadest and deepest sense of meditation, is unavoidable—this may look like a definitive undermining, an abandonment of the most proximate measures and horizons, but this movement alone can I provide the ground for a mature taking up of a position. What is a root which merely lies withered in the soil instead of continuously seeking its ground, constantly measuring its ground anew, and ever more originarily reaching down into that ground—into the not-yet-penetrated darkness? Only as something that in this way digs down and grounds does the root secure for the shoots their highest growth and their safest protection against storms. Certainly, not every shoot is for every other—most shoots rest on the trunk, contentedly or disgruntled but always calmly and without feeling anything of the sap which at every moment must rise into them out of the rooting movement and the unrest in the depths.

71

205

On the most extreme path,
   with the strictest gaze,
   through the simplest word,
   in the most fitting structure,
   to the most intrinsic play,
   for the inceptual (event).

206

Uncommon eras, even if their uncommonness is only the extent of their deterioration, require that which is most alien.

207   72

Style is the self-certainty of "Da-sein" in the latter's creative law giving.

Future style will involve the highest meditation on style; such meditation, if carried out in searching and proceeding, *is* itself already style. (Cf. Ponderings VII,[17] p. 76.)

208

The attempt to calculate what philosophy can and should accomplish is an idle occupation if philosophy is not *already* extant; therefore all that matters is the *one* care, namely, that philosophy *comes to be*; if at some time or other, then philosophy will now remain the strangest, and thus also the most misunderstood, with regard to its way of effectuating.

209

The hardest, yet most unerring, touchstone for determining the intellectual seriousness and power of a philosopher is the question of whether he immediately and radically experiences, in the being of beings, the proximity of nothingness. Someone to whom this is denied stands definitively and hopelessly outside of philosophy.

---

17. {Heidegger, *Überlegungen VII–XI*, GA95 (Frankfurt: Klostermann, 2014), 53.}

210

What we must accomplish for the beginning qua the *other* beginning: radical knowledge of everything essential relative to the first beginning and its history and yet precisely also an overcoming of that beginning. The overcoming I will succeed at all only by way of such
73   knowledge. It will never occur through merely looking aside, for *in that way*, as impotently delivered over to tradition, we come not merely into emptiness but above all into the dominion of what is *not* overcome, is still effective, and is now all the more covered with the semblance of something self-evident and self-thought.

The other beginning is possible only on the basis of the most intrinsic *historical* thinking, a thinking that has overcome all historiology. Yet the most mysterious ground of asking the question of being, as a *historical* asking of the question, resides in the fact that being is now to be experienced and grounded, on the basis of the (event), as what is *most unique* and most nonrepeatable.

211

Will the most originary *appropriation* of the (event) succeed? And if the latter is still to be granted to the coming ages, how could the appropriation succeed except in *preservation?* That word names the *activity of restraint*, which is far from any weary adherence to what is traditional but also distant from any empty driving away of what has just been grasped. Preservation is the highest power for the moment in
74   which what is given as task I first appeals and what is given as endowment compels toward a collision. Preservation is the mystery of creativity. Preservation—names the fact that we are *held* in history out of the (event) only if we ourselves are *holders*—

holding to the compliance and holding out in the moment and so steadfast in being.

Preservation only as Da-*sein*.

Preservation of the carrying out; the history of *restraint*.

Out of the latter arises the former.

212

The *uniqueness* of being and *oddness* of beings—how the uniqueness and oddness raise themselves in their intimacy on the basis of truth—i.e., on the basis of the clearing concealment in what is sheltered.

How the sheltering of the sheltered and thereby that raising happen in preservation as the carrying out of the restraint of Da-sein.

213

Preservation and the forgottenness of being.

Preservation as the gathering of being into the proper domain of the uniqueness of being.

214   75

How common and small such a city Sunday is now; the peculiar blending of this commonness and smallness can properly be said only in the loan word "ordinary" ["*ordinär*"].

215

In philosophy, individual truths are not substantiated by means of proofs; instead, the *essence* of truth is grounded. But what is this grounding? Up to now it has remained concealed and showed itself only in a distorted way and misinterpreted by "science."

The grounding as Da-sein; the latter, however, is steadfastness in the (event).

216

Thoughtful endeavor with regard to the *other* beginning:

Dark, intricate, uncleared paths when the day is over; not a simple way through the fields on a Spring morning.

217

Where what is great opens out as the massive and gigantic, it is smallness, so small that it cannot even *be* small, because it does not see genuine greatness.

218   76

Being and Time is not a "philosophy of time" and even less a doctrine about the "temporality" ["*Zeitlichkeit*"] of humans; on the contrary, it is clearly and surely *one* way toward the exposition of the ground of the truth of being—the truth of *being itself* and not of beings, not even of beings *as* beings. The guideline is a leap in advance into "primordial temporality" ["*Temporalität*"], that in which originary time along with originary space essentially occur together *as* unfoldings of the essence of truth, unfoldings of the transporting-captivating clearing and concealment of truth.

Admittedly the insufficient first draft of the Third Division of Part I, on "time and being," had to be eradicated. A critically-historically configured reflection of it is contained in the lecture course of s.s. 1927.[18]

219

Innumerably many things are "going on" now incessantly, and they immediately become familiar to innumerable persons, in order then to be forgotten already in the next instant and be replaced by the very latest, forgettable, thing. Much is "going on," and the bustle occurring all over the planet, which is still called "earth," is a mere single "going on" which continuously devours itself and turns itself again into fodder.

77   Much "goes on"—and nothing *happens* anymore—i.e., | there are no more decisions set out into the truth of beyng, or even venturing the full sacrifice in this domain, in order to have in view, in the actual downgoing, the greatness of beyng.

Yet if only this—the fact that everything merely "goes on" and nothing happens anymore—had burst forth as a happening and thereby as *the* plight! A *first* thing would thereby *happen again*—and history would have taken itself out of the domain of incidents and their gigantic display and into the calm site of what is unsurpassably great.

220

Will the West still master the second beginning? Or must the West now actually become the land of the evening[19] and do so in the light of seeming to be a morning which finds it so easy to forget the chaos of the night and stumble into the supposed daytime?

221

Why do I have two g's in my name? Why else, except that I recognize what constantly matters:

Benevolence [Güte] (not pity) and *patience* [Geduld] (i.e., supreme will).

------

18. {Heidegger, *Die Grundprobleme der Phänomenologie*, GA24 (Frankfurt: Klostermann, 1975).}

19. {The word for "West" in German, *das Abendland*, literally means "land of the evening," just as "West" is derived from *vesper*.—Trans.}

78

222

If the future history of mankind is still to be a history and not a mad rush of self-devouring incidents which are temporarily arrested only in the loudest noise, and if a history, i.e., a style of Dasein, is still granted us, then that can only be the concealed history of the great stillness in which the sovereignty of the last god opens up beings and configures them. And so what matters:

First the great stillness must come over the world for the sake of the earth. It will come only out of the intimacy of the strife between world and earth, insofar as the intimacy of the contention of this strife is disposed by restraint as the basic disposition of Dasein.

223

If someone does not realize now that *through* his work and *for* it solitude must arise and become ever greater, then his "life" has no worldly place on this earth but, instead, remains caught merely relatively in the current shifts of an onrolling bustle and its incidents and increasingly requires rousing by means of so-called | "consequences" in order to cover up the groundlessness and to ward off the dizziness from all this bustling about.

224

The *actual sharing* in the will to renewal on the part of the Germans consists only in the growing acknowledgment of the plight and in an originary grasp of the extreme tasks.

The *false standard of reliability*: if this standard is acquired out of extrinsic agreement with the precisely current institutions.

It is not necessary that those who find satisfaction in their dealings and machinations and find approval in their "communities" should still know or even surmise anything of that originary alienation from everything egoic, the alienation which must reside in the creative suffering of individuals not primarily as a consequence, but rather as a condition.

225

What do we need first and foremost? The insight that only a long preparation and increased meditation will produce the space and the occasion for the hesitant suddenness of creative moments.

226

Inceptual thinking must make its way *without signs*. If and only if the sheltering of truth in beings devolves upon the thoughtful grounding of the essence of truth, will this thinking be historical and become the fire of the power of what is true.

For itself, this thinking can accomplish nothing and must smolder away if those do not come who can rekindle the flickering embers. This is the sense of the uselessness of philosophy.

227

What is now to be done for philosophy?—That results from its assignment to originary thinking and from meditation on its current state (cf. interplay[20]).

228

Only the extreme futurity of the creative basic disposition in the most abyssal "space" of earth and world provides the guarantee of a great history. Every originarily creative capacity is equally essential to prepare for that history.

229

The mystery is the source of that truth which guarantees us the great breadth of the affiliation to beyng | and makes the inexhaustible into a gift. What previously seemed to be familiar and to be bogged down in habituality is suddenly irradiated by the magic of the concealed essence of beings.

The paltriness of our relations to beings, the susceptibility of those relations to all quick and calculable arrangements, is based on the increasing impotence for great reverence, which arises only from the power of recollection. Recollection is never the backward-directed adherence to something past; instead, it springs from a creative futurity which denies itself every empty immortality and in the finitude of its destiny has found the uniqueness of the essence. This futurity truly outlasts all mere perdurance as the same, and once again it newly rises up toward uniqueness. Only that which is nonrepeatable can effectuate this arising again of something unique. That is the innermost law of beyng.

81

---

20. {*Beiträge*, 167–224.}

230

Not the *proclamation* of a doctrine to present-at-hand humans, but the *dislodgement* of today's humans into their concealed plight of a lack of a sense of plight. This dislodgement is the first presupposition for any recreation of the ground.

231

82

Philosophy can never immediately lead or offer help; it must be prepared historically and be standing by. With what and for what?

With the essential realms of questioning and deciding and of the sheltering of truth in beings.

For a volition which is thereby prepared to strive for its destiny and to do so deliberately as history.

And therefore philosophy *must* perhaps disappear from the sphere of the ordinary public claims and needs.

232

Philosophy is useless, though sovereign, knowledge. (P. 39.)

233

How good that only the fewest, and they so seldom, surmise something of the truth of beyng.

234

Is it not an abyssal and therefore scarcely ever noticeable error to strive by means of institutions to raise Dasein and the history of mankind to their destiny and even to their greatness? An error, because only the configurable flashing of the uniqueness and strangeness of beyng in the hardest assault draws humans to their heights and I can hurl them to their depths, in order thereby to open them to the space-time of their "there." Everything else, not having this event-character, is excluded from the possibility of grounding essential history; the more gigantic everything else becomes, all the more clearly is it only the self-clouding delay of a long-since determined and irresistible downgoing which is denied the possibility of becoming a transition.

How then must a downgoing be, so that it can become a transition?

83

235

We are not only not in possession of what is true (what and how beings are and we—*who?*—as beings ourselves in the midst of them).
Above all, we do not know *truth*; indeed we do *not* even *want* to know
the essence of truth, for we bristle at questioning. As a path into the
uncertain, we distrust questioning and appeal instead to the healthy
proximity to "actuality" and to "life." And this is indeed the most insidious form of resentment against the essence of truth and the most
tenacious mode of the abandonment by being. (Cf. p. 94.) Those who
question.

84

236

Clarity as the snatched-up transparency of what is empty and superficial, or the clarity of illumination—i.e., as the will to the richness and
to the depth of what is concealed—questioning as the will to struggle
over measures.

The increasing mistrust of questioning has its impetus in the hidden anxiety that on the path of questioning one might perhaps have
to encounter one's own unacknowledged groundlessness.

Questioning is indeed "self-decapitation"—namely, of those who
are groundless, who stagger on and on in the semblance of standing
on native ground. (Cf. p. 93, 94f.)

237

Whither are we plummeting? Or is this no longer a plummeting, since
that presupposes height and depth and can have its own greatness
and even its victory—supposing that those plummeting come again
to themselves by way of the plummet, in that they bring themselves
before the truth of beyng. No more plummeting, but only a bemir-
ing and stagnating? Who wants to estimate the vector of our history?
Those last of all who merely cling to its past.

85

238

Who are we? It does not seem necessary to know that; it is better just
that we *are*. But "to be" here means to be a self—to stand out from
selfhood while grounded in it. And therefore our being always occurs
as an involvement or a going out of oneself; in each case in an appropriation to oneself, to which an assignment always belongs. To know
who we are is so necessary that without this knowledge we could never

decide whether we "are" or only strut among nonbeings and find ourselves given there as in the *cogito—sum*! ["I am thinking—I am!"]

239

Which is the extreme decision? It is whether we appertain to beyng—i.e., according to the turn: whether the truth of beyng essentially occurs in such a way that beyng requires us—as ones who are self-altering and who ground Dasein.

240

Genuine *philosophical critique* is always only meditation on the measure (the truth of beyng). It must never be taken myopically as disparagement or condemnation, and certainly not as a detecting of errors.

241

It does not befit a genuine thinker to battle | on behalf of his thought   86
and contrive the corresponding machinations; he must have the higher courage to let his thoughts, well ordained, stand on their own.

242

A philosophy that raises to consciousness only what is extant and what has come to pass is no philosophy—and can never be one in an age of transition where meditation on the necessities of the extreme decision must be carried out—i.e., meditation on the affiliation to being and, prior to that, on the truth of beyng and on the essence of truth. Since, through spiritual decline, we are too impotent for this carrying out and no longer know any high measure, such meditation must first be prepared. And since such decisions have their own time and cannot be calculated according to needs, a high spiritual clarity is required so as not to force something that is premature. One who offers himself for such a preparation of this meditation stands in the transition and must have grasped far in advance and must expect from his contemporaries, | as immediately pressing as this may be, no im-   87
mediate understanding—at most, only resistance.

In meditation and through it, there necessarily happens that constant otherness, and to prepare that is what genuinely matters but would never find the site of the event if there were no clearing for what is concealed.

243

Just as genuine philosophy is never immediately effective in "life" and seen from there stands aside uselessly, whether as eccentricity of thought or as an exercise in splitting hairs, so it is never immediately graspable when and how such philosophy has once been effective in its own proper way. For if this has happened, what is essential to it must in part necessarily have become self-evident in the meantime; and now philosophy proves to be otiose all the more, especially since what is self-evident cannot be recollected. Therefore, only a few are able to surmise what is happening in this concealed history of the truth of beyng.

88

244

It is always risky to give names to the basic positions of philosophical thinking.

My endeavors could be named ones aiming at a *"philosophy of Da-sein"* (cf. Kantbook,[21] concluding chapter). Of course, the meaning can only be that in this thinking the grounding of Da-sein is prepared for the first time and that this thinking itself already grows out of this ground—viz., Da-sein—by unfolding it.

Da-sein and its grounding, however, are demanded by the other beginning of philosophy itself, by the asking of its basic question regarding the truth of beyng and regarding the essence of truth. Only because my endeavors, insofar as they question *in that way*, are philosophy in the other beginning, can it be a philosophy of Da-sein. Thereby all previous notions attached to this term (presence at hand, actuality, existence in the sense of *existentia* ["existence"]) must be abandoned.

Inasmuch as the first attempt to capture the mode of *being* of Da-sein designated the latter with the word "existence" ["*Existenz*"], not least because the word *ex-sistere* ["to exist," "to stand out"], interpreted in a certain way, could indicate | the transporting character of the "there," this attempt was then labeled a "philosophy of existence" in the sense of Jaspers, who placed in the middle of his philosophizing Kierkegaard's concept of existence taken in its moral force (communication and appeal).

89

Fundamentally different from this is the directionality of *Being and Time*. The concept of existence, although indeed cointended as a moment of the existentiellia (hence, care), is here brought into relation with Da-sein, and the latter is determined only on the basis of the

---

21. [Heidegger, *Kant und das Problem der Metaphysik*, GA3 (Frankfurt: Klostermann, 1991).]

question of the truth of being. This questioning stands essentially and originarily apart in the entire history of Western philosophy.

245

Neither the setting up of "ideas," nor the reduction of them to useful "values," nor the problematic alliance with a blind "actuality of life" will bring about a "renewal" of philosophy. For that, the necessary other beginning is required. And the necessity is the one of a change in the essence of truth, and that necessity is in turn necessitated by the most intrinsic and broadest historical plight. This change I is car-   90
ried out in a preparatory way in the thoughtful grounding of Da-sein, a grounding which for its part is incorporated into the structure of the question of being as the basic question.

246

Philosophy in the other beginning is above all the grounding of the abyss qua the site of the moment of the truth of being.

247

The more gigantic the human being becomes, all the smaller must his essence contract, until he, no longer seeing himself, exchanges himself with his machinations and thus "outlives" his own end.

What does it signify that the human masses are worth so little they could be annihilated in *one* stroke; is there a stricter proof of the abandonment by being?

Who surmises the resonance of a last god in such a failure?

248

It might seem that in an age of transition even the grasp of the past and the future would be at its clearest, since knowledge I of these is   91
easiest. Yet the opposite is the case, assuming it is an actual (effective) transition and not one that merely dissects the "present situation."

In an effective transition, the proceeding is already exposed to the thrusts of what is coming and is still bearing what has been handed down. Here in a unique way what has been and what is coming press on beyond each other and press through each other; what meditation (on the transition itself, in service to its effectuation) is able to know of the transition is not—and never is—that which properly is happening in the transition. And yet such meditation, if it grasps in a genuine sense, coeffectuates this happening.

And if that meditation ever proceeds to the extreme and brings the essence of truth itself up for decision, then indeed the effectuation of the meditation will require a long time and will follow paths which those very paths will slowly make unrecognizable and otiose in their upsurging configuration—but there will once again be in a few great hearts an illumination of that beginning. The beginnings withdraw
92   from every will I to seize hold of them; in withdrawing, they merely leave behind the outset as their mask.

249

"Worldviews" remain outside the sphere of creative thinking (philosophy) and of great art as well. They are ways in which philosophy and art are immediately brought—i.e., directed—to use or rather to misuse by everyone. Therefore, philosophy can never be "worldview," nor may philosophy ever think to take over the place of worldview. Indeed philosophy cannot even determine a worldview as such— but must merely tolerate being used—or passed over—by worldview.

The so-called theoretical groundings of worldviews are therefore a peculiar mix of half philosophy and half science; they lack the seriousness of thinking as well as the strictness of research. Both thinking and science are replaced in advance by a desire to postulate the "worldview" immediately. Thus it is always misguided to measure
93   such groundings of worldview with I the standard of philosophy or science, both of which are radically different from worldview.

These groundings have value only as contributing to that use the worldview itself serves. But philosophy is intrinsically useless; "science," in relation to "worldview," has a definite though restricted use.

250

The extraordinary can never be the conspicuous; the most extrinsic must be the most intrinsic.

251

In restraint lies a concealed boldness.

252

How dreadful can that slavery become which arises from the immediate subjection into which all opposition and contention necessarily fall?

How do matters stand with the self-certainty of a people, when this people loses the possibility of guarding, and creatively enduring, its own most proper destiny as that which is most question-worthy? (Cf. p. 84.)

253

Disappearing more and more is the power for great | solitude qua the   94
site of the opening up and founding of being and thereby also of the
ground of the creative affiliation.

But if this affiliation were a mere juxtaposition, then it would require no "power" and no ground.

254

Who is the human being? Only a value-positing animal or only the wrappers for a "soul" that is to float off into eternity—or the unique site of the truth of being and of the relation to beings?

That unique being to whom this uniqueness so seldom lights up to become a grounding possession.

255

Are you a questioner? One of the genus of those who do not stagger and do not crave the new, who know the ground in the abyss and stand more firmly than all who merely have convictions? (Cf. p. 62, 83–84, 102.)

256

These who question form a new rank in the affiliation to beyng. Their alliance—concealed to themselves—does not know numbers | and   95
does not need to be instituted or confirmed.

257

It is claimed that my rectoral address does not belong in my "philosophy," presuming that I have one. And yet something essential was expressed in that address, specifically at a moment and under circumstances that did not at all correspond to what was said and questioned. The great error of the address surely consisted in its assuming that in the purlieu of the German university there would still be a concealed genus of questioners and in still hoping that these could bring them-

selves to the work of inner transformation. But neither the previous personnel, nor the subsequent one, belong to this genus. That they remain excluded from it finds its clearest testimony now in the fact that they have come to an understanding among themselves and have found themselves and above all—have thereby made their careers. The main defect of the address is due to my not knowing this beforehand. And that is also why it could not be understood. Who could
96   have thought out so far forward in order I to know that self-assertion—the reacquisition of selfhood—must be grounded on a questioning of that which is most question-worthy? Can one, thus thinks common sense, build one's house in a storm, in that which would merely demolish it?

The *technological* character—installed in the essence of modern "science," which is related only mediately to Greek "knowledge"—the "technologizing" of all sciences, even the "human" ["spiritual"] sciences [*"Geistes"wissenschaften*], cannot by its very essence be stopped by some sort of "preventive measures" interposed along the way. Even here something rolls or, better, slinks to its end.

258

The procreative succession of generations can keep going on for centuries to come and so perhaps produce ever greater masses of human exemplars—but that does not at all mean there will be a history or a people—for the most intrinsic configurative law of a historical people
97   is in each case temporally restricted to a short span of I ages. Knowledge of the configurative sense of the shortest course does not lead to "pessimism"—but the reverse: to the supreme will to betake oneself out into the extreme possibilities in order to be overgrown by them.

259

Seen in terms of the West and "world history"—is an *ahistoricality* already *arising*? If so, then this arising must especially proceed in the appearances of the loudest and most conspicuous incidents; the ahistoricality as the increasing impotence for history—an impotence deriving from history and still nourished by it—will make every effort to institute deliberately an unprecedented display of historicality. The arising ahistoricality will not in the least ever know itself or admit that it is such. But precisely this self-certainty—in part still apparently sincere in being carried out—is the most uncanny testimony to the fact that already a clear devastation is in the offing—a devastation calculable in long spans of time.

Or is the appearance of the commencing ahistoricality only the sign   98
of the historical entrance into an era of *transition* to a new historical
day in the West? If a *transition* is in progress, then every volition toward gathering and every step toward meditating must be affirmed—
no matter how provisional and obscure and overly certain of themselves these may be. An era of transition requires, as does no other, a
breadth of historical vision and an insight into the pressing dangers.

Must not the transition—whose course is unavoidably zigzag—
maintain itself in an irrevocable self-certainty with regard to its own
doings, such that it must appear to be not a transition but already fulfilled eternity itself? Is this certainty not needed in order to endure
the transition as a whole? Yes it is—but then required to the same degree—indeed to a still higher degree—even if in a different way—are
those who fully live in uncertainty, in that uncertainty which pre-
pares the future | wherein the space-time of the great decisions is   99
thought in advance.

In a transitional era—which by essence is richer and darker than
any other era could ever be—the extreme counterpowers and coun-
terappearances must subsist together out of a deeper ground and must
summon up the following: those who are self-certain, who arouse and
pursue the most proximate and most easily graspable conditions of
historical Dasein, as if this were *the* task pure and simple; the questioning ones, who think far in advance and prepare the basic conditions of
creativity whereby the space-time of Dasein is first grounded for the
entire people; the many, who gather together as alike in the same accomplishments and collaborations and reciprocally confirm one another in their indispensability; and the few, who in solitude take on
the sacrifice of the misinterpretation and consequently, on the basis of
a future affiliation, prepare history and consummate the transition.

The genuine and highest historical meditation on the transition
will come to know that these opponents | will and must ever so often   100
contend reciprocally, as they basically belong together, but always only
mediately achieve unity. Therefore, every attempt to unify—by way
of leveling down—these necessary opponents, belonging together in
opposition, will not only remain a misunderstanding of the historical
powers but above all will weaken them. The only demand is a way
and type of meditation in which this oppositionality is grasped so
thoroughly that it is not curbed and even destroyed by means of extrinsic expedients on the one hand and mere juxtaposition on the
other. (Cf. Of the event: The resonating: The abandonment by being.[22])

---

22. {*Beiträge*, 108ff.}

260

What may be the reason the question of the truth of beyng is not understood? Because it is not taken seriously, and that in turn because one has no motive to do so, and that in turn because the access to this—to the abyss—is not open—i.e., is not a *plight*—in the time of a lack of a sense of plight.

101

261

Is *knowledge* as impotent today as it seems, and is everything merely a matter of "action"? Or is the appearance of the impotence of knowledge only a mask covering an exceptional prodigality of *opinion*, that half-knowledge which apparently concerns the essential and at the same time is comprehensible to everyone while yet avoiding the prime decisions and taking refuge either in action or in didactic preaching. The half-knowledge allows only this either-or to count and is distinguished by its hatred of all interrogative meditation. It is unaware of the originary spheres of decision concerning the affiliation and nonaffiliation to beyng.

This half-knowledge at the same time looks like genuine "belief." And in the end it is indispensable as the basic form in which one steers clear of the real abysses.

262

More difficult than the carrying out of thoughtful questioning is the knowledge of such questioning, knowledge of what it is and must be.

102

263

Who are those who establish beyng and think the truth of beyng? The strangers amid beings, alien to everyone and familiar only to that which they seek; for in seeking resides the most abyssal proximity to the finding, to what alone is intimated to us in self-concealment. (Cf. p. 93f.)

264

The one who is able to think together truly the treatise on being-toward-death,[23] for example, and "On the Essence of Ground,"[24] and

---

23. {Heidegger, *Sein und Zeit*, GA2 (Frankfurt: Klostermann, 1977), 314ff.}
24. {"Vom Wesen des Grundes," 123–176.}

both of these together with the lecture on "Hölderlin and the Essence of Poetry," i.e., is able to grasp the originary and unexpressed relations—those between the essence of *beyng* and its grounding in Da-*sein*—such a one is on the way to that which my seeking has in view.—The extrinsic juxtaposition of the concepts used does not help much; it perhaps provides a desired opportunity to reckon up contradictions. But what matters is never to establish results for sound common sense and its perpetuation but, instead, to find—and proceed on—the *way* through the abyss.

265   103

To remonstrate against *Being and Time* for not taking up or even naming the "people" and the "community of the people" as "cores of meaning" is equivalent to reproaching a fir tree for not attaining the performance of a race car. In the end the fir as fir is capable still of something the race car, as loud and as gigantic as its demeanor may be, will never perform. Thus *Being and Time* is striving for something which, remaining in stillness, reaches far ahead of all idle talk about the "people" in the "pseudophilosophy" suddenly become overzealously "folkish" ["*völkisch*"].

266

Which future of "philosophy" will be publicly ushered in by the already protracted decline of thinking: a file of undisciplined pseudophilosophers will swagger here for a time, cut off from every genuine tradition yet indiscriminately predatory on any accomplishment, without the mature certainty of a craft, lacking any diffidence and reverence, inordinately intent of the pomp of their own vanity, and bustling on and on in a cloud of noisy prattle. In this wilderness, the quiet growth I of the future German thinkers must perhaps most   104 easily find its refuge—on account of its unrecognizability—and become ready for leaping again into the great origins and beginnings, ones never to be touched by those pseudos.

267

Our knowledge always extends only as far as the reach of the steadfastness in Da-sein, i.e., the reach of the power to shelter truth in configured beings. Kant's *Critique of Pure Reason* must presuppose this nexus, though unable to grasp it as such, let alone set it on its ground (the reciprocal relation between Da-sein and being).

And because this ground was not grounded, this critique remained groundless and had to suffer being surpassed at once, with its own help, toward absolute knowledge in German Idealism.

268

My questioning: solely the endeavor to ground *Da-sein* as the ground of the truth of beyng. But the necessity and the ways of such grounding are only alluded to.

105   In light of this task, the previous history of philosophy gathers itself up into the clear simplicity of a few steps. And yet, how disguised and overlaid through reckless "problems" is the essential. Will we be able to find it once again? Do the aversion to thinking and the opposition against it merely constitute the deep breath preparatory to a new leap? The devastation must then be endured, even if it consumes our powers. The victims of this victory do not need a monument; they must remain a model of the great style in which—at times we cannot calculate—the "wheel of beyng" turns once more, only to lie fixed again for a long time.

269

We cannot *know* what is basically happening with us; such knowledge was never granted a historical age. What the age believes it knows is always different from what is happening. But we must grasp two things, specifically in their correlation:

On the one hand, the setting of a defense against the uprooting of the West and at the same time, on the other hand, the preparation of
106   the highest | decisions of historical Da-sein. That defense, in the mode of its procedure and claims, is utterly different from this preparation. The former requires an implicit faith as well as the unquestionableness of the grasping counteraction. Whereas the latter must be an originary questioning, very provisional and almost—seen from there—useless. It is not necessary, indeed is perhaps even impossible, that both of these could be carried out at the same time on the basis of a higher knowledge. It is even probable that in the horizon of the defense—which understands itself at once as a new grounding—all questioning must be rejected as an attitude left behind.

And yet—only if the preparation of the extreme decisions creates for itself a grounded space—as poetry and art in general, as thinking and meditation—only then will the approaching history be more than the mere continuance of the bodily line of descent in a fairly endurable circle of "life."

270

The end of history. History itself is in its essence finite, because affiliated to beyng. The end of history will break in when history perishes on its own. That will | occur when the bombast pertaining to history   107
is applied to history itself.

What is insidious in a bombastic age (cf. the late Roman civilization) is not that everything there is mere bombast and noise, that only through these means does anything count as "actual"—instead, it is that through these means provision is made for what alone shall remain in historical "recollection," namely, precisely everything that satisfies this bombast.

Only if every originary—i.e., still questioning—recollection is undermined, and if nevertheless history and its eternity are spoken about more than ever before, only then must history hasten to its end.

Or is there in these happenings once again another beginning—must we not only leave that possibility open—but also pursue and interrogate it—because we must not presume to exhaust the essence of history?

Does it not then also pertain to historical Dasein that we ever remain behind history?

271   108

Remain behind the times—certainly; the question is only how and where? Whoever assesses "the time" only according to what is timely and consequently has recourse to what used to be timely and adheres obstinately to that—he becomes untimely. But the one who remains behind *there* where resides the ground of "time" and of its timeliness, he goes in front of time. He does not bother about seeming to be "reactionary," which might easily accompany such a remaining behind, nor does he proclaim to be the one who truly bears the future—he remains in his way in the domain of the still-to-be-created ground of history—because we could never know in advance which configuration of public history will arise out of the concealed ground.

272

To *be* in the proximity of the gods—even if this proximity is the remotest remoteness of the undecidability regarding their flight or advent—that cannot be charged to "good fortune" or to "misfortune." The constancy of beyng bears its own measure in itself, provided it at all requires a measure.

273

That "science" is now made "political" is only the consequence of its intrinsic, modern—i.e., *technological*—essence. (Cf. p. 116.)

109

274

Are we too old for what is already new
   or too new for what is still old?
   Or do we stand between everything as transition?

275

What is the origin? That which we do not know—neither its whence nor its age?

276

Is it still decidable for us today what are genuine beings? Is the question of genuine beings becoming needful to us? Does there consequently still exist the possibility of a great destiny? Or will everything wallow in an undecidedness, numb to itself on account of machinations, and proceed to an end which perhaps will still use up centuries?

277

Many are of the opinion that it is the excess of "organization" that effectuates the equalizing and leveling and, in unity with that, the pressing down of all levels into the commonality of what is common. This opinion is erroneous.

110   Organization itself, in its mode and execution, is always only the consequence of the then-current knowledge of, and desire for, the essential.

The disinclination with respect to the essential and unique is the motive of the downfall. Moreover, this disinclination and the aversion to any clarity in the prime decisions are already centuries older than everything of which the present is capable.

An overcoming and modification of this aversion will therefore require even more generations and lines of descent in the future, in case such overcoming and modification can still begin again in a radical way.

278

Machines and *machinations* have neither memory nor recollection. Where machination reigns—and it reigns most powerfully and best of all in concealment, where Dasein is to be constrained and propelled through "worldview"—all the more easily will the *semblance* of historical recollection expand. That it is mere semblance can be seen in the fact that prehistory counts equally with history, like what was taken over from the nineteenth century | with a mere change in application. There is *recollection*, however, only where the past is cherished, i.e., desired and known as something still occurring, in order to place the future into question and hold it up to a measure.

But one who as a "reactionary" against the future is only for the "tradition" has the same aversion to meditation as do those who blindly believe in what is new and through the latest achievements already sense themselves satisfactorily confirmed in relation to the past.

Those who *ever belong to yesterday* and those who *ever belong to tomorrow* meet up in what is essential: namely, the fact that they avoid—with an unsurpassable confidence—every confrontation with what is decisive, i.e., with the question of whether and wherein beyng still is grounded and groundable.

A *young generation* may be called young only when it must forbid itself this avoidance and do so on the basis of its own innermost will to existence. If it is not capable of that, if it cannot even hear an allusion to it and experience the necessity of it, then this generation's senility is insurmountable and easy to cover | over only through bluster in an environment which will only allow either "rest" or the confirmation of its "progress."

279

Sentiments without institutions are impotent; institutions without sentiments are violent.

Sentiments and institutions must arise originarily out of *meditation*, out of that questioning knowledge which as essential knowledge is already volition—but, measured against the cravings of machination, is useless.

This era lacks the power and discipline of meditation and likewise lacks rest and measure. Why? Because in its deepest ground, one concealed to it, it no longer wants meditation? But meditation bears on the truth of beyng and requires that the more originary essence of truth be grounded as the first, again decisive, truth.

Yet is this not presumptuousness—to want to ground the essence of truth again and more originarily? Do not the beings now placed into machination take their inexorable course, without bothering about their truth?

113   Are not the last death throes of the gods coming over the West? Only one who thinks out into this extreme possibility can fathom the plight concealed behind current history, wherein impotence and violence together seem to constitute the law of motion.

280

To arouse meditation, prepare for it, penetrate into it—that is all that matters if the downgoing is to become a transition. Everything else is to be cast behind, for the sake of this one thing: *meditation*.

281

What was the previous path, since the germination of *Being and Time* in 1922, except a seeking and developing of the soil and horizon for the extreme meditation: on the truth of beyng. And for us what can now be coming except meditation in the *same* attitude with greater originality, even if all-consuming; for the moments of meditation are not recurrent. If the historical hours of meditation are neglected, then everything rolls on in the blindness of what is self-evident, which is the most terrible abyss.

114

282

Who still surmises the jubilation and the horror of the compulsion of that plight which has projected mankind, as the projector of the truth of beyng, into beings?

What a blessing is the increasing disdain for all philosophy—for that meditation on the truth of beyng—!

Might this not one day cast a few individuals into a great fright and chase them out to the edges of the abyss, such that they might experience something of the possibility of the ground and thereby be compelled into a questioning—a seeking—of the ground?

283

We still reflect too little on the fate of those solitary ones who had to fall at their advanced outposts, seemingly without exploits and works, without illumination and transfiguration. And how great is their number, how much forgotten their individual names and sacrifices. What has the god of our history here required of the people? And yet—over and against these fallen ones of the Great War, how rare are those who in solitude fall on the path of meditation and of the projection of the projections in the πόλεμος of truth. Or are these few already too many for our weak recollection and | preservation on the basis of an essential transformation? How unreal and remote from history are here all historiological reports about our poets and thinkers and about the most unique ones among them, who had to fall after the shortest of journeys? How will we bring the coming generation before the stillest and most solitary history of our people?

115

284

The thinking of the thinker is a *thinking back* [Nachdenken]—he thinks back over what the poet poetizes in advance. But the creative decision in the thinking that thinks back consists in finding *the* poet and in grasping the one who is found such that he appears as the one who *must* be thought back to. This thinking back is not a mere conceptualizing of what was previously presented poetically—as a thinking back, it must follow the indicated path, i.e., must first pave and ground this path and so at the same time place the poet and his work back into their incomparability. I am speaking here of Hölderlin. (The well-meaning ones of today—the malevolent may be left to themselves—are of the opinion that my discourse on "Hölderlin and the Essence of Poetry" should be taken as | the long-awaited demonstration of how "my" philosophy is to be applied to literary theory and in general to the human sciences and to aesthetics. The poor things! Hölderlin as object of research for a "philosophy" and for its applicability to such science! Where are we, if such opinions are the well-intentioned ones?)

116

285

"Philosophy" must never demean itself to the task and demand of either erecting a "worldview" or "grounding" and "configuring" one that already prevails. A "worldview" is clear about itself only if it sees in philosophy—specifically, in genuine philosophy—an *opponent* and indeed one essentially necessary for it.

The teacher of worldview and the writer about worldview must not be mistaken for the philosopher. Philosophy must always remain a danger for "worldview" (cf. the Middle Ages); philosophical *erudition*, however, with its stupid claims, should not harm worldview. The opposition between philosophy and "worldview" is at bottom a congruity (cf. p. 99.), assuming that neither corrupts its own essence through a perverted setting of goals.

286

Why must the *transitional* ones (who prepare and carry out the transition) be the ones who *go down*? Because the arc of the transition, which must curve over the past and to the future, allows no long stretches in a straight line but instead, as an element in an arc, requires in each case the curved shortness of constant change and thereby the shortest path.

287

The one who seeks comfort diminishes and misinterprets the sacrifice.

288

If only a few ever hold out to the *last god* Da-sein as the site of the moment in which once again beyng needs beings for the sake of works and sacrifices, then the end of history is recoiling into the greatness of the beginning of history. Therefore, all meditation must count toward this one thing: to prepare—mediately and on very roundabout paths—these few ones in whom the truth of beyng gathers itself into the still light of restraint.

It always seems as if they are thinking history in a greater and
118   stronger way, those who confidently promise it an eternity, | if not even more. And yet thereby they rob history of the innermost essence of its uniqueness and its necessarily limited duration. They deny history an end as the uniqueness of a gathering into something ultimate. One expects returns from the superficiality of the "and so on." But this notion corresponds merely to the wishes of the masses, who only in such a way can "think" to themselves a self-transcending and even must do so to guarantee their own continuance.

289

Our history will proceed to its end, or is already at its end, unless once again those *few* come to power who *know and set into work beyng itself*—solely for the sake of itself—and its *truth*. But since the many are intent on determining knowledge from the narrow perspective of "science" and—which is quite in order with regard to an already "technologized" science—intent on making "science" political, the *non*-wanting of that originary knowledge then appears to come to sovereignty as the start of a confirmation of the end. Of course, this end as such can still have a "future" amounting to centuries (cf. China). (Cf. above, p. 108.)

290

The complete "politicizing" of all "sciences" as well as their "underpinning in a worldview" is quite in order, supposing that *essential knowledge* is no longer wanted and that from sheer "heroism" what is most question-worthy is surreptitiously avoided.

But who with knowledge will be surprised that now a "science serving the people" alone counts as what is "close to life," whereas all questioning and a fortiori the questioning of that which is most question-worthy are scorned as useless, if not indeed suspected of being destructive? For—what is now taken to be the "actual"? What is the "actual" according to the common—allegedly unspoiled—taste of those who go to the movies every week?

291

The fact that today's "science" *can* be altogether transformed into "political" science presupposes the *technological* character of modern science. The previous science is not overcome by means of this transformation but on the contrary is first set to rights and brought to its end. Something scientifically "new" (in the *essential* sense of science) can therefore no longer arise; only the direction of the | utilization is new.   120
And even if the utilization suddenly comes to an end and the necessity of "theory" is seen once more, this "theory" will bring about no further change in science, in the sense that the essence of knowledge would be configured more originarily. This is so because what now in general counts as the "actual" would not be placed into question but, instead, would be accepted as unproblematic.

What then can and should *philosophical meditation* accomplish within the university, an institution entirely subservient to science? The more "scientific" the university becomes, all the more definitively must it get rid of "philosophy." Yet philosophical erudition can still be of some use, since it is indeed not philosophy but is in the same class as "science"—whereby now even a "pedagogue" ["education scientist"], i.e., someone utterly untouched by philosophy, can "professorially" altogether "step in" for "philosophy," not to say "trample it underfoot," since there is no longer anything left to be trampled. Some day an agreement will be reached among the previous and current "stand-ins for philosophy," since nothing brings together so closely as the same resistance against the one thing still felt to be threatening here, | namely, philosophical *meditation*. And thus everything on all   121
sides in the university is at rest, and all that is still required is an honest individual who will one day take this institution for what it *is*, an

agglomeration of professional schools with a directionality turned *toward one thing—universus*—namely, utility.

How unworldly and impossible now seems the attempt to draw the "university" back to the task of the peculiar grounding of knowledge as the ground of science, i.e., back to the necessity of originary questioning. How could anyone still believe that such an "institute" would *want* to accomplish a self-assertion of knowledge and should even become law giving?

How was this miscalculation possible? Because courage was lacking to face what I already knew, courage for coming to terms with the "death of God," with the abandonment by being in the current appearance of beings, i.e., because courage to face what we already know is, as Nietzsche says, so rare.

122   *292*

And yet—the essence of our history, the remotest proximity of the last god, is never affected by all this, no matter how it "develops." And therefore the supreme possession remains inviolable, namely, the seeking and abiding within this proximity and the indicative preparing of the preparedness of the future ones for the last god. Every step of thinking and every discourse pertain only to this indication, there especially where they may be silent about what is essential.

And what would still remain to say of beyng in this provisional sphere of preparation, if the few were here the ones who spoke together and through the demand for the highest discipline of knowledge-stimulated questioning? But who are these? How great must the solitude still become? Indeed this is no lamentation or complaint, but only the knowledge of a necessity. And even those would become co-questioners, if the most provisional indication of what is most question-worthy did not first have to roll away the all-obstructing burden

123   of the tradition at every step and thus expend itself in clearing up |
and purifying. Finally there would still be this to accomplish, if not at the end a perversion and a misinterpretation of the innermost volition did not overtake and corrode everything: the interpretation in terms of the "psychological," the impotence to get free of "lived experiences" and to endure Da-*sein*, and the inclination to reckon everything merely as "personal" accomplishment, or else as "personal" inability, and to dissolve everything in demonstrable dependencies on earlier "already" stated opinions. That is the most uncanny. On this basis, the being of work is withheld most pointedly, because most inconspicuously, from every work. If we still want to refind our way to

the truth of beyng, then everything depends on abandoning lived experience and leaping into Da-sein.

But however the unchecked falsification of everything spends itself, there yet remain, to the one who knows, the mature rest of the mountains, the concentrated illumination of the meadows, the silent flight of the falcon, the bright cloud in the immense sky—that wherein the great stillness of the remotest proximity of beyng has already announced itself.

The fountainhead at Stübenwasen   124

A pure streaming from the concealed
base of the mountain.

uniquely the task—

untroubled in misuse—
not heeding the misinterpretation
keeping equanimity in the face of ineffectiveness.

Distance from all bustle
no attempts at immediate help

remaining opaque; the mask.

July 5, 1936

{Index}

PONDERINGS V

Intimations

which carry on the intimation
of something given by way of intimation.

Compliant with the conjuncture of beyng,
we are at the disposal of the gods.

Meditation on the truth
of beyng is the first taking up
of the post of stewardship
for the stillness of the passing by
of the last god.

The last god—is not the end—but is instead the *other* beginning of the immeasurable possibilities of our history.

For the sake of that beginning, the previous history must not perish but must indeed be brought to its end; i.e., its transfiguration must be set into the transition and into preparedness.

The last god—the preparation of his appearance is the extreme venture of the truth of beyng; only in virtue of this truth can the retrieval of beings succeed for humanity.

In appertaining to the last god—the other beginning is to be carried out . . . (Cf. p. 30–31.)

The age in which all things and machinations are unproblematic has begun. The flood of "lived experience" is rising.

Philosophy—the interrogative calling up of the most question-worthy (beyng) is becoming the most alien.

And therefore philosophy is the most necessary, if the other beginning is to arrive.

The most powerful configuration of what is necessary amounts to simplicity.

Let us venture the preparation of the simplest question regarding what is most unique—i.e., regarding beyng.

Seen historically, in this way the overcoming of "metaphysics" commences in furtherance of the truth of beyng.

1

3

What is happening? The destruction of the earth—the reciprocal way-laying of peoples along with a bustling about that lacks a direction and a goal—*lacks the will* to a goal—for the self-preservation of a people can never be a goal but must always only be a *condition*. And it can be this only if the will to a goal—to the truth of beyng—is already the first and radiates as the originary obligation rather than being pursued as something fabricated. Nor can one ever say that the condition must be secured first so that the setting of the goal may follow—no; the struggle over the goal is the first, unavoidable struggle. Otherwise all endeavors regarding "culture," in themselves already late blooms, remain pure machinations and operations of our "lived experience"— "culture weeks," ones horridly and perhaps deliberately imitative of the "sales weeks" at department stores. The destruction of the earth in the guise of what is *gigantically* unprecedented from day to day and always new and in the guise of the running down of all resistance has disappeared—and with it any capacity for awe in face of that which is self-concealing.

2

4

Where do we stand? On the verge of extreme despair? Yes—but here (and here alone for the one who endures this site for a moment) is still the full light of the beacon of beyng, the light in which the last god is concealed.

5

Is Da-sein only a transient streak of lightning beyond the earth, into a world, out of that abyss which contends between world and earth—

or do the most secret earth and the most open world first become extant in the "there" of Da-sein—

or does neither the former hold nor the latter nor both, such that we never sufficiently know the truth of beyng and in our desire for a grounding float adrift like a shadowy dream—

or is this—such awe of the restrained inner turn to the essence of things—the most delicate aspect of Da-sein and the radiance of the intimation of the most remote proximity of beyng?

6

Where are the grounds of nobility, if not in the mature certainty of
3   the ability to be only what I our destiny is in each case?

7

If the towering white clouds mount into the broad heavens.

If the bleak days scare away all shining radiance, and if all breadth shrivels into the paltriness of narrow conventionality, then the heart must remain the source of what is light and spacious. And the most solitary heart makes the broadest leap into the middle of beyng, if on all sides the semblance of nonbeings stops its noise.

8

The other beginning is at first only the waking of the will to *questioning* and the resoluteness to traverse this stretch of questioning. If only the Germans could finally grasp that this most difficult struggle still *stands before* them as always and that for it not even the crudest weapons have been forged. But one will again pass over the memorials of the great questioners—I for one is in blissful possession of the "truth," and   4
questioning, as a dubious sign of weakness, can be kept away from one's soul and even more from one's person.

9

If only the *question* of truth, i.e., the *question* of the essence of what is true, could be kindled in a few, whose task, as poets, thinkers, makers, and doers, would be to draw the Germans out into the space wherein the truth is what is the most true.

If only even the remote impetus to this question could be effectuated in its first steps.

But it seems that there are only two camps: in the one, the many totter, those who firmly believe they are in full possession of truth and all that remains is to spread and consolidate this belief; in the other, the innumerable ones prowl about, those who sink in empty annoyance and uncreative bitterness and cling merely to the past.

Yet where are those few to whom the deepest plight of beings becomes a rejoicing over the originary | affiliation to beyng, because they   5
know that all origination must be excessive and that the excess of mutual belongingness in all beyng is the source of the supreme strife? (Cf. p. 106.)

Only if *this knowledge* becomes the work of the maker, the discourse of the thinker, and the word of the poet, can there once again appear a god who *requires* a people in order to ground beyng in the truth of beings.

And so there must be some few humans who reflect on this necessity and remain an impetus to meditation and do not take umbrage at any misinterpretation of the destination of their short path.

Only *that* people which originates in such necessity is a people. (Cf. p. 35.)

10

Great ages of history have never "had" "culture" nor indeed "made" it; instead, they stand silently under the necessities of a suffering creativity.

6   "Cultural politics," provided "culture" may at all count as a measure of historical Dasein, is a sign of unculture. "Cultural politics" is the last veiling of barbarity.

11

Why is there now lacking everywhere on earth a preparedness for the knowledge that we do *not* have the truth and must again *question*?

12

Remarkably distributed today are the *claim* to and the *participation* in the configuration of things—is this a sign that only machinations of gigantic proportions are forced up, whereby many useful items are produced, as are also such things that previously were not or at least could not be put into effect? But does this testify to a *creative* spirit?

13

Those who would draw near to what is *great* of work and sacrifice and deed must first grasp the *freedom* of all greatness, and that means I they

7   must surmise the *necessity* which shows itself only through an understanding of the most concealed *plight*. This plight, as suffering and pain, incites a transfiguration and prepares a fulfillment. (Cf. p. 17.)

14

Mother—my untainted memory of this pious woman—without bitterness, and in a surmising prescience, she countenanced the itinerary of a son who had *apparently* turned away from God.

15

The earliest ones, *toward* whom we are working, are those of the generation *after* the next. From them will arise the new futurity, because *they* will carry out for the first time the great creative *recollection* of our essential history. For these of the generation after the next—perhaps the future ones of the last god—in order to be able to make ready a few of the impulses, Da-sein is today still given its necessity.

16   8

The fiftieth anniversary of the "torpedo boat" is to be celebrated soon. What should then be done with the putative hundredth anniversary of Hölderlin's death, if even this anniversary will still have its entanglements and disaccords. Then will come soon the fiftieth anniversary of the "motorcycle"—what a transformation in the memory of people and of their "anniversaries." Yet these *must* indeed come, since all *power* of *recollection* has disappeared or been cut off and for a long time must in its stillness force the new roots into the concealment of beyng—where this power is not already dying.

17

Only *maturity* for the inconspicuous and self-withheld is strong enough to be struck by the essence of what is restrained therein. There is no maturity, however, without a scorching in the fires of pain.

18

To learn great joy in little things—is a genuine art of the | transfor-   9
mation of Da-sein.

19

Preparedness and expectation bear fruit more richly than does all fulfillment.

20

Revolutions.—Kant carried out his "Copernican" revolution in the interpretation of human experience and thus in the position of humans toward immediately available everyday beings. Henceforth knowledge no longer conformed to objects, but objects to knowledge. Here indeed insight into the essence of knowledge changed and so did the concept of object (it was now acquired for the first time). Nevertheless the idea of *conformity* was retained. To be sure, the revolution was not a mere reversal, but was an incorporation, of the previous ontological knowledge, into the essence of a more originally—transcendentally—understood *ego cogito:* Platonism incorporated into the essential structure of consciousness.

10   Nietzsche carried out a reversal of Platonism itself: the "true world" of the supersensible became a semblant world—yet one necessary for guaranteeing the continuance of *"life."* The "apparent" world of the senses became the "true" world as the actually effective, creative, self-surpassing world. Even this revolution had to be carried out as a transformation of the "sensuous" and the "true." Yet if this revolution finally—because right from the beginning—is in fact caught up in Platonism, in the opposition between "being" and "becoming," nevertheless, provided it is pursued into its essence, it possesses the power to compel meditation on whether or not the ground of Platonism itself and thereby also the original and not Platonically understood pre-Platonic philosophy are to be put in question.

Yet even more decisive than these changes carried out *within* the previous paths of thought is the change still impending before us and therefore to be prepared by us. This change goes against the entire elapsed history of philosophy, from the inceptual apprehension and gathering of beings as such (in νοῦς and λόγος—Parmenides—Hera-

11   clitus) I up to the incorporation of "beings," as that which is constant and fixed, into "life" qua becoming (will to power). *From the relation to beings*, despite its multiple configurations in the course of history, yet remaining ungrounded in the only possible ground (the truth of being), *to the questioning of being itself.* This revolution is carried out in the productive seeing and grounding of *Da-sein* qua happening of the truth of beyng.

This revolution is basically no longer a revolution but rather the transition to the completely other beginning, which, as the other, incorporates the first one—the ἀλήθεια τῆς φύσεως ["the truth of nature"]—originarily and does *not* disown it.

21

Philosophy in the other beginning—arises as something necessary out of the plight of the abandonment by being. Nietzsche experienced and recognized the most proximate form of this abandonment as nihilism. Yet in order to place the other beginning and its questions into the sharpest decision, we must still think out into the possibility that this beginning, despite its necessity, is only a veiling of the definitive

12   end of philosophy. For it is still not I decided, indeed not even once

asked, whether "philosophy" as well as "art" according to their *essence* have not come to an end with the present age. Their forms might still be "cultivated," and "culture" might be pursued as a means of politics, indeed for centuries to come—and yet no necessity need prevail here any longer. The reason is that cleverness in intermixing and imitating what was hitherto can, like everything else, increase to the gigantic, so that humans, becoming ever smaller, might nurse the opinion that here a creative greatness is in play whereas only a gigantic impotence has been let loose.

The state of the earth can be so transformed in the history to come that everything could merely turn into an untouched passing by of the congealed intimations of the dead gods.

But *if* this possibility of history exists—and many signs point in that direction—then it is more essential to know about this than to deceive oneself by pursuing illusions. Yet this knowledge has historical | power only if it arises out of a *necessity to question* which *nevertheless*   13 ventures the other beginning and its preparation. Assuming philosophy is at an end—assuming the asking of its original question remains denied to it in the sense that this questioning still needs to become a grounding of history—then philosophy cannot simply stop. Instead it must be brought *philosophically* to its end, an end that must be endured, even if broken up by the τόλμα of an other beginning.

22

Can someone become an *impetus* if the work takes him back from every immediate contact with commonality and places him on the side? *Only in that way* can he be this—in an age when everything—especially the ultimate—has dissolved into indiscriminate availability for everyone.

23

Have we already given enough thought to the circumstance that ever since Western philosophy in its deepest meditations surmised its unrolling to | an end, something worthy of wonder occurred, namely,   14 that those who created and suffered this meditation and thus already bore in their knowledge what is completely other—and did so in very different ways and in different spaces—Schiller, Hölderlin, Kierkegaard, Van Gogh, Nietzsche—were torn too early from a lucid existence? Did they merely break apart, as an extrinsic calculation might perhaps determine, or was a new song sung to them, one that could never endure an "and so forth," but instead required as a sacrifice the shortest path?

Where and how do we preserve the open and never-dying fire of the most concealed intimacy?

A grey-white cloud puff is dissipating into the blue sky of a windy summer day on solitary mountains.

24

One who abides in thoughtful meditation is never tempted to make philosophy "practical," because the task of thinking is indeed to make
15 "praxis" philosophical. But how does the I address on "the self-assertion of the German university" stand in that regard? It is not inconsistent with it, for, despite what many believed, the address did not seek to apply "my" philosophy to the "university" and its configuration, but instead sought the reverse, to bring the university to a meditation from the course and in the course of *its* tasks.

Nevertheless, the address and its attitude were a mistake: the university does not *want* to meditate and can no longer want to, not because someone or other has forbidden it to meditate—but because modern science has reached that stage in its technologization whereby "progress" would be impeded by meditation. And what would this "science" still be, if it could no longer make progress?

25

A "philosophy" that openly or covertly seeks validity with respect to politics and significance with respect to "worldview" is merely *calling* itself "philosophy" and remains abyssally separated from what this name conceals more than reveals.

16
26

Only one who has suffered the abandonment by being out of the depths and, in unity with that, has surmised beyng out of the corresponding heights and as so surmising has gone along actual steps of Nietzsche's path—only such a one may transmit Nietzsche to the future. The greatest impediment to understanding is thereby perhaps the task of getting over (without degrading Nietzsche's genuine volition) the almost devilish wasteland which thrust itself forward as what was contemporary in Nietzsche's itinerary and deformed the essential aspect of it. Where a crude "biologism" seems to dominate the words and thoughts, something other than the essential presses itself into the open—but that other is easier to grasp and so supplants the essential. Presumably, however, this relation—merely in different ways—holds for every philosophy, such that the traditional "image" of the history of philosophy is almost completely ruled by superficiality—and only a few know of the concealed history of thinking.

27

The summer day with the great high clouds, in the expansive background of a space that is becoming more blue, over the first regreening of the alpine meadows after | the July haymaking, within which   17
are strewn in broad arcs—like the simplest thoughts—the country houses with their wide and low roofs in the noblest illumination of their silvery restraint.

28

Arbitrariness is slavery to the accidental.

29

Times may arrive in which the plight that makes creativity necessary must be explicitly *expressed*. If the immediacy of a work is still to remain here, then this immediacy is a *higher* one, to be accomplished only through an excessively great creative power.

30

Thinking in the other beginning, thinking which in questioning seeks the founding of the truth of beyng—does this thinking want the *impossible*? Yet what would in truth become of beings if *this* volition were no more? To want the possible—is that still a *wanting*? Yet for us volition means knowledge and thus means the withstanding of the thrown affiliation to beyng itself, beyng which needs us in that it consumes us.

This needing and consuming happen outside the small measures   18
by which goals and purposes are posited and appraised and uses are calculated.

In the happening meant here, we—those to whom it is granted—are appropriated by beyng. Therefore, the sacrificing of those great ones is never a passing away into nonbeings but rather is an appropriation to being itself and thus is being itself. (Event)

31

On the other hand, all "wanting" which—to all appearances very "rationally"—"wants" only the "possible" will always be sure and safeguarded. It will avoid the appropriation—and thus avoid beyng. Nevertheless, it will always seem to attain what is "properly actual" about anything.

Such volition and activity are even necessary—so that the *plight* of the sacrifice might become possible. Yet all straightforward and conventional activity is meant to know nothing of this necessity; instead, it must be able to enjoy its supposedly freely chosen preparedness and accomplishment in its assigned domain. The consuming fire of questioning must remain foreign to it.

Matters are different, however, with:

19   Those wretched squalling ones who see "nihilism" in any actual *questioning* that casts us out of an illusory certainty and who take this "nihilism" as overcome by their supposed "nearness to life." These cannot be helped, because their "healthy certainty" consists precisely in the fact that they do *not want* clarity and yet claim to go beyond the immediately active ones and be philosophers, or at least they claim to deserve that name. Anyone who questions needs to know that and why such illusory forms are indispensable and find their "public" or else are surviving more covertly. But those who question must *never* allow themselves to be led astray into starting or carrying on a confrontation with such a pseudo; for thereby they would already admit to being attacked, whereas they are only—at most—spit at. They would have to lower themselves to a "level" they must never occupy, assuming their mission—although surrounded by great darkness—is sure.

32

20   Need to accomplish the few essential things necessary for the | time meted out. Can creative humans once again turn to the simplicity of what is necessary and endure in that simplicity?

33

Would that a thoughtful grounding again became a sort of compilation of dicta, well protected against idle talk and unharmed by all hurried misinterpretation; would that the opera omnia of twenty or more volumes along with the concomitant snooping into the author's life and the gathering of his casual utterances (I mean the usual "biographies" and collections of correspondence) would disappear, and the work itself be strong enough and be kept free of the disfavor of being explained through a bringing in of the "personal," i.e., kept from being dissolved into generalities.

What transformation of humanity would this presuppose? The uncanniness is not so much that humans are perhaps no longer capable of accomplishing this transformation, but rather that they no longer want to accomplish it, that they might remain unaffected even where impulses could perhaps still strike them, instead of opening themselves precisely there for what is other—still not endured by them—which of course cannot be where one *still* more comfortably I boasts of a possession and irreverently calculates everything according to conformity or nonconformity with that possession—(I mean "Christians" and their "Christianity"—insofar as these keep "cultural activity" in motion).

21

34

The great ossification.—For a long time the struggle over true meditations has been cut off—even more: *anxiety in the face of meditation*, although unnoticed by most, rules the drifting and the getting by from one thing to the next. And out of this there then arises that arbitrary judgment which has never striven for measures, but instead has always merely taken refuge in the conventional measures. What does it signify that young persons now judge Rilke's work and find that he alienates himself from the "community of the people" and has become an "individualist"?

What does it signify that those who are overflowing with "Christian humility" raise self-righteousness beyond all limits and explain—as if they had privileged knowledge—Nietzsche's madness as an instance of the Christian God punishing and I striking down the arrogant?

22

What does it mean if the two main groups of our people as regards worldview, namely, those who "think" in terms of "politics" and those who "think" in terms of "Christianity," take each other to "court" over the most genuine sources of our future history? And if in between these groups the indifferent ones and the perplexed still pay homage to some sort of denial? And if some still cling to an earlier belief? And if, in all this, there is often still much good will and even a capacity to be effective, allowing one to say that the accomplishment here was "not bad"? Is this not indeed, on account of a still extant "respectability," precisely a constriction of domains and a flowing away of the great decisions? Humans are becoming ever smaller.

35

It seems that Hölderlin's words about the Germans at the conclusion of "Hyperion" are *definitive*.[1]

What lies therein? That the Germans remain the ones who make ready the hardest suffering for the greatness of the creators and so— ever again provide an | *essential* condition of fate. And also that "misfortune" and doom would result if this people were one day drawn into a mediocrity that knew everything because it diminished everything. The greatest danger is not barbarity and decay, for these states can be driven out into something external and so can drive a plight to the foreground. The greatest danger is mediocrity and the uniform disposal of everything—whether in the form of the emptiest activity or in the mode of respectable—although no longer compelled by anything—conventionality.

Thought more deeply, Hölderlin's words are not an accusation, or even a reproach, in the usual sense; instead, they name that which reverts and cannot be averted.

Whoever has at any time thought all the way back to these necessities and from them has drawn essential knowledge will remain secure against the danger of falling into a fruitless reproach over contrary states and contingencies. Censure can always only lead to a sharpening of the necessity to affirm the | contrary. And that means: to lead to a holding open of the question of the ground of the opposition and from that to a holding open of the impulses toward creativity. (Cf. p. 111.)

36

Why are humans becoming ever smaller? Because they are denied an arena for growing into greatness and because the grounding of this arena is thwarted. And what is this arena? That which we call Da-sein, that site at which the avoidable is preserved in diffidence and thus is unfolded into freedom on the paths of creativity. And where are the signs of that thwarting? The clearest is *anxiety* in the face of questioning accompanied by a simultaneous suspicion of all "anxiety." And the most dreadful sign is *impatience*, the avoidance of the vocation to be a transition.

Instead of this, where once the name "philosophy" could still have been spoken, there are now a hollow presumptuousness and a noisy

---

1. {Friedrich Hölderlin, *Sämtliche Werke*, vol. 2, *Gedichte-Hyperion-Briefe*. (Berlin: Propyläen, 1923), 282ff.}

superficiality in alliance, and these draw everything into the turbid and arbitrary.

37

That we long ago entered a *completely unquestioning* age is testified less | by those many who *explicitly reject* questioning than by those who allegedly "possess" an irrefutable (i.e., "Christian") "truth" and in addition *act* as if they were questioning in that they can never speak enough about "venture" and "decision." They are the actual seducers of the age, since they are unwilling to let the age be what it is. And these seducers are properly the ones who do *not* question, because they brandish the *illusion* of "wrestling" with the truth.

38

An essential distinction concerns whether humans come to stand before God creatively or whether they merely account "religion" an institution useful for their own ends.

39

In *Being and Time* and everywhere in my thinking, *history* means the prehistoriological and the superhistoriological. History has its ground in Da-*sein*. But because for us today "life" has long been overgrown by all sorts | of apparently "natural" needs and drives, none of which were ever originary, neither can we entrust ourselves to this natural "life" and its currents, nor should we sink into mere dissolution and doubt. Instead, we must—on the basis of the highest volition toward beyng, i.e., in questioning—push forward into the extreme plight of the essential decisions, i.e., into an admission that we do not possess the truth.

The repelling of historiological erudition, i.e., historiological comparison and calculation, is necessary because historiology makes creativity lame and blind. But let us not fool ourselves: this mere repelling still does not guarantee the freedom of the power to create, for such power can in the meantime be distorted or even obstructed through that all too calculative "configuring" of "history"—i.e., through "historicism"—so that what seems to come to us immediately and straightforwardly still does not come from the origin. Therefore, the repulsion of the "historiological" (cf. the "dismantling" in *Being and Time*) is essential only if it is borne and guided by an active meditation. And in terms of essential thinking, that means: only if | the basic position of humans in the midst of beings as a whole is brought to decision, i.e., only if we ask the question of the truth of beyng and in this questioning recognize *that the human being must become the preserver of the truth of beyng* and that the uniqueness of beyng requires the uniqueness of those few who creatively recreate truth in beings. Thereby they illuminate those beings for the first time and bring to them articulation and form—by placing this form into a work or by merely uncovering it anew in creative recognition.

40

Philosophy as thoughtful meditation on the truth of beyng has the single task of creating in advance for the few, i.e., for the creators, the field of knowledge and of a grounding discourse. On these things, namely, one's grasp of this essence of philosophy and one's making oneself necessary as equal to it and not to be turned aside from it— on these is codecided one's affiliation to the few. This affiliation is never something one merely chooses and procures for oneself; instead,

28 | it is in every case laid on one's shoulders as a great burden.

41

Thoughtful meditation on the truth of beyng is *primarily* the grounding of *Da-sein* qua the ground of future history.

Da-*sein* as the contention of the strife between world and earth. This contention, however, is different according to the way the strife itself unfolds as appertaining to the openness for what is self-concealing and the way the "there" is endured as the abyss.

Da-sein must remain alien to all who "live" on the basis of what was hitherto and who continue on in that way.

42

The *"history" of philosophy*—only the creative thinker knows of it, but never does the "historiologist." So that the thinking of beyng may smoothly take its course for a long time to come, there must be *impulses* toward a *displacement* onto the other, at once higher and deeper, course. But how could a person endure both together: undergo this

29 impulse and transmit it for the others | and simultaneously be content to proceed along the already opened and common course itself?

A simple either- or is at issue here:

either the *sacrifice* of the undergoing of the impulses and the sacrifice of the reticent configuration of that undergoing, in that apparently it is always only what was earlier that is spoken of, although the complete otherness of the second beginning is thought—

or the *gift* of immediately proceeding on the indicated course.

Each of these has its own greatness and its own smallness. And all who here stand under these provisions must know they have no choice, but rather the distinction, to belong to their respective ineluctable course and remain faithful to it.

43

We never grasp the *inceptual*; in order not to become something present at hand and thereby forfeit itself, the inceptual must constantly withdraw. Therefore, the beginning can never present itself; it can only be carried out, namely, in the downgoing of recession, such that the withdrawal truly *remains* a withdrawal.

(Cf. lecture on the work of art[2] and w.s. 37–8, p. 12.[3])

44   30

Who is the future human being (cf. p. 34, 47), assuming he would still ground a history? Answer: the steward of the stillness of the passing by of the last god—the grounding preserver of the truth of beyng.

But where and how are these stewards of the stillness to come forth? Can we "breed" them? No! The steward must be able to remain awake and also be the most watchful and the most alert. Stewardship for this stillness, however, is not a mere state in a present-at-hand human being; instead, the stewardship of the truth of being requires a transformation of humanity such that humans in their highest possibilities become nothing less than the grounding of truth, and this grounding happens as Da-sein.

In addition, the concealed relation to beyng itself already belongs to the essence of this transformation—; the attack of beyng must strike deep into Da-sein. Therefore, the coming forth of the stewards depends on a preparation, perhaps a very long one, whose goals will be largely misunderstood. This preparation must think in advance both beyng and Da-sein | in their reciprocal relation and so attain the place   31

---

2. {Martin Heidegger, "Der Ursprung des Kunstwerkes," in *Holzwege, Gesamtausgabe* (GA)5, 2nd ed. (Frankfurt: Klostermann, 2003), 1–74; Heidegger, "Vom Ursprung des Kunstwerkes: Erste Ausarbeitung," in *Heidegger Studies* 5 (1989), 5–22.}

3. {Heidegger, Grundfragen der Philosophie: Ausgewählte "Probleme" der "Logik," GA45 (Frankfurt: Klostermann, 1984), 39ff.}

of stillness, the place the creative ones occupy in work and deed and thus first configure into the free domain. Mere breeding of human exemplars with such and such qualities would be a mistake, indeed *the* mistake pure and simple, because *the grounding of the relation of the human being, on the basis of his ground, to the truth of beyng* must indeed be and remain what is first, to which all education is subservient.

45

Will those *stronger* ones arrive, those who in advance thoughtfully master the mystery of beyng itself *in such a way* that future humans may find their center therein? We transitional ones must still bear all too acutely the often empty burden of the past and discover *in it* a concealed weight, because the *mere casting off* of the tradition only seduces those who are unprepared into taking their contingent present for the eternal, whereas this present might perhaps only be a very weak offshoot of an unmastered past. Yet what is that sought-after center but the *between* in which the discord of the god and of confusedness stand in and against each other?

32

46

Even essential thinking, especially essential thinking, requires long *experience*; and if such thinking has become ever more essential thereby, then the power and certainty of the originary presentiment have also developed for the first time. This experience, however, is concerned not with immediate everyday things, but only with what is to be thought in such thinking: the truth of beyng. The history of this truth—which is never graspable historiologically—must be traversed in all its hidden paths. Therefore, what is essential in philosophy remains closed off to mere "shrewdness." The history of the truth of beyng refers to the way humans undertake an openness for what is self-concealing—withdraw from this openness and cling to something pregiven—or merely posit themselves on themselves as beings and more or less expand these into society, a people, and the like, in order to dispose from these and back to these all other beings. In this last-named way, humans withdraw *completely* from beyng, believing they already have "beings"—"actuality" and "life"—firmly in hand, underfoot, and on their lips. So situated, humans are most safe

33   from the fact that I a god is assailing them or withdrawing from them; they are even safe from the knowledge of their exclusion from the first decision, the one they must make in order to arrive at the place of possible greatness and of the *necessary* creativity surpassing all usefulness.

47

It is in the history of the truth of beyng that the battle—but also the absence of battling—among *mankind, beyng*, and the gods is carried out. According to the status of this *battle*, world and earth lie in *strife*; and according to the type of this strife, beings as a whole are opened, available, subdued, revered, or repudiated. The extreme repudiation, however, announces itself where apparently the opposite takes place, i.e., where nearness to "life" is installed as the "principle" of humanity and the sheer preservation of this "life" is postulated as the highest goal.

The site of the just-named battle, however, is never present at hand; instead, it is always something to be attained through battle and to be grounded in battle.

48

34

We must learn that beyng as the ground of beings cannot be founded on them or acquired from them and that nevertheless just as little can mere volition compel "beyng"—or its truth. That would require what is deepest: resoluteness (preparedness), which is at the same time regrowth into that which bears thrownness.

Beyng is neither the ἰδέα—nor the ostensible opposite of the ἰδέα, "life"—but instead??? We know only this: we are entering the historical moment in which for the first time the truth of beyng is becoming a—indeed *the*—plight as well as the origin of a wholly other necessity—and this moment requires of us the preparedness for its preparation—and this preparedness requires of us an essential transformation—of the human being into Da-sein—a new responsibility—not a reply to the question of who we are. (Cf. above, p. 30.)

But we revere all this preparing silently as the intimation of beyng itself, an intimation that needs the human being.

49

35

People—meditation on ourselves and on our history stands today in the twilight of this name. If we for once put aside all the insidious equivocity of the term, which conditions not only the inaccuracy of speech but also the great variegation in attitudes and procedures, then we must give thought to the following:

with masses of 65 million, does not even the number, as the number of a possible configured class, already set a *limit*? Such that a people with this quantity of members is impossible? Or with *this* scale of number must there not be a corresponding unusualness in that which first allows the "people" to be a people—namely, the *surpassing* into the truth of beyng, the truth that bears and develops a people. Here—with such a quantity that is almost countless for purposes of configuration—must not the surpassing have an *excess*—; and, so that this *excess* can be measured and standardized, must not the number of the creative ones be small rather than great—in the uniqueness of what is most unique? (Cf. p. 52.)

But how are precisely these countless ones, brought to "themselves"
36 | with their claims and measures, supposed to be led not only to recognize those most unique ones as the most futural ones, but also help prepare them? If we do not wish to withdraw from the essential decisions, then what is required is meditation of the basic conditions of being a people—but *this* meditation is indeed only *one* of those radiating out from the still more originary meditation on the ground and truth of Western Dasein.

One must of course not fall into the basic illusion—that everyone's easily possible insight into the biological condition for the breeding of a "people" could touch what is essential—whereas the predominance of this naturally crude and common biological way of thinking precisely suppresses meditation on the basic conditions of being a people.—The knowledge and indeed creation of these conditions require an *excess* of the *surpassing* of a people by itself, the liberation from all calculation of either particular or common usefulness. As preeminently necessary as this requirement is, so little does it touch upon the necessities of the proper Dasein of a people—necessities which are
37   also not grasped by a mere appeal | to the Christian Churches, but are thereby only distorted.

Decisive is whether these masses that are not a people—especially under hard external compulsion—undergo a transition to the *basic disposition* which is to dispose differently (according to the respective groups and classes) ones who grow on the basis of respect and will into a preparedness for the surpassing of the everyday—; the surpassing proceeds neither to the other side, nor does it remain on this side—but it does indeed open the entrance into the truth of beyng—beyng as the event—in which the advent or absence of the last god is decided. This decision will be a long history and so will shake a people back into its grounds and abysses.

Everyone must experience and undergo this plight undisguisedly and must make it experienceable to all the others there with him. The acknowledgment of this plight of the abandonment by being is the first liberation, for it is already a coming into the proximity of the extreme remoteness of that which saves; yet this saving does not mean taking aside and comforting—but rather *appropriation* into the re-creative restoration of beings.

And how long must the patience be, in order to effectuate the excess of awe in the face of beyng amid the unbound frenzy of the mere furnishing of beings for external resources.   38

How false is that reckoning which first of all strives to secure the external resource in order then—perhaps—to retrieve the other.

Whereas the attaining through struggle and the grounding of the truth of being are solely essential, even if "only" to give the downgoing its greatness.

50

The *deepest ground* of today's Occidentally determined global state of the goalless, self-entangled, relentless, avidly progressive "mobilization" of present-at-hand things, as well as the ground of the insertion of all the being of humanity into that "mobilization"—is the *abandonment by being*, inattentiveness to the truth of beyng. Yet this is prefigured in the first beginning, which had to raise beings as such into experience (knowledge and configuration) for the first time.

As a consequence of this attitude, "cultures" arise, and after the disintegration of "cultures," "cultural politics" arises in reckoning with that "mobilization."

51   39

The poet—Hölderlin—stands here in solitude, and he is driven even further back into his solitude if he is now made to be timely "in the course" of "cultural politics"—without our meditating on what it is *poets* are to accomplish—; the aspect of Hölderlin's works that is richest in suggestion is therefore: the poetizing about the poet. But who could fathom this without at the same time radically experiencing the plight of the abandonment by being?

What will happen if out of this deepest ground we do not become ones who ground the overcoming of the ground? If we do not become open and trusting enough to accomplish both: this that is most originary *and* the first step in the mastery of the immediate afflictions?

52

How long already has philosophy lacked the first asking of an essential question which in its uniqueness could ground a new history of thinking? Everything is merely the rectifying of the one already in-

ceptual answer accompanied by increasing forgetfulness of the sup-
porting question.

40   53

Why can no thing any longer rest in itself and in its essence? Why
must everything be inflated and falsified or at least explained as a
"factor of culture"? What is going on here? The *avoidance* of the dead
weight of the essence of things, the *avoidance* of the necessity of becoming a slave to that essence instead of numbing oneself in machinations.

How few know the extent of the destruction of the earth today and
the sort of confusion lurking behind what seem to be surely guided
achievements of "technology"?

Once again—what kind of excess in the surpassing of beings is required in order to subdue the machinations and their unbounded
numbing power and to incorporate them into the truth of beyng?

                                       54

Contemporary humans are convinced that dashing along in machination (machination which is intrinsically and necessarily *incapable*
of setting goals) would be strength and power and the mastery of
41   "life." How little can they know of the fact that a traversal of I even
the shortest course of a downgoing requires an *essentially higher* and
even a *creative* power—because a downgoing can be endured only on
the basis of decisiveness toward the mystery of being itself, i.e., on the
basis of restraint and diffidence toward the essence of beyng.

How is intimation of the god supposed to come to us as waiting
ones, if we idolize the antidivine? Yet how are the waiting ones supposed to cease such activity unless a god appears? Both—the god
and the confusedness—must break forth and appear—and for *that* to
happen the field of *such* appearance must have previously acquired a
unique breadth and depth of openness—i.e., *the truth of beyng* must
be experienced and the preparedness for that truth awakened. We
must enter into the unique plight of that *between* for the god and the
confusedness—indeed must first open up the plight and ground it.
Thereby we are assigned the most difficult task that was ever to be accomplished in human history.

42   This "between," however, is truth as the essential occurrence I of
beyng, beyng understood as the event.

For if we speak of the surpassing of beings, that smacks of "transcendence," which presupposes an experience of beings as present at

hand, whereby the "transcendent" means the consequent "divine" being.

But the surpassing of beings actually means the leap into the truth of beyng. This truth so little *is* a god, or even only vouches for a god, that precisely the essential occurrence of beyng must become and must long remain the site of the decision regarding the absence or advent of gods. Surpassing means getting over the entrenched humanity which, without exposure to an essential transformation, tailors its goals to its own measurements. That happens where, precisely where, one speaks all too loudly of "devotion," i.e., where this remains merely a timely assurance of a definitive certainty.

55

By what do we most easily recognize today's confusion in "thinking" and impotence for questioning? By the fact that everyone is prowling around in inconsistency | and making a game of it: 43

The crudest Platonism ("Ideas," values) is commonly taught, and at the same time so are "lived experience" and "existence," enlivened and made appropriate to the times by the use of expressions—if not the actual thoughts—of Nietzsche. Yet Nietzsche was precisely the adversary of all Platonism. Perhaps such a mixed "thinking" is excusable, however, since Nietzsche himself did not attain an overcoming of Platonism. But then this would have to be known—and also the precise respect in which his battle was not a victory and why not. And knowing that requires grasping why Nietzsche himself still belongs within the history of Platonism—namely, because he did not go beyond the guiding question of beings, which had long been customary, and arrive at the basic question. If those who want to renounce all philosophy attempted to do so, but not with the help of a groundless pseudophilosophy, then they would indeed have to be called the more honest ones in comparison with the inflated pretenders to a "politically" irreproachable "philosophy." In that way, however, both groups belong together. Today, and already long ago, every step of thinking | 44
is endangered above all from lacking the proper space and atmosphere; therefore, every genuine questioning must be clear about the situation of philosophy, without falling into the error of letting such activity count as the opponent in a confrontation.

56

The Germans are *still seeking* for their goal.—Do they actually still seek for it? How so, for if they had truly *sought*, they would have found it, since their goal is the seeking itself. But only one who calculates and chases after usefulness could believe that thereby infinite goallessness is made the goal. What if seeking were the *most constant* sojourning in the proximity of what is self-concealing, out of which every plight falls to us and every jubilation excites us? What if finally we succeeded in *this* constancy, and it was never again *dissolved* through the apparently *affirmative* attitude of engagement, even if the engagement is for the most part genuinely intended?

Where is the speaker or sculptor who first gives this to the Germans as the innermost law for the integration of their Dasein? When will there come forth the | thinker who will raise into grounded knowledge, and incorporate into the simple word, the truth of beyng, i.e., of the beyng that needs us qua seeking ones? Only those to come create the future, and their greatness will be to remain the *future ones*.

Seeking as goal—to be sure, seeking in the highest sense, the seeking of the truth of beyng. In that way, however, humans make the goal not themselves but rather that basic disposition of their essence as Da-sein, a disposition which indeed brings them to *themselves* and in this selfhood brings them precisely to the "between" for the confusedness and the god.

But why must humans have a *goal*? Where is the ground of the necessity to posit goals? In the fact that humans are basically *seekers*? Can that count as an answer?

Yes—for here the *turning* announces itself—such that humans, if they *are* actually and steadfastly seekers, appertain to the turning, which means they are appropriated by the *event* as the essential occurrence of beyng itself. Yet here we surmise that even "goals" and "having goals" are *not* the highest and never are the highest, but are always only foreground—to be sure they are this | in the more originary sense in which the foreground has become the abyss [*Abgrund*] of the "between." In the center of this "between" is concealed and thus "appears" that which we call the intimation of the god and the thrust of the confusion. And this could never be degraded to a goal. The goal is precisely—in the deepest and broadest sense—to find and endure the site of the moment of goallessness—the moment of that which is the most concealed and incalculable in its ineluctability.

That *turning in the grounding of goals* (cf. p. 55) can be grasped concisely as follows: because humans are seekers (cf. p. 30), goals are necessary. Because the necessity of goals exists, *seeking* is the highest goal. This is a remarkable train of thinking and is alien to anyone who thinks only in words without thereby carrying out the leap into the essential occurrence of beyng—i.e., into the turning of the (event), in order to realize ever anew that beyng needs the Da-sein of humans and that *therefore* the truth of beyng is precisely *not* a human fabrication. In this "not" can be found the counterstroke to the turning and at the same time the intimation that here neither calculative | think-   47 ing nor the "dialectic" of concepts can accomplish anything. The former cannot, because it altogether moves only amid "beings" as present-at-hand things. The latter cannot, because it is concerned only with producing the *unity* of the contradictory as a represented and representable unity—i.e., concerned only with truth as "idea" and not as appropriated openness for what is self-concealing.

57

Where is there still any greatness? In the simplicity of the essential out of the power of binding transfiguration? I still see only the gigantic, and that is never the small—which indeed can always maintain a relation to greatness whereas the gigantic destroys every possibility of greatness in that it itself intends to be the great. (Cf. p. 106.)

What can still become of a human throng whose eyes must be blind to the chasm between the great and the gigantic? And what are seers supposed to accomplish, if exaggeration drags everything down into the indiscriminate, wherein the gigantic and the dwarfish are equally empty? Where can that which is flat ever | bestow the dimensions of   48 a space in which transfiguring exaltation and denying downfall are the directional poles of decision?

58

Great corruptors of the spirit are lacking—all the more numerous are the mediocre ones. The most serious and especially the most clever example of these latter is the theologian Guardini.[4] He traverses all the possibilities of the spirit in the great forms of the poets and thinkers, is never trivial and never crudely Catholic—always in tune with the modern "wrestling" with the truth and availing himself of all the means of contemporary thought and discourse. *But nowhere does he venture an essential question* or even attain a question not previously posed—; he merely serves up anew the already secure stock of answers for those who wish to flee all questioning. This even seems to be "creative" in the eyes of the average intellectually lazy person, and yet everything is only a very clever imitation of what the Church Fathers and apologists of the first Christian century already "practiced"

---

4. {Romano Guardini (1885–1968) taught the "Catholic worldview" in the 1920s at the Universität Breslau and at the Friedrich-Wilhelms-Universität Berlin. In 1939 he was forced to retire. He published, among other works, books on Hölderlin (1939) and Rilke (1941).}

in their own way. The current "spiritual life" is so lacking in direction
49   and measure I that it not only finds such pen-pushing satisfactory but
even considers it something superior in comparison to what preceded.

59

Hölderlin—if only we could completely remove him from the present
day so as to assess and save the *fragmentary* character of his essential
work. To experience his work *in this way* as a fragment requires the
highest power, for this experience does not mean calculating and establishing what is unfinished and interrupted and thus is "negative."
On the contrary, we mean fragments [*Bruch-stücke*, literally "pieces
broken off"] in the sense of the *breaking in* of the extreme impulses
and endeavors within a completely new realm—one still not at all
surmised in the West—and the *breaking open* of this realm in accord
with essential domains, and the first *breaking forth* of its essential configurations. That is not something unfinished—instead, it is the highest which can be attained in the depths of the creation of the truth of
beyng. Pieces of the break, of the *breaking up* of the great ossification
and lostness, and this in the apparently impotent *word*. What a re-
learning is necessary here in order to liberate the work of the poet to
50   its most concealed truth. I What a repudiation of everything hitherto
and everything supposedly certain. What a renunciation of compari-
sons (difficult only to stop) and of forms of comparison with other poets. What a power to surmise the breaking forth of the most futural
ones precisely amid those who are necessarily contemporaries. What
a will to bring the sources of the highest riches to gush from what is
apparently negligible about his work.

60

If the unavoidable other beginning is to be reached in *philosophy*, then
thoughtful questioning must venture and abide the hardest confrontation with what is simplest. Today's easily-carried-out discussion of
the apparent riches of a comprehensive "philosophy of culture" is
merely a veiling over of the impotence for questioning. Yet what sort
of education should we facilitate in order to make the generation after
the next at least equipped for the simplicity of the great questions, for
the protracted courage to endure therein and surmount all idleness,
for the seriousness of the word in order to make even the smallest step
51   of thinking self-responsible once again, I and for the *correct* hearing of
one another, which is alien to all rashness and pedantry. On behalf
of the education of these thinkers we must now begin unobtrusively,

and my teaching activity strives for nothing other than the unobtrusiveness of steering toward what is simple and constant.

Those who want to prepare here—they need to know that individual impulses perhaps become effective at first on long byways and then as no longer recognizable in their origin. But what if the compiling of previous opinions in all domains of teaching increases, the cleverness of this empty amassing expands, and at the same time the certainty of the gaze at the hollowness and uprootedness of this activity declines? Even then, and a fortiori then, there must be those who become slaves to the inexhaustibility of what is simple.

And what is the simplest, that which allows no complication or confusion? It is this, namely, *that the essence of beyng needs humans*. In questioning this relation, the essential occurrence of beyng is determined for the first time as I the event and the human being is determined as Da-sein. 　52

But we unfold the simple in its most proper riches when we are able to say the essence of the simple ever more simply. The most disastrous and always easily intrusive semblance of the simple is the *empty*. The insidious inducement to avoid the simple is the seemingly genuine demand to "allow for" diversity.

The simplicity of that relation between beyng and Dasein—the relation which is the essential occurrence of beyng itself as event—comprises the *highest excess* of the surpassing of all mere "beings" by way of a reascent to the site of the moment of decision concerning the gods. (Cf. p. 35.)

61

As soon as a *philosophy* has reached the question of the essential occurrence of beyng—and only then will it be justified in bearing this name—it must necessarily think counter to its own epoch. The one thing philosophy is *not*, and never can be, is the "expression" of its epoch grasped in thoughts.

But that necessary opposition to its times must also never become 　53 the refuge of those who adhere to their times only as bygone and hitherto and are confused and lame with respect to the willing of a configuration of the future because they saddle this willing with the burden of a now uncreative tradition as the standard.

That opposition of philosophy to its times does not arise from any sort of deficiencies or defects in the epoch, but instead derives from the essence of philosophy and does so all the more necessarily the more precisely and genuinely the willing of the future acquires form and direction in the times. For, always, but especially then and indeed

by essence, the productive thinking of the truth *of beyng* leaps *ahead*
of all instituting, preserving, and restoring of *beings*—ahead of all immediate creation and work. Therefore, philosophy—assuming it actually is such—can also never be appraised "politically," neither in an
affirmative or negative direction. A "National Socialist" philosophy is
neither a "philosophy" nor a service to "National Socialism"—but in-
54   stead simply runs behind it as burdensome | pedantry—an attitude
which is already sufficient to demonstrate its incapacity for actual philosophy.

   To say a philosophy is "National Socialist," or is not so, means the
same as to say a triangle is courageous, or is not so—and therefore is
cowardly.

62

Every *transitional thinker*, i.e., one who carries out the transition, necessarily stands in the twilight of the ambiguity proper to him. Everything appears referable to the past and attainable out of the past, and
at the same moment everything is a repulsion of the past and an arbitrary positing of something to come, from which the future seems
to be lacking. Such a thinker cannot be "lodged" anywhere—but this
homelessness is his ungrasped indigenousness in the concealed history of beyng.

63

Nietzsche's *Thus Spoke Zarathustra* an outcry, perhaps the cry—for the
stillness of beyng? And the latter—since a transition is underway
55   here—a unique arching bridge whose piers remain invisible, such
that the swing of the arch traces its path with ever more verve.

64

Thinking in the other beginning is not the setting of a goal as the rep-
resenting of an "idea"—but is the *grounding of a goal* as the leap into the
ground of the necessity of seeking. This abyssal ground is beyng itself
which appropriates *to itself* the stewardship of Da-sein and so appropriates the human being as the seeker of beyng. (Cf. p. 46.) Goal-ground-
ing is the positing *of what is found* in the sense of taking it over. Here
the goal does not stand before and over humans as the "ideal," but
stands behind and under them as the grounding ground and something already carried out. (Cf. p. 65.)

65

Great epochs of creativity have never pursued "cultural politics," nor have they formed a "worldview" from meditation on "heritage" and certainly not from meditation on racial foundations. All that is only a "subjectivism" pursued into massiveness, I the last offshoot of the   56
cogito ergo sum ["I am thinking, therefore I am"], a bad veiling of creative impotence, and it is—and this remains all that is essential, since it grasps into the future—especially a *neglecting* and *undermining* of every possibility of great decisions concerning whether we can still grasp truth in its essence and whether the relation to beyng can still become our plight.

66

The longer I carry out my work, whether badly or well, here in my adopted homeland, all the more clearly do I see that I do *not* belong, and *cannot* belong, to Alemannia as it is behaving convulsively and barrenly here on the upper Rhine. My homeland, the village and farmstead of my mother—the breezes of Hölderlin waft over it all, and his springs stream through it; it possesses the hardness, incisibility, and abyssal character of the Hegelian concept; it is permeated by that "speculative" drive of Schelling which ventures far in advance; and it has nothing of the lying bluster which rages over I the land here and   57
is concerned with making noise. It is then just like the native "Alemanns" to fancy themselves the genuine ones and dissociate themselves from the "Swabians."

But—over and above all distribution into belonging to a line of descent and a class—what alone is decisive is *how* one does belong, i.e., whether one merely gives "expression" to the common and familiar qualities of the line of descent or rather, through one's course of life and achievements, sets forth undeveloped tasks and new possibilities. All of this makes otiose the talk—even rational talk—about belonging to a line of descent.

67

Our epoch, in accord with its smallness and accompanying self-inflation, believes that through dogmatic "reflection" on the past and on "biological" foundations it can posit the beginning of something already antiquated even in its idea—the beginning of a "culture"—instead of actually venturing into the future and posing the actual decisions—i.e., taking the Godlessness I of Bolshevism as well as the   58
moribund state of Christianity as great signs that we have actually

and wittingly entered the epoch of the abandonment by being. Instead, everything is moving in a great lie: now one combats Bolshevism in the name of "Christianity," now one wants to overcome Christianity with the help of doctrines which never reach into the domain of the decisions to be taken—since, for example, race can only be a condition of a people, but never what is unconditioned and essential of that people.

68

How few see clearly enough to recognize that all essential decisions are being avoided. It corresponds to this avoidance that with an unprecedented irresponsibility anyone at all can prattle on and on about the most essential things. Can such a time be "great"—a time which, according to its propaganda, has already assured itself of "greatness"? What does it signify that the "elite" is a thoroughly corrupt multitude? 59 | How easily is there made here a rewarmed and equally timid professing of Christianity, in order to fancy oneself as "better"?

This epoch is nowhere great—but uncanny and unique is the concealed happening to which the epoch must comply, along with all its machinations. Greatness lies in this concealed circumstance, namely, that *a history is pressing to its end and the transition requires bridges.* Yet the first pier needed to sling their arches must be deep-reaching *meditation* on the actual plight of the *abandonment by being.* This meditation must stand in its new ground (the truth of beyng) simply, silently, relentlessly, and deeply rooted—and must resist washing away in the surging mire—and must do so for the sake of a sacrificial preparation for those who most of all will lead the trajectory of the arch through the purified air of genuine knowledge and appraisal and across to the other beginning. And it is altogether within the "order" of today's noisy decisionlessness that these future ones are reviled as traitors to the people and as unreliable.

60   Only the knowledge of the concealed and uncanny greatness of the historical moment furnishes the power to withstand this unique circumstance for a while and not take as important the "critique" of what is contemporary—as necessary as that "critique" may be for meditation. The issue here is to *see* the contemporary inattentiveness to what is actually happening *and yet not to see it*—i.e., on the basis of the certain knowledge of what is completely other—the future—to bring patience into play and seek what is necessary in its own element. Every sort of "oppositional disposition" and attitude, however, sinks at once into the lowland of the customary—i.e., obstructs precisely a grasp of the authentic confusion as that which broadly overhangs all of today's

machinations, whether these are useful or destructive. For even *medi-tation on the confusion* requires noble and futural sentiments.

Therefore, it will always be futile to try and clarify to the common opinion and evaluation what the confusion of being itself is, how it pertains to the essential occurrence of being, and that it consequently can be experienced only on the basis of the originality I required by every constancy in the truth of beyng.   61

The knowledge and naming of the confusion remain untouched by all caviling, resentment, despondency, and lamentation. To illustrate this using the idiom of a past account of beings: *one must be a god in order to know who is the devil.*

69

Sameness.—The masses constantly need something that never was before in order to keep fresh their transient "lived experiences." Accordingly, for the common understanding sameness is that which is to be dismissed with the comment, "Nothing new."

Yet sameness—the simple in its ever-originary essentiality—is the mystery to which creative individuals are committed.

70

Perhaps the most difficult thing is to be a philosopher in the guise of a "philosophy professor." If someone in this guise is actually a thinker, then he would do best to remain hidden; for he will be taken as a I "professor."   62

71

What is *question-worthy* is essentially other than the *questionable*. The latter refers to indeterminateness: vacillation. The former awakens wonder; its binding power binds and strengthens its concealed constancy and greatness. Any arbitrary thing can become questionable, but only what is rare and essential is question-worthy.

At the same time, what is question-*worthy* unfolds questioning up to the rank of a unique knowledge. The questionable feeds only on a customary kind of questioning that is already sure of itself.

72

What is now still carried on under—but no longer *"in"*—the name of *philosophy* is a variation on traditional teachings in the framework of established disciplines, but with reference to contemporary needs, and this is then the "new" and thereby immediately already old.

Nowhere an upsurge from the most proper necessities of philosophy and of its beginning—nowhere a presentiment of the plight into
63   which thinking must first be replaced in order to I receive the deepest impulses and thereby first determine the point of departure for the other beginning.

Now there is no need for a "system" and a fortiori no need for the facile compendia whose comprehensiveness gives the erroneous impression that something is originarily questioned there. (Cf. p. 144f.)

If only we had the most proximate pathmarks for the inceptual course of future questioning and also knowledge of the necessarily "provisional" character of this course!

If only we had the pathmarks, so that in resolutely taking its bearings from them the movement of thinking could stir itself up.

If only we knew *merely what* has gone to its end, *what* is the transition, and *how* the other beginning must be. This knowledge would in itself already be *the* philosophy, not just for our times, but the one that had already borne our times beyond themselves, without its being recognized or recognizable in effectuating this.

Yet the form of that philosophy would have to be very diverse and peculiar. Perhaps such a philosophy is a superhuman task—even in
64   the fact that it necessarily would have to pass by all I things that are now valid, esteemed, desired, and familiar, and could have no contact with these, yet so as to be effective in the future precisely on that account.—

Indeed something *still* more preliminary is assigned to us, in order to waken the memory of what has gone to its end, i.e., what still prevails as having been, not so that we might again make this the measure, but rather so that we could prepare for its creative overcoming. All philosophical education must also turn exclusively in this direction and must not allow itself to be deflected by the transient needs of the day. Yet how many abide in this task, without finally getting bogged down in their own activity as an end in itself and thereby even losing the future?

Where is the one who completely thinks and questions only on the basis of the most intrinsic necessity of philosophy, such that we could hear him and dialogue with him? Everything remains mute. But still noisy are two *apparently* hostile but basically collaborative I brothers.
65   The one, hardly worth the mention, adheres obstinately to the past and makes philosophy pedantry, though seemingly superior to the dissolute scribbling of the "people's philosophers." And the other, just as oblivious to the essence of philosophy, degrades philosophy to "ser-

vice" to the "people," presents a mixture of philosophy (borrowed from the past) and political figures of speech, and behaves in an up-to-date way. But both agree that individuals want to put themselves forward and that for the longest time it has been known what must be "done."

Both agree that one should resist every attempt to bring to light the flawed ground of these "positions" which are not even deemed worthy of a "confrontation."

Who could still be surprised if every originality and seriousness of thinking disappears here, and the endless writing of books goes on more furiously than ever before.

All goals are lacking—not because none are posited, but on account of a deeper reason, i.e., because the *grounding of goals* is not experienced as something necessary. (Cf. p. 55.)

73   66

The ambiguity of everything customary—only with difficulty and in each case in a new way do we ever become equal to such ambiguity. On the one hand, the customary creates a genuine and necessary shelter for all deeds and accomplishments. On the other hand, however, precisely thereby it makes all things "customary" and takes away their originary power—unless we have grounded our Dasein on originary things, which are never customary.

The capacity to experience both (namely, the protecting favor of the customary and also the domination of the customary on the basis of what is not customary), to acquire them and hold them together— that capacity is "good fortune" but then is also, as Hölderlin knew, difficult to bear as misfortune.

But to that being which abides in an exposedness to beings, what is more customary than beings? And what to this being is therefore more uncustomary than beyng itself?

We must ever again transform everything difficult into an impelling and thus into a repelling toward the uncustomary. The latter is the space for | the nearness and remoteness of the god.   67

74

If things have progressed *so* far that the most proper labor is made into a playground for "dissertations," then the moment has arrived whereby for a long time an actual comprehension and especially the volition for such comprehension will remain absent. That moment arrives necessarily.

75

Versus a great work of art, it is essential to philosophy and to the poetry which prepares philosophy that they are comprehended at the earliest only *after* two or three generations. The one who here strives for contemporaneous understanding makes himself *historiological*— i.e., something past—whereas he must be thoroughly *historical*—i.e., something futural.

76

Technology is neither grasped "metaphysically"—in the truth and untruth of beyng—nor mastered at all, by postulating it to be the "total" determination of Dasein. That technology must become this is in accord with its essence—but how is that to be endured? Through mere

68   recognition? No—I in that way we do indeed avoid a false romanticism which merely yearns to go back; but we do not acquire any prospect for a setting of goals, especially if we do not come to terms with the possibility that through the "total mobilization"[5] of the technological itself everything is pressed to its end, especially if the sources of a possible surpassing of this occurrence are nowhere opened up. For that to happen, we must go back very far in *historical* meditation— to the connection of τέχνη, ἀλήθεια, and οὐσία.

Only on the basis of a questioning of beyng and of its truth does the *space* of a confrontation with technology arise for us—otherwise we are merely moving in appeasements or in simple acknowledgment of these. We are still thinking metaphysically and our sight is too short, such that we cannot set the correct meditation here on its course and into power.

77

Technology, as the machination of humans wandering in the abandonment of being, a machination wallowing on in its own abyss and apparently supported and confirmed by "nature," this technology I can

69   be overpowered only, if still at all, from the "event."

The event is more originary, because it is more inceptual, than all "religion"—the happening of the truth of beyng as the wholly other elevation of humanity and as the opening up of the other kind of abyss.

---

5. {Ernst Jünger, "Die totale Mobilmachung," in *Krieg und Krieger* (Berlin: Junker und Dünnhaupt, 1930), 9–30.}

78

My "historiological" lecture courses and "interpretations" are all *historical* meditations, not historiological considerations of the past. (Cf. the current w.s. 37–38, p. 12.[6])

Historical meditation lets the happening be experienced authentically—i.e., in its *inceptual futurity*. Therefore, historical meditation—which arises only in creative thinking—must always *accomplish an anticipation* for what has been, i.e., must show more therein and show something more originary. Accordingly, such meditation is always historiologically false but historically true. For those small in calculation, something gratifying results here, namely, that Plato, Kant, etc., have then indeed all known everything already. Those who calculate this way are totally unaware of the reverence in the presence of what is great, the reverence by which alone we ourselves prepare for greatness. Historical truth of historical meditation I does not mean   70
that the past is correctly presented as it is in itself, but that the future comes to light in what has been, even if and precisely if what has been is suppressed and *not* mastered in its forestalling yet unliberated power, i.e., when the past becomes a task for us, but never the object of a calculation.

Yet some few must come later, those who grasp what historical meditation means for us transitional ones.

This is the overcoming of historiology and of historicism and is not the shameful flight into the timeless and the misunderstood "eternal" by which the ones "understand" mere endless duration and the others mere immobilized completion in itself.

This insufficient—i.e., external—relation to history, as this relation has developed in today's historiology (which in turn resulted in historicism), will not be overcome by a flight out of history, but only by an originary leap into the happening of history.

Admittedly—whereas historical meditation requires the highest rigor, it remains far behind historiological "exactness," since the latter relates only to the scientific form and I to the content determined   71
thereby.

To a large extent, historical meditation looks just like a historiological consideration. That is necessary—but even more necessary is the deep breath and the broad vision the historical must never lose over and against the "historiological." Thus it is a mistake and ruinous of everything to "confront" historical meditation with historiological research and naturally find such meditation too weak and, espe-

---

6. {Heidegger, *Grundfragen*, 39ff.}

cially, "violent." All this points to a completely ill-bred thinking and to a profound incapacity for distinguishing levels of questioning and maintaining standards.

Therefore, even a disputation with such misunderstandings of historical meditation is futile and above all an abandonment of the proper levels.

Pupils always understand their teacher only historiologically; he is for them precisely still the present, yet already the passing and the past, that *they* follow up. In order to grasp the teacher *historically*, one must be a *non*pupil. Nonpupils are to be sure also all those who have 72   never gone through school and therefore I even lack the presuppositions for understanding merely "historiologically" what the "teacher" says.

The true nonpupil is the one who is not *merely* a pupil but one who would himself—*by himself*—be an essential teacher. Yet such are rare. And therefore a philosophy, e.g., is creatively grasped *at the earliest* 100 years *after* it arises. We Germans are now precisely beginning to prepare ourselves to grasp Leibniz. And what still lies in between and altogether before that?—

Nevertheless, the historiologists of philosophy naturally already know everything precisely and even have already prepared titles and labels for most things—; thus my endeavors supposedly belong to the "philosophy of existence," and the following historiologists will gladly utilize this label, since indeed the contemporaries of this alleged "philosophy of existence" must have known best what was *actual* at that time.

In this way, historiology is a constant and indeed necessary falsification and obstruction of history.

Only one who "makes" history is also capable of awakening it.

73   79

Whence the ineffectiveness of philosophy? The prior question would be to decide whether we do still have a philosophy at all. But this supposes that an essential questioning is starting and quite other realms are opening and therefore other positions are taken—yet an unreceptiveness for all this exists at the same time—an aversion which cannot be explained as mere unrefinement. Another force must be at work here, one we miss by pointing to the excess of practical-technical "interests." For these "interests" are primarily the results of a transformation which perhaps must be grasped and experienced as the complete *abandonment by being*—as the decisive outbreak of that abandonment.

In the field of this outbreak, which is the field of beings as a whole, nothing is spared.

80

In the era of the most furious mania for the quick publication and distribution of everything for everyone, is it still possible to *educate* a people | to the people, i.e., to the restraint for their destiny? In the   74
realm of letters, e.g., is it possible that only what is most essential will be written and said and even this only after the longest preparation and in genuine maturity? Whence is the power for such self-discipline supposed to come? And how will the few (who alone could have the ability) be able to master the massive and the machinational, especially since these few must renounce the very ways and means by which those things bring the few into "operation"—must do so, because otherwise the few would turn their most proper being into its opposite.

81

Is it mere flight, cowardice, and weakness to renounce encountering the massive and the machinational immediately, with their own means? Or is it not a matter of high courage, one which pertains to working unseen and unappreciated on the preparation of those who then are there to transform in an actual way for the first time that which is unstoppably approaching its end?

To be sure, the danger of complete destruction is not thereby dis-   75
pelled. That danger will always remain and will give an even stronger impetus to the preparation of the other; for historical configuration has its own law: that which transforms must become another beginning—and can never run alongside what is to be overcome. *The other beginning must run ahead and therefore at present must give the impression of lagging behind, remaining idle, and merely letting things take their course.*

But how few grasp this, and how rare among those few are the ones who in such preparation do not again become mere keepers of what has been, on account of boredom with the present?

82

Why do we have so many authors, some of whom are very clever, some of those very good, and some of those very serious? Why only authors—and no unique poets? Because "one" can no longer want poets. But the poet could be without all this in his | necessity; he *has even*   76
been long ago—Hölderlin—except that we now bring him up to date historiologically, and thereby far into the future we even deny him the possibility of becoming historical—becoming an originary happening of our history.

83

The basic experience of my thinking: the superior power of beyng over all beings—the impotence of beings to bring forth an origin; yet beyng not as an object of thought and representation, and the superior power not as the a priori in the sense of the condition of the possibility of presentification. All of that is only superficiality and the remote consequence of the inceptual—but again visibly foundering—beyng. The superior power of beyng essentially occurring in originary truth—out of which alone and into which alone every being arises. Beyng essentially occurring in the abyss of space-time.

This basic experience is not a "lived experience." Instead, it is the leap into history. Through this leap, the concealed happening of history first comes to effectuate and to demand—at the start, as a question concerning the first beginning. Yet I simultaneously the superior power of beyng requires an empowering and distinguishing of humans—but how? Not as humans—but rather? That was what had to be disclosively questioned at first. And the first answer was: human beings as Da-sein—as that which grounds the truth of beyng and appertains to the groundless, the abyss.

Yet this basic experience, with all its concealed determinateness, is entangled in the past, scattered over it, and clouded and distorted by it every time this experience strives for its proper configuration. And it would be an even higher delusion to maintain that the first approach, in *Being and Time*, had overcome the danger. The entanglement is now still more dangerous, because the self-assertion has ossified in achievements. (Cf. p. 106.)

84

The agreement of beings with beings first arises out of the affiliation to beyng. And this affiliation no longer occurs, unless we traverse the abyss of the truth of beyng.

What counts is not to have "lived experiences" of beings, but to bestow oneself into beyng. Everyone has "lived experiences" of everything, and I no one bestows himself on what is unique—for nowhere is there the compelling work of decision.

85

The tyranny of *technology*—where technology itself against itself is so uncertain, tottering, and fading; surpassed by itself in the instant and without guarantee that it can master and fascinate—which humans does this presuppose? How far must the uprooting extend in order to be carried away by such a thing? For it is indeed not a matter of individuals, romantics who perhaps still offer resistance and yet are concomitantly crushed down.

Technology can protract, delay, and move in this or that way into what is measurable—it can never overcome—i.e., ground—; it itself is becoming more and more that which cannot be overcome, and so it precisely maintains itself in a duration—although it offers no guarantees, especially where it stands against its own kind.

86

The clearest sign that the age is historically uprooted and historically untethered is the Hölderlin vogue; for either Hölderlin is assigned I to the "fatherland," or he is openly or covertly slipped into "Christianity." In this way, the decision which he himself *is* is not only avoided but not even raised to awareness. Yet the semblance endures that his work is now valued at the highest, whereas this is only done historiologically and referred to some use or other.

49

87

Technology and uprootedness.—Whereas radio and every sort of organization destroy the inner growth, i.e., the constant regrowth, into the tradition of the village and thereby destroy the village itself, professorships for the "sociology" of peasantry are instituted and heaps of books are written about nationality [*Volkstum*]. This procedure of writing about such things is exactly the same as a radio talk to farmers about the needs of strangers from the city who are increasingly flooding the villages.

But the most disastrous of all is the fact that no one wants to see those procedures at all, let alone their sameness and their common ground.

88

Technology and its twin sister—*"organization"*—both the opposite of everything "organic"—are by essence driving on I to their proper end, a self-hollowing out. And *we, swept along,* i.e., just as captivated and enchanted or also dragged on by this procedure—what are we doing? We equip ourselves in the direction of technology and organization (said together: we equip for machination). We equip for the end—so as then in the end to be unequipped for the beginning and especially for the great desolation and derangement of everything.

80

Equipping themselves for the end are also those who want to breed the people "biologically"—for, despite the opposite appearance, this breeding and the call for it are only the *consequences* of a previously instituted and unquestioned sovereignty of the machinational in itself (in the sense of a not yet overcome "liberal" notion of progress).

The future ones, in the essential sense, are to be recognized by whether they equip for the end or prepare the beginning and the transition. In the meantime, the most fateful ones exercise their handiwork, the ones who apparently equip themselves *just as much* for technology and for what is of today *as also* for the "other"—those who want to rescue only the past, whether from sheer greed for power and | hatred of everything creative or (which is basically the same) from an incapacity to create.

Therefore, the future ones are difficult to recognize, especially since, if they *are* indeed such, they keep silent.

89

Are we questioning the truth of beyng in order to ground an originary affiliation—or are we setting out to explain beings on the basis of beings and "master" them? Yet this "mastery" is not a sovereignty, but only a poorly veiled slavery within a procedure which must go on to its end.

Why should we halt something which must go on to its end? The end, however, is never the last, if we understand end as the mere running out of the no-longer-conquered beginning. The last, however, is in its necessity the supreme transfiguration of the first.

90

"Culture"—in itself affiliated at all only to the age of the commencing modernity—is today merely an appendage of technology and on the one hand serves to veil the irrevocable tyranny of technology and on the other hand helps anesthetize the masses, who are supposed to be fobbed off with the "cultural assets" previously denied them. The consequence is that, for example, | during a performance of *Hamlet,* a performance which otherwise would lack all necessity, the country people cough and spit and sleep and at the most impossible times break into laughter—this then is called "people's culture." In itself an entirely unimportant occurrence and yet, seen essentially, the sign of a boundless mendacity and perplexity—not of the "people," but of those who furnish the people "culture." And that in turn is only an expression of the universal machination into which humans are displaced—

in which they must remain without a relation to beings—because the truth of beyng is not becoming a plight to them.

91

Plato—but we are not led into the open domain if we merely parrot what was said earlier, misunderstanding it and misinterpreting it and calling for the postulation of "Ideas." That leads as little into the open domain as does the banishment of the Ideas qua the supersensory and the nonsensory over and against what actually demands to be affirmed, the sensory. In either case, there is *no* properly thoughtful confrontation with Plato; such commences only if we are strong enough for the question: what is happening when the ἰδέα is posited as οὐσία, and νοεῖν of the ἰδέα is made the basic determination of the human | essence? To what extent is this still a last unfolding of the *unobtrusive* and *unquestioned* occurrence which the Greeks rather more suggested and concealed with the name ἀλήθεια than actually mastered?   83

That occurrence which first opens and grounds the space round about humans and first makes possible for them a perspective even on themselves—that occurrence is what no one has yet grasped but what we reach out for more originarily in speaking of *Da-sein*. Something which is more inceptual than the first beginning and more futural than its end?

Through his "theory of Ideas," Plato has just as much rescued ἀλήθεια as he at the same time decisively thwarted all questioning into it, so that even Nietzsche was still led by Plato onto a path which had to keep him from a leap into the open domain.

92

Humans are on the point of plunging precipitously back once again into that human being (the conception of the human being) who now pursues the end of the last human: the human being as *animal rationale*.

We extol "worldview," because it is "reasonable," as something endowed with a higher truth!

And we pursue the breeding of the *animal*[7] as the slave of this "reason." And the saving of the West is supposed to come from that?   84

---

7. [Latin word *animal*.—Trans.]

93

The *history* of philosophy—what is more essential: to pave, by way of questioning, the courses of originary questioning, or to present them? But even the presentation could never be a portrayal of what was already attained—it would have to set out on a renewed course and so at every stage lay the level of the previous one deeper—deeper into the ground and deeper into the abyss.

Which courses must a transition tread in order to arrive at that developing and developed ground from which the leap into the other beginning becomes possible?

Here we must speak of beyng as the most alien—; the speaking must not only preserve the alien character undamaged, but must increase it—and yet all this in an artless simplicity. Who will venture something of the sort? Who is prepared enough and rich to the point of excess?

In this realm are discredited all those artifices and calculations with
85   which I up-to-date "philosophy" is now produced.

94

The number of those counted among the younger people is increasing, those who with the help of some snatched-up "worldview titles," for which they do not deserve the credit, set out to refute the previous history of philosophy "from the highest lookout." Actual history is of course not bothered by such tripe. But it is indeed food for thought that, e.g., Descartes is now refuted by small-minded teaching assistants who have never suffered, or even conceived, a proper thought in its necessity, let alone *that thought* which would give them the right to *consider* a confrontation with Descartes and *consider* the *preparation* for such a confrontation. I mean *philosophical* preparation, not the preparation needed to advance one's career as an author. It is food for thought that there are no more teachers who could check such vain pretentiousness or, even further, through the correct education into reverence, would never allow such attempts to arise. Instead—so it
86   might seem—this sort of robbing of corpses within the I "historiology" (not the history) of philosophy is thrust forward in order to attain in that way the "philosophical" fruitfulness of the "worldview." "Battlers" of this stripe will also not hesitate over such activity, taking it as the best and surest way into the "cleared path for those who are fittest." Whither is all this leading?

Perhaps, however, it all belongs under the law of the indispensability of the mediocre and immoderately noisy—that law whose scope we still underestimate too much to keep from falling into the erroneous expectation that a cornfield could arise overnight out of a wasteland.

95

Who of today surmises the *other* law, namely, that what is most essential is first gained conflictually in the particular form it itself demands in order thus to sink back again into concealedness as what is *too* early? And finally: who will venture this detour in an age where indeed only palpable "facts," i.e., uses and results, have validity—where what is sought is not at all truth, but only practicality.

When will we see the pavers of the detours of that which is | too early? (At   87 first only the trumpeters of what is all too late make noise, and they do so incessantly, trying to outshout one another, because the ears for the noise are becoming ever larger and ever more numerous—because ultimately people no longer *want* to hear anything other than the blandishments over organized uprootedness.)

96

If people today and especially professional scholars in "philosophy" grasped something from the fact of Nietzsche's having spoken, then all writing about philosophy and talking about philosophy would have to *stop at once*, and the *silence for years to come* would make manifest: the Germans are beginning to comprehend their most futural thinkers. Instead, "literature" is growing without bounds—and why not, when the *figures* of book production—the greater the better—speak all the more loudly for the growth of "culture." But we are already again standing in the domain of the law of boundless noise.

97

Education is now—in the age of technology—| tasked with "putting   88 out" a new "type" of human being, just as business enterprises "bring out" a new "type" of motorcycle. And this educational business enterprise even enlists the "Greeks."

98

What is coming to be, if frustrated store clerks and misfit engineers make "culture"? *What is already*, if this is resisted only by bringing "works of the past" back into currency? *What must be*, in order to create a change here? Answer: the future ones and the invisible ones, those who are able to think back to the great beginnings without ever running the risk of letting themselves be drawn into bad temper on account of being "misunderstood," and who nevertheless acutely observe everything of today in order to see what therein is history and not a mere incidental. For this that is of today will presumably have a great deal of time ahead of itself and will expand ever anew under all sorts of forms—since it indeed merely wants to make *itself* the "new time" ["*neue Zeit*"] and thus remains the continuation of all "modernity" ["*Neuzeit*"]—a span of the ending of that era.

89   *What is of today*—we do not mean by that a particular political "worldview" or some sort of "cultural politics"—but rather the total European situation in its movements and countermovements.

And what is decisive here is that a reversion to the previous "metaphysics" is setting in everywhere and that the human being is revived as *animal rationale*—as the rational animal (race and reason). (Cf. lecture course, 37–38, p. 36f.[8]) Seen inceptually-historically, this signifies a bogging down in the past, despite all impulses and exertions in individual fields and attitudes. All of that must necessarily remain uncreative, because no decision is ventured on the basis of the inceptual and because no decisional space is prepared—indeed no preparation is even wanted.

Whoever does not see this crude reversion to the discarded residues of the common property deriving from the Western conception of the world and of humanity, whoever does not see that here lies the proper occurrence of what belongs to today and tomorrow, such a one has altogether no vantage point from which to question philosophically— i.e., so that this questioning in what is most remote could measure up to the great thinking of the West. As beneficiaries of this thinking,

90   we I allow ourselves the wretched presumption of being "advanced."

All striking out against Christianity amounts to pseudofighting, since one basically wants the same thing, only turned the other way round.

All appeal to the ancients is vain pretension, because one renounces the questioning that would in general *correspond* to them, or is not even capable of such questioning.

The indolence of historiological cognition and the literary cleverness in mingling everything—

the untrammeled robbery of everything not achieved by individuals—

the appeal to "lived experience," i.e., to intellectual laziness—

---

8. {*Grundfragen*, 140ff.}

all this creates an atmosphere such as the one that broods over swampland and apparently stimulates luxuriant growth.

All capacity for drawing distinctions is dying away. And where there still are distinctions, the general atmosphere is nevertheless determinative. Weak romantics, as also unscrupulous careerists (in the realm of the "spirit") breathe therein.

But even this would make no matter, if it did not happen precisely in the vector and manner of the *running out | of the end* and thereby— which is decisive—suppress the wakefulness for a preparation of the other beginning.   91

The fact that, among us Germans in particular, there is in addition much goodwill and an extreme power at work in nonthoughtful, not-artistic, and nonpoetic "fields" merely makes the situation *still more* question-worthy, for one day the question must arise: wherefore? And what if then those are lacking who have been educated opportunely and long enough to take up this question? And what if it transpires that the *new* "intellectuals" no longer master the "intellect" (i.e., true thinking), but are only furiously publishing charlatans, perhaps even "to the best of their knowledge and belief"?

99

Pleasurably tugging on the strings of their machinations and calculations, the ones who were mentioned above intend to make history and to pursue only the last weaning from the great gods. How is a word of beyng supposed to find a captive ear in these circumstances?

100   92

Science is always distance from the object and thus a fortiori distance from beings, and consequently the instituting of machination and calculation is needed to dispel the distance. The knowledge characteristic of science is therefore a very conditioned one and for that reason is precisely never "compelling" knowledge.

Knowledge in the proper sense is *affiliation* to beyng and requires a leap into the truth of beyng. The grounding of the affiliation is Dasein as history.

101

The further the projection of beyng, all the more originary is the conflict in the appropriation; the deeper the conflict, all the more excessive is the excess of intimacy.

In the projection always something left over, a residue.

In the thrownness in each case already a surpassing and something held in reserve.

102

If it is a matter of handing on something great in the transition, we must proceed very slowly and steadily, without regard to pressing needs and without self-indulgence, for anyone who only wants to save himself up for what is great, instead of "sacrificing" himself for its preparation, has already *renounced* it.

"Sacrifice" admittedly *sounds* boastful and Christian. It is meant otherwise.

93   Today, since the result concerning truth is decisive, no one should be surprised if the first positions on knowledge and ignorance are also immediately judged in the same way. In the transitional era, however, that signifies a complete misunderstanding of what is unique and is therefore allotted only to a few, namely, that an incomparable truth happens in the course of the transition itself. In the transitional era, more than at other times, everything is out of joint, everything is in the hunt for some sort of foothold, and everything is full of claims to a truth for all—and precisely here the truth of beyng shines only in a few, whose affiliation is: self-ignorance in the recognition that such are there in order to prepare the other.

And yet: ever again this "yet"! For, precisely as work, every work, as much as it might conceal its origin, is only a fragment from that fracturing required by the great turmoil in humans—their position between being and semblance.

94   Just as we encounter ourselves in various | forms, according to the respective ontological level we are capable of maintaining, so the same applies to the form of the things appertaining to us. And only from the increasing depth of Dasein can the abundance of forms be mastered and brought into the free play of their transfiguring effect.

103

Nietzsche's *Will to Power*—i.e., what we know as a "work" with that title—is not a fragment, but precisely *the work* of the one who *set* on its first course *the end* of Western philosophy. Therefore, all endeavors—even Nietzsche's own—in the direction of a conventional configuration of the work are mistaken, for the essential end cannot be something finished, as little as can the beginning. Instead, it must remain ungraspable and thus inexhaustible. Consequently, all endeavor regarding this work must aim at securing that most proper "unfinished" character in its historical configuration, so that everywhere at the same time the multiplicity of levels and the intricacy of perspectives can come into full effect instead of getting lost in the monotony of a schema. Only slowly will we bring ourselves *toward* the time in which I a German generation has become mature enough in the power   95 of questioning and in the rigor of meditation to allow this endwork to rest in itself as an impetus into the other beginning. Until then, the still dubiously increasing "biological-psychological" snooping around in the person of Nietzsche must of course be overcome. For, such snooping gives the illusory impression that something would be known of the work as soon as the psychological background was grasped. But that is impossible, because no modern thinker so excessively forced himself to sublate his own "person" through the law of thinking and of meditation. The fact that Nietzsche on the other hand, as no one before him, also constantly speaks of himself and communicates only "himself" in his publications does *not militate against* what was just said, but supports it. For, all that self-communication was only a preparation toward an overcoming. The fact that it had to be expressed merely reveals how pressing his task was—so pressing that an individual could not simply bear with it but had to scream it out. But how erroneous it would be to take this scream for what was properly said and was properly to be said, whereas it is only I a calling back   96 into the authentic task of meditation: the radical transformation of "actuality" and the creation of the presuppositions for that.

The confusion over Nietzsche is almost unresolvable if we heed how his writings and "works" are furiously combed for "passages" which are then strung in some order according to a concocted plan. Meanwhile, the genuine "work" on the "simple" interpretation of beings in their "what" as will to power, and in their "how" as eternal recurrence of the same, comes to a halt. And whereas the question regarding the ground of the correlation of these projective domains is the only essential question, i.e., the only one Nietzsche "merely" left behind, the talking and writing about him rage on with respect to everything that is merely occasioned to some sort of appearance on account of one remark or other. If we consider the purifying labor to be accomplished here, and if we see in addition how in sequence ever again someone or other "treats" and solves all questions in a "work" that must not be less than 600 pages strong, then it becomes clear that in the realm of thoughtful meditation we have not taken one step I   97 beyond the time of the "world riddle"[9] literature of the last decades of the previous century. Except now everything is much more clever,

---

9. {Ernst Haeckel, Die Welträtsel: Gemeinverständliche Studien über monistishe Philosophie (Bonn: Strauß, 1899).}

not so crude, not so narrow—but for that reason all the more insidious, although also some degree less effective because there are too many of those who, in the most boring variations, all flaunt the exact same unquestionableness of all things in the illusion of dealing with the burning "problems."

In such a time, which in regard to thinking and configuring has been deprived of all measures and of every attitude and secures itself merely through cleverness, only one thing can still help: to bring before ourselves once again the most alien, simplest, and greatest of Greek thinking—not so as to renew it, but in order to liberate ourselves from the antiquated, i.e., from what has become usual and ordinary, and to let measures be surmised. There is only a thin chain of such ones who will at first be prepared to venture the assault against what is most tenacious: i.e., against the expansion of ordinariness, against the rapid | diminution of everything essential, against the associated appeal to "intellectual possessions" and "spiritual values."

If Nietzsche had to fulfill his Da-sein today, he could only say the same things he once said, but say them with *even more* hardness and passion. And yet in the meantime a more originary meditation on the beginning of our thinking would have to be carried out: the question of beyng—no longer obstructed by "epistemology" and "nominalism" and no longer devastated by "ontology."

Yet perhaps this more originary questioning can primarily serve only to supply Nietzsche's work with a view into the future in order that from the future his work might first be experienced in its historicality—in that binding power which originarily unites what has been and what will be, so that from this origin the hitherto might be overleaped.

The distinction between the concealed configuration of the work and the expressed endeavor of the work does not at all coincide, however, with the familiar separation between the writings Nietzsche himself published and the posthumous ones, | as if the latter contained the planned work. Instead, that distinction runs equally through both the published writings and the notes Nietzsche left behind.

The concealed configuration of the work is *so* actual that it propels all his reflections and endeavors and even specifically compels the premature communications, where the character of the work shines through only occasionally, like flashes of lightning. (Cf. especially *Beyond Good and Evil*—e.g., "On truth"; "On religious life.")[10]

---

10. {Friedrich Nietzsche, *Jenseits von Gut und Böse: Vorspiel einer Philosophie der Zukunft, Werke*, vol. 7 (Stuttgart: Kröner, 1921), 7–37, 67–90.}

104

A perturbing discord holds sway in all overcoming with regard to matters of thought. At first the overcoming, arising as it does out of that which is to be overcome (e.g., metaphysics) and thinking *against* it, must precisely deal with the content, distinctions, and concepts of the other and so must point into that other. Yet as long as only this occurs, all overcoming [*Überwindung*] is wound back up [*zurückgewunden*] in what preceded, as in a winch [*Winde*], and is not set free. The overcoming is actually carried out only if what it in advance points toward is attained in itself, such that it makes possible its own domain of grounding. But then the overcoming also rids itself of the critical misunderstanding that it would merely be | opposition or a desire to   100
refute or a mania for change, whereas in truth it first liberates what is to be overcome from all appendages and strives to set what is to be overcome back into its proper greatness and necessity and from this necessity raises up anew what is overcome. Only the essential is worthy of such overcoming. The inessential and the pedestrian can perish in their emptiness.

105

Tell me *which* thinker you have chosen as an "opponent" and *how* you have chosen that one, and I will tell you how far you yourself have entered into the domain of thinking.

106

Today nowhere can we find the least exertion which would signify a volition and especially an originary compulsion to project, ground, and secure a basic attitude of questioning in its main lines, an attitude arising out of the task of thinking—what is the meaning of this lack? What does it mean that no one has knowledge of the essential task of the other beginning or could have or even wants to have such knowledge? How can it be explained that there has begun everywhere a pursuit for the most hasty and most current production of "philosophies" which are attempting | to become praised, and validated, as "politi-   101
cally reliable"?

107

"Worldviews" and their promulgation first appear when the "world" falls out of joint, the passion for world projection flags, and everything must remain a mere substitution.

The will to be immediately "effective" seems "natural" in the sphere of the usual human comportments, tasks, and machinations. And therefore "thinking," a fortiori, could very well strive for such effectiveness, as if it must first remain without practical use as "mere" thinking. In the light of this desire for effectiveness, it must then be felt in "pain" when all such attempts founder in misinterpretation and in what is precisely contemporary and fashionable.

But why could I never have felt this process to be "painful"? Because I knew obscurely, what I now know more clearly, that indeed precisely this misinterpretation of all my work (e.g., as a "philosophy of existence") is the best and most lasting protection against the premature using up of what is essential. And it must be so, since imme-

102   diate effectiveness must remain foreign | to all essential thinking, and because such thinking, in its truth, must be prevented from becoming "familiar" and "understandable" to contemporaries. For that would mean what is to be disclosively questioned in thinking had been degraded to something Already commonplace.

So then everything is in the best possible order—i.e., everything is well hidden and misinterpreted and withdrawn from rough fingers and from being rubbed away by the common understanding. Yet it is still an error to believe that this knowledge of the necessity of misinterpretation, like just any cognition, must be simple to acknowledge and easy to bear. But what arises here as a difficulty holds only for the one who has to bear it, in order thereby to become severe toward himself and mild toward the many who still want that which they might "refute" and declare to be "overcome."

108

The greatest struggle rages over the task which is made necessary *by* a first work *against* that work itself. If the grounding of this task succeeds—if the question of the truth of beyng compels a turn to the question of the beyng of *truth*, and if the question of being first vi-

103   brates in *this* | question of truth—then the genuine strife of questioning is roused, the inmost tranquillity is assured through the hitherto, the affiliation to the unique ones is prepared, and the other beginning—has begun.

109

What sort of picture of the present age will be handed down to a presumably ever smaller posterity by the knowingly or unknowingly captivated or uncaptivated writers?

110

The *historiological* presentations of "persons" and "ages" now have the ambition of matching their occupation with *"journalism,"* and newspaper reportage has reached the level of *bad essays in school.* Whither will historiology arrive on such a path? Why do we nowhere see any exertion toward the necessity of an original style?

It is because no necessities are experienced but are merely "lived through," and all talking and writing which have now come to "power" are stylistically from the day *before* yesterday, and therefore they fancy themselves new; for yesterday's things indeed precisely still remain in our all-too-short memory.

111

104

What has become of "science" in the course of a development that reaches far back and is now merely accelerating? "Science" here includes both natural and human science. The former has become *"technology,"* with a still-indispensable appendage called "theory." The latter science has become *"journalistics,"* with a still indispensable appendage called the "gathering of material."

"Technology" and "journalistics" both enjoy the "advantage" of being "close to life," and above all: they no longer bring those in authority before any decision. What counts now is only the pursuit of novelty and the overtrumping of that by the most novel. And inasmuch as both "technology" and "journalistics" now unite, which happens very easily, since the one lacks what the other possesses ("psychic lived experience" and machinelike compulsion), a new sort of "spirituality" arises, about which we say little by calling it dreadful.

The *most insidious* aspect of all this, however, is not that matters have come to such a pass, but that now from here—visibly more and more—it is claimed that this age competes with earlier ages of the spirit I and that those ages are even praised. Instead, if everything were brought to light in its naked devastation, then at least a clear situation would be created and the unavoidable decision prepared. But thereby this impotence gets entangled with earlier goals, measures, and claims, even if only in the *clever* technology of a journalistics captivated by its own incapacity. This European situation is now the only constant in the daily change of "political" relations.

105

112

Yet a little while—and one will no longer battle Nietzsche, since the weapons for it are lacking, but will consign him to oblivion. The most uncanny supremacy of the "they" in the epoch of the community of the people consists in the fact that they are consciously led like sheep. Moreover, the most disastrous way of being led is the one requiring that certain works and their creators not even be mentioned. The deliberate cultivation of forgetfulness—as a protective measure for the benefit of those who are average and those concerned with their own hollowness. Meditation on this procedure—one not entirely new, unique only in its extent—provides a good contribution to a commentary on the statement: "'Human beings' make history."

106

113

What is greatness?—An institution of beyng rooted in a self-grounded ground, an institution from which what strives to be a being must originate and which must remain a scandal to nonbeings. (Cf. above, p. 47.)

Why do we meditate on what is great? Because we are small and want to overcome that which is small. Then is smallness the only ground for the impetus to greatness? That cannot be; for the small and the great and their sovereignty in human doings and sufferings are already the *consequence* of the shrunken and the massive. And these? Do they spring from the *excessive* as its conquerings and the unique arresting of it? And the excessive—where does it hold sway, if not in the essence of beyng itself? Yet how do we say this essence? The appropriation of humans into grounding-there: within the event as the ground of history, beyng overtakes the beings originating from it in that beyng itself must again become I alien. The excess of beyng forces the counterresistance of beings, and this strife is grounded in terms of Dasein as the strife of world and earth, a strife which is in each case variously necessary and carried out on various levels in the shelterings of the truth of beyng—in work, word, sacrifice, thinking. (Cf. pp. 5, 76.)

107

114

Da-sein, into which the future human being must leap, is stewardship for the passing by of the last god, a stewardship that builds (to build means here to erect beyng in beings). Such passing over *eventuates* in that space-time which determines the clearing of the "there." And it can eventuate only if the *event* prevails as the essence of beyng— which in turn happens when the truth of beyng is grounded inceptually, and it comes to that only if truth itself and its essence have become a plight and the oblivion of beyng is shaken. Who can gauge

how far we are from the beginning of this history and how continuously the danger is growing that "results" and "progress" of the "new
time" (*again* a "new time") are thrusting us from the beginning and
from the compulsion to it?

115

When in the deepest plight in Prussia, the enemy extensively occupied the country, and all volition to (as well as, before that, all knowledge of) what is necessary disappeared, the king in East Prussia had
his uniforms and hats altered and to that end set in motion all the
tailors. Thus it also stands now with the German university and "science." The enemy (as "technology" and journalistics, as the pursuit
of what is unproblematic) extensively occupies the "country"—lacking is any knowledge of the essential and the most question-worthy;
instead of this, professorships are established for "folklore" and the
"sociology of peasantry," spatial research is pursued, and "science" is
brought to the "people."

Are we now going through the deepest bemired state, or must
a greater devastation with a simultaneously increased concealment
come about, so that there might be a few who awaken? Yet then the
petrification and massification of the total situation will perhaps be
already so extensive that no offensive by those who are awake and
aroused will help any longer. Even here—and here a fortiori—what
remains is only the possibility of an other beginning, in whose wake
something like university affairs might first change.

Meditation on *science* can only mean recognizing "science" as that
which it had to become, namely, a subordinate technology, | one
which by essence can no longer have a proper future but can only decompose and thereby convert into human comportment. Of course,
this future inessentiality of science does not signify that such unsci-
entificness should be equated with ignorance, for essential knowledge
can never be first acquired and grounded through "science."

109

116

The basic state of contemporary mankind is the disavowal of all *history*, wherein especially the incalculable and overpowering must prevail and every necessity must originate as momentary and freelance.
Instead, in power now is the purely self-cognizant raging on of *machinations*, *rules*, and *types of procedures* which first determine what is incorporated into their concatenations in order to prescribe in that way
alone what may be valid and what not. This is the extreme conse-

quence of the *abandonment by being*, where it seems as if "beings" are indeed in advance ruled by another—very much so by an "other," but this is only the hidden offspring of the beyng that has degenerated into something self-evident on account of a notion of beingness as ἰδέα, whereby one particular being is granted precedence.

110   *117*

The unrestrained power of the machinational is in no way broken by the fact that all who are caught up in it also occasionally invoke "the" *"providence."* For *this* "providence" belongs to the machinational the way the suspension of noise, as alleged rest, belongs to making noise. The invoking of "the" providence, which is merely "cited" incidentally and "makes appeal" to the "lived experience" of the masses, is the strongest confirmation of the implicit trust in rationality and in what is achievable by the "engagement" of the will.

This same outcome can be attributed to the glorification of *"personality."* For "personality" is proclaimed the "ideal" by someone wanting to suppress his inability to get free of entangling rules. Both "personality" and "providence" are the inducements and seemingly higher "spiritual" titles with whose help we configure the most desolate stirring up of empty dispositions toward an "unforgettable" *"lived experience,"* one which in the next hour will vanish without a trace and so needs constantly new occasions of "lived experience." This is a need satisfied most surely by believing that even "lived experience" is subject to rules.

111   *118*

You must endure an end if you wish to prepare the other beginning. The end, however, contains a great deal of failure, obliteration, and disorder— along with the semblance of the opposites. And therefore the enduring of the end must perform a great deal of denial, such that everything might seem to be dissolving into a fruitless "critique." But that denial and every uncovering of insufficiency arise from a *resistance* to the sheer ending of the age, arise *already* from the preparation of the beginning, and serve only the beginning.

On the basis of inceptual questioning, everything that was called a "being" becomes a nonbeing, because the truth of beyng already radiates up and requires the transformation of nonbeings into beings and compels us onto a concealed path. (Cf. p. 23f.)

119

Thinking within the beginning must renounce resting in a well-rounded "work," the way this latter is made possible and required by the *center* of a historical course. The beginning must always—in concealment—*protrude* over all commencements and what comes from them. This protruding I can be reached only in an ascent. Consequently, inceptual thinking is always an ascending (and falling) which by itself first brings the protruding element before itself and up above itself to the protrusion—letting the mountains emerge.

112

Thinking in the other beginning is stepping up (understood as the event of the grounding of the "there") into the excess of beyng.

120

Inceptual thinking is neither a *"work"* nor even a *"process"*—instead, it is a course which disappears as it proceeds and yet, as past, *remains* inimitable and full of directions—*remains*—to be sure, only in that constancy which finds its stance each time in a new leap of questioning.

121

In long and reticent meditation, one must have gone to and fro on the unfrequented paths leading to the concealed *standpoint* of Hölderlin's hymns. Every fixed word is a misinterpretation here, because this standpoint, in its power to provide a ground for space-time I and in its precipitateness, can be taken up only in speech and indication, provided the blocks for its underpinning have been thoughtfully hewn and hauled. For that Da-*sein* which the poet has carried out in grounding it itself could never be attained by *us* through the much-invoked "reliving" of it. It is attainable only if, in the plight of our own itinerary, we once become mature for that Da-sein in which alone the open realm is effectuated for the tarrying and passing by, the flight and absence of the gods in *one* stroke. So we must rather deny ourselves constantly any words about the poetry of this poet, despite all incentives to communicate some things gropingly—statements and references to which it is then in any case granted to be registered somewhere in the "Hölderlin literature." Is not here any kind of silence the most genuine relation to this poetry? Not as if what would need to be said is especially "significant" and "consequential"—but because it is *too* simple and too uniquely requires only the transformation of today's humanity. For there still remains the expedient of saying something concealedly and more in the form of what is usual and in general to

113

114   prepare quite faintheartedly for an | entrance into this poetry. Thus
the renewed elaboration of the first drafts of my lecture course on
Hölderlin (*Interpretation of the Hymns "Germania" and "The Rhine"*[11])
could be of service, whereby I would have to make allowance for all
misinterpretation and especially for all short-sighted thinking.

122

We are too tightly bound to a long provenance, one that is too fully
covered over with historiological cognitions, for essential thinking to
be jostled out into its proper ground and to be allowed to grow purely
out of that ground. Therefore, the other and what is given as task must
always not only be said in the form of what is given as endowment,
but must even be questioned. (A lecture course on "Schelling" or on
"Plato" is indeed what it is called and yet "is" something quite other.)
In this transitional work, we ourselves consequently need the assistance of those who loosen our essence from this concatenation and
posit the other in its simplicity as our standard.

115   Yet here resides the great danger that the form of | what is given as
endowment will alone be directive and what was said will turn back
into what was previously familiar and was perhaps registered as a certain variant. If only "originality" were in play, then this accounting
could pass into the familiar. But at issue is not the "person"; on the
contrary, it is a matter of other possibilities of the truth of beyng itself
and thus a matter of the beyng of truth.

123

We are still always moving in the age of *progress*—except that progress
was for some time pursued as an international treasure and today is
proclaimed as a competition among nations: the "best" films and the
"fastest" aircraft—the "surest" means not to tarry anywhere or become attached to anything—but rather to possess everything casually, and then what? Then to totter in the great emptiness and shout
oneself hoarse.

The progress explicitly proclaimed as a competition is now becoming a still stronger pincer clamping humans in their emptiness.
And what then actually is progress now? The bringing forth and carrying away of beings and what counts for that on the basis of the truth
116   of beyng, | a truth already wretched enough in itself. Then let us look
once with open eyes and ask, e.g.: whither has modern natural sci-

---

11. {Heidegger, *Hölderlins Hymnen "Germanien" und "Der Rhein,"* GA39. (Frankfurt: Klostermann, 1980).}

ence progressed? One could say: for the past three centuries, so rapidly, so far, and so precipitously that no one can survey this movement any longer. And what has basically happened with respect to the knowledge of nature? That knowledge has not gone one step "further," and it could not and should not, if that progress was to have been made possible; for nature is still the spatiotemporal nexus for the motion of points of mass—despite atomic physics and the like.

Indeed inceptually this nature was still held in an order of beings—now even this order has disappeared with the increasing impotence of Christian belief. Taking the place of that order are the "personal" "sentiments" of the researchers into nature, who of course acknowledge, in opposition to the much more forthright "materialists" of the previous century, that "besides" this—"besides" their domain of work—there would still "be" the "inner."

Progress depends on the increasing oblivion of beyng due to the ever more clever, arbitrary, and calculative exploitation of "nature." Soon even | living nature will be so much caught up in this that it will   117
be held in the pincers of planning and destroyed. Yet this procedure is inconsequential, since—insofar as it drives toward this destruction—it always produces the same, because what it facilitates was already exhausted at its commencement—the commandeering of nature into calculation and the displacement of humans into the attitude of self-certainty through practicality. The sole concern with certainty as well as the increase of the masses and the provision of bread and circuses were proclaimed to be cultural accomplishments, so that the progress of culture could henceforth be taken as secure. What is transpiring in this milieu cannot be fathomed, and yet it is always only the same devastation consequent on an already long-since complete uprooting of beings from beyng.

What must happen for history to eventuate again in actuality?

124

What makes for confusion and hesitation and reservation—what prevents an unequivocal outlook—in regard to everything of today lies in the fact that indeed here | and there something genuine is experi-   118
enced, something essential recognized, something substantial done, and something indispensable summoned—and in the fact that all these remain scattered islands and are quickly covered over again by incidents in the public domain.

To gather together all these accomplishments is just as futile as it would be small to try and deny their "value." Or do we still lack the long view which recognizes this as belonging to the transition, which keeps its distance from it despite everything, and which calls beyond this for something more essential—namely, the inceptual? Whence ever again the temptation to mix together and finally associate as the same the beginning, sent far in advance, with today's promise of this or that?

A beginning is what it is only through its *exclusiveness*; but its greatest danger is to exchange itself with the good remainders of the end and believe it can find therein an increase.

How—if the enticement to this sprang from anxiety—to remain only in the exclusivity of the beginning and in all its improbabilities? But what would become of the leap into the beginning, a leap | to be carried out ever anew, without this anxiety?—Barely a game, one that could be certain of never effectuating anything in the future.

119

And so it must be accepted that in the domain of thinking everyone avoids the essential question with the help of the stratagem, one still promising results at present, to repaint in the colors of a "political" philosophy that which was thought hitherto—with a cleverness and insistence that vary. Yet why note this down once again, since now at the earliest only the generation after the next can become mature enough for creative thinking? It is because even this future generation, and it especially, requires a long preparation. And what if instead of that it only plays with borrowed scraps of thought? Then everything depends on those who are living today, precisely because in relation to them it seems futile to hope for the essential, since the ties to the past are much stronger and more hidden than these "new" philosophers surmise.

Then what is to be done? That which you already had to do all along: | exercise relentlessly the simple craft of interpreting the great thinkers, of getting used to long thinking, and think for yourself—in concealment—that which is most necessary for you to think.

120

125

Why is the possible impact of the oldest Greek thinkers (Anaximander, Heraclitus, and Parmenides) so inexhaustible? The further these thinkers move us—all the greater becomes the enigma of what is unique. It is because we do not possess any "complete works" of these thinkers, nor especially any of their "collected correspondence" or any rummaging around in their "soul" and "personality" but instead have only the naked hard words. These allow no escapes and refuges in the "psychological" but in every case merely demand anew the same simple and thorough thinking. From this circumstance, namely, that the secret of history has left us only fragments, will we finally learn something about the way we need to bring a thoughtful work into our presence and then pass that work on to those who will follow?

126   121

Why today are words and above all simply naming-saying-question-ing words so powerless? Why do they merely serve for communica-tion, address, exhortation? Why are they no longer able to strike into beings and into the truth of the beyng of beings and reign there as the ground of an originary and simple position? Why? Perhaps because demagoguery and the misuse of words in every possible respect have reached gigantic proportions? No! For these things are themselves only the remote consequences of the actual reason. Perhaps because "imagery" and "tone"—the immediately, quickly, vividly, and also fleetingly perceptible aspects—have acquired the upper hand over words? No! This too is only the consequence of the actual reason. And that reason is the obstruction of *truth* in its essence and thus the com-plete closure of the relation among word, truth, and beyng. For that relation to prevail, as the place of its history another humanity would of course be required, such that even the priority of imagery and tone could not in any way be indicative of an awakening of the necessities of art in these domains.

Yet how will we arrive, and arrive once again, at the | simplicity of   122
the grounding word? That will become a long path, and many pre-liminaries will have to be accomplished first—including a great re-nunciation of the ordinary and usual.

And first of all a long—creative—*silence* must preconstruct the new space for the future work. And this silence itself must be a developed—but not fabricated or forced—one and accordingly must be grounded and be endowed with a power of self-unfolding and certainty. Where are those who could plant such a power—in view of the fact that they are ones who have to undertake something discordant: use words to prepare silence?

127

No one up to now actually asked in a penetrating way what the Greeks experienced and developed as the beingness of beings. But what I have communicated of this meditation in my writings and especially in my lectures and seminars has in the meantime penetrated into the race of commentators—as something self-evident. I will one day find that I myself am accused of "plagiarizing" these newly promulgated dis-coveries. But that is to be endured. What is almost unendurable, how-ever, is that these circulating new insights do not *effectuate* anything; instead, people merely | trade in them and make a career out of them.   123
This demonstrates that people have not grasped them and never will—despite the quick and agile way of snapping them up. And therefore

we can tranquilly continue to make a present of something left over for the hurried commentators.

That is an unavoidable epiphenomenon of all silence and must indeed always be decided in speech.

128

Thus a philosophy first and foremost effectuates; if it is *reputed*, then it is no philosophy. For philosophy must be able to effectuate by *not* being reputed, by merely standing entirely in itself, and by still having the capacity, as its greatest deed, to revere something even greater and yet not "bow" to it!

129

What is the human being today? That which he is accounted to be. And he is accounted to be the summary drawn from the answers to the many questionnaires addressed to him from all sides—the human being is the result gained through a gigantic calculative approach to him—he is what is offered up by an index-card file. Will this human being still be able to encounter a God; or, more clearly asked: will any God still be willing to enter the atmosphere I of this human being?

124

130

What grounds history is that which is *capable* of having to wait the longest. But what waits longer for its adoption than the *beginning*? For it must at the same time endure the fate that things proceed through it and out of it, i.e., away for it and beyond it.

Adoption of the beginning happens very seldom, and only *through* another beginning.

131

Nothing saves us any more / not in simply continuing, which is inconsequential, but / into greatness—except for the simple grounding of the uniqueness of a necessity of beyng.

132

Historiologists are the real slaves of their respectively "current situation." Looking backward, they intend to be superior to that situation and its instructors, and what they discover is always only their present, from which they powerfully wall off the future.

The bustling about in the past "saves" them from the very | difficult task of insight into the goallessness of their present—one that does have "goals" both "politically" and otherwise but basically does not know the ins and outs of anything. How good it is that the "current situation"—especially now—alters so swiftly; for how else could there remain the possibility of progress?

133

Philosophy—what is most proper to it and always left unsaid in it—is kept open only to a few, and they are used by philosophy and used up by it. The superficial and widespread view of philosophy is but the necessary and long shadow that follows it, and in this shadow many seek recreation and intellectual amusement or some sort of utility. And in this domain there is easily available at any time "philosophy," which anyone can pursue and make into the object of a so-called confrontation. Moreover, there is a rich, well-established, and suitable-to-every-taste "history" of philosophy. On that basis, opinions can be played off against one another and mixed together without an actual *question* ever compelling a return to actual history—to that history in which very little happens and does so very slowly and very rarely. But in it basically one | beginning always rises against another, in order then to know itself as the same, the unique, and the rare and to recognize opposition only as a superficial expedient. To withstand for a moment the truth of being and in its extinguishing to make the fire visible—that is what can never become graspable and "reasonable" to any ordinary calculation. But that is also nothing only those few can of themselves attribute to themselves in order to find in it their apartness and the pride contemptible to all "Christians." Instead, it is the essential occurrence of beyng itself—the temporality of beyng itself, the fact that from time to time in its self-concealment it must come into the light of that fire. What wretchedness and especially what lower, though well polished, bustling about lies in that *summum ens* ["supreme being"] which is to make everything adverse pay a hundredfold and *therefore* gets assigned to the claim to be the genuine being. And if this *summum ens* is not, then this is another idol of the same kind.

All "culture" is indeed precisely that preoccupation with the cultivation of beings, and to this all beyng can only | become something supplementary.

134

Those who maintain that "philosophy" should be abolished in the universities, institutions already defunct anyway, and replaced by "political science" are basically quite correct, although they do not in the least know what they are doing and what they want. Indeed philosophy will not be abolished thereby—that is impossible—but something that looks like philosophy will be eliminated—and philosophy runs the risk of being deformed in that way. *If* this abolition did transpire, then philosophy would be "negatively" secured on this side—it would be clear henceforth that the *substitutes* for the philosophy professors have nothing to do with philosophy, not even with its semblance—*assuming* that that substitute does not lapse even further into the semblance of philosophy. Philosophy would disappear from public and pedagogic "interest." And that state of affairs would correspond to reality, for there is no philosophy at all here—even *if* it *is*.

Why then do we not *cooperate* with that abolishing? We already do so, | in that we are forestalling the possible development in it of the younger generation (no more dissertations). But that is only something incidental and, above all, *already comes too late. Already* one would *again* like to be such a professor of philosophy, and already announcing themselves are "new" candidates for this career—people endowed with the necessary "political" skill who now as "new" *all the more* confirm and strengthen the past in its pastness. For they are all *even further* removed from any questioning and "pledge" themselves to a *sacrificium intellectus* ["sacrifice of the intellect"], over against which the medieval does not count at all, because the Middle Ages did not know any originary questioning whatsoever nor the necessities of such questioning—and could experience nothing of what Nietzsche had to raise to knowledge. But this is even to contemporaries only an expedient and if need be a mine, but not something which could compel them to seriousness or even to meditation on it.

One indeed *"has"* the truth. Proof: one now acts as if there had to be "research." Whenever, and only if, one knows oneself to possess the truth | does the affirmation of "science" claim validity. And matters have never gone so well with "science" before; all that was needed was a brief vilification of "intellectuals"—one only so long that people had come far enough and were numerous enough to replace the "intellectuals." Let us not deceive ourselves regarding the very extensive previous existence of the "new" science—let us not fail to recognize its groundlessness and its remoteness from all philosophy. And let us be aware that to see this is only a preliminary, because we know that the history of the truth of beyng happens in its own domain and has its own "chronology."

128

129

135

Who of us transitional ones (those belonging to the transition) is one who *goes over*? Who is capable of placing the first beginning before the other, and the other before the first, such that both, belonging to each other, protrude more originarily and more inceptually? Only the one to whom it is given to disappear in the cleft between the two protrudings—i.e., to found the *between* of the cleft.

136   130

There are only a few *questioners*. Most people merely want answers, or rather: they would like to be the answerers and to have their reward for that, even if that reward is only fame (coming from *which* "admirers"?—asked incidentally). Few are they who on the long bridge bring into vibrancy the unique swing of the arch and remain in this vibrancy and take no notice of the piers—few are they who know and love the opening-grounding power of questioning and scorn the impotence of the closing and obstructing answer. Few are they for whom the most question-*worthy* is the truest and is the source of all riches.

137

What we must learn: a very long and radical endeavor is required to master, like a game, the craft of thinking. For *only* with this mastery may we venture to think an essential thought and thereby turn onto the path of *history*—i.e., the path of the future of thinking. Erudite cognitions regarding the historiology of philosophy are of course useless and a burden, unless I they are immediately and constantly recast   131
into *historical* necessities—and *that presupposes* we have proceeded from the historical plight of thinking, in defiance of all daily "needs." Thus, in the turning, the work of craft and the compulsion out of what is highest are *assigned* to each other. Neither is capable of something essential without the other.

But what if both these are lacking to us today? Indeed, what if the genuine urge in that direction is suffocated through a pseudopossession of omniscience and through a facile presentation of everything? What must then happen first as a remedy? The taking up of the great models? Certainly—but who can do it? Above all, where are the *eyes* capable of seeing such models, and where is the space in which the *necessity* of thoughtful questioning (not merely its imitation in "worldview" literature) could unfold?

138

Where does the human being stand?—In organized lived experience as the lived experience of organization—and this position is to be understood as a total state which determines contemporary humanity *prior to* and beyond any political attitude.

132

139

What is great can never be determined as "greatness" by such and such a quantity. Through greatness, what is great is only misinterpreted and slighted. All "superlatives" merely tear down what is great. To the great belongs both the originariness of the truth of beyng and that which protrudes—that which, standing in itself, satisfies itself and is the resolute law of free beings, wherein they find their necessity. If we ask what is "greatness," then we have repudiated all "great" things and their calculation.

140

The many forget beyond beings that which to the many is a nonbeing, namely, beyng. The creative ones know beings on the basis of beyng, in that the creative ones set the truth of beyng into a "work" and place beyng under beings, so that they (beings) might become more fully beings in the "work." Consequently, for the many, there must always be *"religions"*—but, for the individuals, there is *God*.

141

Historical meditation is the genuine detachment from historiology.

133

142

If your endeavors in public and for the public have been assigned a label ("philosophy of existence"), then it is time to disappear from public view. Not a false craving to keep fresh this problematic appellation by means of attempts to stay in step with the "development" and "progress" of current "philosophy."

The silent acknowledgment of the *proper time* of every essential step. And what thoughtful step would be more essential and more unique than that of *questioning* the *truth* of *beyng*, over and against all metaphysics, for which beyng—as well as truth—is unproblematic and for which the only step consists in the explanation of beings as such on the basis of the clarity of that unproblematic beyng.

The end result of the impotence of "metaphysics" against itself: the most complete obliviousness regarding what must happen shows itself in the very honest expedient, yet one already lacking any creative power in craft, the expedient of degrading "metaphysics" to a toy for *"lived experience."*

Jaspers—indeed the most extreme example of what could at present appear in opposition to my unique endeavor (the question of beyng). I The fact that his as well as my "philosophy" are accounted   134
instances of the "philosophy of existence" offers the most vivid proof of the thoughtlessness of the age.

Astonishing—that one possesses so little knowledge of *style* that one cannot surmise the abyssal disparity in our entire attitude toward the *history* of philosophy. But the small-mindedness of today's literature shows itself once again in the fact that even if this unbridgeable oppositionality could be made visible to it, such literature would still never be capable of recognizing that between Jaspers and me something "common" does indeed persist: *decisive thinking* in contrast to all mere philosophical erudition on the one side and to "zealous" scholasticism of worldviews on the other—since both of these, before they began, already renounced thinking. But this "commonality" is such a broad—indeed the broadest—condition for thinking that it allows extreme opposites, so that Jaspers's thinking belongs entirely to the *running out* of the end of "metaphysics." Jaspers, as I no thinker before   135
him, *requires* "metaphysics"—for the sake of "existence." Without "metaphysics" everything would decompose into empty "psychology" —which it *nevertheless* is perhaps. For my endeavors, the basic postulate is the *overcoming* of "metaphysics" as such—a questioning in the direction of this overcoming.

Where in Jaspers's *first* work, *Psychology of Worldviews*,[12] which still determines what "philosophy" is, can there be found even only a trace of the *question of being*? Jaspers merely rejects "ontology"; he does not overcome it and does not at all understand that "fundamental ontology" must be the first *deliberate* step toward this overcoming—though saddled with all the questionableness that must inhere in such an attempt.

The sharpest objection against his "thinking" is the comprehensiveness of his publications, where *not one single* essential thoughtful *question* can be found—where rather the concern is only with the historically given answers and positions as something finished, for the mere purpose of "appealing" to them. And yet—the seriousness of his

---

12. {Karl Jaspers, *Psychologie der Weltanschauungen* (Berlin: Springer, 1919).}

endeavors surpasses all former erudition and utterly goes beyond all scholasticism of worldviews.

136   *143*

How many concealing sketches and detours must an essential thought traverse in order to come into its simplicity and then remain all the more unsayable?

144

Why does essential thinking no longer have any power to ground and to implant a configuration? Because it lacks *truth* as the essential field wherein the binding and fruitful relations to beings would first raise this thinking to its essentiality and submit it to the earth. Since the grounding of the *essence* of truth remained previously denied, machination and "lived experience" had to proliferate on the basis of the sovereignty of *correctness* and had to promote the impoverishment of the world and the destruction of the earth as genuine progress. Therefore, everything depends on the grounding of the essence of truth. Truth, however, as the openness of self-concealment, is the essential occurrence of beyng itself. Accordingly, the other beginning of history must come—if it is to come at all—out of the question of beyng (no longer out of the question of beings).

137   *145*

Those who today falsify the last remainder of philosophy by turning it into a scholasticism of worldview in order to make themselves up to date should at least summon up enough insight and enough rectitude of thinking that they make St. Thomas Aquinas their patron— the only patron saint appropriate to them—in order to learn from him how one can be uncreative in the great style and yet can place very astutely essential thoughts into the service of belief and give belief a decisive basic structure. Why is this not happening? Because even this extensive heteronomy of thinking lacks power, and above all lacks the certainty of craft. The confusion is so great that these "political" philosophies, ones "tied to the people," are never recognized as wretched imitations of *scholasticism*.

The grotesqueness is complete when all this confusion is joined by the "struggle" against the Catholic Church—a "struggle" which has still not at all found—and cannot find—its opponent as long as it thinks with too short a sight (and too narrow a mind) of that which constitutes the foundations of this Church: the adapted metaphysics of Western thinking in general, | in which these "worldview strug-   138 glers" are so inextricably entangled that they do not surmise how much they themselves participate with their "opponent" in the same brittle foundations (unquestionability of being, groundlessness of truth, essential determination of the human being).

146

The creative person's bravest knowledge, however, is this: with what he precisely does still understand, he ushers into the light that essentiality and otherness which he is necessarily prevented from experiencing. Therefore, the creative person must be overcome by the creative person and thereby ever again be one who steps into the light of something prevented, testifies to it, and projects the concealing word into the solitary dialogue of the solitary ones.

147

What still awaits us as "spiritual" culture: that the "spiritual persons" of the day before yesterday "deepen" their "lived experiences" through the misuse of Hölderlin, and indeed as regards what is most essential—what is still quite untouchable and can be grasped only through great detours and after a long maturation—they choke off such things with their verbal facility which is "saturated with lived experience." | These saviors of "culture" are more fatal than all necessitated barbar-   139 ity which they do not grasp and to which they are equal only through flight.

What if every glib versifier of lived experience was placed on the same level as Hölderlin and was declared to be able to complete him?

148

Which knowledgeable person will still be able to venture into words, when all words have been exhausted—not only by newspapers—but also by those who are "spiritual," when the apparently unavoidable salvation of our spiritual tradition has merely deteriorated by being degraded into the "lived experience" bustling about in literature, when no one any longer *endures* the knowledge that we do not have the "truth" and even less its essence. But should not the knowledgeable ones then all the more "speak up"—even in face of the danger of becoming a mere object of some sort of "lived experience"? For what purpose? Merely in order to "occupy" these misinterpreters anew?

No—the knowledgeable ones know *their own time* and must be able to wait *in what they leave unsaid*, until their contemporaries have become antiquated.

140   Those oblivious ones—who believe that Hölderlin is "incomplete" and that just any rhymester who has stolen verbal dexterity from the poet could complete him—are committing stupid and impudent "aesthetic" calculations.

What could be more complete than this poet going all the way to the end, i.e., all the way to the space of the decision regarding the flight and advent of the gods? What is more complete than the founding of this still hardly surmised space? And the work assigned to accomplish this, *must* not that work survive in a configuration appearing to all "aesthetic" movements in art as necessarily "incomplete"—only because these movements find what is ultimate to them in the "completion" of their extrinsic measures and "lived experiences" and so cannot know anything of what is eventuating in the work.

149

The human being will draw his routes further in his irresistible massiveness, and for that will ever anew and always more surely invent his purposes and results and satisfactions. He will know ever more
141   faintly—and one day not at all—that I he has unwittingly abandoned—or had to abandon?—the possibilities of an essential history.

What used to be necessities of the highest ventures toward beings—the co-trembling with beyng itself and with its Dislodging Χάρις ["Grace"] into the midst of beings—have long since fallen into oblivion and been changed into objects of good-natured erudition, at times fillers for the emptiness pressing toward a gaping void and fillers of the evasions of that emptiness in all "lived experience."

The measures for beings are becoming ever smaller, the results ever greater, the self-deception ever more complete, the proficiency ever more calculative, and all this at the same time ever more public and common. Or were these always the usual human excesses—except we previously did not see clearly enough and were not coolheaded enough to incorporate them into human history as necessities rather than evaluate and disparage them only from the presumed high points
142   of individual eras. Then it also cannot be gauged I whether indeed, and precisely in the case of this vast excess, something futural and unique might not still be granted to Western humans in their history—perhaps even the greatest thing: the passing by of the last god. About this perhaps no one can inform anyone else, so that, in the simplest stillness in the "between" of world and earth, beyng might tremble in its clearest intimacy and, as the event, might appropriate

all beings and thus the god. What is most necessary, accordingly, is that there are those who can prepare for this and out of the previous extended lostness can liberate the question of being to its originariness and for that purpose can bring all great accomplishments back to their essentiality and restore the humans of the future. For this, however, the decisiveness of the repudiation of everything halfway and leveled off must also be hard enough and must not shirk from intensity and rage, due to a false concern with a long-since-empty "superiority" in every usual "treatment" of the "spiritual."

150   143

Perhaps even only my *errors* still have an impelling power in an age overloaded with correct things and for the longest time lacking in truth.

151

Every history creates itself or abandons itself to its historiology. The question can be asked: is a history all the more unhistoriological, the more historical it is, and all the more historiological, the more unhistorical it is?

That means: the less a history reaches down into the grounding of beyng and into an originary configuration of the human being in the midst of beings, all the more prevalent, loud, and comprehensive will historiology be. But the exaggeration of the historiological is the self-promulgation and self-commendation of a present moment which can be determined by the fact that altogether everything is directed merely toward a kind of objectification and no longer toward the grounding of beyng—because beyng has already abandoned all beings and relegated them to themselves—to their machinational objectification.

152   144

Today's "philosophy," in case this name may be misapplied to the following, is:

1. An erudite and pedantic elaboration of the past in the direction of a progress that corrects and improves everything.

2. Feeble romanticism of an "ideology" of empire [*Reichs-"ideologie"*] in the manner of George, mixed with a half-understood Nietzschean humanism.

3. Unrestrained party-*scholasticism* in many variations, unrestrained but tactically prudent and completely living on the past; there are here, as formerly there were Thomists (to be sure, without Thomas)

and Scotists (to be sure, without Scotus), in any case clever wire pullers, who do not at all move anything from its fixed position, because they merely want to—and indeed do—bring themselves into these positions.

In this overall condition of today, universal cleverness and frivolity are able to cope with everything and apparently even make themselves at home with the great thinkers of past ages. Thereby the semblance is heightened that a naturally hitherto "unheard of" "life of the spirit" is in I the process of development. Nothing is experienced of a plight, and necessity is measured according to usefulness, which even as the common good still leaves enough room for the individual good.

Basically, however, it is better for the masses not to see through all this, and one day they will even be brought to admire these philosophers of theirs.

But for those who are knowledgeable, this means: no perverse attempts at resistance and certainly not at refutation of that wherein nothing is situated and nothing is set down.

How long did medieval scholasticism prevail and was even accompanied, as we hear, with a rich spiritual life? So far as I know, a few centuries—and yet it had—even if very extrinsically—Plato and Aristotle behind itself? Today's scholasticism, which is too weak in thought to place something similar behind itself, will presumably for that very reason prevail much longer. It is good that the truth of beyng does not let itself be challenged by this. (Cf. p. 62f.)

The immediate requirements of providing for needs lead now to insight into the indispensability of "science." Its praises are sung everywhere, it proceeds and hastens everywhere to reach its limed twig in good time I and remain stuck there—a need to adhere which then is "lived" as confirmation of the right "of" science. Unanimity as well as gladness prevail everywhere, and the most marvelous times of the expansive years [ca. 1870–1914] were broadly surpassed in a new configuration—and the necessity of those who go under, those who prepare the transition, becomes greater than ever—without "anyone" able to surmise the least of it.

153

I notice with horror that the rapidity of today's "lived experience" has already arrived at "happenings" and that even "happenings" are already fortunately raised to "lived experience."

And so this word "happening" must no longer occur where something essential is to be said. But *should* the essential still be said?

154

For the most part, historiologists think unhistorically, if they think at all. Since they survey everything that is in development (which means, for them: in the succession of antecedents and consequences), they can and must trace everything back to everything. I Thereby lost to them is the uniqueness of the essential, of what creates history in the "earlier and later" of what is unavoidably contingent. This that cannot be surveyed they then take to be "living" historical actuality. If they wish to grasp this latter as a whole—which then is called historical philosophy—they come upon "ideas" according to which history is actualized or else they fall into a *psychology* of aptitudes and "types" of peoples and persons. And why does history remain closed off to the historiologist? Because he is not a creator but only someone who records the past.

147

155

What must not be mixed up: "philosophy" as erudite pedantry and *the mastery of the craft of thinking*. The former is the end, the latter the means, but a means that converts into that which is to be created— which often can be only a proposition or a dictum.

156

"Ontology" decides nothing, and can decide nothing, about the truth of beyng, because it does not know, and cannot know, the question of that truth but instead obstructs the ways to it; and I where "ontology" does come across that question, it necessarily misinterprets it. One cannot deny "ontology" and at the same time affirm "metaphysics"—for both are based on the question of beings as such and as a whole, and with this question the beingness of beings is already posited as something supplemental.

148

Yet perhaps the age of the abandonment by being (the age of machination and lived experience) might very well need precisely "metaphysics" and "ontology"—even if disguised—since this age indeed originates out of "metaphysics" and can maintain a footing only therein. Accordingly, the concealed backward turn of the history of truth and of humanity and of beyng will become even more pressing and enduring than we—who are already standing in the transition—would like to admit. The fact that Hölderlin must still further await his future is a sign which is more seldom seen the more univocally it shows itself.

157

We face a *double danger*. On the one hand, the fact that historiology is taking the upper hand anew and even more forcefully, insofar as the newly confirmed erudition makes use of this possibility of "assertion" as dissemination. | On the other hand, the fact that where this erudite mere familiarity and the capacity to explain everything are repudiated, this does not stem from a knowledge of history but arises because everything is transferred into a pseudomythology which then necessarily meets up with historiology at that point. What is thereby endangered? The possibility of our still being struck in the future by what is simple and our being impelled into what is essential. And the danger is also that the great sensitivity for what is simple might be definitively lost to us and the moment of persevering in what is essential might not come to pass.

149

158

Modern "science" is now for the first time coming into its own: for it is now becoming close to life and at the same time may more than ever adhere obstinately to its past. It now carries out the feat of being at once "close to life" and also "solitary" and is both of these accompanied by an increasing commendation of the indispensability of such masters of calculation who will presumably still bring about "gigantic" accomplishments.

But what if there were no more "life" (here: essential relations to beings themselves) at all—what would then be the point of "nearness to life" and "remoteness to life" and the feat of | coupling these together?

150

159

The danger for *"science,"* in case it is still worthy of danger, is not that "freedom" is taken from it, i.e., that the form of constraint is merely altered. On the contrary, the danger is that "science" will no longer have the resources to recognize that it is fused into the process of machination, such as even to disappear therein. Yet the danger to it is not this process itself, but the ever backward-glancing disregard of this process, a disregard that expresses itself most readily in a seeking, by way of new "sense bestowals," for something that already no longer *"is"*—to say nothing of how problematic the concept of "sense bestowal" is in general. "Science" lacks the courage for what it itself already *is* as a product of modernity.

It might often seem as if the massiveness pressing forward everywhere, its ever more rigid institutions, and its importunities are no longer to be overcome in the direction of a disclosure of the spatiotemporal field of beyng itself, since beyng requires original creations. I But if it does seem so, then we are already calculating only with the 151 "values" and measures of machination—and are forgetting that here calculation has altogether suppressed meditation. For, beyng and its truth are the incalculable—but this alone requires preparedness— perhaps a very long, perhaps a multifariously intermittent preparedness. What could still bring a path and a rank into human history other than this preparation for the stewardship over the truth of beyng—? Where else is the previous Western history supposed to have had its concealed impulse than in the attempt, with its first beginning, which allowed the human being to become the *animal rationale*, to bring the necessarily derived consequences of that to a creative denouement in order at last to surmise the abandonment of beings by being and to surmise as well what is cloaked in this abandonment, namely, an intimation of the essence of beyng? We do not need to place into history some sort of abstruse "meaning"—we only need a simple enough experience of history in its basic thrust I in order to 152 know what it will furnish to a still unequipped future.

With one stroke, all previous thinking is then consigned to impotence, and all mere mediation and counterbalancing become a clutching at a straw and, stupefied by knowing it all, perceive nothing of the rare and simple concord of the truth of beyng, a concord that—by withholding itself—assigns mankind to a unique stewardship.

Experience the overwhelming power of this assignment! And thus keep open for the gods a spatiotemporal field! The few humans who are capable of this will be defenseless in public. For all *their* powers will be consumed in the self-defense by which they—in offering defense to the urgency of the assignment—first let flame up the plight of the abandonment by being. To them, beyng as the self-refusing appropriation will be utterly inexplicable, because it remains debarred in advance as the still illumination of self-concealment, which liberates the highest power of creative disclosure and transforms the human being from the mere rational animal into the grounder of Da-sein.

But that which is to be created—especially what we call the *work* 153 of art—itself creates a great decision regarding *art*, so that if this decision is made correctly the word "art" becomes insufficient, a mere remembrance of the *animal rationale* and of its τέχνη. Since:

it is one thing for what is "created" to be merely something already present at hand (in knowledge and belief) which wants to be taken as something definitive, confirmed, reinforced, and in general even "expressed" and "attested"—and it is another thing for the work to open up for the first time something inexhaustible and create the domain that broaches yet unsurmised tempests.

160

What if there were an actual speaking of beyng in the most unitary simplicity and in the most beautiful conciseness?

And if the truth of beyng, out of the still unconceived word and the still alienating work, should illuminate all care and discourse, would then the previous "beings" of machination and of "lived experience" not have to collapse and sink away as nonbeings?

But what is so simple that it can be utterly alien to us?

154

161

"*History*" of philosophy: to occur in the most marvelous, long-prepared, and now altogether free upsurge toward and out of the other beginning—and thus concomitantly to revoke an inessential knowledge and return it into the concealment of that self-concealment which radiates as beyng.

At some time or other, and then unrecognizably in its relation to this that is withdrawn, that knowledge must rise toward the work.

In such history, a multiply reciprocal leaving alone of the great solitudes happens, and therein is prepared that uncanny silence which indeed still devours the thunder of the passing by of the god. (Cf. p. 18.)

How well and deeply beyng (the event out of this silence) is concealed in all beings and remains sheltered in them.

The thinker?

A great child—who greatly questions.

{Index}

PONDERINGS VI

The stillness of the essential force of things.
The sobriety of the power for the passion of productive thinking.
The decisiveness of the stewardship of Da-sein.
The frankness of the renunciation on the basis of knowledge.
Renunciation as preparedness for self-refusal.
Self-refusal as the bestowal of beyng.

*   *   *

The abyssally nonrecurrent character of a passion
of thinking is the root for the binding
simplicity of an essential step.

One must come to stand in the most remote in order to find the courage to break the silence over the most proximate (beyng). But even in that way, what is said remains very remote and can never become a common opinion.

The "work" of the one who at this time must be a creator cannot be a work, but only the dispensation that prepares the space for another "work"-world. |

Beings stand ever lighter in the darkness of the conjuncture of beyng; ever simpler becomes the steadfastness in this clearing where there comes to light that which pertains not to us, but to the essential force of beings; ever more necessary becomes the renunciation in relation to the basic configuration of the preparedness for the strangeness of what is unique: i.e., for beyng—the still hearthfire in the forsaken and disarranged house of "beings." The darkest is the fire and the glow—

Deliverance from the *"gods"* means: from the idols to whom belong all "purposes" and "causations" and "causes," all forms and "goals" of machination: "the" science, "the" technology, "the" common usefulness, "the" people—"the" culture.

Why this deliverance, and whence the demand for it? From the truth of beyng—so that every being might again find its way back into its simple ground and manifest in all this the abysses of beyng, which alone suffice as sites of the decision on whether beyng merely bestows beingness to beings or surmounts itself toward the trembling of that which is most uncertain: the advent or flight of the last god.

Beyng.—In the self-refusal of beyng, we transitional ones experience that surmounting of beyng itself which has its source in beyng itself.—

In this surmounting arises the field of the "between," the "between" which allows the self-refusal to eventuate as an assignment of Da-sein. And in the assignment, the "there" as the truth of beyng extends beyond the self-refusal and into the affiliated abyssal character of the trembling.

Out of the *ground* of the people, out of their history, and out of the ground of their history, out of Da-sein, one needs to speak *against* the

people—who never know the truth. Only in that way will they come to their "space"! Whereby we of course always primarily mean the *place* in which the many who are crowded together can spread out. But what if this place were one day given back to us, and yet the necessity of the space continued, indeed perhaps first broke out then? What if the people had as a goal only to be the people, i.e., to remain what they already "are" as present at hand; would this people not then have the volition to be a people without space, without the projective domain in whose abysses they might first find the heights to overgrow themselves and the depths to pursue a rootedness in the dark and to have something self-closed (truly an earth) as that which bears? Or should we maintain that if only the "place" were secured first, then the space would of itself devolve upon the people? Wretched blindness? That "place" for those who are all too many and are ever becoming more numerous would a fortiori have to suffocate completely every necessity of space and thereby stifle the possibility of a histori-
3   cally | creative indigenousness. Therefore, the meditation of the few must go much further, beyond the current shake-up, so that from afar a long goal might strike them and prevent them from being blinded by what is current. (Cf. p. 30f.)

4

Let us not fall prey to empty classicisms which persuade themselves of their "newness" through gigantic proportions and compact means. Let us not become insensitive to the well-concealed emptiness and to the lack of all projective powers and spaciousness in all the smoothness and strictness of the gigantic forms. The latter become ever more easy to learn in the readily increasing cleverness in its domination, and what is alien nowhere finds a place to break in any longer. "Taste" becomes "better," and the capacity to taste—the power to surmise in advance that which is still unsurmised—becomes rarer.

How should we surmise what is beautiful, if the essential ground of beauty—truth as the truth of beyng—is so completely withdrawn from meditation, especially since meditation is detested and obstructed on account of the unquestionable possession of "truth"?

4   5

Mere opposition to historicism leads at most to the unhistoricality of machinational "lived experience" but never to the grounding of an essential history. For, to fill up the coming time with incidents and to interpret these as "happenings" still cannot mean to ground history, because what is necessary for that is the compulsion toward a more originary truth, one that transforms human beings, i.e., displaces them for the first time into the spatio-temporal field of beyng.

6

Thinking—does it remain condemned to grasp itself and in that way take on the projective drive into beyng itself? Or is the thinking of the truth of beyng that creative thinking which no longer needs a concept of itself, because before it developed it already had to project this concept from itself? But is it not already on the point of doing so again through this question?

7

"Psychology" in the sense of the "projection" of everything onto "lived experience" has grasped contemporary humanity with such completeness that only I the step into the transformation of humanity can   5
still suffice to survey the entire omnipotence of "lived experience." The "biological" way of thinking not only fails to break this sovereignty of "psychology" but even strengthens it by making it cruder and all the more available to everyone. This way of thinking also shifts all "work" into the atmosphere of the exudation from peoples and personages. Every presupposition for the possibility of the effectuation of an actual work disappears thereby—for a work indeed precisely effectuates—if it is effective—a displacement into the wholly other space it itself first grounds. *But all lived experience is antagonistic to such displacement and even to the claim in favor of it.* "Lived experience" appeals tacitly to "the" certain "life," the one that is certain of itself and of its incontestable measures and regions. And in relation to all this, what is more "actual" than such "life," which today takes good care that people are enthralled by it? The exalting of "life" to "all-encompassing life" [*"Allleben"*] is at once arbitrary and thoughtless. Nietzsche shows how disastrous this exaltation can become, Nietzsche who is as far removed from biologism as I his biologically physiological way of think-   6
ing, in its manner of expression, seems to confirm the opposite.

8

All "meaning" has become meaningless—if "meaning" is supposed to refer to "Ideas," "values," or some such genuine or ungenuine Platonisms. Why? Because the foundation (all of Western metaphysics as such) of this way of thinking is unstable. Or was "meaning" indeed always already meaningless—inasmuch as the truth of the ἰδέα as the determination of the beingness of beings remained unquestioned? The meaninglessness of meaning and beyng as what is self-concealing constitute the still latent treasures of the history of Western metaphysics—they are distributed into many rooms, and on account of many transformations these treasures are unrecognizable in their simplicity.

9

Very few first endure the meaninglessness of meaning as the great illumination announcing another emergence. On the contrary: all fanatics rage against "nihilism," because it is indeed, if misinterpreted crudely enough, the most convenient background from which even 7   the thoughtlessness I of worldview can stand out.

Where nihilism poses as a crude "materialism," it has got rid of all danger (cf. p. 12). The form of nihilism that for the longest time has not been recognized—let alone overcome—is, as Nietzsche saw clearly, any kind of *idealism*. The most disastrous variety of nihilism, however, is without a doubt "heroic realism,[1] in case we have recourse to machinations and processes and not to mere "titles" and "catchwords."

10

Much is improved "from below," brought to order. The "standard of living" has been raised—the "people" move "upward" from "below." But nothing is eventuating downward from above. It is because nothing can any longer eventuate *in* the "above," since such "above" and "below" are indeed only the ever invariable preliminaries. Yet perhaps all this is becoming a general preparation for a history unknown to us, such that whenever a shake-up and a compulsion toward a resolution start to germinate and effectuate, the *Yes* of the current generation is demanded.

8   The one—frightful—thing to be endured in all this: the fact that the immediately succeeding humans will entangle themselves ever *more* eagerly and *more* impulsively in the unending "sensational" outcomes of their machination. Their "lived experience" will need to become ever more exciting, all this will become the most proper possession of their own accomplishment, and a liberation will be set into this sort of "life." Therefore, the unneediness will become ever greater and at the same time less known—provided the compulsion into the immeasurableness of beyng can at all be termed a need.

---

1. {Cf. Ernst Jünger, *Der Arbeiter: Herrschaft und Gestalt* (Hamburg: Hanseatische Verlaganstalt, 1932), 34.}

All "life" hides itself in its own hidden limits and is lived at any time as something new and unprecedented and nonrecurrent. But is "life" beyng? Especially if beyng is not something beyond life, and subsequent to life, but is instead the contemporaneous abyss of life. Indeed the abysses constitute the most solitary realm. They are borne by what is most alien, of which "life" seems to have no need. Therefore, we will never *immediately* liberate "beings" from machination and protect them from the importunity of lived experience. On the great detour over the abyss of beyng, I beings—which are still only "objects" or "beings in themselves"—first again come to be, vibrant in beyng, vibrated by it, and borne outward into the bifurcation. (*The unneediness of life; the great detour.*)

9

11

Need to be able to forget beings—and whatever things count as beings—and instead meditate on beyng—rather than remaining bound to the opposite: pursuing beings I and whatever things count as beings I and forgetting beyng.

12

Technology.—We commonly confront technology I with the claim that its "philosophy" resides I in this overly facile either-or: either humans are subject to technology, or else they are the masters of it. As if technology itself were something like a "machine," or even a tool, rather than the essential consequence of a basic position toward beings, a position that extends into the abandonment of beings by being, explicitly institutes that abandonment, and entrenches it. As if here we could speak of the subjecting and mastery "of humans," whereas these humans themselves rest on the same ground and groundlessness from which technology arises.

To this ever more common "solution" of the "problem" of I technology, there then corresponds that "journalistic" practice of explaining technology naturally at the same time in terms of a circling around God, so as not to pay homage to the opinion that technology originates out of utility. In fact it originates just as little out of utility as it is a circling around "God"—or it if it is the one, then it is also the other, and both merely in a superficial way.

10

Technology has its root in a collapse of the essence of truth. On account of this collapse, truth is degraded into the correctness of a representation and every being into an object, although this degrading was experienced as an ascending and was later developed as progress.

Such degrading, however, is actually the first shaking of the essence of beyng itself in the beginning of its history. How deeply must we then delve in order to grasp "technology," i.e., at the same time the affiliated human being, and create the preconditions for a transition, which is something other than a "domination" especially since the latter always only amounts to a slavery it itself had made blind. Nevertheless, could someone who is a mere contemporary ever believe that this gigantic technology—not simply its "products"—even could at all ever still be *surpassed*? There pertains to this belief, as its ground, a *knowledge*, and to venture such knowledge induces the proper weights of beings and of beyng.

11

13

The most profound misunderstanding of philosophy: the opinion that we could and should immediately and constantly take up our abode where philosophy opens up the abyss. Because this effort fails at once, we take philosophy—the abysses of beyng—to be refuted. And yet these abysses are the ground of all foregrounds and backgrounds, between which, going back and forth, we save ourselves, secure ourselves, and pacify ourselves. What then is philosophy supposed to offer us? Immediately, nothing at all. We satisfy it well enough if we cast aside that misinterpretation and thereby surmise the abyssal character of beyng in beings—and we are prepared for philosophy if a mission of creativity, always remaining in the domain of creativity, strikes us.

14

What is decided in *history* is not what first happened, but what is attained as last, what incorporates everything that preceded and radiates through it. This that is last unveils the beginning for the first time and thereby unveils itself as an infringement on the beginning. For, the genuine beginning sets the limit of the end corresponding to it
12   and | prevents a mere perishing.

15

Concerning p. 7.—Has nihilism, appearing in the crude form of materialism, got rid of all danger? Certainly—insofar as we no longer immediately fall prey to this nihilism but instead know ourselves superior to it. But—is there not hidden here the even greater danger that this superiority will now be taken too lightly, that the "height" of the superior will constantly take its measure from the flatness of what has been overcome, that everything in this "struggle" will remain hidden, and that the other will arise only out of the opposition and come forth only as long as and as far as the opponent reaches—until in all this the sense for something more originary, as prior to the opposition, is completely exhausted and dissolves into obscurity? The further in advance we think, all the more acutely must we see *this* danger, the danger of obstructing the path into the other beginning, for that beginning can never come to be out of the form of opposition, even if it apparently must be prepared therein.

16

The abyssal sorrow running through Hölderlin's work—is it only the re-sounding of a procreation that is still closed off to us, or is it more essentially the pre-sounding of a basic disposition we cannot assign to any of the usual "registers"—the pre-sounding of that disposition which raises into hesitant truth beyng as the reticent sphere of the decision regarding the gods? Or is that re-sounding only this pre-sounding—a re-sounding we still do not master if we think of it on the basis of what is overcome? As much as Hölderlin himself does seem to move yet within the "metaphysics" of German Idealism, so essentially is his poetry the first overcoming of all "metaphysics." But we will grasp this only when in our thinking we have overcome the essence of metaphysics.

17

Beyng—self-refusal as the trembling of the divinizing of the last god. The trembling is a keeping open—indeed even the openness of the spatiotemporal field of the "there" for Da-sein.

18

14

Beyng—the trace of the divinization of the absconded gods, a trace that broadens a clearing. This clearing sets free the self-refusal as an assignment of Da-sein, whereby the clearing is grounded, humans are transformed, and beings come to be more fully. That tracing of the divinization, the tracing that in itself is this assignment, may be grasped as the appropriation.—To name beyng means to "think" the *event of appropriation*.

19

Thinking in the other beginning is not for the public. Members of the public encounter "philosophy," if they at all lend a thought to this useless pursuit, with the expectation of receiving some sort of answer as an assurance and confirmation of their desire for "contentment." To ordinary thinking, nothing is more alien and suspect than the step into the *unguarded*, because there—according to the usual reckoning—one can only count on losses. The unguarded clearing of the self-re-fusal is the *storm* which blows within beyng itself—the event of ap-propriation itself stands in the storm.—Force—submission and breaking and downgoing are | the signs of beyng. But this storm of the event is the intimacy of the divinization in the trembling of beyng.

If future thinking is *not* equipped to endure *this strangeness* of its mission (the strangeness of the grounding of Da-sein), then it lacks everything needed to place into suitable words even only the most provisional questions regarding the truth of beyng, to wait for the ca-pacity to hear on the part of the few, and to leave aside all clandes-tine ways.

What does this say about the possible communication of this think-ing?

20

Historical Da-sein is going to run under and surmount our political will only if this Da-sein, *from its own resources in poetry and thinking*, finds its other beginning. All mere concurrence with the political will is insufficient and never corresponds to the uniqueness of our mis-sion. From which snarled confusion of obsolete traditions of thinking and representing must we first detach ourselves? And how else can this | detachment succeed than through a prior binding to the com-plete otherness of the beginning?

21

The affiliation of the creative ones to their assignment is all the more intimate, the more properly the origin of the respective domain of creativity finds itself in *its* beginning and unfolds its sovereignty. The sovereignty of creativity is the only appropriate guarantee of its ser-viceability—in case it is at all still necessary to think of and require such a thing.

Usually "service" is considered merely as being subjugated and fol-lowing orders. The purest service is sovereignty.

But what could hold sway with more sovereignty than *beyng*, wherein beings first come to be beings? How does the human being ground this sovereignty? The one who grounds must become someone who is transformed.

22

"*Science*."—It will no longer bring itself beyond the servitude of its activity. And this character is a consequence of its modern | essence (attaining the point where everything can be calculated and explained). The servitude will increase, as the "results" and the "prestige" now become greater—what else does a servitor seek? And the greatness of the "results" and of the "prestige" is assured, because the servitor has entered upon a service that is very rich in prospects: the natural sciences work for technical utility, and the human sciences are in quest of a "German." In every case, one serves the "people," naturally while adhering to the purely "theoretical" tasks and with indignant repudiation of all trade school affairs and in the assurance that one will afterwards be able to return at once to the purely theoretical "problems."

And in fact quite unforeseeable "results" will come to light—and knowledge will become ever more unessential, because one will feel content again in a newly "drawn out" activity (in fact basically stemming from 1890), especially since one now discovers things of which the "liberal" masters from the previous generations surmised nothing. In such an atmosphere, how could thoughtful questioning still have a role? Philosophy has still never arisen out of | "science." Then out of what? Out of itself. And what does this origin give us to think about?

17

18

23

Who stands as a creator in that restrained time of the long transitions between the very infrequent moments of the shining forth of all the strangeness of beyng?

24

"*Temporality*"—the common opinion still sees it as dissipation in change and slavery to the succession of one thing after another.

And yet it is *mastery* of this "time," without flight into the standstill of the empty and of what is ever the same. And it is mastery as steadfastness in the opening up of the truth of beyng.

Time—the trembling of beyng, a trembling that complies with the conjunction and essentially occurs as the clearing of the self-concealment. (Cf. p. 13.)

25

How comes it that something *rare* can no longer exist and that no one is strong enough for what is rare? Because everything has long since been leveled down to mediocrity and everything has been made accessible. Because everything can be produced and in an instant becomes familiar to everyone everywhere.

19   Yet these are only consequences of an incapacity to be prepared for what is rare. The rare mostly and for long periods refuses to show itself and yet in self-refusal intimates back toward itself. Our incapacity to measure the bearing of this intimation, to proceed unguardedly in this measuring, and to follow up the intimation. Yet in all things and in everything, there still persists what is most rare—beyng—as more alien even than nothingness, because it itself first projects nothingness around itself as its own most proper shadow.

26

Need to take account of the possibility that historiology will eradicate history, which means that the only thing historiology allows to count as worthy of representation will be denied any claim to appertain to what is concealed and unique in history. Or in other words it means that *history will go down* and the Sinicism of machination and of lived experience will commence, i.e., the hollowing out of all beings and the unimaginable increase in the capacity to forget this process of the downgoing, the decline, of history. Can there be history where no sooner has something set out than it is proclaimed historiologically as

20   the greatest "event" of all previous history? | The epoch of declining history is by essence presumably a very long one, so long that all recollection becomes completely weary of it and it returns to "chronology," i.e., to the recording of the exorbitant series of exorbitant "lived experiences."—

It is not the West that will go down; instead, its history is threatened with decline, and it itself is in danger of continuing on machinationally and unhistorically, a continuation that can become all the less weary as the human being becomes ever smaller, less in need of recollection, and less capable of meditation.

27

How long will Hölderlin still be claimed for the "classical" age? As long as the classical is taken for the highest and, especially, as long as a relation to Greek antiquity can be demonstrated. This foolish cultural appraisal has indeed today, when "humanism" must be rejected, a bad conscience, for which reason a realistic classicism is invented. If this frivolous juxtaposition of "cultural types" were solely at issue, then it would not need to be mentioned. But this "cultural morphology" in the "human sciences" (crudely imitative of Dilthey, but

with a crude I alteration in outlook) is merely the consequence of a   21
mode of thinking of the infamous nineteenth century, a time allegedly now left behind. Since *along with* the presumptuousness of such
historiological calculating and soothsaying, historical ignorance increases at the same pace, those pursuits then have free scope, especially if they cover themselves in the opportune "politics." (Cf. p. 22.)

28

Today much of the essential tradition must be abandoned, but that is
perhaps unavoidable and not necessarily disastrous. What is sinister
is something else: that the possibility to meditate once again on the
greatness of this loss is becoming ever weaker and will finally disappear, on account of the impotence for meditation and the aversion toward it. (The decline of history because of historiology and specifically
now because of the supposedly first "correct" historiology.)

The disappearance of this possibility is the dawning of an excess
of rigid and crude historiology. And this entrenchment is again only
the consequence of the concealed abandonment of beings by being.

29   22

"*Cultural morphology*" is an inheritance of the nineteenth century,
where it still meant the capacity to set up and even derive a system in
itself (of cultural types). But now one fancies oneself more insightful,
places oneself in one's respective determinate cultural type, and from
there decides about the other types and in opposition to them. That
seems more "realistic." Basically, however, the old deficiency has remained: the avoidance of any essential meditation. One even has an
excuse for this, and the excuse takes on an air of superiority: "meth-
odological" discussions are renounced and the "methodical" is thereby
measured up to that notion of "method" which arose in the "method-
ology" of the "theory of science" of neo-Kantianism and positivism.
Thus it is not at all seen that "method," as a way for grounding truth,
constitutes the most essential part of any meditation on the matter at
issue (in philosophy), i.e., on beyng.

30

A "time" will be all the greater, especially in its own eyes, as those living in
that time become smaller and as this diminution happens more unobtrusively
and rapidly. The necessary consequence of this process is that every
meditation is "lived" as a raising of objections, as mere scrupulosity,
and even as I antagonism. Where this evaluation is elevated to a prin-   23

ciple, all mediocrity and all incapacity for thinking are securely protected and their justification never fails. Meditation is then a sign of
weakness or of mere skepticism. At the same time, what was accomplished in previous meditation is taken over as something self-evident, if not indeed something self-discovered. And the genuine greatness of the age immediately loses every field for the unfolding of its
exemplary power. But what is essential is again not to identify this,
but to recognize how here is formed a proper atmosphere for the self-
stimulating machinational "lived experience" (an atmosphere in
which at once all other "life" is unwittingly suffocated) and to recognize how all this is *not* caused by the accidental failure of today's humanity and that instead here centuries will go to their end, whereby
the mere negative depreciation of these processes would lead to the
gravest errors.

In opposition to this opinion, such a state must be known and
grasped in its essence as the irrepudiable initial position for every step
of the transition.

24   *31*

What "philosophy" now still is:
1. An agglomeration of historiological and systematic *erudition*.
(And from the elimination of all the mistakes of an intellectual tradition of two millennia, how should there not finally be compiled the
"correct" "work" of a very zealous pedantry.)
2. *"Scholasticism"*—but naturally an apologetic treatment of the "intellectual possessions" of the most arbitrary provenance, snatching up
what is newest, *in the service of the Christian Churches*, the mishmash of
a relatively ordered "level" as the principle of the totalizing.
3. *"Scholasticism"*—but one still seeking for its Aristotle—*in the service of the political worldview* (principle: the covering over and disavowal
of all the "sources" from which this philosophy originates). "Community" as principle of theft—the selection of those who are as un-
deformed as possible—you should speak to the oblivious ones as the
"public." The organization of the reciprocal praise.
4. "Philosophy" as *abusive grumbling about philosophy* and about its
rekneading into the hodgepodge of a worldview that lags behind.
25 | (Principle: ostensible battle against Christianity—without one ever
having been a Christian and needing to pass through a confrontation
with Christianity.)
5. Journalistic cleverness in the treatment of all these sorts of "philosophy," with various dosaging according to the circumstances—
(the remainder of the scriveners on the *Frankfurter Zeitung* and other
newspapers).

Utter inconsequentialities—taken for themselves—; but in their not-accidental *nexus* (which extends all the way to express agreement), all these deformations of "philosophy" are indeed what is essential to the "spiritual" and "cultural-political" situation. All together have the same interest—always badly hidden, though differently for each case—in neglecting the actual questioning which presses on to the first decisions and meditations and in closing their eyes to all the question-worthiness of beyng and to every unguardedness of beings. And therefore this "camaraderie" of nonphilosophy is "closedly" ready for the "engagement" in service to the entrenchment of the abandonment of beings by being and the entrenchment of the prime form of this abandonment—nihilism.

Yet I all this would not only be appraised too highly but especially in a perverse way, if one thereby let oneself be led astray to an explicit and immediate combat with it, above all because this "philosophy" remains a necessary means to mediocrity. Everything mediocre, having in itself no weight and never able to strike roots, requires from time to time an obtrusive confirmation of its indispensability, in order thereby to become ever more mediocre and serviceable.   26

What "philosophy" in the just-mentioned types still is may be seen simply in the fact that it has already for centuries been cast away from the great course of its first history and can no longer venture, by swinging onto this course, to give itself up to an essential confrontation by which it would be referred to its groundlessness (namely, the fact that the guiding question of beings—as it is always still asked—has no ground, unless it arises out of the basic question of the truth of beyng).

To be sure, what rises up with this question requires a transformation of the human being and also requires that which is unique and highest in all philosophy, namely, that philosophy take its origin out of a grounding of the truth of beyng and thereby renounce every crutch and dependency and confirmation—. The most difficult to grasp is this: I the productive thinking of beyng ventures the origin   27 out of nothingness (out of the shadow of beyng), namely, beings as a whole qua beings. Beyng is to be ventured—whether humans, grounding the truth of beyng, will transform themselves in this ground and its preservation i.e., its unfolding. Philosophy stands and falls with the preparation and seizing of this task.

To turn to philosophy in this task means to turn away from every attempt at an immediate agreement *with* what is still pursued as valid or even only *from* that and out of opposition to it. Seen in terms of the conventional and its trustees, however, this turning away seems to be peevish enmity and obstinacy.

The turning away cannot demonstrate what is essential and first in it and what bears it: the originarily appropriated turning toward the truth of beyng—the steadfastness of Da-sein.

32

For all future creativity, the *unique* destiny of Hölderlin's work remains a unique predetermination of the affiliation of his work to history. For this work did not meet with a mere ordinary misunderstanding or a mere inability to master it on account of its difficulty—instead, this work as such involves something unique: to establish a decisional do-
28   main far ahead into the future and precisely for that reason | to re-main behind for every calculating present and, as something past, to fall victim to various changing timely interpretations.

33

Misled by the excess of a *historiology* pursued through a mere craving for cognition, we see even history only as the elapsing of stories (in-cidents). We are unable to surmise what is leaping ahead in happen-ings (and the resultant long and concealed remaining behind of what is most essential) and to take from this space our measure for his-torical greatness (from the space of the remaining behind that leaps ahead). (Cf. p. 102.)

34

How strong must a *work* be, in order to remain constantly *untimely* in itself (not merely on account of an incapacity in those who are con-temporaneous with it)? This "untimeliness" is the presupposition of every genuine—i.e., ever invisible and mediate—"effectiveness." The strength of a work is measured by the extent to which it refutes its creator—i.e., grounds something altogether different than that on which its creator himself stood and had to stand. Therefore, all "biog-raphy," "psychology," "biology," and "sociology" are null and void for the work and its "effectiveness." The latter does not at all consist in
29 | being understood, if that means: explainable out of the sphere of what is intelligible to an epoch.

The "utility" of a work is often said to consist in its allowing us to recognize ourselves in the work, to find our wishes fulfilled therein, and to reform ourselves accordingly. The work as *mirror*. The mirror becomes what it is through the one who takes the work as a mirror. The work is thereby degraded to the standards of lived experience.

What does it mean to become mature for the truth of a work? Works shown to us by "art history" in what and how they *are*? "Only" still in recollection? Or is recollection the unique space for growing up into greatness? May we base everything merely on "greatness"? Are we asking all this because "works" are everywhere denied us and are so because the capacity to imitate has become too great and too un-limited? And still greater the contentment with these achievements, which become more prominent as we see history less.

35

Behind everything now transpiring, if it is more than a political re-organization, must be prepared that which we do not know and from which all creative decisions I are to be determined: the transforma- 30
tion of the essence of truth.

36

"Give to Caesar what is Caesar's and to God what is God's" {Mk 12:17}. This "slogan" is now becoming a "political" one but is indeed Chris-tian. The ethnic-political [*volkspolitisch*] worldview has stepped into the place of "Caesar," and God is still supposed to be the Christian—i.e., ecclesiastical—i.e., Roman one. This distribution of claims and "authorities" to the "earthly" and the "heavenly" is indeed intrinsi-cally already—according to its very articulation—Christian. Whoever concurs with it and orders his behavior in accord with it—assuming this is based on a decision and not on a mendacity imbued with the Enlightenment—is, despite everything, standing on the soil of "posi-tive Christianity." In other words: the possibility of an originary crea-tion of a quite other "world" and truth is thereby definitively cut off. Yet this prospect perhaps offers nothing strange—since indeed the ethnic-political worldview grasps itself for its part as "eternal" and fin-ished. On the side of "Caesar" and of "God" and in the very distinc-tion—one has "the truth" everywhere. Everything is solved and an-swered. A completely unquestioning age is dawning. All I questioning   31
—the "problems"—shifts completely into the field of the accom-plishing, instituting, disseminating, and entrenching of "worldview" and "faith"—and the domains of "creativity" in the sense of "art" and poetry merely have the corresponding role of expression, confirma-tion, and attestation and are therefore already secure in themselves. Even here there exists only the one "problem": how can everything be aligned "unitarily" in service to the "people" and brought to the "people"?

The complete lack of questioning is the basic trait and indeed the necessary trait of a "world" in which mediocrity is supposed to reign. Yet mediocrity never brings itself to reign; on the contrary, it requires the corresponding great achievements distinguished by their leaving the most essential decisions (on being and truth and Dasein) unconditionally untouched—and by adhering instead to the customary domain of the tradition.

The age that completely lacks questioning must of itself press toward "eternity"—for what else remains to this age except the *self-continuance* that yet bestows on all things that which in a certain way still allows a "futurity" in every temporal point and in every situation.

Yet this age—against | its own will—can now be the preparation for a complete revolution into a new beginning. How so? Because Christian faith—despite the earnestness of individuals—has (through the centuries-old tactics of assimilation and vindication) forfeited all creative power as well as the power to wield such powers and because on the other hand political purification and unification create a ground on which something else can become necessary, over and against and beyond what lacks questioning. What is coming no one knows. Yet one thing is certain: the attitude of balancing off what has been handed down and the calculation of the "truth" in terms of the (Christian view of the) earthly and heavenly must be broken off, if indeed *the truth is once again supposed to become the truth*.

37

In all creativity, the rule holds: few things and these good, and what is good accessible only with difficulty; and not rather: many things, bad and easily accessible. But what if now a new rule were found, one apparently definitive since it settles everything: many things and these good and everything readily accessible?

That is in fact a possible demand. If it acquires exclusive validity, then the *rare* is foreclosed. The rare—meant not only | in a temporal sense—as that which remains absent in long intervals of time. The rare is above all the unusual and difficult and something accessible only to a few. Whence arises the mediocre good, if not from an *inability to attain the rare any longer*? This good always remains only the "not bad"—and thus necessarily the supplement of something unique which has extended into the easy and frequent.

The demand for many things, good, easy—as a principle of the "configuration" and "attitude" of "life"—destroys its own possibility, if it would also disavow the rare and the unique. But must it not do so, in order to remain prescriptive? Of course. And this intolerance on the part of the good mediocrity and indeed best mediocrity is even necessary, so that the rare and difficult can in themselves remain difficult in accessibility. These "laws" of creativity, and of its working out, have their ground in the essence of *history* itself, and history is grounded in creativity:

History: the openings, alien to one another, of what always remains absent (cf. p. 19). The alienation itself founds the nexus of history. What always remains absent—is not, however, something emptily selfsame—but is instead what is unfathomable of the richest ground of beyng, in the midst of which beings are struck and abandoned | by   34
the divinization of the god. We first experience this essence of history when we have forgotten historiology—have entirely dismissed it as a mode of thinking and calculating.

38

There are two ways of attaining *history* (not merely of what is past)—
as that which is still unfathomed and still entirely strange to us and as the abyss of the rarest and most unique divinization of the still undecided god of gods. The latter way is the complete overturning of beings and the transformation of beyng. Yet in each case, there is decided, along with the human power for Da-sein, the manner in which this power is attuned and determined through overturning and transformation, and so is decided the good fortune that this power still comes into play at all.

The way of overturning is short and breaks out suddenly with all the danger of a rapid devastation while swaggering in what is merely "new" and "unprecedented."

The way of meditation is long, hidden, and to all appearances never effective.

Or are both ways necessary and indeed such that they must never meet? What then | does this mean: the assignment of the two ways to   35
each other? It means that we today, already quite distant from truth and beyng, merely follow the traditional and the calculable, when overturning *and* transforming events are required in order to place humanity once again *before* the silent essential weight of things and *into* the capacity for the passion of creativity and then to ground this open realm as the "there" of the clearing of self-refusal—and thus to attain the abyss.

39

The genuine superiority is the radiation—indeed the invisible radiation—of *rank*. Rank—taken essentially, not by degrees—belongs to *Da-sein itself*. For Da-sein alone may leave to things the greatness of their essential weight and may be shocked by their illumination. Genuine superiority therefore derives from the power to magnify things—; to magnify means here: to lend and allow greatness (cf. p. 83). Nongenuine superiority lives on the diminution of things, and this diminution presupposes monotony and mediocrity. (On greatness, cf. *Ponderings* V, p. 106.)

36   *40*

Where do we stand?—This question asks *directly* about the "place" within a supposedly familiar and surveyable historical space which is itself supposedly present at hand. The error of this view becomes clear only slowly and with difficulty for an age completely brought up on "historiology" and "psychology" (in various forms), especially when arbitrary circumscriptions of the "spiritual," "political," and "cultural-political" "situation" of the time are easily available and produce a thoroughly intermixed variety of cognitive values. That this "psychological" and "culturally agitative" geography already allows a—perhaps very poor—preconception of "history" and "situation" to be determinative and makes every such calculation question-worthy is the least of all that must be considered here forthwith. Yet perhaps what is halfway and thus quite insufficient and fatal and semblant in this question ("Where do we stand?") can be seen most readily if we once *dwell* for a moment on this rushing directly at the "where" and at the determination of the "where." This pause to dwell | will be brought home to us by the simple reflection that here something else still remains to be disclosively questioned: where do *we* stand? "We"? We who? It seems as if this were clear and decided and needed only an indication of the standpoint for "us." But whatever does not lie in this unquestioned "us"? Perhaps already the answer to the sought-after *"where"* in which we stand. And then the question, which is accustomed to casting around itself such a great semblance of thoughtfulness and profundity, would in earnest not be a question at all—but only the last sign of a humanity drowning in "historiology," a humanity that claims to be master of history.

Accordingly, if a question is to be posed here, it must run along these lines: Who are we, that we cannot dispense with the determination of a "where"? Yet this question throws us back to a more originary one: why must *we* ask about ourselves in the question of the "who"? What is already opened up with the projection of the who-question? Answer: the selfhood of what is taken into the question. But what is selfhood, and how does a "where" belong to it? Is the self not an "expression" of "personality," and the latter the "spiritual," and thus the nonspatial?

But does the "where" refer to "space" in the usual sense, and is self-   38
hood not rather the ground of "personality" instead of its expression—
and this ground so essentially that the grasping of selfhood already
accomplishes the overcoming of "person" and "personality" and thus
also the overcoming of thinking in terms of the distinctions of body,
soul, spirit?

Who are we—such that the determination of the "where" inflicts
us? The ones who ground Da-sein? *Are* we these? Or do we seek the
first step in the grounding when we transform that question: where do
we stand? Do we surmise at this position something of the projective
power and transformative weight of an actually developed question?

"Who are we—such that . . . us?" This question is different from
the immediate one: who are we? But can this question, in whatever
form, be asked at all with the prospect of an answer? In other words,
does an age ever know itself? Or is it known only by posterity? And
what does "knowledge" mean here? The question—rightly understood—does not at all ask about a present at hand or past humanity
or about a type of humanity. This question is so unique that it must
first ask about that which is to be interrogated and must | *disclosively*   39
question only that. This points of course to an unusual human situation which is impossible to describe separately. Where do we stand?
Do we stand at all—if "standing," as an ontological characterization
of humanity, means more than being present at hand? If "standing"
means the carrying out and enduring of steadfastness in Da-*sein*?—
We do not yet stand but, instead, cling to the animality and rationality
of the *animal rationale*.

And who would want to contest that not much "happens" thereby,
yet that the consequences become so gigantic that they take away our
need for goals and especially any need for the truth of what is true.
(Cf. p. 84ff.)

41

The "breezy" wind of timeliness is now taken more and more out of
the sails of all "labor" for Nietzsche's work. That is good. But it does
not suffice to liberate this work in itself to its truth.

Perhaps this work, after its liberation from noise, must still pass
through forgetfulness, in order then | to be renewed. The fact that   40
Wagner and Chamberlain[2] now claim victory over Nietzsche cannot

---

2. {Houston Stewart Chamberlain (1855–1927), author of *Die Grundlagen des neunzehten Jahrhunderts* (1899), married to Wagner's daughter Eva, anti-Semite, early promoter of Hitler.}

be surprising and must be interpreted as a way of protecting Nietz-sche's work from public opinion.

42

Every creator, as a creator, stands necessarily in opposition to every sort of "worldview." But this opposition is to him thereby something always inessential—never even his motive, let alone his goal.

43

The folkish [*völkisch*] worldview has its own necessity with regard to the task of a historical compilation. In accord with its range of vision, this worldview can make its "totalizing" character immediately and easily recognizable and intelligible—especially with respect to all creativity. A people is the *ground* on which all creativity proceeds; a people is with regard to the process of creativity even the *root* out of which creativity arises and stands. A people is finally the *goal* and the *domain* of the working out of creativity.

41   As definitive as all this seems, so certainly does it remain superficial—unless that around which this worldview circles, the people, is moved into the *truth*, placed into the question of beyng, and thus jostled *out* into the contingency of its essence. The character of a "people," which makes this "people" appropriate to bear a "totality" (in the manifold sense already mentioned), does harbor the danger (if this character is consciously expounded as a unique one) that a people itself in its individuals will no longer be able to tolerate its own question-worthiness, will become trapped in its "totality" and thus be closed off from the "whole" of beyng, and will thereby make itself unsure for the decisions which may perhaps be demanded one day in this domain. (Cf. above, p. 2f.)

44

What if the occasionally justified mistrust of a certain "intellectualism" unwittingly hardened into an untrammeled diminution of the power for essential thinking and knowing? What if the surmising of the silent power of idle meditation disappeared? And what I if it even

42   came to a contemporaneously new and strengthened *affirmation* of "science" as an indispensable form of technology, such that science, prior to everything, disseminated a distorted concept of knowledge and readily prevented a renewal of essential thinking?

Yet who could decide whether or not this stilling of essential meditation is necessary and even creates for it a unique possibility to set to work once again? And in all—who deranges the work of thought? No one—in its weaker endeavors, it merely deranges itself though the false desire for public validity.

Can beings as a whole be transformed through the productive thinking of the essence of truth? What could mere "thinking" accomplish, in view of the rapid swirl of incidents and facts? Yet why should "thinking" accomplish nothing, if it, as before, thinks what is essential and grounds truth anew? What would even a very rich effecting and pursuing be, if they lacked the domain of their goals, claims, judgments, and values? Out of what does this I domain originate? Out of a grounding of an essence of truth, a grounding that lies far back, has long been forgotten, and today is no longer in the memory of the many. Nothingness, as mere nothingness, could never incorporate despair, if there were no truth.

The origin of the productive thinking of the essence of truth is always imperceptible; it cannot be recorded—immediate promulgation is denied it, denied by necessity, and therefore all thinking seems ineffective, the more completely as its object is more essential. This danger does not threaten thinking from the outside; instead, thinking is threatened through itself, through its being denied its required self-certainty in forgoing what is immediate.

It is repugnant to the essence of beyng and to the productive thinking of its truth to be known in their essentiality by the many and to become something that can be said. The denial of the self-certainty nevertheless always arises because thinking does not leap ahead far enough, ventures too little into what is strange, and is involved too soon in making itself understood.

43

45   44

We need a new god! No! This "no" is not because the old god would still suffice and could still be a god—but because this god is not at all the one that is in need of us. The other god needs us. That is not a simple reversal of the previous relation—instead, it is the sign of something completely strange, a divinization, for whose articulated domain the past gods—the "ancient" ones as well as the Christian one—are of no help, especially if we take them as ordinarily interpreted.

We are—the future ones must be—the ones who are needed, those who, in grounding, *hold* beyng open and urgent and developed in the truth of its essence—beyng which discloses itself as the appropriating event of Da-sein, whereby the latter is then appropriated and its truth (the "there") is itself grounded. The god needs *us*—but not merely the current, present-at-hand humans as they stand and move, and also not merely humans in general in some sort of unification and im-

provement—but what is meant here is "us," those humans whose essence is first decided in the pursuit of the truth of beyng *on the basis of beyng*—thus not merely another and higher "type" of humanity—but
45   rather a ground of humanity (as Da-sein), I a ground arising out of the extreme relation to beyng itself, a ground previously closed off by necessity.

The other god needs us—this sentence can also be reformulated: beyng, moving out into its truth as the event of appropriation, and as the "between" for the divinization and so for "beings," compels humans to a displacement into Da-sein and into its stewardship. Will humans still be "strong" enough to become these compelled ones? In other words, will they still respond to the abyssal character of beyng, or will they definitively adhere to their "own," i.e., to "machinations" and "lived experiences"?

In this regard, to be needed is higher than "needing" (requiring). The other god needs us—*requires* the grounding of Da-sein and dispenses this grounding into the shortest path of a sheltering of beings in the simplicity of their structure.

46

Now even the "solitude" of the creative ones has already become a catch phrase, and what still remains well and purely guarded in the circle of the radiation of beyng? But—although the talk of this "solitude" has become common property—does that affect the solitude itself? Yes—insofar as it now becomes *still more* solitary and I thoroughly
46   inaccessible to itself. Solitude does not arise or persist—as is known—through the *absence* of those pertaining to it, but through what? Through the advent of another truth, in the invasion of the fullness of the merely alien. Therefore, the solitude can never be "removed" from the outside; it would and could still slip away.

Yet which solitude must be there where the issue is to abandon metaphysics and to arrive at beings out of the truth of beyng—better: to bring beings into arrival out of that truth?

47

The sign of *greatness* (cf. *Ponderings* V) is never gigantism as the merely quantitative aspect of effected accomplishments but, instead, is the— unrepeatable simplicity of the resolutions. In the domain of *thinking*, these resolutions are the essential and thus rare *questions*, i.e., the stillest ventures to ground the self-assertion of humanity on the question-worthiness of beyng. If we consider the rarity of such questioning— centuries feed on the drawing back and forth of an already posed and

thus expired question—⏐ and if we meditate on the fact that indeed   47
only a halo of the flashing up of such questioning can ever become
visible again—and that only for a few—concerning what philosophy
is—then we will not wonder that we—to be sure, even with our excess of omniscience in the historiology of philosophy—are shut out
from philosophy so completely and will be for a long time to come. Is
this destiny the source of our obliviousness with regard to beyng, i.e.,
the source of our approaching beings on our knees and our dancing
before beings (of everyone's actuality)? Are all of today's "thinkers"
thus in the most concealed forms merely "psychologists"—giving anthropological explanations of what was formerly thought—whether
this anthropology is now oriented toward "biology" or toward the
"history of the spirit"—and whether this history of the spirit is oriented toward Dilthey or toward the "folkish" ["*völkisch*"]? Is that why
history and its powers and forms are now calculated according to
"types" and classes? And does it depend on all this adhesiveness and
impotence for all questioning, and thus on the unlimited bustling
about and "creativity," that every attempt at meditation remains
without a firm footing, like the slightest step in a swampland, ⏐ and   48
therefore is itself immediately drawn into the universal quagmire?

48

"Ideas"—taken as truths of beyng—are the "best" ones when they *cannot* be "realized" immediately.

"Ideas" as representations of what should be, on the contrary, are in
themselves always powerless. The truth of beyng, however, does not
need power, because it is in itself power—the ground of power—assuming we seek the essence of power nowhere else than in beyng itself, in order then to know that the essence of beyng no longer needs
to be labeled as power.

49

We see little enough of the spaces, courses, and paths in which a
grounding of Da-sein vibrates, rushes, ascends, slips, tumbles, stalls,
and in renunciation accomplishes what is greatest about it. What could
be the point here of the cleverest syntheses and calculations of "psychological" and "physiological" "data," of life's "outer" and "inner" circumstances and ⏐ influences? What would be the point of a reference   49
to the "creativity" of action? But is it not in good order that all these
explanations remain misconceptions? Yet what if they are not taken
as such, but if on the contrary in them the "lived experiences" of a
human being are themselves supposed to be brought to a pure re-

"living"? And why should these explanations be erroneous? Is not the human being the "rational living being"—is not all of "biology" and "psychology" and "morals" as such cut to the measure of this being? Certainly—but this "psychology" and its sustaining sovereignty of lived experience are conversely at the same time the *whirlpool* into which that conception of the human being is drawn ever again and thus is twisted and hardened.

What trap resides in the fact that the oldest determination of the human being secures itself and endures? Is it the oldest—and does it originate out of a fullness of knowledge of the human being, or out of a failure of this knowledge? Whence comes to the human being his own interpretation? When will come to him finally a deep mistrust of it? And how will he come upon the source of this necessary 50 mistrust—I upon the question of the truth of beyng, the question which alone can become the place of the essential origin of the human being?

50

"Lived experience"—the reason these *words* are entrapping is not that they are now used up and have become a mere catchphrase. This using up is only the consequence of the fact that indeed everything has become a lived experience, that one now encounters oneself in the most superficial form of the *cogito me cogitare,* that now in the most concealed way the certainty of lived experience has become the measure of actuality and thus the measure of truth. The result is that soon, perhaps already, "lived experiences" will be redeemed through "happenings" and that therefore in continuous increase everything will be poured into the mill of lived experience and be ground up, and that this will more and more count as that reality providing the measures for the projection of "all-encompassing life."

Indeed the use of this term, "lived experience," has risen into the unendurable—but that would not be worth noting if it did not indicate that lived experience has entrenched itself therein as a form of 51 humanity—i.e., I of modern humanity as the organizer of nihilism.

51

Every day sees increasingly gigantic numbers in the speed of machines, in the mileage rates of autos, in distances mastered, in audiences at the cinema, and in listeners to the radio. But what if we once wanted to calculate what we fortunately cannot, namely, which distance from beings and from the essential power of things is carried out in becoming entrenched and in the increase of those "needs" after the increase into the gigantic, which hollowing out of beings is gaining ground here? This process, prepared for centuries, has seized all "cultures" and "civilizations." This process drives in itself toward an end and indeed is today perhaps only the very long-enduring and more and more self-ignorant entrenchment of an end state, one which according to its type still has great "progress" in prospect.

52

Nietzsche.—Perhaps Nietzsche's authentic work—in the way that it had to remain unconfigured—| is full of determinative power, except that   52 we are unable to face up to it. A finished corpus of work indeed allows an overview and a presumed mastery and thereby the usual "disposition." An unfinished body of work naturally tempts us to an arbitrary compilation of apparently random passages and thus to an ascendancy of arbitrariness in another direction. In every case, with such an appropriation the still-concealed movement of thought (the questioning, along with the domains it ventures into and the ones it shies away from) thus remains unliberated. The thinking nevertheless remains well guarded and kept open, until those come along who are strong enough to be swept away by it.

In the meantime, one will take delight in "images of Nietzsche" and through the production of Nietzsche-"literature" will degrade his work to an exercise ground for ever worse and more directionless "dissertations."

53

Neither the progressive hollowing out of all beings nor the parallel yet outscreaming exaggeration of every matter and every word deserves our focus; | what does instead is that occurrence which shows all this   53 as merely concomitant and which itself has not yet come forth. How should we designate it? The ordinary things of all history and of its incidents lend us no framework or field in which they would be reconciled; instead, we are ones who are compelled—finally—to project out of itself this that is not coming forth and thereby to break apart our past.

The hollowing out and exaggerating of "beings" as derangement into nonbeings are the consequences of the fact that beings have fallen into machination. They were predestined to this fate, ever since beingness was sealed as representedness (ἰδέα). The derangement into nonbeings, however, does not seek to know itself but, instead, must renounce itself and falsify itself into a conquest of the true actuality of "life." And this outscreaming of itself—it arises from the most con-

cealed anxiety, which is too weak to become ready for the shock
whose trembling lets gape open the breadth in which beings (having
become nonbeings) are abandoned by beyng. The occurrence I of the
abandonment by being, if granted its voice and its disposing force, testifies to the abyssal character of beyng. Admittedly, not for the many
and the stuck fast, since these for a longer and longer time still grasp
at all things and make everything great accessible and therefore small.

54

Only a few are still able to traverse the cleft between the gigantism
of machination and the reticence of beyng. And who is able to endure both at once in their extreme oppositionality and necessity, in
order to know therein the bursting forth of the divinization and thus
to possess—to renounce—that which refuses itself as self-refusing?

55

In order to sense what is weighty, one must be weighty oneself.

56

There are slave markets at which the slaves themselves are often the
greatest dealers.

The gigantic as a quality of the quantitative.

If futureless violence and retrograde spirituality determine the *age
as one that is completely unquestioning,* and if those two—of the same
origin and with the same unrecognized goal—falsely turn each other
into opponents, and if on this basis Dasein's lack of truth becomes
more severe and all signs point to a long and delayed end—then where
must the beginning be posited? (Cf. p. 60.)

57

The Christian "Churches" have passed over—already long ago—into
the service of a world Christianity that smacks of the Enlightenment
and thus also of romanticism and that decks itself out with everything
Hölderlin and Nietzsche (and their successors) creatively suffered in
thinking and poetizing. The goal is the *complete suppression of questioning,* the repression of all the question-worthiness of beyng into the unknown and negligible. And all this still under the aegis of a struggle
against Bolshevism and every sort of "totalizing" claim—the trivialization of nihilism—as its most dangerous form.

54

55

58

Technology—a common misunderstanding is leading to an erroneous position regarding it. Technology and its sovereignty are believed to be unspiritual and "materialistic," on account of the presumption that technology is necessarily bound up with matter. But technology itself is a preeminent form of the "spirit"—a preeminent form of knowledge and decision.

Its sovereignty is of a peculiar significance, because technology assumes a form by virtue of which it overpowers all previous configurations of the spirit and does so all the more obtrusively as the power to inner mastery on the part of the spirit subsides. Thus we no longer have realms out of which a mastery of technology could be carried out. Mostly we vacillate between a pure idolization, whether negative (Spengler) or positive (Jünger), and an incorporation of technology into a folkish [*völkisch*] or other totalizing purposiveness.

Yet these things themselves are already consequences of the concealed sovereignty of technology. We should not appraise technology according to the obvious forms in which it has been carried out but, instead, must grasp it as the peculiar configuration of the modern essence of truth (certainty) and as grounded in the essential determination of I beingness as machination. (Cf. p. 9f., above, and p. 80.)   57

59

The *twilight of the idols* is drawing near. But not as a harbinger of their sinking into the night—instead, as an announcement of their unimpeded entrance into their day. It is not yet the evening twilight; coming first is the morning one. The assembling of the idols is the sign of a long and conclusive flight of the gods. Beyng itself is entering a new age—beyng is coming to be as the self-refusal of the most concealed hearthfire in the day that is outshouting itself.

60

Proof of God (in case such nonsense is allowed for a moment): why is there no "God" according to Christian measures? He ought to have appeared long ago against the gigantic idolatry. Since the idolatry has already reached the point of calculating how it might still overstep and overshout its bounds and its own excesses and yet the Christian God thereby continues in his activities, it then follows that he does *not* exist and only an idol conducts this activity.

No longer beings in their beingness, but beyng in its truth must be disclosively questioned; therefore all describing, exhibiting, explaining,
ordering, and deducing are refused. What matters is the fathoming
of an abyss. The form of knowledge can no longer be determined on
the basis of some sort of erudition. All science draws back decisively
into its proper domain: technology. Philosophy enters into a first, Occidentally unfamiliar, most decisive opposition to "science," wherein
all "worldview" also belongs.

If *philosophy* passes over into a *distorted guise*, it becomes *"scholasticism"* or *"worldview."* The future scholasticism, however, is no longer
an *ancilla theologiae* ["handmaiden of theology"], but a *servus anthrop-
ologiae* ["servingman of anthropology"]. It must be named with some
such masculine form of "server" or "assistant" in order to indicate its
"heroic" character. A question: what is "heroic" about this philosophy?
Perhaps the thinking? But a thinking that forbids itself any questioning and completely disallows the question-worthiness of beyng—how
can that be "heroic" or even only an actual thinking? The only thing
"heroic" here is the | *servitudo* ["servitude"] of the *servus*. Compared to
this *servitudo*, the *sacrificium intellectus* of a Roman prelate is of course
still pure freethinking.

59

                                    62

The metropolitan man of letters, good at everything but nowhere "ex-
pounding" himself even with a single thought, tolling at all bells and
in doing so never becoming past, everywhere pushing forward supe-
riors and drawing from all waters, this man in the mask of a "heroic"
"thinker" steeped in blood and soil?

                                    63

Nietzsche asks—mankind a mistake of God, or God a mistake of
mankind?[3]

Or are *both* a *mistake of beyng*, both taken in the empty Christianity
of modernity? A mistake of beyng, because ever since the first beginning of thinking, beings in the beingness of the idea disguised all the
truth of beyng and every beyng of truth—a mistake of beyng that does
not depend on this but on the fact that up to now beyng could not be-

---

3. {Friedrich Nietzsche, "Götzen-Dämmerung," in *Der Fall Wagner: Unwerthung
aller Werthe I, Dichtungen* (Leipzig: Kröner, 1919), 62.}

come the "between" for beings and for the field of decision regarding the gods. But what if we are to be witnesses to this abyss of history— to the mistake I of *beyng*—; how casually and simply does there flut-   60 ter here the "greatest" agglomeration of incidents in beings.

And the mistake of beyng—must it not be interpreted into the comprehensive character of beyng itself—the mistake: beyng as event of appropriation not becoming comprehended? (Mistake here nothing human, but all humanity only in the domain of what is proper to beyng?)

64

The age of programmatic heroism and of an absolute lack of questioning must—so it is to be expected—become the express enemy or at least must appear to be such an enemy of every basic disposition arising on the basis of terror and anxiety (not anxiousness). Only a few can recognize that the fanaticism of the complete lack of questioning is nothing other than *the outshouted anxiety in the face of the question-worthiness of beyng*. And still more rare will be the knowledge that this age which is completely unquestioning necessarily draws into an attitude whose supreme and therefore unexpressed principle becomes one of avoiding every essential decision (even the decision about the essence of truth) and of interpreting this flight as strength of will and unconditionality, as belief in the "eternal" I values. The assuring of the lack   61 of a sense of plight represents itself at the same time as the saving of culture.

The rare thrusts within the history of *beyng* are so strange and so incomparable to all beings that even the "greatest historical events" sink beforehand into the nullity of beings. Therefore, the gaze of thinking must never be diverted from this, and the maintaining of the unique decisional standpoint must never be deranged. Not even if this knowledge remains unapproved and is attained by no one. Whatever for? Can the affiliation to beyng itself ever be surpassed?

65

What now still encloses a power of becoming must grow into its own primarily annihilating space.

66

All endeavors regarding *"science"* suffer from the fact that they still have not seen into the essential inessentiality of "science" and above all cannot do so if they are supposed to be able to take themselves seriously as "cultural accomplishments."

62

67

The height attained by thinking at any time is measured primarily and ordinarily against that which must be overcome. If this that is to be "overcome" is low and desolate, then so also the highest triumph remains a defeat and a disastrous one, especially inasmuch as it cannot recognize itself and above all does not want to recognize itself in what it is, and because it must therefore take itself to be an unconditioned consummation.

68

If we posit the requirement to appraise essential history according to what eventuates in beyng and as beyng and to bypass beings ("actualities") despite their most clamorous obtrusiveness, then we are compelled to the admission that we still lack the *truth* in whose clearing beyng as the event of appropriation overpowers us. In the assignment and disposal of this event, the divinization draws past like the flight of a swift bird—the moment of the intimation toward the undecidedness of a—of *the*—decision.

69

Those "spiritual" ones who can never complain enough that "the
63 spirit" is "in danger" are | themselves the endangered ones—nay, the lost ones; for they know nothing of a spiritual decision, since they have long been firmly secure in an "educated" possession of an "education" in everything "true, good, and beautiful." Furthermore: "the spirit," *if it did still exist* as spirit, could be brought into danger only *through the spirit*. And *that* danger is not at all extant. Here and there can be found mere pseudobattles over the "spirit."

70

The "totalitarianism" of what is superficial ("people," "politics," "race") and the destruction of every grounding or even any admission of a decisional possibility in the essence of truth and of beyng. Whatever does not in advance reach out into this realm remains superficial and all the more unconditioned in its claims as it is more destructive in its accomplishments, precisely *because* a semblance speaks in favor of a constructiveness and a renewal.

71

As long as the truth of beyng is not grounded and thus the essence of the human being is not decided, the derived form of knowledge—science—in whatever configuration and usefulness I it may appear—remains without a ground. "Beings" are surrendered to the arbitrariness of the throng. But the more irresistible the human masses, all the more indispensable is "science." *This* sort of necessity, as it increases, includes an ever more extensive hollowing out and degrading of the essence "of science." On this basis can be gauged the significance of the now-spreading satisfaction of the "researchers," with which they record the inevitable recognition of their accomplishments and tasks. Through this wretched self-satisfaction, they betray themselves as the genuine enemies of knowledge—i.e., enemies of meditation and of the passion for the question-worthiness of beyng.

To be sure, they themselves in this attitude are already no longer free but instead are serfs of something irresistible, which they are simply unable to behold in its essence, because they are blinded by its unlimited success and because success is the greatest lure cast out everywhere by machination.

The insidiousness of considerations of an epoch when they get bogged down in comparing and "typifying" and do not from the beginning arise out of meditation.

72

Only one who knows can *question*. To endure the question-worthiness of beyng requires a *knowledge* of the essence of truth as the clearing of self-refusal. Any sort of "belief," held up to *this* knowledge, is still an instance of doubt. Such knowledge—untouchable by science and useless for science—stands in the event of appropriation and, in questioning, fathoms the abyss as the denial of a ground.

Denial, however, is the supreme gift—for those who know, those who question. "Ground" as borrowed soil is a comfort to one who does not know, who needs what is unquestioned and is to make use of it. Genuine questioning seeks only that strangeness it already knows, without being the courage derived from it *and* without first unfolding it into truth. Questioning is displacement into the event of appropriation. (Cf. p. 67f.)

73

As long as we still insist on "lived experiences," we deny ourselves the displacement into truth. Or would indeed the increasing frenzy of "lived experience" make truth impossible and thereby assist the usual possessors of truth, the Christians, to a new supremacy? Christianity is victorious *once again* through the production of the opponent in subjection to it, whose only option is the *overturning* of the Christian view of mankind. Yet overturning is indeed a coarsening and constricting of the essential relations (for Christianity, essentially the relation to the creator God). Overturning is inversion and reversion—but never overcoming as liberation.

74

The attempt to restore an essential truth to "science" through its reacceptance into "metaphysics" must one day (that day has come for me) be seen as a futile endeavor. For, every reacceptance into the question-worthiness of beyng signifies a dissolution "of science," and "science" will precisely resist this and would prefer a new servitude in
67   order to save I this "cultural value" and indeed, in view of the zeal for "cultural politics," will encounter no impediments to that servitude.

75

A comprehensive, complex work (such as Hegel's *Phenomenology of Spirit*) seems to place a greater demand on thinking than one of Nietzsche's concise "aphorisms" that can be read in a trice. But it in fact merely seems so. And we will remain subject to this seeming as long as we are not exercised in actually contemplating the delimitation of a thought in its proper limits instead of merely compiling "aphorisms" thoughtlessly according to the ostensible "content" and in that way making up for the missing "system." The leap into the essential statements and the releasing of their latent truth require a knowledge that has matured slowly and surely and a sense for things held in reticence. How few feel the draughts of reticence wafting round about even some of most paltry statements. And with how much difficulty does that reticence become effective, since it is more ambiguous than anything said explicitly.

Overly accustomed to what is grounded and all too directed to what
68   holds good, overly subject to "actuality" and I all too addicted to what is present at hand, we grasp only the nonoccurrence and nonpresence at hand of a ground—for us, that is how the abyss opens itself (Dasein). Our grasp is too short and we are too immature for preserving or even experiencing the abyss as the *refusal* of the ground and the refusal as the gift of the lighted event of appropriation itself (cf. p. 65).

If this gift affects you, then the "there" flashes up, and as one who has been affected and who apprehends, you are appropriated to Da-*sein*. Yet at the same time you need to know thoughtfully that this flash never affects in such a way that you would not need to make yourself, through constant meditation, affiliated to the essential power of simple things (and to have, e.g., a knowledge of the essence of equipment). Only by traversing the widest breadths in the simplicity of their lineation is this flash ignited.

76

An unbridgeable gap separates the courage for *transiency* and the flight into *"eternity."* The latter is required—at least as a lure—by the masses. To the former appertain those who are rare. Yet still closed off is that domain of history in which what is transient (not as the "actual," but I as law-giving) requires its respective congeners and places itself uniquely into renunciation in the awakening of the one who is transient as well as the others. (Cf. p. 89.)   69

77

Art.—The question is not whether art should be free or bound, but whether art can or cannot be art. Bound art is like a farm dog, specifically a tame one on a long leash leaving it free to run through the whole farm at any time in any direction. Why should this not be called "freedom," and why should it not even be conceded that this freedom is more useful than the unboundedness which would merely bring the tame, previously leashed dog into perplexity and useless straying? But such a sort of free art is never art, assuming we assign to art something else, something the eagle shows us in seeking the summits and rarely becoming visible.

(Dog or eagle?) Of what use—if indeed usefulness is at issue here— is the best race, if that is merely a race of dogs, while the decision is avoided as to *who* then are supposed to be the ones for whom, and even justifiably, a good race must be required?

78   70

Where do you belong?—Among those who cleverly ruminate on the past and are always satiated, or among those who are only of tomorrow and have already become certain of their "eternity," or among the transitional ones, the lost ones, who have no fixed place in what is customary but nevertheless share in the convulsion of beyng and thus are the transient ground of future space?

79

The *self-meditation* of the dawning age of transition from the first beginning to the other beginning is a peculiar one—because the self-acquisition to be prepared here must become strong enough to give up the past and the usual, including especially that which at present is made "accessible" a fortiori to the many as a "cultural acquisition" that was held back from them and is now again for a time entrenched thereby. This self-meditation will find its special difficulty in the fact that it always and precisely comes to stand in the shadow of what it has recognized as its severest adversary: i.e., in the shadow of "psychology." Yet only as displacement is future self-meditation what it must be. It must first place the current humanity, which is severed more than I ever into the distinction between the "individuals" and the "community," out of this superficial and derived distinction and must place humanity into the domain of decision regarding truth and the essence of truth.

Seen in this way, the momentary assembling of the people is necessarily ambiguous; it *can* arise from modern machination, one which is radically transferred to humans themselves and which "makes" everything through institutions and lived experiences, and it can strive to persevere in this task as an "eternal" state, with the inclusion of the previous "cultural" activity of mankind.

But this assembling—necessary precisely in this form—can also be a mere preparation for leading the "people" (i.e., above all, the opponents of what always threatens the people, namely, to be caught up in themselves), leading them through to a decision by virtue of which an originary domain of the truth of beyng could once again be opened up and fathomed. All self-meditation must already be decided in favor of the displacement into this decision; for only the decided are ones who can decide.

Yet these are again double-headed: the decided ones facing backward, who defend a rigid ideal (race, community) as definitive, I and those decided forward, who reach out into the question-worthiness of beyng and prepare for something still unsurmised.

80

The "question" of the *"university"* has now brought this place to light for what it has long been: an institution for bustling about. Basically everyone who is active there strives to be left in peace in the sphere of his researches and their prospects for results. Nobody wants to be turned seriously toward a *one*, to belong to a *uni-versitas* ["something turned toward unity"]; to be turned toward and transported into the truth of knowledge—as having to venture something at this place and for its sake. But all are just as vehemently *against* turning the university into a trade school, in which guise it has long existed in complete security under a very thin and threadbare cover.

And why are all *against* this dissolution? One could as it were publicly and in "society" still maintain for the university the appearance of a "culturally determinative" and even "spiritual" power; one could still—naturally in solidarity with all the people—appertain there as the place of "higher" education, and one could, with the help of this affiliation to something "higher," still invoke a certain "consecration" onto the otherwise all-too-clear pursuit of ordinary usefulness.

But one does *not* at all want and *can* no longer want a *self-assertion*,   73
which could only be a self-venturing. For this, those who were earlier lacked the courage and the capacity, and those of today lack any need for venturing, since they believe something great has been ventured politically and so it is sufficient merely to affirm it, whereby the rest will get along by itself. But *even less* than in the political can one dispense with the deed in the spiritual (not in science). Here the deed is *questioning*—it is the capacity to question long and perhaps always without a "satisfying" answer, and it is the will to unfold this as a creative power.

Seen from the viewpoint of those who preceded and those who are now, this can count merely as "romantic," and it *is* so, as long as the opinion and the attitude are that in the university itself something is still to be accomplished *against* it. That is not only impossible in effectuation, but above all it remains in intention an error, though insight into this error will admittedly come about very slowly. (Cf. the propositions about science.[4])

This insight will arise only from an experiential knowledge of the previous overturning of the university and from the unsuccessful attempt to overturn today's university—assuming both are borne and led by an essential knowledge which lies ahead of all the "sciences" and from the beginning | stands outside of them.   74

81

History.—On those who ground and effectuate, only that is effective which they themselves, through their unique backward-glancing

---

4. {Heidegger, *Beiträge zur Philosophie (Vom Ereignis), Gesamtausgabe* GA65 (Frankfurt: Klostermann, 1989), 145–158.}

love, have raised out of the tradition and into the sphere of an effective work. And this respective new grounding of what has been belongs for itself again in the domain of the accepted future and cannot become the object of a public historiology and stock of platitudes. The earlier grounders are contemporaneous with all later ones through these later ones themselves. What has been is "effective" only in the moment as the necessary and equally noble opposition to the struggle for the proper determination encroaching on the grounders, a determination which remains back in darkness at first and which can never be proclaimed contemporaneously.

In history, there is no "causality." But—what if there were for once those who know and speak, who are over and done with all backward and forward calculation according to causalities in history, or even in nature, as capturing only the superficial, machinational essence of
75   beings and of truth as correctness, | i.e., the centuries-old exclusion of mankind from the truth of being?

82

Nietzsche.—The calculation of the influences on Nietzsche's thinking according to the contemporary and earlier philosophical erudition is merely something incidental—busy work for the scholarly news service. Essential for knowing Nietzsche historically—not historiologically—is familiarity with the unexpressed and thus all the more proffered transformation of Hölderlin, Leopardi, and Stendahl. The establishment of dependencies says nothing here; it can only be a point of departure for questioning over to something else: to the motives for the movement of the most concealed history of a dialogue in the abysses of beyng.

Historiologists of philosophy and journeymen on the "newspapers" have, fortunately, no ears for such discussion; all the more cleverly do they know how to awaken "interest" in gossip and thereby at the same time produce the appearance of a "human" explanation of the thinking of this thinker. And what does one not give up today, if only something "human" is brought closer.

76   ## 83

Philosophy.—The more essentially philosophy creates its essence on incalculable paths, its ambiguity becomes more insidious and more difficult to sublate. Philosophy appears to be like the inconsequential, ineffective, and frivolous opinions of a hopeless eccentric. Philosophy is the unique knowledgeable guarantee of the essential occurrence of beyng and therefore is so "actual" that it does not at all first need actualizing. In the one case, philosophy is sought and appraised within the public horizon of human pursuits (where science also belongs). In the other case, as the grounding of the truth of beyng (thus as affiliated to beyng), philosophy has already repudiated every assignment to the institutions of beings. Both cases collapse into one if and only if philosophy *is*, and in that way for the first time they make the case of philosophy complete.

Rarely do we grasp the uniqueness of this case. Instead, in public we accord philosophy a certain prestige and almost the character of something unconditioned. Neither of those cases is taken in its decisiveness; we make it easy for ourselves by following a middle, comparative course.

And the atmosphere of patronizing toleration becomes the doom   77
of philosophy, whenever it is unsure of its essence. Philosophy then oscillates between science and worldview, whereas these two formations are equally unable to determine the essence of philosophy.

Philosophy is philosophy, nothing less and nothing more. Often enough, however, it is liberated from the clutches of those two misinterpretations of its essence and therefore must involve itself in them, especially when it presses to provide itself explicitly with validity. But if philosophy forgoes that, specifically on account of its inner superiority, then it must also be able to wait until its proper essence, drawn from philosophy itself, becomes a creative possession of human existence.

84

We pursue everywhere a raising of the "level" of the average, along with a simultaneous diffusion of the average level itself in all operations, in all accomplishments, in all institutions, in taste, etc. Therefore—one concludes—the *above* average level must *also* be attaining a greater height.

But that is in many respects a *false conclusion*.

1. What is above average, if it is supposed to have normative rank,   78
cannot be forced up from below to a greater height but, rather, must be of its own origination and must be unconditioned with respect to the average. For, if calculated in terms of the average or even the superior, the genuinely above average can very well be a reversion and a regression, because the standards of averageness cannot at all be prescriptive for the above average. The above average posits altogether different measures and another essence.

2. The higher the average level becomes, the less needy it is in relation to the above average, and the more suspicious of any attempt to attain it. The elevation of the average does precisely *obstruct* the *above* average.

3. The apparently clear conclusion from the elevation of the average to the greater height of the above average is itself a treacherous sign of the calculative character of an attitude which is thereby already excluded from the possibility of grasping the essence and origin of the setting of ranks and thus of preparing them in the correct way. Progress even here I is always only a mask covering a decline, in the sense of the increasing abandonment by being.

79

85

Does there not now spread like a contagion through all that is human the habit of organizing everything according to an established calculability and producibility, of seeing therein the prescriptive mode of all dealings, and of denying effective power to any other sort of development?

Should creative ones, in case there *are* still such, as grounding and beginning ones, yield to the pressure of the age toward calculability, utility, and breeding, and transfer what is essential to themselves into these domains and forms, in order to abolish definitively what cannot be produced and cannot be bred? No. But a quite different decisiveness and persistence of the cognitive attitude is required in order to be the steward of the gift and self-refusal of truth, the steward of the unforeseen and the strange.

86

You must be able to renounce being measured with the measures, even the highest ones, of that which is destined to be overcome.

80

87

The new politics is an intrinsic essential consequence of "technology" and is so not only with respect to the ways and means of proceeding which are set in motion by it. On the contrary, in itself this politics is the machinational organization of the people to the highest possible "performance," whereby even people are grasped with regard to the basic biological determination in an essentially "technological"-machinational way, i.e., in terms of breeding. A result of this essential nexus is that "technology" can never be mastered through the folkish-political [*völkisch-politisch*] worldview. This that in essence is already a slave can never become master.

Nevertheless, this birth of the new politics out of the essence of technology, insofar as we grasp these nexuses not chronologically-historiologically but in terms of the history of being (as arising out of the machinational distortion of the essence of being), is a *necessary* birth and therefore not a possible object of a short-sighted "opposition" assisted by appealing to the previous "worldviews" and to standpoints of faith. Necessary are only the concord of originary possibilities and the impetus to concomitantly creative meditation, which today, otherwise than ever before, can think only in terms of centuries. (Cf. p. 56f.)

88   81

Does a *truth* arise from the coupling of two errors? No. Then a third error? No. Instead, something much more dangerous, because more pertinacious, namely, the *semblance* of a truth and indeed mostly a semblance which cannot be surpassed with respect to self-evidence.

89

Why is now, and already earlier, every *truth* which is supposed to be a common possession becoming unexpectedly an untruth? Is it due only to humans, namely, their inability to seize the truth and adhere to it? Indeed it is not, for in the *common* seizing upon a "truth," this "truth" would otherwise have had to come to light even more purely, whereas in the community each one already assists, and is supposed to assist others to, that which bears all.

Or is it due to the essence of truth, because truth is always also untruth, such that something individual does not remain equal to it and precisely then least of all when it is a matter of seizing its full essence (which includes its distorted essence)? The question above is therefore insufficiently posed, because by using the term "truth" it assumes there is and would be its pure "essence."

But—according to what do we in general value the | "essence" of   82
truth and the truth of the essence?

Whither must we and can we place ourselves in questioning, if we once radically distrust—not on "psychological" grounds, but on the ground of the history of being—the actually emerging immediate insight?

90

Why does the proclaimed and the extolled (in short, what is in some way *public*) attain so often the rank of "truth"? Perhaps because "publicness" is still a paltry remainder from the lost and past essence of truth as the openness of beings? Because—the less the latter itself still prevails, all the more insidiously does the former proliferate, behave as a stronghold of correctness, and entrench itself in various configurations.

91

Entrusted to *philosophy*, the thinker stands in opposition to an *enemy* (the distorted essence of beings, which belies itself in coming to be), an enemy that, without ever abandoning its malevolence, shows itself as *appertaining* to what the thinker must radically *befriend* (the essence of beyng). And because I there is no way of avoiding the enemy, and because reliability toward the friend is everything, the thinker has an *ambivalence* toward a unique homeland, an *unbearable* ambivalence that indeed does precisely *bear* him. Indigenousness in the homeland is an unconditioned one, because it is rooted in the spatiotemporal field of beyng. (Cf. p. 92f.)

83

All who approach philosophy only from the outside, nibble on it or grumble at it, make use of it or fret over its uselessness, must wonder how a thinker can *stand* at all, since they never find his stand"point"— and never suspect that the "point" bearing the thinker might indeed be that ambivalence. How can someone stand within an ambivalence, in the "either" *and* in the "or" at the same time, unless he pertains to those who ground the abyss at whose edges all things valued and proven preserve what is most proper to them as first assigned and can bestow their magic in the span of time remaining to them out of the duration of the taciturnity of their essence. (Cf. p. 35.)

The standpoint of philosophy, of every philosophy that finds itself in its essence, is visible and attainable only if philosophy, as indeed is proper, is grasped philosophically. To be sure, one can today, and today more comprehensively than ever, easily verify every philosophy that at any time emerged in Western history—by verifying its anthropological presuppositions and others related to its worldview.

84

Especially since Montesquieu, this frivolous hunt has become a very accomplished and self-evident practice. Such reckoning up of presuppositions, which today is promptly carried out by anyone preparing a "dissertation," gives our contemporaries a stronger and stronger impression that this is the proper way—as digging into the "depth" and "background"—to come close to a philosophy and even

to "fathom" it. Who then can still wonder that such a demonstration of presuppositions now already suffices to refute a philosophy—e.g., that of Kant—without one ever undertaking the exertion required to involve oneself in the actual work of thought and in the paths of that work, paths that never terminate, since they lead into the abyss. Such exertions toward an appropriation, indeed even the requirement for them, can become so alien that already a prehistoric bone, | of which   85
nothing is known except that it is a bone, works more reliably as testimony to a supposedly familiar culture. But what if for once this very anthropological-psychological calculative hunting "fathomed" itself? Yet, as fortune would have it, the proper fortune allotted to it, this "heroic" thinking lacks any power to take a questioning step beyond itself. Which displacement would be required here to extend over the void yawning "unfathomed" under all anthropology?

Thinking must first stand beyond all anthropology and psychology if it wants to be equipped for the question of who the human being is; for as soon as and whenever the human being is "questioned" anthropologically and everything is related back to him (whether as individual "subject" or as "people" makes no difference in this fundamental domain), then a decision has already been made about the human being, and every possibility of disclosively questioning the essence of the human being on the basis of very different relations (to the essence of beyng) has been excluded. Even all doctrines (e.g., the Judeo-Christian) of the human being which determine him immediately on the basis of the relation to a "God" are anthropological—| whereby indeed in non-Christian anthropology, and in ones that   86
would be such and cannot, *Christian* anthropology and its doctrinal content must play an essential role, even if only by being inverted.

On the other hand, Christian and in general Western anthropology (determination of the human being as *animal rationale*) is in *Being and Time* related quite differently to the grounding of Da-sein, since the question of what it means to be human is determined there through the *question of being*, and all anthropology is in principle—i.e., from the very outset—overcome. Therefore, in *Being and Time* Kierkegaard and even Augustine can very well play a "role," but in a quite different direction of transformation than would be possible for a modern anthropology which, *as* anthropology, places itself—seen metaphysically—on the soil of Christianity, though it might otherwise behave ever so heathenishly. (Cf. p. 36f.)

92

Meditation on philosophy is usually taken to be *"philosophy of philosophy"* and even might be branded an extravagance of "reflection."

Now, however, in a meditation on philosophy the first question is in-
87   deed where I philosophy (to which meditation does appertain) stands,
i.e., where it is posited to be through the type and direction of its "reflection."

Our current meditation on philosophy is related to that out of which
philosophy itself arises, i.e., related to the truth of beyng and to the
history of beyng. This meditation is anything but an empty self-relat-
edness—instead, it is in all respects something entirely unique, appertaining only to the current "situation" of philosophy *in the transition*
to the other beginning—it is meditation on this transition itself as the
realm of the history of being, a realm inaccessible to all historiology.

What in the horizon of today's opinion (which remains psychology
everywhere) appears as mere self-analysis is, if borne by the question
of the truth of being, the disclosive thinking of the essence of beyng
itself, not "philosophy of philosophy."

(Perhaps we must in many respects already read Nietzsche's endeavors in this direction—even if for him still something else was in
play; cf. *Ecce Homo*.)

93

How would a modern Middle Ages have to look? What would be the
form of its "scholasticism"? In what way would the conciliar-dogmatic
88   condemnations of the propositions I of thinkers be carried out—in
case it came to that? What form would be assumed by the modern
prelates and abbots of this Middle Ages?

94

Bureaucracy in full swing as an essential *consequence* of *technology* and
at the same time as incitement to it.

95

Conundrum.—An age that is thoroughly borne and determined by
technology and thus is the actualization of the most extravagant form
of *mechanism*—how can such an age conceive of itself as an age of the
organic worldview, since "organism" is supposed to signify the living
character of what is alive, thus the nonmechanical?

But "organon" indeed means tool! And it is not at all decided, in
fact not ever actually asked, whether the "organism" could determine
or at all even touch the essence of what is alive. Perhaps the mechanical and organic are the same—and perhaps the most extreme
exaggeration of modern technology—mechanism—demonstrates

precisely what is proper to an "organism," namely, the capacity to be stimulated by what it itself posits and determines as its own conditions. Every technological result stimulates itself to its own overcoming. This complete intermeshing of the mechanical is the "organic."

What does not at all show itself in this is a fundamental property of life: growth. In the mechanical—say: in the "organic"—there is not even death—because the mechanical possesses altogether nothing of life.

89

96

One who is serious in thinking *biologically* needs to know that the forms of life indeed do demand spans of time but are finite and never "eternal." The *"eternal"* is the pretext of those who cannot cope with time, i.e., have never grasped time. Therefore, eternity is the monopoly of Christianity, and the "eternal people" is thought neither biologically nor seriously in a Christian way. What instead? (Cf. p. 68f.)

97

The addition of the determination "eternal" is accidental to the *historical* essence of a people and is a degrading of the possible greatness of a people, a greatness that consists in the uniqueness of a nonrecurrent and perhaps brief course (see the history of the Greeks). Perhaps, however, "eternity" is the indispensable lure employed to bring the essence of the people I close to the "people."

90

98

Ambiguity adheres to the essence of a public "truth"—if it could still be "truth." The allusion to this ambiguity is therefore not necessarily an objection against "truth."

99

But if beyng abandons all beings to themselves (apparently in order for them *to be*), if mere numbers and their calculation gain the upper hand, if the massive and its satisfaction must become the principle of all "ruling," if ruling is determined from below, if for this perversion of its essence a masking is required in order for it to endure before itself, if what is small, empty, decisionless, and in awe of nothing betakes itself into the form of the gigantic and of the determinateness of the calculated and settled and thus establishes the standards for the masses, then all this cannot simply be judged as a deterioration, as little as the self-interpretation of this procedure as an ascent out of the superficiality of self-praise can be found back in the domain of meditation.

91   The process is all the more unique inasmuch as through it, with the help of the hasty and facile disposition of past history (a disposition made possible and incited by historiological pursuits), everything great of earlier ages can apparently be installed as background and illuminated with a certain light whereby all measures become the seeming personal property of this procedure. For the latter, according to its kind, cannot allow the greatness and essentiality of the past to tower up, i.e., allow what is current to be placed in question at any moment—instead, everything past is ordered as a mere foil to set something off in relief for the arbitrary use of everyone.

Even this unique procedure is again not the fabrication of some individual operative agents or other, who have accidentally lost all measures while taking in all the flaws of machination—on the contrary, these individuals and these many are only the last weak splashes of a wave whose movement is to be sought only in the essence of beyng and in the humans who are affiliated to that essence. The *history of being* is shifting into a state which we could never assess according to the incidents of the day and according to fabricated public opinion,

92   because even these are I consequences, indeed ones that precisely do not admit of a conclusion drawn on their grounds.

100

Ordinary thinking, i.e., calculating, calculates this way: the more fully a being the human being is, and the nearer he comes to himself as this being and is able to relate everything to this being (i.e., the more "lived experiences" the human being has), all the more certain and secure of *beyng* must he become.

Why do we so seldom come to know the opposite, namely, that beyng is illuminated all the more, the less fully the human being is "a being"? The human being must be able *not* to be, in order to grasp the truth of beyng and on that basis assess the beingness of all beings in their essential power. Because the human being also appertains to beings and indeed establishes himself more and more in *this* "affiliation," the way to the truth of beyng is thus barred to him, and if partially open, yet only so much. But this seeking for a way and paving of a way therefore constitute his highest dignity and the kindling of the glow of his essence.

Through the mere renunciation of beings, which is always only the flight to some being, naturally the "supreme" being, humans never

become the lords of beings, | which means stewards of the question-   93
worthiness of beyng, those who are steadfast in the discrepancy, the
ones who ground the abyss (p. 82), and masters of the downgoing.

"*Downgoing*" and "end" are—so it seems to everything "natural"
and "healthy"—horrors; therefore arises all the resistance of every
"optimist" (i.e., pessimist) to the disposition of downgoing. This resistance is now for the most part remote from any knowledge of the essence of downgoing. It looks upon—calculates—downgoing as a relation to beings, a cessation of beings, a mere absence of beings. But
downgoing—conceived as the supreme victory of history in the relation of history to the essence of beyng—is nothing "negative" whatever. Where downgoing is necessary and is affiliated to the history of
being, it cannot be resisted through the crudest and most massive possible diffusion of a problematic and ephemeral "optimism."

"Downgoing," as a moment of the *history of being*, pertains only to
those who are strong, strong enough not to make noise over "heroism."
(Cf. p. 99.)

101

It required a thinker of the rank of Hermann Lotze[5] | to show the best   94
of the nineteenth century at its midpoint. He was a nobleman who
preserved the richest tradition of German philosophy, transformed
that tradition according to what was new and "positivistic" of his era,
and not accidentally undertook the last genuine interpretation of Pla-
tonic philosophy. Neo-Kantianism transmitted only a thin broth of
Lotze and already had no sense for the silent "substantiality" of this
thinker in whose work all the limits of his century become visible in
a higher form. Lotze is the thinker I always loved ever since my student days and loved even more despite the growing oppositionality;
for the *Great thinkers* cannot be loved—the icy solitude which must
surround them, and which can be penetrated only by an interrogative battle with them, repudiates any restful and protected relation.

Every philosophy is inhuman and an all-consuming fire. Only a
humanity that wants to be more than itself can place itself occasionally in the glow of this fire in order then to bring to completion something well-conceived, keep it for the longest time in the safeguarded
light of understanding, and then find | some sort of "happiness."   95

---

5. {Hermann Lotze (1817–1881), author of *Logik* (1843) and *Mikrokosmos: Ideen
zur Naturgeschichte und Geschichte der Menschheit; Versuch einer Anthropologie* (1856–
1864), especially influenced the neo-Kantianism of the 20th century.}

There gleams in Lotze a shimmer of the hard fire of the great philosophy in the light of a benevolent solicitude for the thinking of everyone. Could he not be correctly discussed today and still in the future, and not merely be dissolved into historiological relations— a leader and friend of all young people entering onto the path of thought? Or will the youth for a long time lack the daring to venture into the serene and broad meditativeness of such a thinker, to whom at the same time language was a lyre for his reserved averageness?

102

Who would not want to rejoice that the number, integrity, and ability of the German *authors and chroniclers* are clearly increasing today? And yet it remains open whether these writers can bring into play a power to form the people, or whether they do not merely labor at the preservation of an entire irrelevant idyll which precisely for a while is gladly sampled in the frenzy and excitement of today's reality, although it never becomes determinative. Indeed, what is "formative" today—if the noble word "form" ["*Gestalt*"] may be misused here a 96   moment—is the movie | theater; the most trashy American films are what "form" the still formable people today, and not only extrinsically (which could easily and quickly be well covered up at any time with some sort of "uniform") but also as regards the people's—to speak in the ordinary way—"psychic-spiritual interests." What sort of increase in the distortion of the essence of the film must still happen in order to fill in the void which seems to be spreading concomitantly and to delay the breaking out of the great wasteland? But perhaps it will not come to that; perhaps it is a law of the massiveness of human beings that they become so flattened in their essence that the least illusion already seems to them an "elevation." And here are then always the many good authors who even come to be allowed to recite in front of larger and larger audiences and become for many individuals a "lived experience."

Yet the most intrinsic fatal character of this state is not that films are triumphing over literature and both are dissolved together in the shallow waters of "lived experience." More uncanny is something else: 97   that precisely the integrity and above all the | great number of good authors will more and more prevent the possible arrival of a *poet*, because the latter is the one who requires a great plight and the freedom of courage for the affliction in those realms which are increasingly excluded from reality by modernity.

And what if now immediately in accord with the example of these respectable authors, even the poets who are equal to their task are slowly and falsely turned into authors? Perhaps it is time to reflect again on the ambiguous role played in this process by publishers and by the entire publication industry!

103

With the increasing torrent of "lived experiences" and the ever greater craving for them, *"beauty"* becomes more "beautiful"—i.e., more loved—and what disappears more and more is the possibility of finding the essence of beauty in *truth*. Truth is of course not today's or yesterday's or the very old correctness of representation, but is the clearing for self-concealment—the open realm of self-refusal—the truth of beyng. The leap into the essence of truth is tantamount to the overcoming of modern humanity.

104

The basic error excluding all modern and contemporary views from *history* and from a knowledge of history is the view that the happening of history is "development." Precisely what is *never* there in all essential history is development.

The thought of development, however, remains the soil that nourishes all historiology, and because the use of this "thought" as the guideline of research leads inevitably to "results," the correctness of this thought and the corresponding notion of history are almost ineradicable.

105

Decline of the West[6]?—Why is Spengler wrong? Not because the heroic optimists are correct, but because they establish modernity on a basis of eternity and want to raise this age of a complete lack of questioning to an enduring state pure and simple. If it comes to that and as long as it remains that, then in fact a decline, a downgoing, is not to be "feared," for the essential presupposition of a historical downgoing is greatness—but historical greatness is possible only where the question-worthiness of beyng is in an essential I form the ground of history. The West will *not* go down, primarily because it is *too weak* for that, not because it is still strong. (Cf. above, p. 93 and below, p. 99, 103.)

---

6. {Oswald Spengler, *Der Untergang des Abendlandes*, vol. 1 (Vienna: Braumüller, 1918); vol. 2 (Munich: Beck, 1922).}

106

Historiology, in the consummation of its modern essence, is becoming *backward-directed* newspaper science—*propaganda* that "belabors" the past.[7]

107

The present age in the West is the onset of the decisive phase of *modernity:* the unfolding of the essence of modernity into its essentially proper gigantic and compulsory commandeering of all realms of beings as institutions of beyng qua machination: the onset of the longest and most enduring pause of Western history *prior to* the downgoing into the other beginning.

108

Downgoing—for calculative and avaricious understanding always something disvalued—is the confirmation of the uniqueness and of the solitary gratuitousness of everything great.

109

Genuine history is the closed empire of the downgoings that know themselves among themselves but that yet | are unfamiliar with themselves. (Cf. p. 33.)

100

110

If *philosophy* in the current moment of the history of being had recognized its unique duty to put itself back into the history of being and on that basis to say what is transpiring with beings (the abandonment by being), and if philosophy likewise had some knowledge that this saying lies essentially prior to all critique of culture and altogether prior to any critique, but that it itself is the decisive step into the truth of beyng, then philosophy would have renounced the pursuit of all erudition about itself and of all advancement of itself and would have become a master of silent meditation. Is there an "education" for this attitude and toward this attitude, or must even such "education" be renounced—since here only an unconditioned leap attains something valid?

---

7. {The first institute for newspaper science was founded in Leipzig in 1916. At the University of Freiburg, such an institute was founded in 1925. Newspaper science was the precursor of communication science.}

111

History of philosophy—how would it first come to power, if the essential truth of the greatest thinkers was ever disseminated according to all possibilities and was so without "naming" the thinkers, and if all writing "about" them was suspended at one stroke?

112

The rigid attempts to prove, even in public, that there still is a *"university"* are not only pitiable (which could be endured) but are above all entirely in opposition to the current of the age and of its irresistible unfolding. Something else entirely, reaching in advance quite beyond the age, is *meditation* on the question-worthiness of beyng and on truth. But that which is gathered under the umbrella of the "umbrella organization" called a "university" is precisely what has neither the power nor the will nor, above all, the knowledge required for this "self-assertion" (not in instituting—but rather) in knowing and questioning.

113

Every *critique* of a present time is justified only as the mediate clarification of the knowledge of *future* necessities. All adherence to grievances clouds the gaze into the essential and lacks that which alone can bear a critique: the capacity to differentiate based on a decision in favor of a still unactual status—i.e., a status still not present at hand but for that very reason already all the more originarily *extant*. But therefore even a genuine critique, when reckoned from the outside, undergoes in | large measure the misinterpretation of being a sheer faultfinding, at most an annoyed one. An era that has become "historiological" in gigantic proportions, i.e., reckons up everything to itself and its own progress, can be brought out beyond itself only through the most originary *critique*, i.e., through the acceptance of a status in what is extreme—the decision concerning the essence of beyng.

This "critique" squanders its innermost power if it believes it must concern itself with the present instead of grasping the necessities of the present, lending them concessions, and keeping its gaze open for their gigantic exertions.

114

Hölderlin.—When will he become a precursor? Today he is simply degraded to a past corroborator of a present. Precursors are not ones who were formerly and have been superseded, but are ones who cannot be superseded, the ultimate ones. They are the most rare, because they are destined to say only very little in the last extremity, and what they say is withdrawn from any applicability.—

And out of what sort of precursor must the last god then come forth?

103

115

The *gigantic* as the mark of the "consummation" of modernity. But the gigantic is nothing "quantitative"; on the contrary, it is that quality which "qualifies" as a "quale" the quantitative in itself, i.e., in its utter endlessness and measurelessness. Only now is everything numerical attaining its uncanniness, namely, that of emptiness and decision-lessness. The gigantic is the genuine antigod of what is great (cf. 99). Therefore, the gigantic is also a *unique* form of historical greatness.

116

Does human *massiveness* follow from human *goallessness,* or vice versa? Or are both valid, and does that therefore require a deeper ground? Which deeper one?

117

If humanity posits itself as its goal, in the sense of assuring its capacity to endure, it has become goalless, and then one day lived experience as such must become the "greatest" lived experience. And if in this establishing of all activity and thought upon a "self-assertion," every-thing is correct, and if this correctness becomes an essential conse-quence of that self-establishing, then indeed *all the correctness* of "life"

104   I might be founded on an untruth.

118

In the presumably very constant duration of the imminent pinnacle of modernity, the clock of history has already raised its clapper for a decisive tolling. Uncannily slow and obscure is the raising of the weight of the clapper.

(As a lad, often alone in the oppressive loft of the old carillon, I saw daily this actual clapper, now still as it was back then.)

119

Does not the age, and everything that serves to usher it in, require this great indulgence, namely, that everything question-worthy be kept at a distance? For in the purview of this age, what is question-worthy can only be something subversive. And who among those that must ground Da-sein would merely want to subvert?

But what if all questioning of beyng were futile? What if beings, as they now are and are becoming, felt they were most comfortable in their negligent tranquillity and then unfolded themselves most successfully? What if even the questioning I of beyng were an error? Yet 105 even then there would have to be those who endure the error, so that beings could be confirmed in their rights, even through this otiose futility. Or is even the latter only the remote appearance of the essence of beyng—the remote appearance of the self-refusal renounced by modern humanity ever more decisively?

120

What then nourishes this zeal that makes a career out of the "problems" of philosophy, that does not even shy away from "being" and in fact produces whole series of books about it? If such a thing ceased, and the name and tradition of philosophical erudition were forgotten, and if this proved to be a genuine cessation, then a surmising of beyng must have still remained in power. And this "not" would be great enough, where otherwise only what is small disseminated itself. But if such a surmising can no longer have any power and "philosophy" continues on as an activity, then indeed vain erudition and its law of inertia offer no sufficient ground of explanation. Perhaps this process, in itself already inconsequential, is but an exaggerated attempt on the part of the abandonment by being to make itself ever more unfamiliar and I thus ever more tenacious and definitive.   106

121

Has *beyng* decided in favor of its more originary essence—its self-refusal? And this so originarily that beyng has deprived this essence of the truth? Then enclosed in this deprivation of the self-refusal would be the supreme event. And the other beginning would be deferred to a remoteness whose measure and direction we do not know. Everything great and rare in poetizing and thinking would now for the first time be placed back into its space to which only the stillness of expectation would confer all the riches of extension. And only the power to keep silent would decide about the affiliation to the event. This affiliation, however, would be most difficult to recognize. But why should beyng not then finally become what is the most difficult pure and simple? Why should not this difficulty become the principle of philosophy in the other beginning?

If the great, purely self-contained silence over beyng once ceased, and the beings abandoned by beyng only fluttered yet in the slight draft of their own noise, and if what is small has definitively calculated and secured for itself its appropriate sort of greatness and its own 107 | gigantism, what then has become of the human being? Answer: a being who knows everything and can do everything, who has instituted this knowledge and ability so completely in a boundless capacity to master everything, that nothing present and nothing past any longer escapes him. Now everything and he himself included can be directed only toward averting the unique and perhaps only still increasing danger: that their proper boredom might no longer be boring to humans. This averting must strive to make beings ever more "beautiful" and everything ever more instituted, in that the institutions proceed to become for their part objects of an instituting, whereby humans can convince themselves that they are opening up ever more elevated and thus "higher" fields of activity. And yet—the boredom becomes ever more empty and sullen—for it is indeed the unique shadow of beyng, a shadow that is not to be eliminated and that can still be thrown in the space of the abandonment of beings by being.

In the meantime, however, there *is* a call of the great to the great— and there *are* unknown ones who apprehended this call of the silent callers and secrete it in a solitary embrace for the stillest day of beyng. 108 We still know little enough of how | far the individuation of humans must leap out in order to take in the affiliation to beyng and found a completely different grounding—one that questions on the basis of the truth of beyng.

122

The human being as subjectum ["subject," "what is thrown under"].— Why does one "think" of *humans*—ever more exclusively—according to what is present at hand and what long since has been present at hand, according to aptitudes and conditions? Why not according to what is unconditioned, which is not that ability to calculate usually called "foresight" but, instead, is beyng?

Whence do the present at hand and its present-at-hand conditions derive their power of attraction allowing them to count as the "actual" and to count as this for beings and for beyng? What is the human be-ing, such that he succumbs to this enchantment precisely when he be-lieves he has completed the disenchanting of all superstitions?

The human being is taken as what most lies before, what is given (*subjectum*), such that he surrounds himself with all attainable pres-ent-at-hand things and fills up every space in between, which still lets him surmise that a "between" holds sway, one which perhaps even-tuates as beyng itself—the "between" whose openness I first lets ap-pear in the light the simple essential power of beings and lets beyng become truth.   109

And now *Being and Time* is "read" and disposed of as "subjectivism." Or does one feel, without admitting or knowing, the threat to all an-thropology in that book? What is anthropology but the glorification and entrenchment of the human being as *subjectum*—of the present-at-hand human being as the cynosure of everything present at hand.

123

Ways are at times more decisive than "results" in simulating goals. What is more essential: to hunt around in the levels of self-consis-tency and utilize all the connections with everyone hunting there, or to resolve to climb an ever more solitary mountain trail, no matter whether the climber ever sees the summit? But does he not know *in climbing* that he is proceeding to a goal which never lies on the level of a resting stage? In climbing, he is drawn by the heights above him and looks—always moving higher—from above to below. How could an agreement with the level be possible there? Only in the space of climbing do the summits tower up as the intangible guarantee of the "goals."

124   110

If *philosophy* is again to find its way to its essence, i.e., if this essence is to appear again in a more originary beginning, then philosophy must arise uniquely out of the truth of beyng and especially out of the de-cisive question of that truth. Not as if beyng were merely the object which had to determine philosophy pure and simple—beyng is never objectivatable. Instead, beyng itself determines that which philosophy has to question disclosively and also determines this very question-ing—for beyng as event "is" immediately and unitarily the ground of questioning and of what is questioned.

The only possible preparation for philosophy is now still to master the few essentials of its history: the dictum of Anaximander, the dicta of Heraclitus, the "doctrine" of Parmenides, Plato's *Phaedrus*, Aristotle's *Metaphysics Z–Θ*, Descartes's *Meditations*, Leibniz's *Monadology*, Kant's (threefold) *Critique*, Hegel's *Phenomenology of Spirit*, Schelling's treatise on freedom, Nietzsche's "posthumous writings" as his "main work." Need to have these ever present in dialogue in their uniqueness, without falling into historiological erudition and calculation.

111   Such I mastery can arise only from an originary questioning that has become necessary due to the plight of beyng itself and primarily due to the abandonment of beings by being. A complete detachment from every previous form of philosophy is the result.

In the meantime, "interpretation" has become *the* fashion in today's bustling about with philosophy. The whole world "interprets"—and becomes ever more forgetful of meditation, on the basis of which, out of the necessity of which, and with the justification of which, the interpretation is carried out.

125

If the motives to continue on with this bustling disappeared suddenly, and so did the possibilities of producing something "new" through the modification of the past as calculated in various ways, and if what counted was to question on the basis of the essential necessity of philosophy itself, then at one stroke the puffed-up bustling about with philosophy would cease. And it would have to come to light how little was grasped of the great history of philosophy and how much (namely, everything) was considered only in the horizon of "science," "worldview," or "conduct of life" and not at all on the basis of the essence of

112   philosophy itself—i.e., on the basis of the fact that I beyng at times flashes up, only to become extinguished once again in beings.

All production of "works" will make us ever more unfit for grasping the question of being—because the evasion into erudition is at once urged upon us.

126

If it is in the form of objectivity that beings are primarily referred to being, and especially if this objectivity is meant in a "realistic" sense and beyng is snatched up just like a glove found on the roadside and is investigated straightforwardly, then it first comes to light that beings have already long since been tacitly degraded to presence at hand and that *thereby* the essential volition has been suppressed, the volition for what the truth of being harbors, for work and deed, for meditation and self-renunciation.

127

What would happen if the actual thinkers had to experience once in its entirety how their questioning is borne and illuminated by beyng itself?

128   113

Awaiting those who are preparatory is a battle over something completely other, dimly surmised; nowhere a support and a solid path, no beacons from anywhere, and absolutely never a confirmation—only misinterpretations and—still more intolerably—a good-natured benevolence. And this that is surmised, if it must not be the truth of beyng itself, does, as the spatiotemporal grounding, illuminate the essence of this truth—Da-sein, wherein the human being as *subjectum* is nullified and is compelled to the establishment of an abode, even if only the one of his own downgoing.

But what if the human being destroyed for himself even the possibility of a downgoing!

129

"*Care*"—the unimprovised space for that standing of the human being within the "there"—in the openness of which what is concealed as such refuses itself and yet shows itself in this self-refusal—but in that way never becomes an object. Care—means almost the opposite of what "they" in general know as "cares"—hurrying about in and attachment to desires and pursuits. Care—but it means indeed that concentration of the human being on the basis of the simplicity of   114 that undesirous, simple, creative relationality to beyng—almost serenity, but in its tensile power, then again not serenity, because *it* (the tensile power) is not creative.

Care—the name for the fact that we are not—yet—able to name the grounding of the human being in *Da-sein*, and even where such a name is ventured, everything comes from what was hitherto and even strives to be explained on that basis (*cura* ["care"]). And yet everything is thought on the basis of something other—the fact that the *truth of being* has already become what is disclosively questioned, that the human being is no longer the *subjectum*, that beings not only are not objects and a fortiori not the in-itself—above all, that the human being is not the origin of being and thus not that which ultimately misinterprets being itself as something which could be arrested directly by the opinions of a calculative acumen, as if being were a wandering fugitive, and then could be locked up in a system of categories.

Yet perhaps the habituation to this mistake has grown so strong,
115   and perhaps the whole age of modernity lives on this I habituation,
such that a liberation of thinking from these lignifications—through
an exertion of thinking—is no longer possible. Yet perhaps a prelude
is possible, if it is played out with as little insistence as could be, such
that it especially raises no claim to be included in philosophical bustle or even in worldview scholasticism. But who could hear or read a
"lecture" otherwise than as the usual pursuit—except perhaps a pursuit somewhat more avid for the "other" and the "new"?

130

Truth is never a goal and an "ideal," but always only the self-concealing beginning, the abyssal ground. The danger of distantiation from
the truth is so insurmountable because human beings believe they
have the truth—as a goal—before themselves, whereby they completely mistake and forget its essence. But if the truth is the beginning, then it *is* only for rare moments of great decisions, indeed it *is*
only the projection of the disposing space of the decisions themselves.
And these? They stretch between the affiliation of humans to beyng—
whether humans are able to provide an abode for beyng—or whether
they let themselves be satisfied with beings.

116   ### 131

Has what is *great*, in remaining great, ever been effective? In order to
be so, it would need to involve itself in a diminishment. "Effectivity"
is inappropriate to everything great. What is great does not require
our concerns, and it alone has ever again a pure, unique, and basically relationless relation to what is great.

132

If the impossible—that which is withdrawn from calculation—has
become impossible, then humans have falsely turned their smallest
smallness into greatness.

133

To be self-evident is the form of the "happiest" possession of "truth."
But what is "happiness" here, and what is "truth" here?

134

But beyng—keeps itself concealed in its essence and in that way guarantees that its abyss always remains untouched—if thinking, by renouncing all objectification and surmising the reticence of beyng, learns that beyng is not the abstract and empty, that "beings" | in the   117
generalized forms of nature, history, and mankind can no longer accomplish anything at all toward bringing about an intimation of beyng—that rather only *a domain of what is decisive*—the ungrounded open realm of the nearness or remoteness of the gods—lets the first step be ventured into the truth of beyng.

Indeed how remote are we from that domain—how severely is our gaze misled, especially if we believe our gaze encompasses everything? And what remains? The human being—the people: this monster of vital impulses, which pursues cultural politics, declares itself eternal, and degrades all history to the mere preparing and presaging of its "own"—the human being, who is impotent to place himself into the free realm of question-worthiness.

135

If the power for historical thinking yet remains, then this thinking must accomplish only the one thing: to set up in its entire strangeness that which is historically great and from the heights of this strangeness to appraise the shallowness and flatness of what is self-evident, wherein modern calculation conducts itself and renounces every volition toward meditation.

The most uncanny, however, occurs when what is flat and empty   118
becomes apparently weary of itself and begins to discover what is great and to teach about it, and to take on airs as its guardian. Then the tyranny of the small is complete for the first time, and the confusion becomes impossible to untangle.

136

Yet all this must happen for *beyng* to resolve itself once again toward a global hour in which a celebration of the discord of beyng comes to resound and all calculation and fabrication, having first simply swaggered about, collapse as insignificant cravings.

Who can nevertheless take up that resolve into a configuring abode for the sheltering of truth; who can entirely perceive this resolve beforehand, and can abandon everything learned, for the sake of appropriating what is Completely other?

Whence would that verve of the vibrancy of his past waft over *to* a human being? In view of the fact that precisely this and the historiological arrangement ever more permit him to enjoy the "beautiful" of every kind and every time and from the establishing of this | enjoyment, to attribute to himself an accomplishment and so take cultural politics itself as "culture," which for its part must already be the onset of the abandonment by being. How unrestrainedly he is now relieved of even the least aptitude to make anything whatever and to find the heralds for that—exactly as if the human being merely expected to be continuously entertained by such imitations and even to see in them an appropriation of "refinement."

"*Refinement*" is indeed justifiably despised as the privileged possession of a class; yet if in opposition one wanted to make "refinement" accessible to the *whole* "people," then one would be affirming in advance precisely that distorted concept of "refinement." The distinction holds exclusively in the domain of drawing limits for the breadth of communication—which is now supposed to be *without* limits.

No one begrudges "refinement" to those previously excluded. But nothing happens thereby for the "refinement" of the "people." For what is refinement? It is the meditative placing of oneself back into the hiddenly compliant abode of the creative spirit—refinement is primarily meditation—the interrogative sufferance of the concealed, on which beyng itself muses; as meditation, | refinement is preparedness for transformation, but as this preparedness it is the unrest of "care" concerning the affiliation to that which, as beyng, presses on to the essential decisions about humans—where they take their origin, what they renounce, and for what they sacrifice themselves—; this, however, not for the sake of humans, but for the sake of Da-sein as the grounding of the space-time of the global hour of beyng.

To be engaged in "refinement," to become one who belongs to that affiliation—is difficult and rare.

And "refinement" is not a question of a "possession," but of destiny. And from afar the destined ones must step into a strange "present," which can be for them always only a passageway and not a stopping place.

119

120

137

If humans have found their range of vision and their field of accomplishment only in "culture" and have made the "conservation" of cultural "*values*" their goal, then one day even this "culture" must become a means of entertainment and pleasure for the "people." "*Culture*" *is the organizing of* | "*lived experiences.*" And the capacity for

121

such organization is the measure determining whether a people is a "culture-people" or not. The organizing of lived experiences, however, has a goal that is hiddenly the goal of all "culture"—to make meditation on beyng otiose through the pursuit of beings and to strive for meditationlessness as the state of universal contentment.

One could not escape this conclusion by referring to the fact that everywhere "good" and "tasteful" things are accomplished and that in comparison to previous times an advancement has been achieved. These calculations are only all too correct—but they remain calculations *within* the pursuit of culture, and precisely *the fact that* they are made out and brought forward proves that one has never thought to place into question "culture" as such—i.e., the modern mode of the being of humanity, denominated by this word "culture" but not thereby fathomed. Thus it comes about that precisely the striving of the "orderly" ones fails, because it only seeks gradual change *within* a comprehensively conditioned state of modern humanity and misuses even every originary meditation merely as a means to *such* | a remedying of "mis-states." But the mis-state is the state and position of the human being as *subjectum*.   122

What if events *such as* the first World War do not unhinge humanity but, instead, leave humans all the more established in their "essence" as *subjectum*? Or is not this world war, like the next, also only the consequence of modern humanity and, despite all the greatness of the silent sacrifice of individuals, still a meshing of beyng itself into the hardening of beings?

Which event must *then* arrive, and be prepared, if humans are to be drawn back from the incessant diminution of their *essence*? How can they themselves even start to surge up, if this diminution must appear to them as a magnification in the form of the gigantic?

However the decision may fall out here, those who are the "best" (ἄριστοι) will act contrary to their "best intentions" if and as long as they move on the level | of a calculation which is devoted to "culture"   123
and "refinement." They will all the more surely work toward a hardening of the current human essence, the more energetically and sedulously they dig up everything "good" and "beautiful" of former times and make these available in tasteful form. Much will become "better," and yet this betterment is only the habituation to the more and more concealed abandonment by being and to the total lack of meditation. And perhaps in this way will arrive once again only a harvest time for a base but very sly and resourceful curial structure of a Christianity which has become "amenable to culture" and which is sent forward by the destructive and confusing powers to be a first battler for "culture."

138

That "they" *no longer* want, *even implicitly,* to be the "people" of poets and thinkers—does this not prove the way is open to affirming *without reservation* that modern essence in which the destructive powers could first and foremost be completely entrenched and could proliferate? What if the Germans by way of self-renunciation fell into the most co-

124   vert and most immune circumstances | ever confronting them? Especially since it is so easy to renounce that poet-thinker essence, for promoted "culturally-politically" are movie actors, pianists, and authors of all sorts. Who begrudges them a decent livelihood or begrudges the "people" a well-managed supply of lived experiences? Especially since it is not enough—within the multilayered pursuit of culture—to let their place be taken in the least even "naturally" by "poets."—

Yet here meditation strikes up against a question which, if expressed, for the first time shifts everything into the range of the prime decisions: of what "use" are poets and thinkers when the "substance" of the "people" is threatened from within and without? Must not this "substance" be secured first, and in such a way that at the same time "culture" is pursued further? But what does it mean to secure the "substance"? Is a people only a "living mass," in which and on which a culture can then be built up? Or does precisely here lie the ground of a failure to recognize that precisely the "substance" itself is first to be determined in its rights and in its mode and disposed on the basis

125   of its essence—| that here this "essence" of the people—for the Germans—consists in meditation on what beyng itself has in mind for them?

Must not all thinking first be twisted free of those notions of the human being as *animal rationale*—i.e., today, as the living community pursuing culture—if the Germans want to find their essence and thus for the first time save their "substance"? Must not the "substance"-character and the "subject"-character be rescinded, as misinterpretations, and the human being placed into the open realm of the truth of beyng—into the question-worthiness of his destiny as one who must not become a present-at-hand cultivatable thing but must rather be a *transition* into the actual downgoing, i.e., into the downgoing that originates in an essential volition? What if dread of the "downgoing" should derange the essential volition and make what is simple impossible?

Thus far forth must meditation be ventured—and long and longer must tarry there and perhaps spend an age at that point—and wonder whether, instead of "culture," beings might not—unexpectedly—

126   come | into growth out of beyng. Yet we do not want to calculate but,

rather, to wait—on the basis of knowledge of the essence of beyng—
or perhaps merely be a sign for those who wait.

139

The more essential, i.e., the more inceptual, a philosophy is, all the
more decisively must it ask, beyond "forms" and "contents," about the
start and directions of the steps of the *movement of questioning*. For this
movement itself and it alone creates and disposes the space for thinking, and the mastery of this space is all that counts—for those who
must again question, while for the others it is inconsequential from
which "side" and on which "level" they misinterpret a philosophy, i.e.,
account for it in their customary ways of "thinking."

140

Beyng as event of appropriation "is" the grounding of space-time—
and thus of every "where" and "when." Therefore, beyng never "is,"
and nowhere and in no way is it "valid"—for validity merely constitutes the objectification of value, and as an objectification constitutes
a distorted essence of beingness.

What never and nowhere "is" appears to us—people avid for beings—to flow away but, projected on the basis of Da-sein, is the most
unique and most dispositional and thus the most determinate—over
against which, all "logic" is merely a stammering of "exactness" and
"univocity."

Beyng is neither a topic of "research," nor an "object" of dialectical
calculation, nor a thing of a "deciphering" which remains a calculating transferred into "lived experience," with the prior concession that
it would not yield any results (the "foundering"[8]).

141

To which misinterpretations would it first have to lead, if *Being and
Time* were completely communicated—since there the volition to originariness has round about itself a garment of "research" and "demon-
stration." And yet—as soon as thinking speaks—it seems a rigidity
comes over what remains saved up for great poetry, which may say
even again and again the one thing that is proper to it and that is still

---

8. {Cf. Karl Jaspers, *Philosophie II: Existenzerhellung* (Berlin: Springer, 1932),
411.}

new each time it is uttered. How dry and empty are the propositions
of thought here—since indeed from them the respective origin and
128   the dispositional movement, I wherein the essential occurrence of
beyng becomes an impetus, are precisely renounced.

142

Greatness—its various configurations (cf. above, p. 46).

The gigantic: the calculation that is resolved on the machinational-
ity of beings and that denies the impossible.

The titanic: the violence of inflexibility, a violence that chooses to
revolt against the gods.

The inceptual: the grounding of the origin of what is simplest in its
uniqueness and unsurpassability.

143

The supreme power of the purest constancy bestows the nearness of
what is most question-worthy—and that is *beyng*. But the drawing
near to beyng qua self-refusal is the pure relation of self-withdrawal,
wherein the entire wealth of the nearness is granted and all indifference as well as all avidity are overcome.

Whoever is thrown into the path of the history of beyng must one
day speak only on the basis of the space-time of the self-refusal and
must abandon all calculating with things accomplished and possessed.
If humans are to experience the essence still reserved for them—to
129   *become* ones who ground the truth of beyng—a great I fracture must
happen, breaking the chains by which modern humanity is trammeled
in objectification and its pursuit. The human being does not need *new*
values; instead, he needs to detach himself *from* values as background-
less presentifications of his "ideals," which themselves have become
possible only after he was withdrawn from the essence of beyng (as
φύσις) and from the essence of truth (as ἀλήθεια). Where "values" are
still "at issue," there the human being is still *entangled* in *calculation*,
and indeed so dreadfully that he believes his positing of *"values"* as his
goal has freed him from all mere "use" and "calculation."

What if then a pseudophilosophy even reckons up for him the presence at hand of "values," just as if they were objects! But they are
indeed "objects"—things the human being sets before himself in a
calculative way and could have stand before him—and therefore all
"philosophy" of "values" is illusory and for sensitive ears a travesty of
philosophy. This travesty is of the same "origin" as the hostility to philosophy on the part of "anthropology," for which reason both "understand" themselves so well. The "revaluation of values"—of whatever

sort it is—merely presents a form of the ever-more-blind entanglement in the modern essence of the abandonment by being.

Both are unacquainted with what is question-worthy, except as deformed into "problems." The question-worthy, however, is what is most profoundly barred and never to be snatched up. To deem worthy that which is question-worthy means to *question*—to place into the open realm—indeed to first found the open realm and set it up. Deeming worthy is radically different from valuing, which always remains a calculating.—

To deem worthy—to step into the effective sphere of the worthiness—of that—whose worthiness and supreme rank are manifested in its demanding for itself the question—the disclosive questioning—the grounding of the truth itself and of its essence—whereby beyng—which appropriates—its truth—as its most proper essence—is nothing other—than this: the event of appropriation.

144

The *abandonment of beings by being*—even in that way the essential occurrence of beyng is still protected on the basis of beings. Thus it could seem that the only necessity is: to recover beyng for beings (such as they are now interpreted and calculated)—or to liberate them from objectification and machination.

Yet—what if beyng itself has turned away from beings and withdrawn from them? And what if a sign of this withdrawal is that beyng furthermore does not allow itself to be known and appraised from the truth of its essence and that I accordingly all measures of today's humans apply in no way to beyng but only to their own "lived experiences" in pursuit of which the human being rotates as a hollow globe of self-fleeing boredom.

If matters are such—then indeed concealment must be allowed beyng, even first founded in beyng. Only rarely then could human volition and the human capacity to bear take on the reticent gift of becoming disposed by the abysses of beyng and of experiencing in the most silent thing the appropriating eventuation of the openness of the "there": the essential occurrence of beyng out of itself.

145

Mere calculation takes the future as something standing ahead, as a fixed goal—an object to which the paths are already computed. But when it arises, the future becomes *in*calculable. Yet the grounding of the future is another process, still alien to us, whereby the grounded becomes a still untrodden ground and an abyss cleared only in a leap.

The leap leaps over the abyss, yet the overleaping is here not a *setting of oneself over* on the opposite shore and establishing oneself there (perhaps as a reversal of what preceded: a revaluation of all values); instead, it is a leaping *over* the abyss which lets the abyss be the abyss it is.

132   Who is capable of such a feat? Those who as grounders are abandoned by every ground and in this abandonment perceive the other—no, perceive only the abandonment itself and experience the simplest affiliation to the appropriation and set this appropriation into thoughtful discourse, into a poetic, constructive, and formative work.

146

"University."—Today's university teachers; they want *neither* an originary questioning of the completely other historical *beginning nor* a decisive gaze at modern science in its essence, in its essential fulfillment in bustle, and its long delayed *end*. They want neither the beginning nor the end but, instead, that which is blind to both, namely, the past and its perpetuation. They want to count as up to date and yet pretend to be ones displaced beyond "time." They do not want to meditate but only to have "their leisure"; "science" needs leisure in order to get going. Therein they are all, the politically reliable and the backward-directed, in agreement in the same harmony and reciprocal mendacity. But this mendacity is only the impotence for recollection.

133   ### 147

"Art and science"—the utterance of this combination of words must be accompanied by Wagnerian music.

But that / "art *and* science" / is at once a degradation of art and an overestimation of science. Such false lowering and raising is nevertheless only the consequence of an ever-greater leveling of all the things drawn into the sphere of the pursuit of "culture" and its "values."

148

Education and schooling.—*Education*: to displace humans into the sphere of influence of what is great.

Schooling: to make those who can count skillful in what is small and calculable.

149

Great and Small—what is small betrays its smallness most visibly in its choice of an opponent, for it chooses as an opponent only what it already believes it can accommodate, whereby it can anticipate finding approbation in its scorn. But whoever scorns is always diminished down to the level of the scorned. Only one who is able to overcome scorn has no more need of the feeling of superiority in order to be great; i.e., to *be* and I to let the other lie where and how it lies.   134

One who chooses as an opponent something great, something greater, can indeed be defeated in battle but in all his inferiority can never become small as long as he adheres to his choice, for that choice has already decided about him.

150

Propaganda is the reverse side of a "defamation" not sure of itself.

151

Where all *meditation* is avoided as a matter of principle, "good conscience" is attained by falsely turning the lack of meditation into strength and health—which succeeds all the easier inasmuch as this interpretation is in the end "practically" correct in relation to the ones concerned.

152

Thinking. What is most difficult is to recognize the *distorted* essence in the essence of beyng and *thereby* to grasp (not merely "dialectically") the distorted essence as a necessity of the essence: to posit the *distorted* essence and in the positing to keep oneself free of all negativity. The "development" of a thinker consists in the unfolding of this capacity to ground the distorted essence. Of course, this affirmation of the distorted essence is, I for ordinary opinion and its "optimism," immediately imbued with the appearance of "pessimism."   135

153

Meditation: the *courage* to know one's own presuppositions and to question disclosively the space of one's own goals. The *power to pay heed* to the genuine seeking and to the venturing of long errancy.

But most people need to avoid meditation, since even this avoidance is necessary for something to happen. Beings never come to being on *one* path. But the lack of meditation, in the form of an affirmation of a complete unquestioning attitude toward all things, can never take the place of meditation, provided humans are supposed to remain in history.

154

One who today proclaims that philosophy is otiose and impossible has the merit of honesty over all those who pursue a "National Socialist philosophy." The latter is even more impossible and much more otiose than a "Catholic philosophy."

136

155

On account of Descartes, "philosophers" concerned with the existence of the "outer world" are brought into a situation where it is supposedly necessary to prove the "reality" of beings "in themselves."

156

"Culture." It is no longer possible for the youth to follow errant paths in questioning and to struggle through to themselves by penetrating into obscurities and things presumed self-evident. How is a creative power to become necessary here? Where does anyone risk one or two decades in meditation, in order perhaps to acquire by struggle a small ray of light? All are trained to sit asleep and wait until one day from somewhere pap is spooned into their mouths.

The less growth and the less soil, the rarer the ploughmen and those who clear the fields and those who go astray, then all the more is there cultural politics and all the more numerous become the "institutes" and "academies" for theater and film, for oratory and for newspaper reportage.

137   The individual nations "make culture" basically only because they do not need to feel ashamed in front of the other "culture" nations. "Culture" has become a matter of rampant competition and a business. And how edifying it is when any worthy mayor of a village is "culturally" active. But one has no "misgivings" even about this; it is enough if one possesses one's leisure and one's bit of public prestige. Where is the ground of this extent of the good-natured and "respectable" spiritual depravity of the Germans? For, something "good" is indeed accomplished everywhere in the conveying, restoring, and renewing of—what was created earlier, and one even believes, if one has been occupied long enough and deeply enough in this mere restoration, that some day one must thereby become a "creator" oneself. It may be—that some day the "violinist" and "pianist" will become *the* artist pure and simple—and the "poet" only a person who "supplies" the "scripts" for "films" and "operettas."

That the "world war" settled over the earth was indeed manifestly
still too small a plight—I since it brought forth no necessities of crea-   138
tivity and produced only opportunities for expedients.

So where lies the ground of this deviation from one's proper essence? In the fact that we are no longer willing to meditate? But
whence this unwillingness? Is it *indeed* the uncanny power of the
golden mean in all things that presses us down into the shallow waters of what is uncreative yet is indeed always "not bad"? What is supposed to liberate us from this power, since it in fact wears the mask of
that which precisely wants to be sought and striven for? What sacrifice must be performed so that *this decisionlessness* in all things might
once be broken? Or—is precisely this—the simultaneous and commonly enjoyed splashing about in the shallowest puddles and the silent sinking of a few individuals in the unknown broad river—is this
the unsublatable essence of the Germans?

Yet then there would be a danger for this essence in the fact that
such "splashing" would receive a certain "depth" for everyone and the
"broad rivers" would be canalized and I made universally navigable.   139

157

Cleverness in everything has already progressed so far that any particular can be immediately taken up, assimilated, and given out as
"new." That means nothing is any longer unfolded into its essentiality
and into its decisional greatness and raised up to a genuine oppositionality. Therefore, the great resistances remain absent, and accordingly
so do the possibilities of being overturned by something alien. That
all extensions in time and space can be snatched up with the greatest
certitude is merely a consequence of the fact that everything essential is snatched up not into the distorted essence but rather into the
a-essentiality of the average. The average has facile superiority as its
distorted essence and possesses a clever kind of avoidance of the essential and therefore has a peculiar suitability to give an impression of
something "good," *that* good which has already concerned itself with
what is to count purely and simply as the best.

The average in all beings is the most acute adversary of the gods.
Yet the Christian God is perhaps—I himself only the unconditioned   140
average and for that reason up to now the most endurable one in the
West.—Moreover, this God is, so to speak, tailored for modernity,
since people can "reckon" with him and "deal" with him. And so he
can even be taken up in a worldview as the "Lord God" and "Providence," and the "denominational confessions" to him (or to something

else?) even form "fronts," and he is even first "authentically" grasped in "lived experience" on boat rides sponsored by power through enjoyment.[9]

158

Long meditations and roundabout ways are required to recognize what at the present moment of philosophy (when philosophy is in its first end and is without the future other beginning) must above all *no longer* be "undertaken," although precisely now with the profusion of all "historiology" and the ingenuity of all "psychology" the possibilities and enticements are particularly favorable to some sort of expansive "classicism" (a pedantic and, especially, correct—faultless—elaboration of the earlier philosophy through erudition). To err in this regard and to draw the youth completely away from questioning, under the slogan "solid labor," are much more disastrous than I the crude and clear elimination of philosophical erudition from the universities. All straying—the more originary, the more consequential—in the direction of a preparation for the other beginning is fruitful and simulating—but precisely that is what remains absent. People have already become much too astute and too learned for them to move off forcefully and stray under a necessity in thoughtful questioning. To be sure, that recognition of what must *not* happen any longer, the possession of this "no," is more difficult than any undisturbed piling up of erudite pseudo-"productivity"—which feigns a "yes" to philosophy.

141

159

Since the years of the groping preparation of *Being and Time*, I have gone a little forward—which, in philosophy, always means *backward*. The one *question* of the "meaning" (i.e., the domain of projection and thus the truth) of beyng—has become still simpler in its necessity, the historical dialogue with the greats still more essential, and the other beginning clearer—but the *paths* of thinking through, *prior* to every premature and untimely utterance, have become steeper and longer and more gratifying—I in case the solitude of these paths could be called "gratifying."

142

---

9. {"Power through enjoyment" ["*Kraft durch Freude*" = *K.d.F.*], sub-organization of the "German labor front," which arranged group excursions, etc.}

160

To comprehend: to strike upon what is unsaid in something said—and to transform it into a more originary question—and in such questioning to press into those domains which are walled up more and more by every conventional way of answering.

161

Anthropology and Descartes.—Every anthropology in which by necessity the previous philosophy was indeed abundantly utilized, though at the same time declared to be otiose *as* philosophy, has the advantage of knowing what is required of it. It is incapable of only one thing, to overcome Descartes—as little capable of it as the consequence would ever be strong enough to confront that which it itself still bears as its opponent—i.e., to confront its ground.

162

The interrogation of the average in its proper grandeur imparts to the average a special sort of constancy. The power for this is not a new influx. It consists rather in the fact that the contentment in the avoidance of questioning is not exhausted but, instead, | reserves itself more   143
and more for the carrying on of the contentment, which becomes ever more secure in warding off everything inappropriate to it (especially what is question-worthy) and also becomes ever more confirmed by common opinion.

163

One hears that the Germans, once a "people of poets and thinkers," have become a "nation of poets and soldiers."[10] The same orator some years ago abjured the "dear God" of the Christians in favor of Wotan. With the incorporation of Catholic Austria, however, the "dear God" has now promptly reappeared in the speeches of this orator. If God can be "cited" according to need, then a fortiori so can the "soldiers" and eventually even the thinkers—if the orator perhaps needs to speak at a rally for a "thinker."

Moreover, there were indeed among the Germans, so far as we know, soldiers *prior* to those wise words. And so, despite this "proc-

---

10. {Baldur von Schirach, "Vom musischen Menschen," in *Revolution der Erz-iehung: Reden aus den Jahren des Aufbaus* (Munich: Eher, 1938), 187.}

lamation," there will *afterwards* still be "thinkers" among the Germans. But how could such declarations not constantly produce confusion in the "youth"?

144   Yet perhaps even our young people no longer take such speech seriously, speech that varies according to the occasion.

164

Dilthey: does not belong among the philosophers, but still less among the historiologists; he is a historical thinker of the type whose greatest form was realized in the nineteenth century by Jacob Burckhardt.

165

The other beginning. To *repeat* the inceptual question of Western philosophy means to begin the *other* beginning. And that requires: to arouse questioning. And that means: to move into the horizon of the question-worthy.

Far from all this is the opinion that that other beginning could simply be posited by a "doctrine" and effected with the help of a "text." We barely surmise which preparations were required until the first beginning could be expressed in words. And how should the question of beings find an ear now—the "ontologists" are the genuinely deaf—when a representational and productive calculation has been inserted
145   between beings as "objects" and humans as "subjects," I and the being of beings had to become machination, and decisionlessness suppresses every truth?

Let us merely consider once again the fate of Hölderlin—to be so caught in misinterpretation, to be so fully deprived of all futurity.—

But the fate is *that* we do not at all consider this fate and meditate on what lies enclosed therein, namely, that everything still comes too early and is too quickly engulfed into historiology.

166

The more and the more quickly humans come to know everything, all the more completely does memory disappear. And *recollection* is something alien, something humans no longer master. "Culture" becomes the basic form of barbarity.

But appraised as essential are indeed these actual (though indeed merely dispersed) thrusts of the last detachings of now superficial beings from concealed being.

167

The steepness of the descent into death can be measured from the height of the nearness to beyng. The space-time of this measurement is Da-sein.

168

146

What is happening if something *great* must be such as to refuse its greatness to everyone—i.e., count only as a "foil" and a precursor? Or does this pertain to everything great?

A confusing ambiguity: is not everything necessarily found to be small and dwarfish in meditation on greatness? Or in such meditation *can* there lie concealed a *great* necessity—to be sure, neither dwarfishness nor greatness—but a creation of space and a preparation of time for the essential decisions?

169

Artworks can be historiologically "considered" and "enjoyed" on the basis of history only if we come to know—more strictly than in "lived experience"—that in relation to art we lack the great plight and also the preparedness to be assaulted by a completely other truth. But how can historiological consideration of the "history of art" *mediately* prepare such knowledge? For this can happen only mediately, because in accord with the attitude of the age, everything *im*mediately uttered is calculated and is poured out into "lived experience." And if I the "plight" is first the object of a "lived experience," then it has become sterile and can never give birth to a necessity.

147

170

If the *philosophy* of the future is a steep and fissured mountain range, then many a one must lose his way therein and remain untraceable.

171

A question: if modernity in its worldviews must deny itself the power and possibility of a reversion to beings (i.e., to the truth of beyng), and if its strength consists precisely in establishing itself in a complete lack of questioning, then is modernity not preparing for itself a swift end? No—what is most perfectly average endures the longest. What is essential is always only for a moment. Historiology, as the genuine pacemaker of modernity, gives this impression only because it adheres to the past, and thereby even what is "great" *"would be"* this as well; because one can have a "lived experience" of it, one would be "great" oneself or at least be touched by greatness and be affiliated to it. Unhistoriological ages are spared this temptation.

Philosophy and words.—Because philosophy ever has to *ground* being itself in the truth of being, the discourse of philosophy must itself become the origination of beyng. This discourse does not describe beyng nor tell of beings. But at first—according to custom—all language *seems* to apply only to beings; therefore, all discourse is apprehended in that sense—and the misinterpretation of philosophy has taken place, even before the content of what it says has been considered.

For philosophy—especially for the philosophy that overcomes all metaphysics as superficial—*words and their configuration* are the event of beyng itself, beyng as event. Accordingly, here the most inconspicuous sequence of a few sentences must already have a structure whose law is not to be read off from beings but, instead, is accommodated to beyng. The originary nominative power of words must be imparted to thoughtful discourse in a transformed way, and from "mere word meanings" "something" cannot be derived. The thoughtful word always thinks beyng, and the latter holds sway in the essence, in the distorted essence, and in the absence of an essence in what is average;

149 | therefore, the thoughtful word never coincides with merely *one* meaning but rather coincides with the entire oppositional essential occurrence of the essence of what is said. For example, if truth is thought of and named, then *un*truth and average opinion are cothought, yet not merely "dialectically," but in the sense of an entrance into the projective domains and their bifurcation, and the latter is not something that could ever be covered by a mere sublation in the "not only . . . but also." If philosophy names the distorted essence, then that distorted essence will be apprehended, in the horizon of everyday explanatory reckonings and pursuits, as a devaluation and as something to contend against. But philosophy can never reject the distorted essence and instead must precisely know the necessity of such an essence, and only with that necessity *and* with what lacks all essence can philosophy know the abyssal character of the essence and thus the full essentiality of the essence.

Even if art is *essentially* different than philosophy, nevertheless the perhaps quite "unphilosophical" artist can very easily grasp something of thoughtful discourse and of its grounding style. On the other

hand, however, because philosophy as knowledge has moved into the proximity of "science," and "science" I is not determined on the basis   150
of knowledge, but the latter on the basis of the currently pursued "science," then "scientific" "thinking" remains at the furthest remove from the possibility of surmising what takes place in philosophy. Already for that reason, the attempt to philosophize within the university is a conscious leap into a sphere of an inevitable misinterpretation of all philosophy. This misinterpretation occurs without ever needing to be made explicit; it is abetted by the inclination to place "philosophy" together with "worldviews" and to depreciate it thereby. The misinterpretation is finally completed through the effort, harkening back to the Middle Ages, to make "philosophy" useful for an up-to-date refurbishing and repainting of the "Christian worldview" and thus naturally at the same time to "refute" "philosophy."

Or is perhaps today's university, precisely because in it this manifold possibility of misinterpreting philosophy is stowed, the most suitable place to venture ever again what is alien? This venture is facilitated by the fact that "philosophy" is furthermore made unrecognizable in advance, insofar as it appears in the usual form of I philo-   151
sophical erudition and thus always unfolds a certain "activity" which can at times even prove useful.

173

Today the "beginners" either are already "complete," such that they "straighten out" everything and "settle" the "supreme problems" and even already in dissertations confute the greatest thinkers and poets— or else in another sense they do not begin at all, inasmuch as they merely parrot everything and make a "scholasticism" out of what they heard. Why do we nowhere encounter those who start with something small and superficial and yet are driven by an unmistakable passion? Presumably, they are there and have their reasons for withdrawing from all guidance!

"Philosophy of philosophy" has now become impossible, because there is no longer *the* philosophy, *"about"* which one could philosophize; but is there that philosophy which philosophizes and thus makes itself ready for the other beginning?

174

It might seem that *the Germans* are no longer deemed worthy of being *abandoned* by all the gods. I What if we, with all the historiological dis-   152
play of resurrected Germans, are at the point of driving the essence

of the Germans into a gigantic perversion—because all this no longer grasps the *root* and has no room for growth—not on earth and not in heaven—but has only the "restlessness" and unconditionality of an *institution*, concealed behind which are emptiness and uncertainty.

Must *more originary* events not arrive as well as *more essential* notions of history and being, if now—in the "world" completely destroyed by institutions—there is still to be a structure which guarantees great destinies?

175

As long as the opponent prescribes the weapons and the kind of battle, a defense is perhaps possible, but not at all a creative overcoming. What pertains to such overcoming is an ancient freedom out of the plight of the most concealed joy of the stillest creativity.

176

What do we know of the origin of power, knowing so little of its essence?

177

If *beyng* can never be read off from any domain of *beings* and certainly cannot be derived from laws and steps of *thinking*, then whither will philosophy be placed once it has understood this? The carrying out and configuring of this experience comprise the grounding of the space for beyng itself.

Can a human ever be exposed to beyng in this manner? Has he ever sought the ways leading there, which are ways of his transformation? How could this transformation otherwise receive its impetus, if not by the history of being becoming "visible" for the first time in human history and determining the essence of its era not historiologically, but historically?

178

Why does the *most abyssal*—the moment—love what is *most fleeting*? How is the most simple breadth of the truth of beyng traversed here— while yet remaining *un*grounded? How do space and time in their most oppositional essence rise into their originary unity, a unity not at all graspable in ordinary concepts?

People—first of all "a people" in the ambiguity of its essence undertakes the fulfillment of the character of the human being as subject, a character modernity holds fast in advance and without knowledge. The essence of a people never becomes an originary historical force as long as the unexpressed subject-character underlies that essence. And any deliberation with respect to a people achieves on this "soil" at most an exposition of various meanings of the word. The "folkish" ["*völkisch*"] first attains its proper—which always means *conditioned*—truth when the essence of a people [*Volk*] is itself recognized in its manifold inner contrariness, according to which that essence must become the site of a fate: a people as the masses, a people as ground of life, a people as belonging to history, a people as incorporated into being—all this not in the juxtaposition of the "also," but in the reciprocality of the concurrent and of what must ground Dasein in its ground.

Instead of this, however, "people" is becoming a name for something that is always only unity, that unifies, and that sublates oppositions; *in this way*, a people veils its most proper essence as a site of destiny and in addition still conceals its previous "subject"-character under the mask of the thought of a community, a thought which allows the "subjective" | to count only as the "egoic" and thus denies itself the possibility of taking up its former interpretation of the essence into a meditative gaze.   155

Yet the subject-character still undergoes a special hardening through the priority of the biological (i.e., in truth, unbiological) interpretation of a people, a "biological" interpretation that is particularly comprehensible to the multitudes and so must very often be expounded in reference to them.

This suppression of the essence of a people in an inadequate (not merely "theoretical") interpretation is all the more disastrous in view of the fact that since Leibniz there are possibilities enough in German "metaphysics" for a relatively originary interpretation. To be sure— they remain—"metaphysical" and thus essentially insufficient for an overcoming of the subject-character.

Even if we say a people cannot be something unconditioned but only something conditioned while conditioning, are we not already thinking "metaphysically" and ontologically in a way that is untrue, inasmuch as we have in advance taken a "people" as an object?

Perhaps all this amounts to trifling with concepts—but perhaps we will once come to surmise that what is intended is only *the decision* of the West—whether a people experiences itself as needed by "beyng" and as sacrificed to it—or as the gigantic arena of a supposedly "eternal" machination.

156   *180*

The forms of *modern Christianity* as the genuine configurations of Godlessness.

Catholicism, which no longer has anything whatever to do with medieval Christianity.

"Confessional front": Roman curialism in the form of German Protestantism; the youngest form of cultural Christianity: Christianity as a mask for the assertion of a now-brittle global domination.

German Christians: an un-Christian and anti-Christian misunderstanding of the Germans.

And yet: Christianity has created and aroused powers of the spirit, of discipline, and of strength of soul, powers which are not to be thought of as missing from Western history, especially since, even if only in reverse, they continue to be effective and still offer "support" to individuals.

But: the great decisions do not occur there. Christianity has long ago lost all power of origination; it has made its own history historiological.

157   *Uncanny play of historiological dates in the foreground of abyssal German history*:

1806 Hölderlin is put away, and a German confederation begins.

1813 The German sway reaches its height, and Richard Wagner is born.

1843 Hölderlin leaves the "world," and a year later Nietzsche comes into it.

1870–76 The German expansive years are founded, and Nietzsche's *Untimely Considerations* appears.

1883 *Zarathustra I* comes out, and Richard Wagner dies.

1888 End of December: Nietzsche's "euphoria" before his breakdown, and—

(9-26-1889).

{Index}

Editor's Afterword

The first series of what Martin Heidegger himself called the "Black Notebooks" ["*Schwarze Hefte*"] is here published in section IV of his Complete Works [*Gesamtausgabe*] as volume 94.

"Ponderings X," included in volume 95, contains a remark on the character of these "ponderings" that unfold in fifteen notebooks. They are not a matter of "aphorisms" as "adages" but of "inconspicuous advance outposts—and rearguard positions—within the whole of an attempt at a still ineffable meditation toward the conquest of a way for the newly inceptual questioning which is called, in distinction from metaphysical thinking, the thinking of the history of beyng."[1] "Not decisive" is "what is represented and compiled into a representational edifice," but "only how the questioning takes place and the fact that being is questioned at all."

Heidegger also refers in a similar vein, in his "backward glance over the way," to "especially notebooks II, IV, and V," i.e., to the respective Ponderings. They are to capture "in part ever the basic dispositions of questioning and the directives into the extreme horizons of attempts at thinking."[2] The emphasis on the "basic dispositions of questioning" reinforces the indication that the Ponderings are a matter of "attempts at thinking."

Following this up, I have inserted as an exergue to these first published Black Notebooks a later remark (presumably from the early 1970s) to the effect that at issue in the "black notebooks" are not "notes for a planned system," but rather "at their core" "attempts at simple designation." It is striking that in all three characterizations of the Black Notebooks, the word "attempt" claims an essential significance.

As "inconspicuous advance outposts—and rearguard positions," that is, as pre-ponderings and post-considerations in the confrontational thinking of being, the Black Notebooks assume a form not yet seen in Heidegger's many already published writings. If what is indeed "decisive" is "how the questioning takes place," thus how the question of the "meaning of being" finds expression, then we are en-

---

1. Martin Heidegger, "Ponderings X," a, in *Ponderings VII–XI, Gesamtausgabe* (GA)95. Frankfurt: Klostermann, 2014. The page references correspond to the pagination of the original manuscripts, which is printed in the margins of the published volumes.

2. Martin Heidegger, *Besinnung*, GA66. Frankfurt: Klostermann, 1997, p. 426.

countering in these notebooks a new writing "style," a concept often mulled over in the "notes."

Besides the published work of the 1920s, the courses, seminars, essays, lectures, and treatises on the history of being, we become acquainted in the Black Notebooks with a further way of expression on the part of Heidegger. The question of how all these various modes of speech cohere does perhaps belong to the most important tasks of a thinking which would seek to understand Heidegger's thought as a whole.

The Black Notebooks present a form which in style and method is possibly unique not only for Heidegger but also for all of twentieth-century philosophy. Compared to generally known sorts of texts, it comes closest to an "idea diary." Yet if this designation thrusts the writings that come under it mostly to the margin of the total work, the significance of the Black Notebooks in the context of Heidegger's "way for inceptual questioning" will still need to be examined.

According to the literary executor, Hermann Heidegger, and Friedrich-Wilhelm von Herrmann, Heidegger's private assistants between 1972 and 1976, the Black Notebooks were brought to the German Literature Archive in Marbach around the middle of the 1970s. On the occasion of the shipment, Heidegger stated that they were to be published only at the very end of the Complete Works. Until then, they were to be kept "doubly secret, so to speak" (von Herrmann). No one was to read them or look them over. The literary executor has decided against this directive, because delays in bringing out the still-unpublished volumes of the full project of letting Martin Heidegger's thought appear in due form should not prevent the publication of the Black Notebooks at this time.

Why did the philosopher want to have the Black Notebooks published only as the last volumes of the Complete Works? The answer might very well be related to an already familiar stricture according to which the treatises concerned with the history of being were to be published only after all the lecture courses. For these courses, which intentionally do not speak about what is contained in the writings on the history of being, prepare for what these latter are saying in a language not accommodated to public lectures.

The Black Notebooks are thirty-four in number. Fourteen bear the title "Ponderings," nine are called "Annotations," two "Four Notebooks," two "Vigilae," one "Notturno," two "Intimations," and four are named "Provisional Remarks." In addition, two further notebooks with the respective titles "Megiston" and "Basic Words" have come to light. Whether and how these belong to the Black Notebooks must still be clarified. Volumes 94 to 102 of the Complete Works will in the coming years make available the thirty-four manuscripts first mentioned above.

The writing of the notebooks spans a time frame of more than forty years. The first extant notebook, "Intimations x Ponderings (II) and Directives," bears on its first page the date "October 1931." "Provisional Remarks III" contains a reference to "Le Thor 1969," so that the notebook "Provisional Remarks IV" must stem from the beginning of the 1970s. One notebook is missing, namely "Intimations x Ponderings (I)," which must have been composed around 1930. Its whereabouts are uncertain.

*　*　*

Volume 94 of the Complete Works is the first of three volumes in which the Ponderings are published. It comprises "Intimations x Ponderings (II) and Directives," "Ponderings and Intimations III," as well as the further "Ponderings" IV to VI. The first notebook of the volume begins in the fall of 1931; the last notebook of "Ponderings VI" concludes in June 1938, judging from a reference to a talk given by Baldur van Schirach[3] on the occasion of the opening of the Weimar Festival that year.

This series of Ponderings therefore encompasses the time Heidegger was rector of the University of Freiburg, from April 21, 1933 to April 28, 1934. The "Ponderings and Intimations III," which begin in "Fall 1932," contain many entries in which Heidegger takes account of his rectorate. It becomes clear that his decision to take office—with all the revolutionary acquiescence—came to be doubted by him very early on. Altogether it is clear how much the thinker remained in inner remoteness from the historical happenings. But it is also unmistakable how assuredly he proceeds from there to the view that philosophy, with the "revolution" at an end, must be advisedly and decisively detached from the "metapolitics" of the "historical people."[4]

Connected here is also the thought that a "Vulgar National Socialism"[5] could be distinguished from a "Spiritual National Socialism."[6] This latter, however, is not different from the former as theory is to practice. The only possibility of making sense of this admittedly seldom-used concept of "Spiritual National Socialism" is that Heidegger understood it to be a National Socialism which follows upon

---

3. "Ponderings VI," 143.

4. "Ponderings and Intimations III," 22.

5. Ibid., 52.

6. Ibid., 42.

the "metapolitics" he develops. But the "metapolitics" can basically be nothing else than Heidegger's ponderings on the relation of the "first beginning" to the "other beginning" in the history of being.

An essential feature of all the Ponderings is Heidegger's attempt to gain insights for the history of being out of everyday "signs"[7] or "characteristics" of National Socialism in "science," "religion," politics," and "culture." This feature is so salient in the Ponderings that it at least codetermines the general impression made by the entries. Heidegger finds anticipatorily in the everyday occurrences of the 1930s "signs" of an ever more catastrophically prominent "forgottenness of being." Furthermore, it is evident that this procedure of finding traces of the history of being in the everyday is what runs under the distinction Heidegger emphasizes between historiology and history.

It is also relevant to this interpretation that by the summer of 1936 at the latest, Heidegger took distance from the actually existing National Socialism, inasmuch as he could recognize and disdain the "worldview" of "desolate and crude 'biologism.'"[8] Moreover, from the beginning he stood out against the National Socialist critique of so-called intellectualism,[9] i.e., a supposedly senseless extravagance of theoretical questions. The Ponderings of this time therefore show how Heidegger extricated himself step by step from his earlier support for National Socialism.

Standing in the background of Heidegger's interpretation of the everyday phenomena of National Socialism in terms of the history of being are certainly all those thoughts we are familiar with from his treatises of that time on the history of being: *Contributions to Philosophy (Of the Event)* (*Gesamtausgabe* 65, 1936–1938) and *Meditation* (*Gesamtausgabe* 66, 1938–1939), as well as the later *History of Beyng* (*Gesamtausgabe* 69, 1939–1940), *On the Beginning* (*Gesamtausgabe* 70, 1941), and *The Event* (*Gesamtausgabe* 71, 1941–1942). Again and again, echoes of these writings resound in the "Ponderings."

* * *

The Ponderings appearing in volumes 94 to 96 of the Complete Works comprise fourteen of the thirty-four (or possibly thirty-six) notebooks with black oilcloth covers. The pages are in an unusual format: 5¼ × 7½ inches. The originals reside in the Heidegger literary remains at the German Literature Archive in Marbach am Neckar. I as

---

7. "Ponderings VI," 15.

8. "Ponderings IV," 31.

9. "Ponderings and Intimations III," 103.

editor had available copies bound in blue linen, with the titles printed on the spines.

The present volume 94 brings together the following texts:
"Intimations x Ponderings (II) and Directives," 141 pages;
"Ponderings and Intimations III," 144 pages;
"Ponderings IV," 124 pages;
"Ponderings V," 154 pages;
"Ponderings VI," 157 pages.

Added to these pages are indexes Heidegger provided at times for the notebooks. When available, they are published at the end of the respective text.

The manuscripts are fully worked out. They display hardly any slips of the pen. There are no inserted sheets.

Luise Michaelsen prepared a typed transcription of "Intimations x Ponderings (II) and Directives" and of "Ponderings and Intimations III"; Detlev Heidegger did the same for "Ponderings" IV, V, and VI. Hermann Heidegger proofread the typescripts.

I transcribed everything once again from the manuscripts, while constantly looking at the already prepared typescripts. Then I proofread the typescripts. Finally, the galleys and page proofs were checked both by me and by my collaborator and student, Sophia Heiden.

Heidegger numbered the individual entries in the "Ponderings," perhaps imitating his own treatises on the history of being, perhaps following the example of certain writings of Friedrich Nietzsche. This changes, however, beginning with "Ponderings XIV"; it and all further Black Notebooks no longer display such numbering.

Letters ("a," "b," "c") with which Heidegger sometimes designated the first pages of a notebook, as well as the numbers that begin thereafter, are reproduced here in the margin of the text. The vertical stroke in the middle of a line indicates a page break. A question mark within braces ("{?}") flags an uncertain reading. All cross-references in the text are to notebook page numbers. Heidegger uses the symbol "□" for "manuscript." All underlinings found in Heidegger's own text have been changed to italics; underlings in cited texts, which would be italicized on their own, have been printed in bold.

More than in other volumes of the Complete Works, certain of Heidegger's remarks, especially ones referring to historical events, were supplied with an editorial explanation. Thereby the reader can see at which time Heidegger composed which of the "Ponderings." Also, with regard to persons and institutions, ones which might be unfamiliar to younger readers, I have attached concise clarifications.

There could obviously be no completeness here, in an edition that is supposed to come "straight from the author's hand."

In some cases, though very sparingly, I brought Heidegger's idiosyncratic spelling as well as his characteristic syntax into conformity with current rules. At the same time, I intentionally retained certain peculiarities, for instance that of occasionally capitalizing adjectives (e.g., "Great enemy"[10] or "Grounding vibrancy"[11]). Also, Heidegger's notorious coinage of hyphenated words was not standardized but, instead, with a few exceptions, is reproduced just as it appears in the manuscripts.

*   *   *

I thank Hermann Heidegger for the trust with which he conferred on me the task of editing the Black Notebooks. Thanks are due Jutta Heidegger for proofreading the present volume and for checking the page proofs. I thank Detlev Heidegger for making available the first typescript. I express my appreciation to Friedrich-Wilhelm von Herrmann for many discussions in which various editorial issues were decided. Such gratitude is also owing to Arnulf Heidegger and to Vittorio E. Klostermann. Anastasia Urban, of the Klostermann publishing house, always offered me capable and friendly collaboration, for which I am grateful. I am indebted to Ulrich von Bülow of the German Literature Archive in Marbach for assistance with regard to questions concerning the availability of the manuscripts. Finally, Sophia Heiden deserves my gratitude for her careful proofreading.

Peter Trawny
Düsseldorf
December 13, 2013

---

10. "Intimations x Ponderings (II) and Directives," 7.
11. Ibid., 41.